IMPRIMI POTEST:

John J. Foley, S.J.
Provincial, Wisconsin Province,

Linus J. Thro, S.J.
Provincial, Missouri Province

IMPRIMATUR:

✠ Joseph Cardinal Ritter
Archbishop of St. Louis
May 13, 1963

GEORGE P. KLUBERTANZ, S.J.
MAURICE R. HOLLOWAY, S.J.
Saint Louis University

BEING AND GOD

An Introduction to

The Philosophy of Being

And to

Natural Theology

New York

APPLETON-CENTURY-CROFTS

Division of Meredith Publishing Company

Foreword

IN RECENT YEARS many scholastic philosophers have been taking stock of their curricula. As a result of this scrutiny, a growing number of schools has decided to compress the systematic sequence of courses and expand their offerings in the history of philosophy. This trend has forced some changes in the traditional course structure. Specifically, more and more philosophy departments have decided that two semesters of general metaphysics and natural theology were more than they could afford and so have designed single semester courses which include both general metaphysics and natural theology.

Although these departments have expressed general satisfaction with this combined course, instructors who leaned toward an existential Thomism have had great difficulty in finding an adequate textbook. Many of these teachers admired Father Klubertanz' *Introduction to the Philosophy of Being* but felt that it did not cover enough natural theology to justify adopting it. By and large, these same philosophers considered Father Holloway's *Natural Theology* to be the best text for the second metaphysics course.

It was natural, then, that someone should suggest to Appleton-Century-Crofts that they bring out a combined edition for use in a one-semester course. Fortunately, the publishers and the authors liked the idea of a combined text and have carried it through to the publication of the present volume, *Being and God*. This new text will undoubtedly rank as high for the one-semester course as the individual volumes have ranked in their respective fields.

By way of bonus, the suggestion for a single volume abridgement of the two texts came just as Father Klubertanz was preparing a second edition of his metaphysics text. Consequently, instructors and students will be able to profit from Father Klubertanz' second thoughts and from the suggestions of his colleagues which he incorporates in the new edition. The new text, of course, also benefits from Father Klubertanz' mastery of the latest Thomistic scholarship.

When the idea of a combined text was first suggested, some thought that the work of the two authors might not fit together well enough to make a successful volume. This fear has proved to be groundless, for Fathers Klubertanz and Holloway both come to metaphysics with the same basic viewpoint, that of an existential Thomism. Consequently, the natural theology portion of the volume picks up where the general metaphysics leaves off. The transition is smooth and easy. In a word, the two parts weld into one book, the best in English on *Being and God*.

The task of selecting the sections to be included in the single volume was fairly easy. Nine of the first ten chapters in Father Klubertanz' book give precisely the important points which have to be covered in any metaphysics course. In addition, the structure of Father Klubertanz' argument was able to be retained, so that nothing had to be wrenched out of context. For the natural theology, Father Holloway's excellent summaries made it possible to cover the whole course in brief. The full text had to be included only for those questions which could be treated fairly fully in a one semester course: the existence of God, the nature of God, and the perfections of God. The summaries put these sections in context and so make them more intelligible than they would have been if isolated from the rest of the treatise.

All in all, *Being and God* should be a boon to those who teach metaphysics and natural theology in a one-semester course. The book is doctrinally and pedagogically sound; it has behind it two experienced and well known Thomists of proved competency; it is written in a clear and direct style.

James V. McGlynn, S.J.
University of Detroit

Preface

THIS IS A TEXTBOOK of metaphysics. By calling it a textbook, we wish to indicate, first of all, that it is not a scholarly treatise, but an introductory exposition at the college level. Historical questions, recondite refinements, and scholarly documentation are not its concern, yet some reference to current views and their historical origins is illuminating even for the most basic exposition.

A textbook is for students. It is intended to help them *learn* something. To learn to be a philosopher is more than to mouth the words philosophers commonly use, yet unless we have a technical and even a sophisticated vocabulary we cannot even talk about metaphysics. But because it is intended to help students get started, it is at best only a beginning. If a student would perfectly master this book, he would be a competent beginner; competent, we hope, but certainly a beginner. A textbook can do no more than bring the student to the point where he can intelligently and therefore profitably read the masters. To attain this goal more perfectly, we strongly urge teachers to assign and students to read the suggested readings. We hope that at the conclusion of the course the student could be somewhat capable of self-instruction under the guidance of St. Thomas Aquinas.

The subject of this book is "metaphysics." Aristotle called it "first philosophy"; by this term he and St. Thomas Aquinas mean the full philosophical treatment of being and its Cause, of Being and God. Metaphysics begins with the beings of experience. Its preliminary concern is with the beings of direct experience, not with concepts, not with emotions or guesses (no matter how noble), not with some logical pre-conditions of experience (often dignified with the impressive term "a priori conditions"). In the beings of experience, and there only, we find what *being* is, and by an inductive analysis we come to know its intrinsic and extrinsic principles as well as its common attributes. But metaphysics, in its full sense, is more than an "immanent metaphysics," as some recent philosophers would wish it to be; the principles the metaphysician finds in the beings of experience lead him beyond experience.

And yet the philosophical study of God, which is expounded in the second part of the text, is a continuation of metaphysics and constitutes with it a single science. In natural theology the student uses principles inductively grounded in the beings of his experience to see the necessity for an ontological source of these beings. In demonstrating the existence and nature of this source, which is the fullness of Being, the full scientific value of metaphysics is achieved. The ways of arriving at God, which in this book are the five ways of St. Thomas, are developed in some detail. And this for two reasons. First, that the student grasp with as much force as possible the necessity of finite being having a here and now ontological ground; and, secondly, that this ground be appreciated in some of its fullness. To come too quickly to God through creatures is to come to Him empty-minded. In fact, what we later go on to say about the nature of God is only a careful explicitation of the metaphysics of the five ways. Our effort in the section on natural theology is to make the student realize the theocentric condition of being, and understand that this center has the mysterious fullness of a source that is at once completely transcendent and immanent. How well the student will realize this depends upon how well he has understood his general metaphysics.

Yet philosophy is not the *whole* of knowledge; it is limited on the one side by the sciences which have their own autonomous validity, and on the other by faith. The sciences, by their proper techniques, are able to give man a detailed knowledge of sensible things which is impossible for philosophy, as well as a practical control over the use of these things. On the other side, a philosophical treatment is inferior to faith in completeness and certitude; it is intrinsically limited to what can be known about being and God in the light of the principles which are discovered in experience.

The metaphysics which is here expounded is a *Christian* metaphysics. Realistically, most of its readers will be Christians, or at least theists, in the Judaeo-Christian tradition. As such, they already have ideas and convictions about the nature of the universe and its relation to God, about themselves and *their* personal relation to that God. Because faith is not philosophy, a believer is still open to a completely honest and fully critical investigation of objects which in fact he believes.

Finally, it is in some sense a "Thomistic" metaphysics which is here presented. We do not mean that the authority of St. Thomas is the reason for accepting it; in philosophy, it is neither sufficient nor necessary to quote St. Thomas. Nor is any claim made to a privileged or uniquely correct interpretation of St. Thomas. But the authors have learned their metaphysics chiefly by studying St. Thomas, though they have been helped by teachers, friends, and students.

A special word of thanks is due to the Reverend James V. McGlynn, S.J. Effectively it was his suggestion which gave rise to the idea of a combined text. It was his suggested selection of passages which was followed, and his order of treatment which gave the form to this book. His generous and gracious Foreword is but the final gesture of encouragement and support which he has given to the whole undertaking.

M. R. H., S.J.
G. P. K., S.J.

Contents

Foreword by James V. McGlynn, S.J.　　　　　　　　　v

Preface　　　　　　　　　vii

PART ONE: THE PHILOSOPHY OF BEING

I. INTRODUCTION

1. Purposes and general ways of knowing　　　　3
2. Kinds of theoretical knowledge　　　　6
3. Characteristics of scientific knowledge　　　　7
4. Why should I study philosophy?　　　　12
5. The philosophy of being and the other parts of philosophy　　　　15
6. Philosophy and religion　　　　17
7. Thomistic philosophy　　　　21
8. Definitions　　　　22
9. Readings　　　　25

II. THE MEANING OF "BEING"

10. Various senses of the word *real*　　　　30
11. Phenomenalism and the meaning of *being*　　　　32
12. Materialism and the meaning of *being*　　　　33
13. Essentialism and the meaning of *being*　　　　37
14. Existentialism and the meaning of *being*　　　　41
15. The Thomistic answer to the question, "What is it to be real?"　　　　42
16. The primitive notion of being　　　　47
17. The metaphysical knowledge of being　　　　50
18. The first principles of knowledge　　　　54

19. Definitions   57
20. Summary of the argument   57
21. Readings   58

III. THE ANALOGY OF BEING: FIRST APPROACH

22. The fact of knowledge in common   64
23. Univocation and its basis   65
24. Is being a universal?   65
25. "Being" is common to many   67
26. The formal structure of analogy   69
27. Analogy of individual beings   71
28. Person and thing as beings   73
29. Definitions   76
30. Summary   76
31. Readings   77

IV. BECOMING—CHANGE—MOTION

32. The problem of change   80
33. Identity, distinction, and difference   82
34. The correct way to talk about change   85
35. A changing thing is composed   87
36. Definitions   89
37. Summary   90
38. Readings   90

V. THE INTRINSIC PRINCIPLES OF CHANGE AND BEING: I. IN PARTICULAR

39. Accidental change and the substance-accident composition of being   93
40. Substance and accident as beings by analogy   98
41. Substantial change and the matter-form composition of substance   100
42. Individuals in a species and matter-form composition 103
43. That-which-is and the act of existing (esse)   111
44. The agent and his activity   114
45. Definitions   116
46. Summary of the argumentation   117
47. Readings   118

VI. THE INTRINSIC PRINCIPLES OF BEING: II. AS ANALOGOUSLY ONE

48. Comparison of the three sets of intrinsic principles 124
49. Theorems of act and potency. I: Act and potency are distinct in their order 127
50. What is the potency for activity? 128
51. Theorem II: Act and potency are not strictly beings but principles of being 131
52. Theorem III: Act, in the order in which it is act, is unlimited in itself and limited by the potency in which it is received 132
53. Theorem IV: Act can be known by itself, potency only through act 136
54. Theorem V: Act and potency divide being in general 137
55. Concluding remarks about act and potency 137
56. Exercise 141
57. Readings 141

VII. THE EXTRINSIC PRINCIPLES OF BEING: I. THE AGENT

58. Principles of change 144
59. Causal factors 146
60. The causality of the agent, or efficient cause 147
61. Types of agents: univocal and equivocal causes 152
62. Types of agents: principal and instrumental causes 154
63. The exemplar cause 155
64. The theorem of causality 156
65. The analogy of causality 162
66. Definitions 164
67. Proofs 167
68. Readings 167

VIII. THE EXTRINSIC PRINCIPLES OF BEING: II. THE GOAL OF ACTION

69. The goal of action 171
70. Orientation in being 179
71. Chance 180
72. Definitions 183

73. Proof   184
74. Readings   184

IX. THE TRANSCENDENTALS

75. Being is a transcendental   187
76. Possibles   190
77. Beings of reason and pure intelligibilities   192
78. The transcendental "one"   194
79. Being-in-itself and being-for-another   196
80. The transcendental "true"   197
81. The transcendental "good"   202
82. Definitions   210
83. Proofs   211
84. Readings   211

PART TWO: NATURAL THEOLOGY

X. THE EXISTENCE OF GOD

1. The nature and characteristics of natural theology   219
2. State of the question   219
3. Explanation of terms   219
4. The proof   222
5. Readings   224
6. Selected passage from St. Thomas Aquinas   224
7. The nature and validity of *a posteriori* demonstration   225
8. Statement of the question   225
9. Explanation of terms   225
10. Readings   228

XI. PROOFS FOR THE EXISTENCE OF GOD

1. The first way: proof from the existence of motion   229
2. Statement of the problem   229
3. The solution   229
4. Whatever is changed is changed by another   230
5. In things that are changed by another an infinite regress is impossible   231
6. This first unmoved mover is pure act or God   233
7. Answering the objections   233
8. Summary of the first way   236

9. The second way: proof from the existence of efficient causes   239
10. Statement of the problem   239
11. The solution: step one: efficient causes essentially and accidentally ordered   240
12. Step two: general characteristics of a *per se* ordered series of efficient causes   241
13. Step three: special characteristics of a series of *per se* ordered efficient causes   243
14. Step four: Why there cannot be an infinite regress in *per se* ordered efficient causes   246
15. Answering the objections   246
16. Summary of the second way   249
17. The third way: proof from the existence of corruptible beings   252
18. Prenote   252
19. Solution   252
20. Answering the objections   259
21. Summary of the third way   263
22. The fourth way: proof of God's existence from grades of perfection in beings   265
23. Statement of the problem   265
24. Solution   266
25. The proof of the fourth way   271
26. Some added considerations   274
27. Answering the objections   275
28. Summary of the fourth way   277
29. The fifth way: the proof of the existence of God from the finalized activity of natural beings   280
30. Prenote   280
31. The problem of the fifth way   281
32. Solution   283
33. Answering the objections   288
34. Summary of the fifth way   295
35. A general proof for God's existence   299
36. Readings   303

XII. THE NATURE OF GOD

1. Man's knowledge of the divine nature   304
2. The problem of knowing the nature of God   304

3. Solution to the problem 305
4. Statement of the question 305
5. Explanation of terms 306
6. Adversaries 307
7. Proofs for our position 308
8. Readings 312
9. The problem of naming God 312
10. Can God be named? 312
11. Solution to the problem 312
12. Statement of the question 313
13. Explanation of terms 313
14. The proof 315
15. Readings 317

XIII. THE PERFECTIONS OF GOD

1. Prenote 318
2. Divisions of the divine perfections 318
3. The divine perfection of simplicity 320
4. God is absolutely simple 321
5. Solution 321
6. General proof 322
7. Answering the objections 323
8. God is completely perfect 324
9. Proof 324
10. How the perfections of creatures pre-exist in God 324
11. Prenote 324
12. Solution 325
13. Second solution 326
14. Answering the objections 331
15. God is infinite and supremely good 331
16. Prenote 331
17. Is the being of God really infinite or without limit? 332
18. Solution 332
19. Answering the objections 333
20. Is God supremely good? 334
21. How the divine perfections are distinct from the divine essence and from each other 336
22. Does the plurality of meanings that the divine attributes have exist only in our intellect or also in God? 338
23. Solution 338

24. The opinion of Avicenna and Maimonides   341
25. The opinion of the Pseudo-Denis and St. Anselm   342
26. Reconciliation of these opinions   343
27. Answering the difficulties   345
28. Summary   346
29. Readings   349
30. The omnipresence, immutability, and eternity of God 349
31. Readings   351

XIV. GOD'S KNOWLEDGE AND WILL

1. God's knowledge of himself and other things   352
2. Statement concerning God's knowledge   352
3. Explanation of terms   353
4. The proof   354
5. Readings   356
6. The perfection of will in God   356
7. Statement concerning God's will   356
8. Explanation of terms   357
9. The proof   358
10. Readings   361

XV. GOD'S CREATION AND PROVIDENCE

1. The manner in which the world comes from God   362
2. Statement concerning creation   363
3. Explanation of terms   363
4. The proof   364
5. Readings   365
6. Divine providence   365
7. Statement concerning God's providence   366
8. Explanation of terms   367
9. The proof   367
10. Readings   368

XVI. GOD AS THE END OF MAN

1. Defining some terms   369
2. Applying these terms to God   369
3. Conclusion   372
4. Readings   372

Index   375

PART ONE

THE PHILOSOPHY
OF BEING

I

Introduction

1. Purposes and general ways of knowing

A college student has already learned many things and may often feel that what he knows is more than enough to last a lifetime. He may indeed be aware of the necessity of continuing his studies in the field he has chosen for his special work; but why take up another subject which, at first sight, will have no practical value? Before this question can be answered, it is necessary to consider the relationships among the various kinds of knowledge and of these various kinds of knowledge to a human being.[1]

One way of dividing and distinguishing kinds of knowledge is by reference to the *knower's purpose in knowing*. He may wish to know something for the sake of the knowledge itself, or he may be interested in knowing in order to act successfully or to produce something. The former kind of knowledge is called "speculative," "theoretical," or "pure" knowledge; the latter, "practical" or "applied." The former is typified by the scholar and research scientist; the latter, by the wise man and the artist.

Next, we can have different *modes* of knowledge about a particular subject (for example, life, number, man). The first mode of knowledge is that of unreflective, untutored, day-to-day, spontaneous knowledge. For examples, we can consider our direct acquaintance with the objects of daily experience—food, weather, clothes, other people, animals, machines. This kind of knowledge

---

[1] The three modes of knowledge are discussed by Robert J. Henle, S.J., "Science and the Humanities," *Thought*, vol. XXV (1960), 513-36.

3

is similar to those immediate, simple judgments in the practical order which are often called "common sense."[2] Most spontaneous knowledge is practical; but there are also some theoretical truths contained in ordinary knowledge. Some of these latter truths are of interest to us here. In our day-to-day dealing with concrete reality, we have an incontrovertible evidence for the existence of a distinct world of extra-mental reality. We see that this world is made up of things which are also distinct from each other; that these things belong to different kinds or classes; that they undergo change; and that there are different kinds of change. These truths are more or less the immediate results of perceptual experience. Moreover, immediate experience delivers to us a massive, constantly repeated and reinforced evidence for some general propositions (for example, that changes are brought about by causes), and some few conclusions (for example, that the world is dependent upon, and under the control of, some greater being). Of these things and truths even the untaught and unreflective man is certain.

Spontaneous knowledge, however, has very definite limitations. The certain truths that it contains are isolated from each other; spontaneous knowledge is not organized through principles. The reflections of an undisciplined mind tend to be rambling, disconnected, and repetitive. Spontaneous knowledge very often cannot tell why it has the truth; its reasoning is often implicit. Spontaneous knowledge is unable to defend its truths against objections and attacks, and can easily be weakened and even overthrown by passion. Hence, even when spontaneous knowledge is true, this truth is at a subscientific level of development.

The second mode of knowledge is refined. For example, knowledge in the second mode is that which an educated person has of human nature through poetry, history, drama, and so forth; briefly, it can be designated as the product of a liberal education. Most humanistic knowledge is practical in the sense that it is knowledge for living, though it is usually not immediately practical in the way in which techniques and vocational training are practical. Indeed, precisely in this latter sense, humanistic knowledge is called "liberal," because it befits the free autonomous per-

---

[2] On the various kinds of Thomistic epistemologies, see G. Van Riet, *L'Epistémologie thomiste* (Louvain, Institut Supérieure de Philosophie, 1946).

son and perfects him in his own being. Merely useful knowledge —the kind that used to be called "servile"—is directed rather toward the excellence of the final product, or artifact itself (the painting, the table, the automobile), or to the skill (as in running a machine, managing an athletic team). This refined mode of knowledge has two essential characteristics. One is that it possesses some organization through principles. The other is that it is not merely knowledge; it is addressed to the total human personality, and for this reason it often is called "humanistic knowledge." A liberally educated person has learned intellectually; he has also developed his sensory, emotional, and volitional life. Because humanistic knowledge usually develops out of a contact or inter-action with culture, it is more complete than spontaneous knowl-edge, for it draws on the contributions of a social group. For the same reason, many of the crude errors and misconceptions of spontaneous thinking are eliminated from refined knowledge. Very many men find this mode of knowledge sufficient for living a full human life and never achieve any other type of knowledge.

Humanistic or refined knowledge, though it is a necessary and irreplaceable part of a full human development, has some limita-tions as far as knowledge itself is concerned. As knowledge, it does have some organization, but its organizational principles are either understood in the spontaneous mode or in terms of concrete imagery, its structure tends toward the rhetorical, and its deepest understanding tends toward metaphor or myth. In humanism, man has found one pole of his perfection, and yet there is a direction in which the full rationality of human reason has not yet been reached.

The mind's drive toward the conscious exercise of its power to know has led to the development of a third mode of knowl-edge, the scientific.[3] This mode of knowledge is relatively com-plete and has freed itself from the subtler as well as the grosser

[3] In the first part of this book, the term "science" is used in its modern, restricted sense, as a name for a special kind of demonstrative, "third-mode" knowledge. The adjective, "scientific," however, is used to mean not only "belonging to, pertaining to, a science" but also "similar to a science." Thus, the entire group of third-mode knowledges can be called "scientific knowl-edges," because all of them are similar in having an organized structure, and "science" is best known to most people. But later on, the term "science" can be used in a broad sense even for philosophy.

errors of everyday knowledge. Moreover, it is organized by intrinsic principles that are proper to its subject, and therefore it can really demonstrate its conclusions. As a further consequence, it is at least to some extent a certain knowledge.[4] The most familiar examples of organized knowledge are the natural sciences. In physics, for example, there is first of all a carefully checked and relatively complete body of facts; there is secondly an organization of these facts into systematic units by means of general principles and theories: all the facts about light are unified and put into relation with each other through the systematic theory of light; all the facts about falling bodies and planetary motions are unified through the laws of motion. It is only when knowledge has been developed into the scientific mode that we can clearly distinguish the various kinds of knowledge.

In this mode of knowledge, speculative and practical knowledge are clearly distinct. The merely useful sort of knowledge itself cannot be developed into this mode, just as the ultimately practical knowledge of prudence cannot be turned into pure knowledge. Yet there can be practical sciences; in the order of action, there are ethics and political philosophy as well as moral theology; in the order of production, there are the various branches of engineering, and so on. All the other demonstrative knowledges are theoretical, and it is with these that we will be concerned from here on.

2. Kinds of theoretical knowledge

Every knowledge is about something; we can talk about "knowledge in general," but there cannot be any knowledge in general. So, too, every demonstrative knowledge is about something; for example, various "subjects" are studied in school, and each one of them has its own "matter." When we want to explain what we are studying, we give some name or description of the "things" with which the subject is concerned: for example, arithmetic deals with numbers, biology with living things. We call this "the concrete subject matter"; by itself it gives only a very vague and general way of identifying a knowledge.

[4] Selected Passages, No. 3, touches on this point.

If we wish to distinguish more accurately the various demonstrative knowledges, we must examine (*a*) precisely what they intend to investigate and (*b*) how this is to be done. These two questions will accurately determine the specific, or proper, matter of a demonstrative knowledge. The concrete subject matter designates the "things" a knowledge is about indeterminately and in their entirety. What we precisely consider about these "things" is the *abstract* subject matter: number (not, the numbers), life (not, living things). For example, we might say that the abstract matter of the natural sciences is "what can be known about the things around us which come into being by natural processes," and that of the social sciences is "what can be known about men in their relationships to each other, especially as they are formed into groups."

But such a limitation does not yet distinguish demonstrative knowledges. For we find that there are distinct knowledges about the same matter; for example, biology, psychology, and the philosophy of human nature have, at least in part, the same matter, man. And they all intend to find out what can be known about man. What then is the difference between them? Their ways of knowing and the kind of knowledge they obtain are different; this sort of difference is the abstract matter considered explicitly according to the way or ways it is known in the particular knowledges. That is why the manner of our knowledge, the principles we use, the kind of argumentation we employ, are included in the adequate notion of a particular demonstrative knowledge. The abstract matter explicitly designated as it is knowable will be called the "proper subject matter" (or, "proper matter") of a knowledge, and the "particular way in which an abstract matter is knowable" will be called its "formal intelligibility." Thus, to give a complete and accurate description of a demonstrative knowledge, we designate its proper matter, that is, we name its abstract matter together with the formal intelligibility under which it is considered.

3. Characteristics of scientific knowledge

Not only is a scientific knowledge unified and organized by having a complete set of similar data, by having a self-coherent or internally consistent set of propositions in which these data are expressed, and especially by having a single set of principles (in some knowledges this is merely an ideal not yet realized) by means of which everything in that field of knowledge is related, but there must be an explicit *showing* of these relationships. A man who has a scientific knowledge not only knows something, but he knows that he knows. In other words, an organized knowledge is in some sense a *certain* knowledge. From this point of view, an organized knowledge contains not only data or facts but also conclusions, which are arrived at by some form of reasoning or demonstration; hence, organized knowledge is properly a *demonstrative* knowledge (*scientia*).

A second characteristic of organized or demonstrative knowledge is that (with the exception of history) no demonstrative knowledge deals with a singular thing as singular. Physics, for example, is not interested in the individual peculiarities of this falling body (for example, that it is a dark-green object falling at 11:03 A.M. in a second-story classroom in Idaho); similar examples can easily be found in the case of biology, chemistry, or mathematics. (An exception might seem to be "individual psychology," but the individual is included in this science not as *this* individual—for example, John Smith—but in terms of the common characteristic of being *an* individual with an individualized set of values or common variable traits.) In other words, organized, demonstrative knowledge is not of the individual and consequently is not expressed through the use of proper names. Put positively, demonstrative knowledge uses general or common terms. Sometimes, also, an equivalently universal proposition is expressed in the form of an indefinite particular (for example, "A man is a rational animal"). We should not be misled by the grammatical form of propositions into thinking that some sciences do not use universal or at least common terms. In the fifth chapter we will examine the implications of universal knowledge more fully.[5]

But first it will be necessary to consider other demonstrative knowledge with which we are more familiar in order to see similarities and differences. Knowledge, of course, is not a thing

[5] See below, sec. 42.

in itself. As an act, it is the act of a man who knows by his senses or his intellect or both; as a habit, it is a quality of a man. (Here we simply accept the fact that sense and intellect are different; in the philosophy of human nature these powers are considered in detail, and the kind of difference between them is proved.)[6] The knowing subject is a man, not an intellect or a sense. It is by a figure of speech that we say, "The senses know this," and "The intellect knows that." It is, however, a convenient, shorthand way of speaking, and we shall often use it.

We have already seen that no demonstrative (scientific) knowledge concerns the singular as singular, in other words, that demonstrative knowledge is common or general in character. We should be careful not to assume from the start that all scientific knowledge is general in exactly the same way.[7] Most demonstrative knowledges are universal, in the sense that they employ univocal concepts and terms.[8] Univocal concepts deal with one characteristic of things that is common to many and leave differences out of consideration. Univocal concepts are derived, either immediately or mediately, by abstraction from material things.[9] When, in the understanding of a material thing, we consider one characteristic, trait, or aspect of it and omit others, we are said to "abstract" from the latter. The two simplest kinds of abstraction are called "total" and "formal."

The very name, "total abstraction," is a kind of misnomer, but it is traditional and has a certain value. Suppose we consider the existing individual or being as fully determinate (for example, Peter) and then drop out of consideration the individual deter-

[6] By spontaneous knowledge we know that intellect and sense are different. For a philosophical examination of the nature of the difference and a proof that intellect and sense are essentially different, see G. P. Klubertanz, S.J., *Philosophy of Human Nature* (New York, Appleton-Century-Crofts, Inc., 1953), pp. 158–164.

[7] The kind of generality which metaphysical knowledge has will be examined in Chap. III.

[8] A univocal term, as we know from logic, is one that is applied in exactly the same sense to many individual things, for example, "gold," "frog," "chair."

[9] There are various ways in which univocal concepts arise. Those derived immediately from sensible things are gained by simple abstraction. Other univocal concepts are made by combinations of the first kind, by second-level abstraction, and by mental construction.

minations and limitations; the result is an abstract consideration of the whole being indeterminately. When I look at a particular pencil, a particular piece of paper, a particular human being and know them as pencil, paper, and man, I have performed an act of total abstraction ("total," because each of these nouns designates a whole and entire thing [not merely a part]; "abstraction," because the definite individual characteristics are omitted from consideration). Total abstraction can be carried further than this; that is, the being can be known more indeterminately, according to a more and more ultimate genus. For example, Peter can be known not only as man but as animal or living thing. The limit of this kind of abstraction is "material substance";[10] this is the *matter* with which some physical sciences deal. Total abstraction is sometimes called the "first degree of abstraction."

"Formal abstraction" is almost a reverse type of abstraction. In this second type, a formal determinant is considered apart from, and independently of, others. A very clear example is found in the knowledge of number, figure, and surface, which can be considered by the intellect apart from the sensible qualities with which they are associated in the real order. This kind of abstraction consists in considering an accidental form (or a perfection considered after the manner of an accidental form, such as "action," "passion") apart from the other perfections of a being, provided that this accidental form does not depend upon these other perfections for its intelligibility. "Formal abstraction" is often called the "second degree of abstraction"; it is connected with such operations as counting and measuring.

In general, abstraction[11] in its proper sense is an act of sim-

---

[10] If we attempt to carry total abstraction further, we no longer have knowledge of a real thing; perhaps we come to a being of reason, "no-thing conceived of as the indeterminate possibility of being" (cf. sec. 77, on beings of reason). It is true that we can understand "substance" without understanding it as material, but this is done, not by way of abstraction but by way of separation; see below, sec. 17.

[11] In addition to these two basic types of abstraction, there are other, more complicated types of abstraction, which for convenience' sake we will call "second-level" abstraction. Whereas both total and formal abstractions have their point of departure in the real thing, a second-level abstraction has its point of departure in a previous knowledge; for example, "humanity," which is the intelligible form (intelligibility) of man, arises by second-level

ple and absolute consideration, which consists in apprehending one characteristic or intelligibility (*ratio*) without another with which it is associated in the real order. Now, we learn in logic that an act of absolute consideration belongs to the first act of the mind, the simple apprehension. We also know from logic that the object of simple apprehension is an essence or quiddity.

In summary, a consideration of most scientific knowledge yields these general conclusions. Most scientific knowledges deal with strictly universal and univocal concepts. Such concepts are the result of at least total abstraction; formal abstraction may also be involved, as well as other types of abstraction. In any abstraction something is always omitted from the object, and an abstraction, in the strict sense, is an act of simple apprehension directed to an absolute consideration of an essence.

We can now, using the definitions of other sciences as models, give a preliminary and descriptive definition of the philosophy of being. Its subject matter, in general, is reality, or real things; its abstract subject matter is reality as we find it in experience; its formal intelligibility is what is real inasmuch as it is real. Its proper matter can therefore be stated briefly: what is real as real. We can see at once that most other knowledges deal with, or are concerned with, some particular aspect or part of reality (for example, physics, biology, sociology). Thus at first sight the philosophy of being seems to differ from all other organized knowledges even by its general subject matter, for it deals with all of reality, and the others with aspects or parts of reality.

But we may wonder whether there is anything more to the philosophy of being than the sum total of all other knowledges. Is there any room for, and any point to, an alleged organized knowledge about the real as such? Some people (positivists, empiricists) say that there is no such thing at all as the philosophy of being. "It is usually supposed that if you publicly

---

abstraction from "man," which is itself a product of total abstraction. Second-level abstractions are more properly called constructions than abstractions, but there is some similarity, in that the products of second-level abstraction also contain less than the initial stage from which they are derived.

dismiss ontology, it will go away quietly. . . ."[12] Others hold that there is a kind of collected and digested summary of all the various kinds of particular knowledges and that this digest could be called a philosophy of being. Perhaps the best preliminary way to see that there is a place for a distinct and special kind of knowledge called "the philosophy of being" is to look at the type of question that is asked in it. For example. What is it to be real? Why do we call a thing a being? Is there more than one kind of reality? What is change? Is every being changeable, or is there unchanging permanent reality? Is being simple or complex? Is being limited or unlimited? Is a limited being caused? How many kinds of causes are there? What are truth and goodness? What is an individual? A person? Is there a cause of the various beings which we experience? Is this cause God? What kind of being is God, and what is His relationship to us? Even if we do not understand these questions now, it is easy to see that no other organized knowledge asks or answers them and that no collection or summary of other knowledges touches on them.

4. Why should I study philosophy?

For these reasons, there are persons who admit that there is a kind of knowledge called philosophy of being, but think it is an unnecessary luxury, like the pastoral poetry of the eighteenth century or elaborate lacework. We may put this position in the form of a concrete question: What does the philosophy of being mean to me? What difference does it make to me whether I bother answering these questions at all or answer them wrongly? Here a distinction must be made. Some kind of knowledge of the real, at the lowest level of our everyday knowledge and as the implicit background of all our other knowledge, is the absolutely indispensable condition of all other knowledge in any mode—this we hope to see more clearly at the end of the course than we do now. But even now we can see that in a sense every man is implicitly a philosopher. For everyone distinguishes between fact and fiction, between dream and reality; everyone deals with reality, takes it quietly or rebels against it.

[12] James K. Feibleman, *Ontology* (Baltimore, The Johns Hopkins Press, 1951), p. 100.

But to satisfy the profound needs which man has, the intellectual sphere of his activities must be enlarged. What he is, what the world is which not only surrounds him and supports him, but also influences him—these are questions which sooner or later come to a reflective person. Consequently, to reach the perfection of his rationality, a person must come to grips with the ultimate questions which are asked in philosophy.

5. The philosophy of being and the other parts of philosophy

Besides the philosophy of being there are other branches of philosophy. Frequently these divisions are used: logic, which deals with second intentions (beings of reason) that pertain to correct reasoning; cosmology (the general philosophy of nature), which deals with a particular kind of real being—that is, material, corporeal, or changeable essense as such—and considers the nature and activities of this *kind* of thing; the philosophy of human nature, which deals with the real being, man, and explicitly treats of his nature and activities; epistemology, which deals with knowledge itself; ethics, which deals with human action. These various parts of philosophy differ in material object among themselves and also differ from the philosophy of being, which deals with all real beings.

Since each of the other philosophical knowledges, however, does within limits deal with something which is, they must all be governed by metaphysics. The principles and conclusions of the philosophy of being are all-pervading. Not that metaphysics can substitute for other kinds of knowledge, not even for the other parts of philosophy; nor can the truths of any other branch of knowledge be deduced from those of metaphysics. This negative description must suffice for the present; we will again consider the relationship of the philosophy of being to other knowledges at the end of the book.[13]

One particular problem of relationship, however, can be taken up at this point. In order to be a complete knowledge of the real, metaphysics must also deal with the absolutely first principle of all other being, that is, with God. The philosophical study of God is often given a special name, that of "natural

[13] Selected Passages, No. 2, takes up this point.

theology," and is usually studied in a distinct course under that name. Is it distinct, though, from the philosophy of being in the same way that logic, the philosophy of human nature, or ethics is? Natural theology treats of divine things not as the subject matter of the science but as the principle of the subject matter (that is, being itself); consequently, it cannot be adequately distinct from the philosophy of being. The philosophy of being, taken in its full sense, deals with whatever is in its entirety and with all the principles of the real. For convenience, however, the philosophy of being is often divided into two "integral parts":[14] introductory philosophy of being and natural theology, which is the complementary and crowning part of the whole philosophy of being. The following comparison may clarify the relation:

THE WHOLE	THE PARTS
The philosophy of being is a distinct philosophical knowledge dealing with the real as real and with the principles and characteristics of the real.	*Introductory philosophy of being* starts with the real which in fact is caused, indeed with the caused sensible real. From a study of this kind of being, we derive our knowledge of what the real is, of what its characteristics or properties are, and of its principles as this kind of being. Finally, since this kind of reality shows itself to be caused, we can move by way of causality to a knowledge of the uncaused Real as the first principle of the reality of experience, and so to a knowledge of that Reality as real.
	Natural theology deals with uncaused reality as the first principle of all other reality, and so with that uncaused reality as itself real.

[14] An "integral part" is a quantitative or quasi-quantitative part, which together with the rest of the parts makes up a whole by addition and so cannot be predicated of the whole; an integral part can continue to exist when separated from the whole (though it may change its nature in being separated).

6. Philosophy and religion

Philosophy and religion sometimes seem to concern the same things. For example, religious teachings mention good and evil, God, the immortality of the soul, the obligation to do good and avoid evil. Philosophy also deals with these same points. Does that make religion and philosophy the same thing?[15]

By religion, in general, we mean "the sum total of man's relations to a higher being on whom man depends in some way." These relations include both knowledge and action (and the latter is made up of a moral code and some kind of cult or form of worship). Religion can arise as a result of men's effort to find out the basic truths about themselves and the universe and as a result of their desire to act in accord with what they know. A religion that arises in this way is called a "natural religion." In our Western culture, however, this is not what the term "religion" generally connotes. Ordinarily, religion means "revealed religion," that is, a religion which arises both from man's own efforts and a revelation from God. The content of revelation, as far as knowledge is concerned, may include both truths that man's reason could reach by itself and truths that are entirely beyond the powers of human reason. These latter truths can be known only by *faith* (the free intellectual acceptance of a truth on the authority of another); the former objects can be known either by reason or by faith.

When we ask, "Are religion and philosophy the same thing?" obviously we are asking about the relation between religious knowledge and philosophy. To answer this question, we must distinguish not only between natural and revealed religion but also between subject matter and formal intelligibility. As we saw in section 1, knowledges are defined by their proper intelligibilities and distinguished one from another particularly by their formal intelligibilities, even when they have the same material objects. Now, all the knowledge-objects of a natural religion are also dealt with by philosophy; but philosophy deals with some things (for example, the nature of knowledge itself) with which

[15] See G. P. Klubertanz, S.J., "Metaphysics and Theistic Convictions," to be published in *Proceedings of the 1962 Workshop on Teaching Thomism Today* (Washington, Catholic Univ. of America Press).

a natural religion does not deal. The knowledge-objects of a revealed religion, on the other hand, are partly held in common with philosophy and partly are special to revelation (for example, the Trinity, the Incarnation). Thus there are some common points in natural religion, revealed (supernatural) religion, and philosophy.

What about the formal intelligibilities of these three knowledges? The knowledge contained in natural religion may be held on the ground of a man's own personal insight (on any one of three levels of knowledge) or on the authority of another and wiser man. The knowledge of natural religion, therefore, does not necessarily involve personal insight; it is merely necessary that it contain truths attainable by human reason. Hence, in the case of a philosopher, his natural religious knowledge and his philosophy would be the same, even though natural religious knowledge is not necessarily a demonstrative knowledge. On the other hand, it is the special characteristic of a revealed religion that its truths be accepted by faith. Now, faith is knowledge resting on the authority of a witness, such that the evidence for the assertion bears directly *not* on the truth of what is known but on the character of the witness as such (that is, on his knowledge and truthfulness. When the revealing witness is God himself, the faith by which we accept His revelation is supernatural faith. But in philosophy the situation is different. All the branches of philosophy (indeed, all organized knowledges except history and theology) rest on evidence that bears directly or indirectly on the truth of what is known. A philosopher as such takes something as true because there is evidence bearing on the truth itself; he does not take something as true *because* someone has said it. On the other hand, the knowledge of revealed religion is taken as true precisely because God has said it. Consequently, philosophy and revealed religion have formally different intelligibilities and so are really distinct one from the other.

One consequence of this difference is that a man who has everyday knowledge plus faith can tell an error from the truth. He cannot, however, tell why an error is an error; he cannot answer an objection; he cannot easily apply his knowledge to unforeseen situations or difficult problems. This is just the kind of thing a philosopher as such can do. Hence, it is practically necessary, even from the viewpoint of revealed religion, that some believers become skilled in philosophical thinking. So philosophy indirectly helps faith. Secondly, a believer, because he has an intellect with an innate drive toward understanding, wants to understand the content of his faith as much as possible. The organized effort to understand faith is called theology, and a large part of scientific theology consists in the use of philosophical principles and methods to help in the understanding of faith.

On the other hand, historically speaking, faith has helped philosophy. For example, a man who believes what the Christian revelation has to tell him about the nature of God cannot make the philosophical error of thinking that God is an impersonal force. Theology thus is a "negative norm" for philosophy, inasmuch as a man's faith may warn him of errors he is making in philosophy. It must be noted, however, that faith can tell a man *that* he is making an error; it does not tell him *why* the error was made or *how* to correct it—this is a properly philosophical task. Secondly, there is a positive influence of faith on philosophy. Faith suggests new problems to philosophical reflection (for example, Christian thinkers go as deeply as they do into the nature of personality because of the problems raised by the Incarnation and the Trinity); and faith often presents truths that serve as hints for the properly *philosophical* solutions of problems (for example, St. Thomas's statement, *"Deus est ipsum esse,"* owes much to the revelation of God's name, "I am who am," in Exod. 3:13).

Akin to this is the advantage that a Christian student has in the very learning of philosophy.[16] Through his faith and the Christian traditions, a Christian has accepted as certain and has become familiar with truths like the dependence of the sensible universe on God, the immortality of his soul, and the existence of God and other spiritual beings. He has a firm grasp of these truths, though he may have only a slight understanding of them. Yet this much at least he does understand, that reality includes much more than is contained in the narrow limits of his own sense experience. Be-

---

[16] See "Metaphysics and Theistic Convictions."

cause of his firm acceptance of truths about nonsensible reality he does not find it hard to raise scientific questions about the nature of the real or to follow a purely intellectual argument whose conclusions go beyond the limitations of immediate sense experience. But what a Christian young man or woman accepts and can understand with a measure of fullness, it may take an unbeliever years of experience and study to grasp. Even with the best will in the world, it is the hard work of years to arrive at a full understanding of being, of the existence of God as a nonmaterial and unlimited being, and so forth. For this reason, Aristotle has said, "Young men have no [intellectual] conviction about [the objects and principles of wisdom], but only use the proper language" (*Ethics*, Bk. VI, 1142a19).

But this by no means implies a formal dependence of philosophy upon revelation and faith. Both the Christian and the unbeliever philosophize in the light of rational evidence; both, though with varying degress of difficulty, can arrive at an intellectual understanding of being and its principles and can acquire rational convictions about them.

Unbelievers sometimes imagine that they alone are real philosophers, for they think that they are the only ones who can call everything into question. Now, no one can question anything except from some starting point, for, as we shall see more clearly as we go along, man is a being-in-a-situation, not an absolute and isolated being. If the situation from which one questions is part of the reality which could be called into question, then one's questioning in principle cannot be complete. The contemporary unbeliever raises his questions in the context of this historical moment of human culture, a moment that has as much need of being questioned—and in just the same way—as anything else that he does question. But the believer who wishes to philosophize situates himself in the context of his faith. From here he can raise questions about any and *every* being accessible to reason. Because the believer has an other than merely rational security, he can question more completely as well as more serenely. He is never in a position to yield to panic, nor need he ever be dishonest about a problem. This, however, does not mean that it is easy for a Christian to be authentically rational, but only that he is in a better position to attain complete authenticity.

St. Thomas Aquinas has explained the relation between reason and revelation very satisfactorily in the fourth chapter of the first book of the *Contra Gentiles*, and a careful reading of this fourth chapter will be most rewarding.

7. Thomistic philosophy

As we shall see much more fully in later chapters, there are many ways of considering reality. Every grown person has an outlook on life (sometimes called a *Weltanschauung*) that involves an implicit metaphysics. Philosophers explicitly state and develop their philosophical view of reality—and come to differing conclusions. Some of these philosophers are wrong, as we shall also try to see; but most often it is a question of how adequate a philosophy is to express the totality of the real.

Moreover, we have seen that what is most characteristic of a demonstrative knowledge is the formal intelligibility which it seeks. This formal intelligibility is concretely specified by the principles and the methods which are used. Thus, what we try to do in philosophy is partly determined by what we think it means "to understand something philosophically" and partly by what we think we have to do to reach that understanding. Here, too, there are differences. We can hardly speak of "errors" of aim and method, except when they would be obviously inept, and this is not likely to be the case very often.

As beginners in philosophy, we are not yet in a position to judge all the various philosophers. It is foolish not to try to make use of the help we can get from a good philosopher, and it is impossible to start out entirely without any metaphysics—a normal eight-year-old is already developing an outlook on life. But because our knowledge of reality as such is still on the everyday level, it is likely to be mixed with much error. For practical purposes, therefore, in order to get started in philosophy with some hope of developing a reasonably good philosophy of our own, we must take someone's lead. What kind of criterion can we use to pick a guide? (*a*) He must know that he is building a metaphysics; if he has only an implicit metaphysics, he will not be of much help to us. For this reason, many thinkers who deal explicitly only with specialized problems (for example, with logic or ethics or theory of knowledge or philosophy of science) will not be practical guides. (*b*) He must know the various kinds of philosophies that have been constructed and have seen their advantages and shortcomings through their historical development. (*c*) His philosophy must violate no evidence; it must be in harmony with all the evidence and certitudes that are available. These conditions are excellently fulfilled by St. Thomas Aquinas.[17] (Note that we are not going to take his philosophy as true *because* he said it. To do this would be to acquire not a philosophy but an opinion.)

This temporary procedure, however, should be replaced at the end of our entire philosophy course by our own personal understanding of the truth and adequacy of our philosophy. In judging the adequacy of a philosophy, we must measure the correctness and adequacy of definitions, principles, and conclusions in relation to the proper matter of the demonstrative knowledge within which they function. To some extent we can be doing this even as we go through the course, especially when we have completed a unit.

8. Definitions[18]

The matter (subject matter) of a knowledge designates indeterminately and in its entirety that which a knowledge is about. Concretely, it comprises the "things" that are studied; for example, the matter of geometry is the lines, surfaces, solids, and angles. Abstractly, the matter designates what is common to all these "things"; in plane geometry, this would be "figures drawn on a surface."

The formal intelligibility pertaining to a kind of knowledge is what is specifically knowable about the matter, and this involves

[17] See W. Norris Clarke, S.J., "The Contemporary Character of Thomism," *Workshop on Teaching Thomism Today*.

[18] This first set of definitions of terms is simply a vocabulary or glossary, giving the meanings of these terms. These definitions settle no philosophical problems; they only make it possible to talk about such problems. Italicized terms are the ones that will be used most frequently and therefore ought to be memorized.

the way or ways it is known and the principles that are used. For example, the formal intelligibility of geometry is the construction, measurement, and investigation of the properties and relations of its matter. Note: most "things" of our experience can be known under more than one formal intelligibility.

The proper matter of a knowledge is its subject matter as specified by the formal intelligibility. For example, the proper subject matter of plane geometry is the construction, measurement, and investigation of the properties and relations of figures on a surface (which concretely are the lines, bounded surfaces, angles).

Demonstrative (or scientific) knowledge is an exactly stated knowledge with a single proper matter, organized through self-coherent definitions and, especially, by a single set of principles and shown to be accurate and true by some kind of reasoning process which lead to a certain assent or at least to a well-founded assent. For example, physics, philosophy, geometry and history are scientific knowledges.

Science is a kind of demonstrative knowledge concerned with the observation of facts, the establishment of general laws, and the explanation of these facts by means of general concepts logically constructed and deductively verified. Only the natural sciences are sciences in this strict sense.

Philosophy, descriptively speaking, is the collective name of metaphysics, philosophy of nature, epistemology, and ethics, taken together. Defined according to its abstract subject matter, philosophy is a (quasi-) genus of demonstrative knowledge about reality and the major kinds of reality taken as inclusively as possible. Defined according to its general formal intelligibility, philosophy is a (quasi-) genus of demonstrative knowledge that seeks (to draw from experience by means of direct insights, ontological concepts, and causal analysis) as complete and coherent an explanation of its matter as is possible.[19]

[19] To define "philosophy" essentially is a very difficult task. Many so-called definitions really define metaphysics; dictionary definitions are not of much help. The third definition given above will not be understood by the beginning student; it will, it is hoped, become clear by the time he finishes this book. Note, in the meantime, two things: (a) philosophy is only one among all the demonstrative knowledges; (b) philosophy draws from

Metaphysics is that "part" of philosophy whose proper matter is the real as real.

Experience is our direct encounter with and knowledge of the persons and things in our world.

Reasoning, in general, is any process of knowledge by which definitions and judgments are reached which are (1) not simply perceptual judgments, or simple essences reached by total abstraction, (2) nor simple insights. Briefly, reasoning is all mediate knowledge.

Total abstraction is the consideration of the nature or quiddity of a thing without consideration of its individual determinants.

Formal abstraction is the consideration of the formal determinants of a thing apart from other determinants of that same thing.

A univocal concept is one which is true of many individuals in exactly the same sense.

Abstraction is the act of considering one intelligibility of a thing without considering others with which it is associated in the real order.

Intelligibility is a characteristic, trait, or aspect (of a thing) which can be understood by the intellect (*ratio*).

Thing is a whole or a complete individual (as opposed to something that is merely a part, as for example, a hand; or to a collection, as a heap of stones). For example, a tree, a dog, a man.

Sensible thing is a thing capable of directly affecting our senses and therefore something capable of being immediately perceived in external experience. The three examples given of *thing* are also sensible things.

Material thing is a thing among whose intrinsic properties are (*a*) that it is capable of being measured and (*b*) that it is able to undergo gradual change; it is not necessary that we be able to sense it. (This is merely a descriptive definition; an essential definition will be given later.) For example, the air 50 miles above ground, a free electron, all sensible things.

---

ordinary natural experience, and so does not in principle exclude faith and revealed theology nor necessarily conflict with them. In consequence, philosophy is not *the* explanation of everything, nor the highest wisdom, nor a doctrine of salvation.

Principle is that from which something else follows. For example, the dawn is the principle of the day; fire is a principle of heat; the structure of a watch is a principle of its movement.

A *principle of being* or reality is that from which or through which something is or comes to be. For example, the principle of a house is its builder and also the bricks and other materials that make it up.

A *principle of knowledge* is some knowledge (usually a judgment or a proposition, but not necessarily so) from which some other knowledge follows, according to some kind of connection between the two. For example, in a syllogism, the premises are the principles of the conclusion.

9. Readings

St. Thomas Aquinas, *The Division and Methods of the Sciences: Questions V and VI of St. Thomas's Commentary on the* De Trinitate *of Boethius* (Toronto, Pontifical Institute of Mediaeval Studies, 1953), q. 5, art. 4. This text deals with the relation between metaphysics and natural theology; *Commentary on the Metaphysics of Aristotle*, trans. John P. Rowan (Chicago, Regnery, 1961), Bk. I, lesson 1, Nos. 1–35, pp. 7–16; Bk. II, lesson 1, Nos. 273–288, pp. 115–119; Bk. IV, lesson 1, Nos. 529–543, pp. 216–219 (on the object of metaphysics).

A large number of passages from St. Thomas Aquinas are translated and collected by James F. Anderson, *Metaphysics of St. Thomas Aquinas* (Chicago, Regnery, 1953).

E. F. Caldin, *Science and Christian Apologetic*, Aquinas Papers, No. 17 (London, Blackfriars, 1951), pp. 1–12, on the method of science. This is a simply written yet accurate presentation by a prominent British layman, who is a professor of chemistry.

Etienne Gilson, *The Unity of Philosophical Experience* (New York, Scribner's, 1940), pp. 299–320; "Historical Research and the Future of Scholasticism," *The Modern Schoolman*, XXIX (1951), 1–10; *Reason and Revelation in the Middle Ages* (New York, Scribner's, 1939), pp. 67–84. The first of these selections deals with the distinctive nature of philosophy, the second and third with the relation of faith to reason. The author is an historian of philosophy as well as a philosopher. Besides teaching in his native France and lecturing in many other countries, for many years he directed and taught at the Pontifical Institute of Mediaeval Studies in Toronto.

D. J. B. Hawkins, *Approach to Philosophy* (London, Sands, 1938), pp. 1–22. Father Hawkins is a British philosopher.

Jacques Maritain, *Degrees of Knowledge*, trans. Gerald Phelan (New

York, Scribner's, 1960), Introduction. This section concerns the place of metaphysics among the various knowledges. The author is a well-known French Catholic philosopher, who lived and taught for many years in the United States.

John Wild, *Realistic Philosophy* (New York, Harper, 1948), Introduction and historical section. This passage deals with the relation of philosophy to other forms of knowledge and shows the origin and development of philosophy. Professor Wild is an American philosopher; in this book, he follows Aristotle, though with some relation to St. Thomas Aquinas.

SELECTED PASSAGES FROM ST. THOMAS AQUINAS

1. On the Nature of Metaphysics

As the philosopher [Aristotle] teaches in his *Politics*, when some things are ordered to one, one of them must be the regulating or ruling one and the others the regulated or ruled. This is clear in the union of soul and body, for the soul naturally commands and the body obeys. This is the case also among the powers of the soul, for the irascible and the concupiscible powers are in natural order ruled by reason. Moreover, all the sciences and arts are ordered to one; namely, to the perfection of man, which is his beatitude. For this reason it is necessary that one among these sciences and arts be the director of all the others, and this one rightly lays claim to the name of wisdom. For it is the prerogative of the wise man to order (that is, regulate, or dispose) others.

Which demonstrative knowledge this may be and with what it is concerned can be judged if one diligently observes how someone is fit to rule. For (as the Philosopher says in the aforementioned book) just as men of remarkably superior understanding are naturally rulers and lords, and men of robust body but wanting in understanding are naturally servants, so the knowledge which is in the highest degree intellectual ought to be regulative of others. And this [knowledge] is the one which is concerned with the most intelligible objects.

Now we can take [the expression] "most intelligible objects" in three ways. First from the order of the [act of] understanding. For the things from which the intellect obtains certitude seem to be the more intelligible. Hence, since the certitude of scientific knowledge is acquired by the intellect through causes, the knowledge of causes seems to be in the greatest degree intellectual.

Second, from the comparison of the intellect to the sense. For since sense [knowledge] is the knowledge of particulars, the intellect would seem to differ from sense by reason of the fact that it comprehends universals. Hence, that demonstrative knowledge is in the highest degree intellectual which deals with the most universal principles.

These are being and what follows upon being, such as one and many, potency and act. But such principles should not remain entirely undetermined, since without them there cannot be had a completed knowledge of those principles which are proper to some genus or species. Nor should these principles be dealt with again in some one particular demonstrative knowledge, because, as they are requisite for the understanding of each and every kind of being, they would, with equal reason, be dealt with in any particular knowledge. It remains, therefore, that principles of this sort should be treated in one common demonstrative knowledge, which, since it is in the highest degree intellectual, is regulative of the others.

Third, from the intellect's very knowledge. For since each and every thing has intellective power from this, that it is without matter, it is appropriate that those things be most intelligible which are in the greatest degree separate from matter. For the intelligible and the understanding must be proportionate and of the same genus, since the understanding and the intelligible in act are one. But those things are in the greatest degree separate from matter which not only abstract from designated matter, "such as natural forms taken in the universal, with which natural science deals," but which altogether abstract from sensible matter—and this not only according to their intelligibilities (such as mathematical objects), but also according to their act of existing, such as God and the intelligences. Wherefore the demonstrative knowledge which considers these things appears to be in the highest degree intellectual and the chief and master of the others.

Now, this threefold consideration ought to be applied to one demonstrative knowledge, not to different ones. For the separated substances that have been mentioned [in the third place] are the universal and first causes of being. It is, moreover, the work of the same knowledge to consider the proper causes of a given genus and the genus itself; thus, natural science considers the principles of natural body. Hence, it is proper that one and the same knowledge have as its function to consider separate substances and being in common, which is the "genus" of which the substances mentioned are the common and universal causes.

From this it is clear that, although this demonstrative knowledge considers the three classes of objects spoken of [common principles, universal causes, separate substances], it does not have any one of them at all for its subject, but only being in common. For that is the subject of a knowledge of which we seek the causes and passions [properties]; but the causes themselves of a given genus are not the subject. For the knowledge of the causes of some genus is the end to which the consideration of a knowledge finally attains. Still, though the subject of this knowledge is being in common, the whole of it is said to be about those things which are separate from matter according to their act of existing and according to their intelligibility. For not only are those things which can never be in matter said to be separate from matter according to their esse and their intelligibility (such are God and intellectual substances), but also those things which are able to be without matter, such as being in common. But this could not be, if [the latter] depended on matter for their existence.

According to these three classes of objects which have been mentioned, therefore, from which we weigh the perfection of this demonstrative knowledge, it comes to have three names. It is called divine knowledge, or *theology*, insofar as it considers the above-mentioned substances. It is called *metaphysics*, insofar as it considers being and those things which follow upon it; for these transphysical things are arrived at by the way of analysis, as the more common are arrived at after the less common. It is spoken of as *first philosophy*, insofar as it considers the first causes of things. Thus it is clear what the subject of this demonstrative knowledge is, in what way it is related to other knowledges, and by what name it is named.

Commentary on Aristotle's
Metaphysics, proemium.

2. *Metaphysics and Other Knowledges*

In all the sciences and arts, whether speculative or operative, it is proper that what is higher and what orders others should consider [the] more universal intelligibilities, since principles are few in number and very great in power, and those that are simple are extended to the most objects. For example, military science is subject to political science, and cavalry science is subject to military, and so on successively. Political science is subject to the consideration of human good, simply. But military science considers this same good inasmuch as it is determined to matters of war, and so on. Because of this the lower takes its principles from the higher, and this is a kind of *propter quid* [causal] proof. This relation is more indisputably evident in the speculative knowledges, because metaphysics, which orders the other knowledges, considers the intelligibility of being absolutely, while the other sciences consider being according to some determination.

Commentary on the Second
Book of the Sentences, dis. 3,
q. 3, art. 2.

Habits are specified by their objects according to that intelligibility to which they principally attend. . . . Even though something is common, there is a particular and proper intelligibility of object. Thus, first philosophy is a special demonstrative knowledge, though it considers being inasmuch as it is common to all things, because it considers that special intelligibility of being inasmuch as it does not depend on matter and motion.

> Commentary on the *Third*
> *Book of the* Sentences, dis. 27,
> q. 2, art. 4, qa. 2.

Metaphysics . . . considers all things inasmuch as they are beings, not coming down to a proper knowledge of morality or nature. For the intelligibility, "being," since it is different in different things, is not sufficient for the specific knowledge of things.

> Commentary on the *First*
> *Book of the* Sentences, pro-
> logue, q. 1, art. 2.

3. *The Certitude of Metaphysics*

The more a scientific knowledge is prior in nature, the more certain it is. This can be seen in that those sciences whose object can be said to be an addition to that of other sciences are less certain than the sciences which take fewer things into consideration. For example, arithmetic is more certain than geometry, for the objects of geometry have something more than those of arithmetic. This is clear if we look at what each of these sciences takes as its first principle; namely, the unit and the point. For the point adds location to the unit. For the intelligibility of the unit is constituted by undivided being. This notion, when it is taken as a measure, is the principle of number. But the point adds location to this.

The particular sciences are posterior in nature to the universal sciences, because the subject of the former adds to the subject of the latter. For example, "being as changeable," with which the scientific knowledge of nature deals, adds to "being (without qualification)" which is the subject of metaphysics and adds to "quantified being" which is the subject of mathematics. Therefore that scientific knowledge which is about being and the most universal objects is the most certain. Nor is it to be objected that metaphysics is here said to be about fewer things, though it was said above [earlier in the same section, not quoted here] that it knows all things. For the universal comprehends fewer things in act, but more in potency. And a science is the more certain the fewer actual considerations are necessary for the consideration of its subject. Wherefore, practical sciences are the most uncertain, because they must consider the many circumstances of singular operables.

> Commentary on *Aristotle's*
> Metaphysics, Bk. I, lect. 2
> (ed. Cathala, No. 47).

II

The Meaning of "Being"

10. Various senses of the word *real*

We have seen that metaphysics can be described briefly as the demonstrative (scientific) knowledge of the real inasmuch as it is real, and that therefore its basic question is, "What is it to be *real?*" Before we can go further into this question, we must distinguish the various senses of the word "real."

In the proper sense of the word, a real being is an actual being, one which is not merely an object of the mind or merely possible, but *is* actually in itself. This preliminary description will be made more exact later on. The best way to clarify the proper meaning of *real* is by contrast: an existing airplane is a real machine, an interplanetary spaceship is not real (not in 1962 at least); Carry Back is a real horse, Pegasus is not; Sir Winston Churchill is a real human being, Ichabod Crane is not; microbes are real beings, leprechauns are not; an orange is a real being, a perfect sphere is only an object of thought.

Sometimes the word "real" is used in an extended sense, for example, in logic and epistemology, to designate not only what is actually now but also whatever has existed, will exist, or can exist independently of thought. In this extended sense, a dinosaur is a real animal, but a centaur is not; Hamlet is a real character, Pogo is not; the battles of the Greeks and Trojans were real, the quarrels of Jupiter and Juno were not. This extended meaning of *real* is used to make a distinction among objects of thought: real objects are those that actually exist or could exist; unreal objects are those that cannot exist.[1]

Henceforward, *real* (and forms derived from it) will be used only in its proper sense; that is, to designate the actual things which are now. Thus, when we speak of "knowledge of the real" we will mean "knowledge of things which are here and now actual," and when we speak of "the real order," we will mean "the order (or totality) of things which are actual here and now." If we want to use the extended sense of the word "real," we will always attach the qualification, "in the wide sense."

Since metaphysics is the demonstrative knowledge of the real inasmuch as it is real, and since we can know and talk about things that are not real, obviously our first question must be, What is it to be real? The question, "What is it to be a real thing?" is not a question about our knowledge[2] but about the thing known.

---

[1] For example, a man can think about a dog he used to own which died last year; the dog is no longer part of the real world in which he lives today. A man can think of a purely fictional character; again, no actual, properly real being corresponds to his thought. But the one who thinks about these things can recognize that in the case of the dog there *was* an actual real thing to which, if it were now, his thought would conform; he can likewise recognize that in the case of the purely fictional character there *could be* an actual thing to which, if it were actual, his thought would also conform. In both cases, absolutely speaking, there is no actual real thing of which he is thinking; in both cases there is simply no-thing in the real order. Nevertheless, the word "real" has been extended to designate objects of thought such as these in order to mark off a distinction between them and still other objects of thought to which *no* real thing *can* correspond: for example, the internally inconsistent objects mentioned in the earlier paragraphs of this section (leprechauns, centaurs, Pogo, the world of Greek mythology) or such objects as necessarily involve purely mental objectivity, such as logical genera and species ("the species, man"; "the genus, animal"). A diagram may help to show the relationships of these terms:

$$\left\{ \begin{array}{l} \text{real in the wide sense } \ldots\ldots \\ \quad \textit{as opposed to} \\ \text{the mere object of thought} \end{array} \right\} \left\{ \begin{array}{l} \text{the properly real, the actual} \\ \quad \textit{as opposed to} \\ \text{the past, the future, the possible} \end{array} \right.$$

For a further explanation of this, see below, sec. 77.

[2] Questions about our knowledge of the real are questions like, "How do we know real things?" and, "How can we tell, from looking at our knowledge, whether an object of knowledge is real or not?" These questions can-

11. Phenomenalism and the meaning of *being*

To help ourselves see the meaning of this question and the basic importance of the answer, we will look at some historical answers before we look at reality itself.[3] Our purpose is to understand these philosophical positions, not to refute them.[4] But to help ourselves to see that these are not things that one could affirm or deny without any change in his basic outlook on life, we will point out some consequences that are logically connected with them.

A first answer to the question is: A thing is real because, and inasmuch as, it acts or does something. A philosophy which answers the question of the meaning of reality in this way is called "phenomenalism" (from the Greek word meaning "appearance"). Phenomenalism, or "actualism," does not mean, "Every real thing acts in some way" or "We know that something is real because we find it acting" or "We can tell what kind of thing

---

not be answered or even considered now, for the answers to them depend at least in part on the philosophy of human nature.

[3] To make these different answers more concrete, we will refer to various historical positions. We are, however, not studying the history of philosophy, and so we are not bound to an adequate exposition of the thought of the great philosophers or to a refutation of their systems as wholes. We are interested only in clarifying the question and seeing what is involved in it.

If a reader should desire further information on some of these basic positions, he can find a full introduction and a guide to further reading in the following books. James Collins, *A History of Modern European Philosophy* (Milwaukee, Bruce, 1954), pp. 109–117 (on Hobbes and materialism); pp. 204–207, 226–228 (on Spinoza and the relation between reason and reality); pp. 267–277, 279–281 (Leibniz and the world of intelligible essence); pp. 707–710 (on Comte and positivism); pp. 408–409, 415, 433–436 (on Hume and phenomenalism); pp. 509–512 (on Kant and the possibility of metaphysics; a highly recommended section). Etienne Gilson, *Being and Some Philosophers*, 2d ed. (Toronto, Pontifical Institute of Mediaeval Studies, 1952), pp. 83–96 (on Scotism and the particular); pp. 51–73 (on Averroës); pp. 74–82 (on Avicenna, another kind of essentialist).

[4] It is unfair to attack something which a person does not understand. Moreover, instead of refuting the position, one is likely to miss the point entirely. So the first requisite is to understand both our own position and those of the philosophers who hold different positions. And once we have a thorough understanding both of our own philosophy and of other philosophies in their historical context, it is usually unnecessary to engage in a refutation of them. To some this proposition may seem a paradox; the only answer is a real study of the history of philosophy.

something is by seeing what sort of actions it performs." These three propositions are perfectly true, but they are not the basic statement of actualism. Actualism holds that action is the reality of the thing. According to this doctrine, for example, "I" am real, in the sense that there are some thoughts, desires, movements, and so forth, which in some inexplicable way belong together. The sources of this doctrine are an incorrect understanding of substance and accident and a misuse of the ability of our mind to consider an action without considering the agent and thus to consider the action as if it were a thing.[5]

To assess the value of phenomenalism we need only to consider attentively the whole real things which are actual. How does an actual real thing manifest itself to us in our experience; for example, a human person? A human person manifests himself to us as something real which acts; a person can act precisely because he is real. A thing is not real in consequence of its action; rather, it can act because it is real. We will have to investigate the relation between a being and its action later on,[6] but for the time being it is sufficiently clear that acting is not the very meaning of being real.

If reality essentially consists in activity, and if activity is in continual change, there can be no permanent personality and no immortality for the human soul. Further, if in such an explanation of reality a philosopher still talks about God, this will not be the transcendent, creative God of Christian thought but perhaps some ideal action or complexus of actions.

12. Materialism and the meaning of *being*

A second answer to the question, What is it to be real? is the answer given by materialism. As a preliminary approach to the materialistic view, we can ask ourselves what the difference is between an architect's idea of a house and the real house which is the result of that plan. It is that the plan has been "realized" in the material components of lumber, cement, stone, clay, and so forth. According to the materialistic view, a plan, order, or structure is not real of itself; matter is the principle of reality.

[5] See below, sec. 39.
[6] See below, sec. 39.

Superficially, we may think of materialism as an explanation of reality based on human productive activity.

Materialism can take several forms. The most extreme sort of materialism holds that only matter exists and simply denies that anything else is or can be real. Dogmatic behaviorism, for example, denied that men really had thoughts and feelings; general semantics, today, admits that men have sensible feelings but persists in the denial of thought.

A more moderate sort of materialism admits that there are some realities, such as ideas, which are not simply material. But it is still a materialism, for it holds that these nonmaterial realities arise from matter, depend entirely on matter, and vanish completely when they are separated from matter. This moderate materialism is professed by some who call themselves "modern materialists," as well as by the Marxists, who call their system "dialectical materialism."

According to all materialists, all the things we see are material, and the differences between them arise from various combinations of simpler material elements. The ultimate elements are then the principle of reality for them. The older materialists and the Marxists think of these principles as material, substantial particles which always existed by themselves. Others, trying to bring philosophy more into line with what they consider to be the best scientific views, think of ultimate reality as a large amount of "free energy" which can be either structured into things or left "free," "unattached" (for example, in the form of radiation).

For the moment, we are going to consider only one point: the meaning of *real* as given by materialism, "To be real is to be material or in matter." It is true that the things which we experience are material. Why should we even question the identification of reality with matter? We question it for the simple reason that we have equally immediate experience of our own conscious activity, especially that of intellectual knowledge and of choice. These activities have as much claim to be called real as any activities of the things we find that are distinct from us. If we wish to respect the evidence, we must admit that both the activities of physical things and our own conscious activities are truly real. If we look attentively at our own acts of knowledge, they do not present themselves as sensible. They have no directly discoverable relation *as actions* to any material characteristic. Intellectual understanding has no sensible qualities; it presents itself as simply different from, and not describable in terms of, mass and motion, chemical action, electromagnetic activity, or in one phrase, any activities of nonhuman things. Take the act of understanding what a square is (or what justice is or that a given syllogism is valid). Examine that act. It is real; you do understand. Yet that act remains indescribable except in its own supersensible terms.

Hence, it is good to ask: "Is matter *identically* reality?" "Is matter the principle of reality in all real things?"[7]

Matter, as the extreme materialists talk about it, is not something which we can experience. Matter is "in itself" always determin*able*. It becomes this or that, it acquires this or that structure. *Real* matter is always some *kind* of matter. As far as direct sense experience is concerned, we experience minerals, plants, animals, men, air, the planets, and so forth. But the determinability of "matter in itself" is more strikingly seen in the case of the supposedly ultimate particles or energy: these ultimate particles have definite electrical characteristics and a definite size;[8] energy is always of some definite kind and quantity; a particle is always an electron or a proton or some other kind of particle (or "wave packet" or whatever other term scientists may find better). In other words, the "matter in itself," which is alleged to be the principle of reality, is itself a determinable genus that is determined by some other principle.

But to be real is to be fully determinate. Why? Because to be determin*able* has a double implication: (1) to be *able* to be something or other and (2) at the present moment *not* to be it.

[7] The first of these two questions implies the position of extreme materialism, the second, of moderate materialism.

[8] At the present time (1962), physicists hold that the electron (and other subatomic particles as well) does not have a completely determined position. Without going into an explanation of the nature of scientific theory, this much at least is clear: subatomic particles have a definite quantum and kind of energy; their size is not completely indefinite but can be known within some limits; their location cannot be determined at the same time as their velocity, but it also is not completely indefinite.

We must then ask the question, Does it make sense to say, "That in virtue of which a real thing is determinable, and consequently *not* yet a definite reality, is simultaneously that in virtue of which every real thing *is* real"? Recall again the precise point of the present discussion. It is not to determine whether there is or is not an individual existing thing which is purely spiritual (without any matter at all); it is simply this, Is a real thing (material or not, as the case may be) real in virtue of some indeterminate "matter in itself"? In other words, Is there something even about a material thing which is not merely "matter in itself"?

If matter is not the whole of reality, is it at least the principle of reality? Another way of putting the question is, Is matter the reason for all reality? Modern materialists and dialectical materialists say that it is; at one time, they contend, there was only matter. Through the course of millions of years, this matter acted and reacted with itself, and so plants, animals, and men came about. But in the last analysis, the simple elemental particles of matter are the self-sufficient cause of all reality; they are eternal, indestructible, active, as we gather from the statements of these philosophers. This position will need to be examined from several different points of view as we go on.

Materialism involves a number of consequences which we are not going to take up here, but which it will be useful to point out. It involves (*a*) the denial of any spiritual reality or person; (*b*) at least logically, the denial of any essential differences in the activities of things; (*c*) the explanation of life and consciousness in terms of the nonliving and the nonconscious. The first of these consequences is evident. The second follows from the admission by the materialist that matter is an undifferentiated principle. Differences can therefore be only accidental. Those materialists who hold that consciousness, desire, and so forth, are really different from nonconscious activities do so at the cost of logical consistency. For—and this is the third consequence—if matter is the principle of reality, then real activities are material, and the activities of nonliving things are the constitutent elements of all activity. It is fine rhetoric but poor logic to insist that materialism fully respects the evidence of life and knowledge.

13. Essentialism and the meaning of *being*

A third solution offered to the question, "What is it to be real?" is not quite so simple and naïve as the first. In general, it consists in saying, "For a thing to be real is to be the *kind* of thing it is." For example, to be a *real* chair is simply to be a *chair;* to be a *real* dog is simply to be a *dog.* In formal and general terms, this doctrine can be summed up by saying, "To be real is to be an essence (quiddity)." We will label this type of explanation "essentialism." Historically, essentialism has taken five major forms.[9]

(1) Platonic essentialism ascribes full reality to the "essence in itself"—for example, to the "horse in itself," "man in himself," "good in itself," and so on. These essences in themselves are the fully real things, but they are not immediately experienced. On the other hand, the things we immediately experience are real by sharing (participating) in the fully real things. Consequently, the principle of reality in the things we experience is that which is fully real in itself by being what it is. The essences in themselves are also called "separated forms" or "ideas." But this Platonic explanation replaces a question with a puzzle, for what is asserted is that the reality of *x* lies in its relation to *y* which is in itself and *also* somehow in *x.* What is this relation? How can the idea be both separated from particulars (in order to be real, in other words, to be a pure essence) and united to them (in order to give reality to them)?

(2) Because this relationship is essentially ambiguous and obscure many modern Platonists have abandoned the separation of the ideas and maintain that an individual or a real thing is constituted by the combination or intersection of many universals (for example, Peter is that particular thing constituted by the coming together of man, white, tall, slender, curly-haired, and so forth). But this theory has two defects: although a collection of universals may be less common than any single universal, it is still not really an individual (and we certainly have direct ex-

[9] Many more divisions could be given, but our present purpose is sufficiently served by a consideration of these types. It is important to note that not every essentialism is realistic; in fact, many types of essentialism are purely idealistic; that is, they maintain that reality consists only of ideas. It will be interesting to recall this observation when we make our critique of essentialism.

perience of individuals, ourselves for example); secondly, there is no effective way to distinguish between a real thing in the proper sense of the word and an essence or a possible thing (which is real only in the wide sense of the word). The Lone Ranger can be more fully described by many persons than Julius Caesar; yet the first is a fictional character and the second was real.

(3) The most subtle of the essentialist explanations is the Scotistic. According to the followers of Scotus, there are various kinds or degrees of reality (the *proper* meaning of "reality" is not directly admitted by them). The minimal degree of reality is that of an object of thought; the next, that of an essence; the highest is that of an essence with haecceity (that is, the ultimately actual singularizing principle). For example, "man" is real with the reality of essence; "Peter" is fully real, having the reality both of essence and of singularity (in other words, he is "*this* man"). Now, it is true that the properly real is the singular (as we shall see later), and Scotism alone of the essentialist systems has seen the importance of preserving the singularity of things, but it has done it at some cost to the unity of the thing. The Scotistic method of analysis which distinguishes singularity from the nature as a real positive perfection, involves necessarily the multiplicity of formal properties (every thing is composed of many "formalities"). Consequently, the essential nature of these things is not itself singular, but rather common. So, though Scotism asserts that things are individual, it also holds that the natures of these things are not formally singular but common. Thus singularity cannot be the basic principle of reality, since the common nature is real prior to the haecceity. Finally, if singularity makes the properly real, and if we can have fully determinate singulars among the fictions of the mind, then even in this system we have no unambiguous answer to the question, "What is it to be real?"

(4) There is another way of understanding the statement, "A thing is real because it is what it is." This way differs from all Platonic systems in interpreting differently *what* a thing is. For the sake of convenience, we shall attach this theory to the name

of Averroës.[10] According to the Averroistic theory, an essence is composed of two principles: matter (the potential principle of essential change) and form (the actualizing principle of specific determination). Neither matter nor form is real of itself; only the composite is real. This theory is not a materialism, for it holds that matter is only the potential principle of essence that individualizes the essence and so in the thing is the reason why it is *this* thing. Nor is the theory a simple essentialism, for form is not real of itself, but is the actualizing and specifying principle, which in the thing is the reason why it is this *kind* of thing. The Averroistic theory explains how material things are in different species and are capable of essential change. It does not answer the question, "What is it to be real?" and Averroës explicitly says that this is not even a good question.[11] Why is this so? As far as nonmaterial things are concerned, he says that they are actual by being what they are. Material things, for their part, are such as are generated, that is, caused in time from pre-existing things. This, of course, is true with regard to the things of our present sense experience, but it is not to the point. When we ask, "What does it mean to be real?" we are not asking about the efficient causes which produced the real thing. True, we understand something about the *kind* of reality a thing has when we know that it is not perpetual but has a temporal dimension. The reason that this answer satisfied Averroës is that he interpreted all questions as "*what*-questions," that is, questions about the essences of things. But to know that essences are different is not the same as knowing what it means to be real. Hence, any philosopher who says, "To be real is to have been caused," no matter how many valuable things he may have to tell us on other points, has missed the precise bearing of the question.

(5) Among the philosophies of today there are some which can be called "phenomenological." Phenomenology can be considered as a method, and as a method it can be practiced by philosophers of various kinds. One of the ways of using phenomenology is to "bracket" the question of existence. Now, what does it mean for

---

[10] For further information on Averroës, see the bibliographical references in n. 3.

[11] In his *Destructio Destructionum*, disp. 5.

philosophy to put aside the existence of the objects which it so carefully describes? In some cases, at least, it implies that existence is not intellectually knowable or is of absolutely no importance in a scientifically elaborated metaphysics; the only thing which is of scientific value is the formal description. These phenomenologists, then, are "methodological essentialists"; they do not simply deny that there is anything beyond essence, but their method will not allow them to reach anything but essence, so essence is scientifically speaking, all that is real.

All the essentialists agree in this one point: to be real is to be *what* something is. It is perfectly true that of all the things of our experience, the question, "What is it?" can be asked. But when we answer the question, we still do not know *whether* it *is* or not. No matter how complicated the answer to the question, "What is it?," we still do not know whether the thing *is* or not. "Is it?" cannot be answered by telling *what* it is. For example, whether I say very vaguely, "I am thinking of something," or very concretely, "I am thinking of Queen Elizabeth's older brother," I cannot judge whether these objects are properly real or not by the extent to which they are determinate. In other words, I do not know, from even the most complete formal determination, whether I am thinking of something real in the proper sense of the word. In other words, essentialism provides us with no effective criterion for distinguishing between a properly real thing and a thing that is real only in the wide sense. And, since our original question was, "What does it mean to be real, in the proper sense of that word," we see that it is still unanswered.

The consequences of essentialism, in general, are not as extreme as those of the positions we have previously reviewed, principally because they have excluded less from their considerations. Yet there are two difficulties. The first is the problem of the nature of man. If we strictly follow an essentialist analysis, and also distinguish body and soul, we have a dualistic view of man, and in this view it is very difficult to keep from seeing man as two things; if we try to avoid dualism, we seem to be driven to a monism which would deny the distinct reality of either body or soul. The second problem is that of the proof for the existence of God. Can we prove the existence of God starting with finite essence? This has been tried; at best the proof is extremely intricate, and it seems to make use of an illegitimate leap from essence to existence. Most essentialists rather work with motion when they come to this point, but motion has a dubious metaphysical position in a philosophy of essence.

14. Existentialism and the meaning of *being*

Some contemporary philosophers are called "existentialists," though there are very few common conclusions that can be attached to all of them. If we speak very generally, and stay away from detail, we can make some statements about existentialism. (1) Persons and things are basically different. (2) Man either has no essence at all, or his essence is insignificant compared to his "existence." "Existence" is that characteristic of man by which he freely makes himself to be what he is. (3) Things can be known by scientific, "objective" knowledge. But persons—ourselves as well as others—can only be known "subjectively"—that is, as centers of self-determination and free response. Heidegger seems to say that the reality of a sensible thing is "to-be-for-a-knowing being." The knower, then, is primary, and material things derive their reality from their relation to a human knower.

If the radical disjunction between person and thing is meant to deny any community between them, then metaphysics is ruled out. There could be perhaps a philosophy of sub-human things, but this would be only a philosophy of nature. If "subjectivity" is meant literally, then there cannot be a scientific, demonstrative knowledge of persons but only personal experience of ourselves and personal encounter with other persons. Perhaps such knowledge could admit of a humanistic elaboration. If "subjectivity" does not exclude the possibility of some kind of generalization, then a philosophy of man might be possible. But the philosophy of man and the philosophy of nature would be irreducible, and so there could not be a first philosophy. If, on the other hand, one were to insist that the philosophy of man is the first philosophy, one would be answering the question, "What does it mean to be real?" by answering another one, "What makes a person be a person?" And thus, strangely enough, in the otherwise laudable attempt to avoid essentialism, one would tumble backwards into an inverted essentialist position. Heidegger's view has additional difficulties. As a criticism of the self-sufficient "matter" of the materialists, his point is well taken. The intelligibility of material things cannot indeed be explained by the later, accidental, derivative appearance of knowing beings, according to the materialists' account of nature and man. But by the same token, the independent reality of sensible things cannot be explained by their reference to human knowers, either.

In summary, then, these are the inadequate answers to the question we have considered: to be real is to perform some action, to be material, to be or to have an essence (whether this essence be universal or singular, in the things or separate from them, whether it is of itself or is caused), to be "for-man." These various views show clearly the inadequacy of some or all of the others. We cannot, therefore, satisfy our intellect by choosing one of them. Moreover, because these views contradict one another in some points and are incompatible in others, a compromise between them is not really possible, and an attempted combination of all would be worse.

What are we to do? We have already seen that we cannot simply avoid all ultimate questions. Could there be another kind of answer which is not involved in these contradictions, and which will make it possible to salvage the truth that these various philosophies affirm?

15. The Thomistic answer to the question: "What is it to be real?"

Certainly, the way to find out what it is to be real is to examine the real. But the real is everything that there is; it is of many different kinds and has many aspects. Where are we to start? What are we to look for in order to examine the real *as real?* An indirect but nonetheless useful way of beginning is to let previous philosophers indicate the points that we should not overlook. The philosophical controversies about the meaning of being can help us to understand being better. So we will begin by sharpening the controversies as much as possible.

THE DIALECTIC OF DISAGREEING POSITIONS

We have noticed a disagreement about the reality and significance of material things. Materialism is one of the recurring parties to the dispute; it has a special attraction because of its direct appeal to the reality of the body and because it gives a reason for dedication to a program of action in this world. Idealism, on the other hand, appeals to reflective and intellectual people; it gives a reason for discounting the errors and excesses of sense. Both systems must contain a truth, else they would have no interest for thinkers; they are in conflict because each sees its partial truth as the whole.

The truth in materialism should be evident to each one of us, because man has a body. Yet there are those who deny this aspect of their experience, doubt it, or relegate it to some insignificant corner as being merely practical, biological experience, not to be even mentioned by an intellectual. Yet what we see, taste, and touch—this food, that car, that television set, this boy, that girl— are real even in their materiality. They are real in that they are independently existing subjects, and their independence of us is manifest to us in that they are spatially exterior to us and act upon us or undergo our action.

Yet idealism and essentialism have a point to make: the sensible is not the real without qualification. If we were only animals, we could not even be materialists. Idealism and essentialism assert that the intelligible is the real and that the intellect is the proper judge of reality, not the senses. Being, after all, is known. Yet what is material and sensible is to that extent changeable and subjective— it is not so much "what is" as "what seems for a fleeting instant to be." Being, as we find it in ourselves, is both knowing and known, and this is as it should be. For any being worthy of the name should be present to itself, with itself, in possession of itself, and these are the marks of a knower. Matter—that sheer extended, barely qualified, senseless reality—thus appears as entirely impossible (Berkeley), as a projection from subjective sensation (idealism), as irrelevant to intelligibility (essentialism). An exaggeration, no doubt; yet essentialism can point to the history of science: as long as science established itself on the basis of sensible qualities it made little progress; after it abandoned these qualities in favor of purely intelligible mathematical relations it made great progress, both in understanding and in its successful creative effort to deal with things. If physics deals with anything real (atoms, forces, etc.) it deals with something intelligible, not something sensible.

Existentialists in their turn admit that man must rise above the limiting and confining biological interests before he reaches his stature as a man, who can know being. Thus, they have no intention of becoming materialists. Against essentialism they object to the lifeless and heartless abstractions with which science deals, but think that this is a necessary result of all ordinary scientific knowledge. They wish to find reality, too; and they find it in human personality, known not scientifically but "subjectively," as personal, in a personal dealing with the world, especially in the person-to-person encounter.

The values of these three positions lie then in these points: material things are real; the real is the intelligible, and in understanding we must in some way grasp an essence, yet the intelligible and the essential are *in* the things which we sense in the first instance; abstraction is useful and necessary, but it is not the way by which we arrive at the real as real; only judgmental knowledge is sufficient; but judgmental knowledge can be the basis of a scientific metaphysics.

DIRECT CONFRONTATION OF THE EVIDENCE

With these lines of thought in mind to help us keep our attention on significant points, we need to look again at some real thing.[12] We should—each one of us—take some really existing singular immediately present to us (not something imagined, not merely some words describing something which was present to someone else). Let us take ourselves in our immediate situation, or some person here and now present to us. This person is performing *actions* by which we become aware of him; even in our own case, our awareness of ourselves arises from something we do or undergo. A person—ourselves also—is something which has

[12] The discussion of three basic philosophical positions in the preceding section was not a proof of the Thomistic answer nor a full philosophical refutation of the opposing positions. The discussion was intended to clarify the meaning of the question about the real and to direct our attention to the various factors which should be considered.

As for starting with the real itself, rather than with some a priori notion we might concoct in withdrawing from reality—the reason we do this will become clear as we proceed.

at least something about him that is *material* and sensible. A person is some *kind* of reality; he has a human nature and not some other kind of nature. Yet a person is also different from the things around him; he is free and *self-determining;* he is the one *for* whom things are; and things for their part are related to his knowledge because they are knowable.

These propositions are true, and the evidence for them is precisely the acting material existents, some of whom, but not all, are persons. Yet all of these truths are just as intelligible when we consider them abstractly—the relation of action to the agent, materiality, nature, and the relation of knower to known can be intelligibly signified without saying that they are actual. Only when we say that they *are* do we signify them as actual. My reality is my actually existing as a free knowing being, and so too the reality of other persons around me is their actuality as knowing and free; finally, the reality of the things in my world which are variously related to me is their actually existing as such things.

Our being expresses itself in action; it is limited by materiality, by the nature which we have, and by the situation in which we find ourselves. Yet when we reflect on our own awareness of ourselves, each one of us sees immediately in his own highly personal experience: I am not simply any one of my actions (much less a collection of or sequence of actions). I am material, but that *I am* is not what I mean by materiality or vice versa. The same evidence will appear, though in a different way, if we attentively consider another person or thing.

On the other hand, when we say, "I am," "you are," "it is," we are not speaking equivocally. Whenever we apprehend some real thing which we sense, at the same time we also perceive ourselves as knowing and as reacting in various ways to the thing we know. Our own actuality is involved with our world, including nonpersonal things, and our world's actuality cannot be perceived by us except in an act by which we also perceive ourselves. This world is sensed and not only understood to be real. In our "being together with people in the world," we have at once the evidence that "to be real" is primarily "*to be*," and at the same time that "to be" is neither to be material nor to be some particular essence.

Confirmatory consideration

An indirect reflection may clarify this proper meaning of "real." Suppose we compare a real human person here and now present in our experience with a fictional character, for example, Sherlock Holmes, and a real thing or animal with the Hound of the Baskervilles. The real person and thing as well as Holmes and the Hound are singular or individual; all have an intelligible essence—Holmes and the man even have the same intelligible essence, that of humanity; all have the sensible qualities by which we know matter; all have particular actions of their own, and the qualities and actions of all of them are described by the same words. Yet the difference between them is more important than all the similarities: the person and the thing we are experiencing are real, Holmes and the Hound are mere objects of thought. And the statement that precisely shows this difference is this: the person and the thing *are*, exist, whereas the fictional character and the fictional animal do not exist, do not have their own proper act of existing.

Grammatical analysis

From the statement, "The properly real is that which is," we get its proper technical name, being. The verb *is* has as its infinitive *to be* (for which the variant form *being* is sometimes used[13]), as its participle, *being* (note that the participle implicitly includes some subject for the verb), and as its corresponding verbal noun, also *being*. Hence, the verbal noun, *being*, in its first sense means "that which is" or "something having an act of existing."[14] For the phrase "act of existing" we will sometimes use the noun "esse"; for example, we might define "being" as "something having esse."

[13] In other verbs, the formation is somewhat different: run, to run, running, runner. The context will usually determine which form is to be understood; in ambiguous cases we will shift to a nonambiguous form or to an equivalent phrase.

[14] The term "something" means "an individual object, known and expressed in an unspecified way." A real thing can be called "something"; so can fictional and mathematical objects. Hence, we can say technically, "something" directly signifies an indeterminately known essence and usually connotes existence. See above, sec. 8 on the definition of "thing" and below, secs. 16 and 75; see also *Summa Theologiae*, Pt. I, q. 30, art. 4.

Since the properly real is that which *is*, and since metaphysics is the demonstrative knowledge of the real as real, we can express the object of metaphysics fully and accurately by the phrase "being as being" or, in the fuller form, "whatever has an act of existing (esse) inasmuch as it is." That is why we call metaphysics the "philosophy of being."[15]

This grammatical analysis looks easy enough, but there are many problems concealed in it. How have we done this? What sort of knowledge of being do we have?[16]

16. The primitive notion of being

We must approach the problem of our knowledge of being in two stages, for there are two knowledges of being. There is, first, the primitive notion of being, "something which is as the things of my experience are" (which St. Thomas mentions in the expression, *ens primum cognitum*), and, second, the being which is the object of metaphysics, namely, being as being.

We noticed in our grammatical analysis that we move from a statement (or statements) to a verbal noun which no longer contains a definite subject. Have we therefore made use of an abstraction?[17] First of all, abstraction, even total abstraction, always

---

[15] This point is treated in Selected Passages, No. 4.

[16] See also below, sec. 24; the treatment of our knowledge of the being even of sensible things will not be completed until sec. 43.

[17] See above, sec. 1.

The subsequent discussion is a straightforward phenomenological analysis of experience. For those who approach this problem with preconceptions (philosophical or otherwise), the following points may be made. (*a*) The human *intellect* (not just the human knower) does know singulars. (See G. P. Klubertanz, S.J., "St. Thomas and the Knowledge of the Singular," *The New Scholasticism*, XXVI [1952], 135–166). (*b*). The doctrine of the three degrees of abstraction is not a complete analysis of *all* knowledge, but only of scientific knowledge; it ignores perceptual knowledge. (*c*) The metaphysician, the philosophical psychologist, and the epistemologist will see that the "commonness" of metaphysical conceptions, principles, and propositions is not arrived at by abstraction (properly so called) but by separation and related processes. The logician (who ignores processes and meanings and considers only terms) calls all nonsingular terms abstract and measures their "distance" from sensation in terms of degrees. Hence, since metaphysics can conclude to beings which cannot be sensed at all, the logician will consider it the "most abstract" of all sciences, in the "third degree of abstraction." For a person to insist on doing metaphysics as if it

leaves some part of our initial reality out of consideration. Now, if we were to say that "being" is reached by abstraction from a real being, we would imply that there is in the real thing some not-being, which is left out of consideration; but since not-being is nothing, nothing can be left out of consideration. Second, abstraction pertains to the first operation of the mind (simple apprehension), for according to its definition it is a "nonconsideration of . . . ," and so it concerns only essences.[18] But, as we saw above, an essentialist view of reality is not adequate. There is "more" to being than essence, and that "more" is its act of existing. Thus, *to be* is other than and different from the definite essence in the being. Hence, we can consider the essence by itself, and such a consideration is properly an abstraction. But the thing with its act of existing cannot be the object of an abstraction (nor can the act of existing by itself be the object of an abstraction, either, as we shall see later); and unless the act of existing is included in being, we do not have being in the proper sense of the word. Hence, for both of the reasons advanced above, being cannot be reached by abstraction. In other words, the knowledge of being is not a simple concept (apprehension) of an essence.

There are, however, other forms of intellectual knowledge, namely, judgment and reasoning. Judgment is that act of the mind by which we assert (or deny) that something *is*, or is modified in some way or other. Judgment, therefore, directly reaches the esse of a thing, for in the judgment we know *that* a thing is. The judgment, it is true, virtually[19] contains an apprehension of an essence. We cannot assert "is" without at least implicitly understanding "something" ("this," "it," and so on) as a subject for that verb. But what is special and peculiar to the judgment is that a

---

were logic is to doom the whole metaphysical enterprise to ruin from the start.

[18] By the term "essence" we mean that which we name, describe, or define (that is, as *what* it is). The term "quiddity" is an unfamiliar term for "essence." The statement in the text is not meant to imply that all the objects of apprehension are simple concepts; there are some very complicated objects which we will consider below briefly in sec. 77.

[19] The term "virtually" means here: "does not actually contain an apprehension as a distinct act but has a function equivalent to that of an apprehension."

direct perceptual judgment is a knowledge that some existent is.

The things that we directly and immediately assert to exist are the sensible things of our experience, as we have seen above, and the judgments that we make about immediately experienced things are called perceptual judgments. The act of existing thus attained is the esse of a material, singular thing.

At some time in our lives we can explicitly realize that many things are and that we have said, "This is," "That is," and so on. The second thing we notice and assert *to be* makes us realize that the "is" is not identical with either the "this" or the "that"; the "somethings" are many; the "is" is somehow general, since it is truly applied to two different individuals, and so also meaningful in itself. When we have done this, we have denied that "is" is identical with any one of the singulars we have experienced, though we have also implicity affirmed that "is" has a common intelligibility in all cases. Yet we have not denied that there is a subject; we have only denied that the subject of "is" must be this or that in particular. The result of this denial coming after an affirmation is a generalization: we go from (1) "this is," "that is," through (2) "neither necessarily this nor that," to (3) "something is." Thus, we have disengaged a common intelligibility from its original presentation in the completely singular sensible thing. But we have not *abstracted* it; we have not left anything out, we have not failed to consider anything. The term *something* is not strictly abstract; rather, it is a term which contains the singular implicitly. It expresses indefinitely a completely determined, singular thing, or, as is sometimes said, it has an indefinite reference to the singular as such. The denial which is the second term of the process we have been describing we will call "the negative judgment of generalization."[20]

In this discussion, we have been assuming that usually a person will have experienced many beings and asserted the existence of a number of them before he ever comes to the kind of reflection we have been describing. Certainly, the negative judgment of generalization is considerably facilitated by the experience of two

[20] Some authors, borrowing an expression from Cajetan, call the process "abstraction by confusion." A student—at least an English-speaking one—will be confused by a misleading translation of what was at best an awkward term.

or more beings. But we might suppose a person skilled in logical analysis, who has seen that whenever we have a direct concept, whatever we can express in a single concept is strictly one, and when we cannot do this, then we are dealing with two really distinct factors. He would, for example, realize that "white man" cannot be reduced to a single concept, and that therefore "white" is not a constituent of "man," but really distinct from it. Next, if he had sufficient grasp of the object, he could see that "white" is not a logical property of man, but a contingent attribute. He could therefore come to see that man is not necessarily white and that white things are not necessarily men. Now, in making the judgment, "This is," he could similarly see that this cannot be turned into a simple concept of an essence; that "is" is not a logical property of any finite thing. From this it does not follow that other things exist; our logician could not even infer that other things are really possible. He would be limited to this: since "this is," and since "is" is neither a constituent nor a logical property of "this," then there is no reason deriving from "this" or from "is" that this be unique. But even this very limited negation would enable him to proceed to the generalization, "Something is."

From the judgment "Something is," we can form a complex apprehension[21] of "something which is," "something having esse." This complex apprehension implicitly contains a real judgment, and so properly is expressed by the participial noun, "a being." However, we can also stress its noun function; in that case, it is expressed by the noun used absolutely: *being;* and if we wish to make this emphasis clear, we will use a hyphenated expression, "that-which-is," "something-which-is."

17. The metaphysical knowledge of being

But the being that we derive from sensible things by direct perceptual judgments and the negative judgment of generaliza-

---

[21] A simple apprehension or concept is an act by which the mind grasps a nature or quiddity without affirming or denying, but simply considering it absolutely in itself. In addition to this sort of understanding, there is another type of conception, which, although not an explicit judgment, has arisen from a preceding judgment in such a way that the judgmental function of knowledge of esse remains. Cf. Klubertanz, *The Philosophy of Human Nature*, pp. 178–180.

tion is precisely the being of *sensible* things, not being as being. Though we have not explicitly said so, what we experience is not an unqualified being; sensible things as sensible do not merely have a sensible essence but a sensible mode of being (the reason for saying this will become clearer later). We could say, "This man is-sensibly," "This dog is-in-matter-and-motion." Hence, we have not yet reached the being of metaphysics. Can we move from being as sensible to the being of metaphysics by abstraction? If we suppose that we do, we would imply either (1) that a sensible thing contains both sensible being and being as being, so that we can abstract from the former to have only the latter, or (2) that the "sensible" part of *sensible being* is nonbeing and so can be abstracted from to leave only pure being. Both of these alternatives have no basis in our experience: we directly see a sensible thing which is, and that-which-is in a sensible thing is-sensibly. Moreover, the second of the two alternatives is self-defeating once we have arrived at the conception of being as that which *is*. Hence, the supposition that we reach being as being by abstraction is false.[22]

Let us re-examine the process we used when we tried to determine what it means to be real.[23] We used the reflections of many philosophers to illuminate our own experience, and with their help examined the beings that we immediately know. We saw that these beings are sensible and material. Yet being is not merely material, for among beings are persons, who are intellectual and free. We therefore carefully examined a being (or many beings), and we noticed that a being (mere thing or person) is (1) some particular kind of thing, which is (2) acting or being acted on, (3) knowing or being known, (4) singular, and (5) sensible and material. We examined each one of these aspects of a sensible thing, and saw that either singly or taken together they are real—provided that the thing in question truly *is*. But, upon reflection and analysis, it became equally clear that although the thing which we immediately experience as a matter of fact (1) always is a particular kind of thing, it is not real because of its essence, for there are many different kinds of essence, essences are sometimes

[22] One of the reasons for this is mentioned in Selected Passages, No. 7.
[23] See above, secs. 11 and 15.

merely possible and merely understood, and things with essences change. (2) Action and being acted on are found in all beings of our experience, and are the immediate reason why we experience them; but action presupposes the reality of the agent and (in our experience) also of the patient; action changes; and there are many different kinds of action. (3) Things are known; persons know and are known, and a thing is not real *for us* except to the extent that it is known; and if we wish to say that the possibility of knowing and being known belongs ultimately to the constitution of persons and things, we can truly say so; yet, as far as human knowledge is concerned, it ultimately presupposes the reality of both knower and known, and the possibility of knowing and being known must ultimately be grounded on some actuality, if it is to be a real possibility and not merely a logical relationship. (4) Things and persons are singular, but so also are mere objects of the mind; moreover, there are many singulars, so that reality cannot be the same as singularity. (5) Things are sensible and material, and so, too, to an extent, are persons; yet, in the last analysis, sensibility and materiality are fundamental traits in the order of essence (for they belong generically to *what* things are); they do not account for the possibility of the things' knowing or being known; they are ultimately the root of the continuous change of things, and so are fundamentally mut*able* and determin*able;* hence, materiality cannot be the ultimate actuality by which things are real.

The discovery that "is" asserts the actuality of all of these and not their nature—what they are, including, as we must, action and materiality in the order of essence—leads to the discovery of the act of existing as not identical with any of them. And this discovery of the act of existing—esse—is the moment of discovery of metaphysics. In other words, after the direct perceptual judgment, "This is," we make a negative judgment, "And its actuality is not identically its materiality, and so forth." This special negative judgment we will call the "judgment of separation,"[24] for by it we separate the intelligibility of what it means *to be* from the

[24] Some authors call separation "abstraction in the wide sense" or the "third degree of abstraction." This latter expression is confusing (see above, n. 17); it could even lead to abstractionism and essentialism.

intelligibility of what a sensible, material quiddity or essence is.[25]

Perhaps it will help us to understand the judgment of separation if we consider it as a summary negation including a series of specific negations which are probably not made all at once. Most likely, the first of these negations is the understanding that reality is not a "property" of any particular thing or due to any form of singularity. Next, we may come to realize that activity is not identical with reality when we learn that things remain real even when we do not experience their action. Then, we come to understand that sensibility is not identical with reality, for even popular science tells us of realities that we cannot sensibly experience. As we come closer to a philosophical grasp of being, we see that matter is not simply the whole of reality or the principle of reality, even in a material thing; this we see when we come to understand that matter is potential and determinable. Finally, by a still more difficult reflection, we come to understand that essence is not identical with reality and being, and this we do partly by reflection on the many, widely differing kinds of things that exist and partly by reflection on essences that are mere objects of thought.[26]

In the formation, therefore, of the complex intelligibility of "being as being," we make two judgments.[27] (1) "This (sensible) thing is," and (2) "Even for this sensible thing *to be* is not the same as for it to be a particular sensible or material thing with a definite essence." This judgment does not imply that we know that an immaterial being exists or that we think that such a being is possible.[28] At the present stage of our investigation, we do not

[25] This point is discussed in Selected Passages, No. 5.

[26] This consideration is clinched by a detailed investigation of real change, for if "to be an essence" were identical with "to be or to exist" change would be impossible; see below, sec. 43.

[27] Two judgments are necessary, not three, because the judgment of separation can do all that the judgment of generalization does and more. However, someone may take this in three steps: (1) the perceptual judgment; (2) the judgment of generalization; (3) the judgment of separation.

[28] It is extremely important to note that just as a material being is not a being because it is material, but because it *is*, so, too, an immaterial being (if such there be) is not a being because it is immaterial, but because it is. In general, the *kind* of essence a being has does not make it a being; whatever its essence, it is a being because and inasmuch as it is.

Hence, it is illusory to attempt to base a knowledge of being as being on

know demonstratively that there are immaterial beings. The second of these two judgments—the judgment of separation—may sometimes be only implicit, in the way in which it is implied, for example, in the explanatory phrase, "Being as being is something which is *inasmuch as it is*."

In this analysis of the beings of our experience and of our knowledge of them, we have been dealing throughout with sensible, material existents. The point of our consideration has been to establish a scientific knowledge of the properly real. We have seen that a real thing which exists, is material, has a singular essence, and acts is *real* precisely because it exists; and that in such a thing, that in virtue of which it *is* is an act—its act of existing. The scientific understanding[29] of the properly real, "being as being," is formed through an implicitly double judgment, in which we have our first explicit knowledge of existence.

18. The first principles of knowledge

A principle of knowledge is some knowledge from which some other knowledge follows or flows. In reasoning, the premises are the principles of the conclusion. But not all principles are *first* principles, for some principles are themselves conclusions from some other premises. A first principle is one that is not proved from or developed from some other, prior principle. There are first principles in every demonstrative knowledge, though it can often happen that some of the first principles of some science (for example, physics) are developed in another science (for example, mathematics). If we want to speak of first principles, we must therefore distinguish between first principles in some particular order and absolutely first principles. In the absolute sense of first principles, sense experience is a first principle of human knowledge.

---

the demonstrated existence of immaterial things. Either "is" is freed from its sensible and changing context (prior to the proof of the existence of immaterial being, and thus is meaningful when we conclude to the existence of such being) or "is" remains as we first find it immersed in sensibility and change. In the latter case, "is" means "is sensible, material and changeable," and to assert that "An *immaterial, immobile* thing is *sensible, material and changeable*" is a contradiction.

[29] See also below, sec. 25, on the "unity" of the knowledge of being.

In the order of intellectual knowledge, there are two types of knowledge, apprehension and judgment, and each of these should have its own first principle. When we began this chapter, we noticed that there are various senses of the word *real*. We noticed there that metaphysics deals with the real in the proper, or strict, sense of that word. But there is a wide sense, which is about the same as that of the word *possible*. The *real*, in the wide sense, or the *possible*, is whatever can be, whether it ever was or not, or whether it ever will be. To this there corresponds also a concept of being—not the being of metaphysics, nor the primitive notion of being, but that "being" which is the simplest of all, which all other notions presuppose, and which itself presupposes no other intellectual knowledge. But then, by definition, this is the first principle of all apprehension, and so we can truly say that being (in the sense of whatever can be) is the first principle of knowledge. In the philosophy of human nature, we will see that being in this sense is the proper object of the intellect and that every concept other than being is understood in some relation to, or as an elaboration or determination of, being. Moreover, since human knowledge begins from sensation and from sensible things, we can also define "being (as first principle)" as the quiddity of sensible things.

Judgments, for their part, implicitly contain apprehensions; therefore, to that extent, being is also the implicit first principle of all judgments. But judgment, in addition, is an affirmation (or negation), and so its proper first principle will be concerned with this characteristic. We can state it this way: "Affirmation is not the same as negation," or, in a fuller and more usual formula: "It is impossible to affirm and deny the same thing of the same subject at the same time." We can also state it in terms of being: "A thing cannot both be and not be at the same time."[30] This principle is called "the principle of contradiction."

Because metaphysics is the demonstrative knowledge of the real as real, we must briefly consider, in a preliminary way, a question that has been asked by various philosophers throughout the whole history of philosophy, namely, "Can there be a reality

[30] Per se known principles are mentioned briefly in Selected Passages, No. 6.

which cannot be known by us?" If we are working with a concept of essence or with the primitive notion of being, then we will not be able to answer the question at this point, and perhaps we would have to give an affirmative answer. But if we are working with being as being, then we can say immediately, "Any alleged or proved reality, since it will be, in some sense of the word, *something*, and since it will *be*, can be known by us as being."[31] And in the same way the principle of contradiction will be applicable to any present or proved or alleged reality.

The truth, as well as the absolute applicability, of the principle of contradiction is known simply in understanding that principle. We discover that a thing cannot both be and not be at the same time when we experience something which is, understand it, and reflect and compare it with its opposite. If we ask, "Where and how do we find the principle of contradiction?" the clear answer is: "Inductively, in experience." If we ask, "How or where do we know the truth and universality of that judgment?" the answer is "In itself, that is, in what we understand when we affirm that a thing cannot both be and not be at the same time." In other words, when we experience a being and understand the act of existing, it is precisely that act and our insight into it that grounds our judgment. For this reason, a principle like this is called "per se known" or "analytic."[32]

Sometimes it helps our understanding of a per se known proposition to take a negative and dialectical approach to it, in other words, to try to see whether we can suppose it to be false. Suppose a man were to say, "It is true that affirming and denying the

---

[31] This point will be taken up again in sec. 77.

[32] An analytic principle is one which can be discovered to be true from an analysis of what it says. When the term "analytic" is used as here defined, it is correct to call *first* principles analytic. But there are other meanings of the term which are not suitable. (1) The Kantian meaning ("An analytic proposition is one in which the predicate is drawn out of the subject by analysis") cannot be applied to any of the principles of metaphysics. (2) There is another meaning which implies that both of the terms which compose the proposition are first known separately by two distinct simple apprehensions, then the content of each apprehension is analyzed, and finally the judgment is made. Such a process is possible in some per se known propositions (for example, in the proposition, "Incorporeal things do not occupy space"), but certainly it is not possible with the principle of contradiction or with many other principles, such as the principle of causality.

same thing can be done at the same time." In that case, his affirmation itself is affected by what he says, so that the affirmation does not exclude a simultaneous negation—in other words, his affirmation turns out to be meaningless. In other words, no man can really *think* the opposite of the principle of contradiction, although he can form a meaningless string of words which looks like a denial of that principle.

19. Definitions

A *real* thing, in the proper sense of the word, is an actually existing thing, one which exists in itself and is not merely an object of thought.

A real thing, in the wide sense of the word, is something which is, was, will be, or at least can be.

Materialism is the philosophical doctrine that things are real inasmuch as they are material.

Essentialism is the philosophical doctrine that things are real inasmuch as they are or have an essence or quiddity.

Being is something having esse (an act of existing).

Being as being is something having esse inasmuch as it is, exists.

Judgment is that act of the mind by which we assert (or deny) that a thing is (was, will be), or that it is modified in some way.

Simple apprehension is the .simple and absolute grasp of *what* a thing is (concept).

Complex apprehension is an intellectual grasp of an intelligibility by way of or through a judgment.

Separation is a negative judgment: a judgment by which we deny that one (thing or intelligibility) is another.

20. Summary of the argument

A. The real is properly being.

The real things of our immediate experience, though they are sensible and therefore material, are real, not because they are material or because they are what they are or because they are singular but because they are, exist.

Comment. To be real does not mean to be material, because matter in itself is determinable and is not the principle of actuality and determination; nor does it mean to be acting, because acting follows being; nor does it mean to have an essence or to be singular, because quiddity and essence do not serve to distinguish the properly real from the real in the wide sense and so cannot be the principle of the properly real.

B. Being as being is not reached by abstraction but by separation.

The act of abstraction belongs to the first operation of the mind, which concerns quiddities or essences and leaves something out of consideration. But being is not merely a quiddity, and there is nothing outside of being which could be left out. Yet being as being is not the same as being material, and this denial or negative judgment is called separation.

21. Readings

St. Thomas Aquinas, *On the Power of God*, q. 7, art. 2, ad 9 (that is, the seventh question, the second article, answer to the ninth argument; this answer is a very condensed but comprehensive expression of the primacy of esse); *Contra Gentiles*, Bk. II, Chap. 54 (especially the paragraphs beginning "First" and "Secondly"; this passage explains that the *whole* thing is that-which-is); *Summa Theologiae*, Pt. I, q. 5, art. 1, ad 1 (the meaning of "being," in comparison with the meaning of "good"); Pt. I, q. 16, art. 4 ad 2 (things are known before one knows one's self); Pt. I, q. 29, art. 1, art. 3; q. 30, art. 4; and q. 98, art. 1 (on the meaning of "person" and the metaphysical status of persons); Pt. I, q. 40, art. 3; *Compendium of Theology*, Chap. 62 (these two passages speak of the two types of abstraction); *Commentary on the Metaphysics of Aristotle*, Bk. VI, lesson 2, Nos. 1171–1190, pp. 465–470 (on the meaning of being).

Max Charlsworth, "The Meaning of Existentialism," *Thomist*, vol. XVI (1953), 472–496; a good introductory article.

W. Norris Clarke, S.J., "What is Really Real?" in *Progress in Philosophy*, ed. James A. McWilliams, S.J. (Milwaukee, Bruce Pub. Co., 1955), pp. 61–90; argues that the possibles are not the primary objects of metaphysics.

Etienne Gilson, *Being and Some Philosophers*, 2d ed. (Toronto, Pontifical Institute of Mediaeval Studies, 1952), pp. 203–205, on the difference between the simple concept and the judgment, and on our knowledge of esse; *The Christian Philosophy of St. Thomas Aquinas* (New York, Random House, 1956), pp. 29–45, on the meaning of "being."

Robert J. Henle, S.J., "Existentialism and the Judgment," *Proceed-*

ings of the American Catholic Philosophical Association, Vol. XXVI (1946), pp. 40–53. This is a detailed and very penetrating analysis of the importance of the act of existing in the philosophy of being and of the judgment as our only adequate knowledge of esse; "A Thomist on An Experimentalist on Being," *The Modern Schoolman*, vol. 35 (1958), 133–141; an enlightening rejoinder.

Jacques Maritain, *Existence and the Existent*, trans. L. Galantiere and G. Phelan (Garden City, Doubleday, 1956), pp. 20–55, on the notion of being.

Oliver Martin, "An Examination of Contemporary Naturalism and Materialism," *Return to Reason*, ed. John Wild (Chicago, Regnery, 1953), pp. 68–91; an excellent study of the inadequacy of materialism.

Van Cleve Morris, "An Experimentalist on Being," *The Modern Schoolman*, vol. 35 (1958), 125–133; a pragmatist critique of the Thomistic notion of being.

Elizabeth Salmon, "What is Being?" *Review of Metaphysics*, vol. VII (1954), 613–631.

Kenneth Schmitz, "Toward a Metaphysical Restoration of Natural Things," *An Etienne Gilson Tribute*, ed. Charles J. O'Neill (Milwaukee, Marquette Univ. Press, 1959), pp. 245–262; a very fine treatment of what the metaphysician discovers in directly experienced reality.

Erwin Schrödinger, *Mind and Matter* (Cambridge, Cambridge Univ. Press, 1959); brief, somewhat difficult reading, but can be helpful in overcoming materialistic monism.

Wilmon H. Sheldon, "Critique of Naturalism," *Journal of Philosophy*, XLII (1945), 253–270; pertinent to our present interest is the critique of naturalism as a form of materialism.

Gerard Smith, S.J., "Before You Start Talking about God," *The Modern Schoolman*, XXIII (1945), 31–32; the importance of a properly metaphysical understanding of being.

Paul Tournier, *The Meaning of Persons*, trans. Edwin Hudson (New York, Harper and Bros., 1957), pp. 179–198; on the differences between the world of persons and the world of things.

John Wild, "What is Realism?" *Journal of Philosophy*, XLIV (1947), 148–158, discusses the meaning of "real"; the main stress of this article is on the opposition to various more or less mitigated forms of idealism.

SELECTED PASSAGES FROM ST. THOMAS AQUINAS

4. What Is the Subject of Metaphysics?

. . . [Aristotle] says, first, that there is a demonstrative knowledge, which considers being as being, as its subject, and considers also "those things which of themselves [per se] are in being," that is, the per se properties of being.

But he says, "as being," because other demonstrative knowledges, which deal with particular beings, do indeed consider being—for all the subjects of knowledge are beings—yet do not consider being as being, but as it is some kind of being, that is "number," or "line" or "fire" or something of this sort.

He says also, "which of themselves are in this," and not simply, which are in this, to show that it does not belong to this demonstrative knowledge to consider those things which accidentally are in its subject, but only those things which of themselves are in it. . . . This demonstrative knowledge, whose subject is being, should not consider all the things which accidentally are in being, because thus it would consider everything which is considered in all kinds of knowledge, for everything is in some sense being, but not inasmuch as it is being. . . . The necessity of this knowledge which considers being and its per se properties, is clear from this, that these things should not remain unknown, since the knowledge of other things depends on them, as the knowledge of proper objects depends on common ones. . . .

Here he shows that this knowledge is not one of the particular knowledges, from this consideration. No particular knowledge considers being universally as such, but only some part of being divided from other parts. And about this part it considers the per se properties. . . . But the common knowledge considers universal being as being, and so it is not the same as any of the particular knowledges. . . .

Here he shows that this demonstrative knowledge, which we have before us, has being as its subject, this way. Every principle is of itself the principle and cause of some nature. But we are seeking the first principles of things, and the highest causes (as was said in the first book); and these are of themselves causes of some nature. But this is only the nature of being. And this is clear from this, that all philosophers, investigating the elements inasmuch as they are beings, sought this kind of principles, namely the first and highest. Therefore in this demonstrative knowledge we are seeking the principles of being as being. Therefore being is the subject of this knowledge, for every demonstrative knowledge seeks the proper causes of its subject.

> *Commentary on Aristotle's*
> Metaphysics, Bk. IV, lect.
> 1 (ed. Cathala, Nos. 529–
> 533).

5. Abstraction Contrasted with Separation

The response. It is to be said that for the evidence of this question we must know how the intellect can abstract according to its operation. We must know therefore that according to the Philosopher in the third book of the *De Anima,* there are two operations of the intellect: one which is called "the understanding of indivisibles," by which it knows what anything is; the other, by which it composes and divides, that is, by forming an affirmative or negative proposition. These two operations correspond to two [principles] in the thing. The first operation considers the very nature of the thing, according to which it has a definite place among beings, whether it be a complete thing, like a whole, or an incomplete thing, as a part or an accident. But the second operation considers the very esse of the thing, which follows from the coming together of the principles in a composite thing, or accompanies the simple nature of the thing, as in simple substances. And because the truth of the intellect lies in this, that it is conformed to the thing, it is clear that according to this operation, the intellect cannot truly abstract what is joined together in the thing, because, in abstracting, a separation according to the esse of the thing would be signified, as, if I abstract man from whiteness, saying "man is not white," I mean there is a separation in the thing. Hence, if in the real order man and whiteness are not separated, the understanding will be false. And so according to this operation the intellect cannot truly abstract except such things which are separated in the real order, as in saying, "Man is not an ass." But according to the first operation of the mind, it can abstract things which in the real order are not separate, not all indeed, but some. . . .

Thus the intellect distinguishes one from another in different ways according to different operations, because, according to the operation by which it composes and divides, it distinguishes one from another in this, that it understands one not to be in the other. But in the operation by which it understands what everything is, it distinguishes one from another, inasmuch as it understands what this is, understanding nothing about something else, neither that it be with the other, nor separated from it. This latter distinction, therefore, is not properly called separation, but only the former. . . . Since abstraction cannot take place, properly speaking, except of things which are joined together in reality, according to the two modes of conjunction (that is, the way in which the part and the whole are united, or form and matter), there are two kinds of abstraction: one by which form is abstracted from matter, the other by which the whole is abstracted from the parts. . . .

And so there are two abstractions of the intellect: one which corresponds to the union of form and matter or accident and subject, and this is the abstraction of the form from sensible matter; the other, which corresponds to the union of the whole and the part, and to this there corresponds the abstraction of the universal from the particular, which is an abstraction of the whole, in which some absolute nature is considered according to its essential intelligibility. . . . But in such things which can be divided according to their esse, we rather have separation than abstraction.

Thus, in the operation of the intellect there is a threefold distinction. There is one according to the operation of the intellect composing and dividing, which is properly called separation, and this belongs to the divine knowledge or metaphysics. There is another according to the operation by which the quiddities of things are formed, which is the abstraction of a form from sensible matter, and this belongs to mathematics. There is a third, according to the same operation, of the universal from the particular, and this belongs also to physics, and is [in some way] common to all knowledges, for in every demonstrative knowledge we omit what is accidental and take what is per se.

Commentary on Boethius's
De Trinitate, q. 5, art. 3.

6. Principles Known Per Se

Those things which are per se known to us, are made known immediately by sense experience, for example, when a whole and a part are seen, we immediately know that every whole is larger than its part, and we know this without any investigation. Therefore the Philosopher says, "We know principles when we know their terms" (*Posterior Analytics*, I).

*Commentary on the First Book
of the* Sentences, dis. 3, q. 1,
art. 2.

7. *Abstraction and the Knowledge of Immaterial Substance*

A certain philosopher, called Avempacé, held that through the understanding of material substances, following the true principles of philosophy, we could arrive at an understanding of immaterial substances. For, he contended, our intellect has such a nature that it can abstract the quiddity of a material thing from matter; if there is still something material left in that quiddity, the intellect can abstract once again; and since there cannot be an infinite series of material principles in a quiddity, finally the intellect can arrive at an understanding of some quiddity which is entirely without matter. And this, he maintains, is to understand an immaterial substance.

This reasoning would be effective, if the immaterial substances were the forms and essences of the material things present to us, as the Platonists maintain. If we do not take this position, but rather take the position that immaterial substances are of an entirely different kind than the quiddities of material things, then, however much our intellect abstracts the quiddity of a material thing from matter, it will never obtain anything even similar to an immaterial substance. Therefore through material substances we cannot perfectly know immaterial substance.

. . . immaterial substances cannot be known by us in such a way that we apprehend their quiddities, but we can learn something about them through the way of removal [separation] and of relation to material things.

Summma Theologiae, Pt. I, q. 88, art. 2 and ad 2.

III

The Analogy of Being:
First Approach

22. The fact of knowledge in common

In the preceding chapter, we have begun with the many things of experience, and after a long and complicated analysis have arrived at a conception of being as being, thereby establishing the object of metaphysics. Now, we can consider this as a movement which arises from the broad base of many individuals to the unity of one complex apprehension. In this, we have shown that metaphysics fulfills one of the requirements for an organized, demonstrative (scientific) knowledge, that we can reach some kind of common knowledge of individuals. But, having reached this peak, we must ask ourselves how this common knowledge is related to the many individuals. For, by "common knowledge" we mean a single knowledge that is true of many things. For instance, it is true of any sample of water that water is H_2O. So, too, the law of freely falling bodies is true of any and all such bodies; the laws of learning are verified in their way in every case of learning; the theory of the cellular structure of living things is applicable to a great variety of living things. And similar examples of common knowledge can be drawn from any science, from mathematics, logic, and philosophy. (The individuals to which a common knowledge can be applied are sometimes called the "inferiors" of that knowledge.)

Logicians and grammarians sometimes speak of equivocal terms as common. An equivocal term is one and the same term (same in sound or spelling) that has different senses and signifies different kinds of things. An example of an equivocal term is "bank," which can mean the ground bordering a river or an establishment for the keeping and lending of money. We can speak of an equivocal term if we refer to an external sign. But an equivocal term does not imply common knowledge, because equivocal terms have entirely different meanings.[1]

23. Univocation and its basis

The kind of common knowledge with which we should be most familiar is *univocation*. By univocation we mean the use of one and the same term and its corresponding knowledge to apply to each of many individuals in the same sense. Examples of univocation can be found in the use of everyday terms like "water," "sheep," "tree," as well as in scientific terms like "vertebrate," "triangle," "syllogism." A univocal term is given its name because of the identity of meaning (*uni-* means one; *-vocation* here means naming). Often a univocal term is called a *universal* because it can be applied to all the individuals of a given kind in exactly the same sense.

How can one and the same term rightly be applied to a number of individuals which are different? How can one and the same act of knowledge include (explicitly or implicitly) many different individuals? There must be a double basis for this. We have already seen the basis for univocation when we considered abstraction; because some knowledge abstracts from particularities we can deal with what-things-are univocally. But in order that abstraction be legitimate, there must be some kind of distinction between what-a-thing-is and its particularity. For the present, we are not going to consider what this distinction is or on what it is based. It is enough if there is some kind of distinction between the essence of a thing (*what*-a-thing-is) and its particularity.[2]

24. Is being a universal?

We have already seen that our knowledge of being is not an abstract one. It is nonabstract, because it is rich enough to in-

---

[1] Kinds of common terms are spoken of in Selected Passages, No. 8.
[2] This distinction is considered in detail in sec. 42.

clude all things and in all their diversity. It is therefore always growing and is able to go on growing indefinitely. But, because it is nonabstract, it cannot have the same kind of community that an abstract knowledge has. We must examine this relationship more closely and also see what its basis is.

First of all, individuals are, or exist. But, we may wonder, do any nonindividual things exist?

Now, a nonindividual is either a *formal* (or reflex) *universal* or a *simple universal* (an absolute nature). A formal universal is defined as that which is known to be common to many and predicated of them (for example, the species "man," the genus "animal"). If a formal universal were to exist as such, as existing it would be not common, but a distinct thing in itself. But it is a contradiction to suppose that one and the same thing should be both common and not common at the same time. Hence, the supposition that "A formal universal exists" is false.

A simple universal or absolute nature is that which is absolutely meant by terms like "man," "horse," "animal," "car," and so forth. It is that which we predicate, a logician would say, whenever we predicate a noun or attribute of a subject. As such, it is not formally universal (else it could not be predicated of singulars) nor explicitly singular (else it could not be predicated of many); it is neither really existing nor a mere object of thought. Now, some thinkers suppose that such absolute natures exist, either in themselves or as distinct elements in things. For example, in the horse Carry Back, there are said to be as many distinct nonindividual elements as there are distinct ways of knowing what Carry Back is (for example, horse, swift, rangy). But this supposition involves a number of unintelligible or contradictory consequences: that something which is potential (can be either singular or universal) is also actual, namely, an actual element of a real thing; that something can be neither singular nor not-singular (that is, not merely be *considered* abstractly, but *be* abstractly), and therefore that contradictory propositions are not completely opposed to each other; that the real thing is composed of distinct elements, each of which taken singly is indifferent or neutral to reality. But any supposition that involves impossible or unreal consequences is not true. Therefore it is not true that an absolute nature or essence exists as such.

Hence, only individuals exist, or, all existents are individuals. Being means that which is, and so it includes the particularity of that which is. But being does not determinately include the particular; in other words, being does not necessarily mean this thing or that thing; it means *any*, or, *a* thing. This special way of signifying the particular as particular we shall call "indefinite reference," because it makes use of the indefinite article to signify a very definite, concrete, singular thing.

Consequently, being is not a univocal nor a universal term. Being is not univocal, for whenever we assert that something *is*, we speak of a unique individual which has an act of existing all its own. Hence, being is not universal, for no two individuals can be exactly alike inasmuch as they exist.

25. "Being" is common to many

Thus far we have seen a number of points which are the data for the problem of the community of being. We will consider them in summary form.

(1) Only concrete individuals exist and can exist in the real order.

(2) An individual real thing is an existent and formally a being because of its act of existing, not because it is material or is what it is.

> Nevertheless, the beings of our experience are material things of a particular kind.

(3) *Being* that is presented to us by the real existents of which we have direct experience includes both a thing-element and esse.

> *Being* is an intelligibility, the *ratio entis;* it is that which we understand when we know a real thing as a being.

(4) Each existent presents itself as an individual thing distinct from all other things, that is, as a unique subject of esse.

> In other words, each individual thing is a unique way or mode (manner) of having esse.

(5) As the subjects of esse differ from each other, so also do the existential acts.

> For example, this dog's existential act is different from that dog's, just as this dog is different from that.

(6) Hence, each individual thing exists with *its* own act of existing.

It would be foolish to imagine that one thing or person could exist with the act of existing of another.

(7) And yet *being* is realized in each existent.

Every real thing is manifestly a singular definite thing having its esse.

Thus, *being* is common to all things.[3]

But the problem is *how* being is common. Being, in any singular existent, cannot be entirely and exactly the same as it is in any other thing. It must in each instance be and be known as a definite singular thing uniquely ordered to its own act of existing. It must in each instance include all that is unique and proper to the singular individual, and so it cannot be an univocal intelligibility. Since, on the other hand, the intelligibility, being, is presented to us by, and verified in, any singular concrete existent, being cannot be equivocal. (As we have already seen, no intelligibility can be equivocal; only terms can be equivocal.) Being, therefore, is somehow midway between univocation and equivocation, and hence we say it is *analogous*, that is, similar.

[3] Though most Thomists subscribe to the formula of Cajetan, "being is simply many, but one *secundum quid*," they also maintain that it is one concept and is *predicated* analogously. Is there one *concept* of being? Of course, there are all sorts of "concepts of being," from Hegel to Sartre; even some self-styled Thomists have a "concept" which they call "being"—one, unique, confusedly containing all its inferiors, and so on. Such a *concept* is *not* the being which is the subject of metaphysics.

Because beings are analogous, they cannot be correctly understood in any *one concept*. But long familiarity has accustomed us to use the unity (even if it is only partial and derivative) and ignore the multiplicity (even though it is basic).

Most philosophers want to go too rapidly; they overlook the basic importance of the verb *is*. For the first problem of metaphysics is, "What does *is* mean?" "How do we predicate *is* of differing individuals?" The verb-predicate "is" should be investigated before we even ask about the attributive noun, "being." We understand and assert *is* analogously, and this analogy demands our first attention. The failure to realize that *is* can be a verb which expresses existential act is the capital fault of logicism (or essentialism) and distorts both the ordinary spontaneous experience of individuals as well as metaphysics. To substitute a noun and a concept for the verb is a serious error. At best, the problem of metaphysics is poorly expressed as a problem of unity amidst diversity; at worst, *being* is turned into an essence or form in order that it may have a true conceptual unity.

See also below, sec. 75.

Univocal terms signify an absolute nature or, at least, something understood after the manner of an absolute nature. They have a definite meaning by themselves, and so can be used alone; for example, the items in a grocery list are meaningful, clear, and distinct, even though they may be just single words. When univocal terms are used in a proposition, they have exactly the same meaning. This is to be expected, for, since they are abstracted from individuals, their meaning does not change when they are applied now to this individual, now to that.

But being is not an abstract concept. We have seen that when we come to know a thing as a being, we know it in such a way that none of its reality is left out. Therefore, being means the whole being. Now, individual beings differ. Consequently, being, when predicated of one being, cannot have exactly the same meaning as it has when predicated of another. Each time it is used its meaning is *proportioned* to the subject of which it is used. We can express the thought of this paragraph by saying, "Analogy is proportional predication."

Yet we do not call the second being "being" by a mere fiction of the mind or by some kind of extrinsic reference of one to the other. (When we do this, as when, for example, we speak of the "right" or "left" side of the road, we are using what is called "improper predication.") Each one of the two has its own intrinsic act of existing which is its own; consequently, each one of them is properly called a being. Consequently, the analogy of being, when we are talking about real things, is proper predication.

26. The formal structure of analogy

But if we are to use one term to signify two things which are not (logically) identical, then there must be some relation between those things. It is not relevant here to say that the predicate is always related to its subject, for we are asking why the same predicate is applied to two really different things. So there must be some foundation in the things themselves.

The unity of univocal predication—to start with the simplest and most easily understood kind of unity—lies in this, that *in* each one of the "inferiors" there is a "part" which, at least abstractly considered, is formally the same. This kind of unity is the strongest of the logical unities—the logical identity of the "part." But the various "inferiors" of an analogous conception—the so-called analogates—cannot be unified in this way. Nor can we have recourse to various strictly ontological unities, such as the unity of an undivided being (the unity of a single person, for example)—these are irrelevant, since we are concerned with individuals which are ontologically many as beings.

There is left, for our purposes, only the unity of relation. Now, relations among things can fall into three, and only three, patterns. First, one of the things may be directly related to the other; we will refer to this as a "one-to-one" relationship. Second, the things may not be directly related to each other, but they may be variously related to a common third; this is the "many-to-one" relationship. Third, the things may not be directly related to each other (either as wholes or in their parts), but they may have internal relationships which are related; this is the "many-to-many" relationship. And this enumeration is exhaustive: "many" and "one" can be combined in only these three ways, while more elaborate combinations will easily reduce to these simpler ones.

For a better understanding of what is meant here, we can look at some examples. A traditional example is that of "health"; the relationships are extrinsic, but this is not important here, since what we want to see is the *pattern* they form. First, an animal is healthy, and various other things are correctly called healthy, for example, food as preserving health, complexion as manifesting it, and so on. Food is directly related to the health of the animal as its partial cause, and thus stands in a one-to-one relationship. Second, in this same example, we can compare the predication of the term *healthy* to the food and to the complexion. There is no direct relation between the food as health-producing and the complexion as health-showing, except through the animal which is healthy.[4] Therefore, food and complexion do not stand in a

[4] There apparently *are* direct relationships between the food and the complexion. But the precise point is: as far as *health* is concerned. The complexion may be ruddy, smooth, oily, and so on, and these qualities may be directly connected with the diet. But they are not the qualities of a healthy skin except in reference to the health of the animal itself, and this is relative

one-to-one relation to each other, but in a many-to-one relationship, where the "one" is outside the many, and yet is the reason for the common attribution. Third, we can consider the predication of the term *good* to a wine and to a ballplayer. There is no direct relationship between the one and the other; there is no common third. There is no common quality, no common action. Is then the term merely equivocal? Not at all. For in each case the term designates a relationship. A wine is good when it is such as to be well adapted to human taste and digestion. A ballplayer is good when his actions are well adapted to his function in the game. The two relationships, however, are not identical, since the very meaning of "adaptation" differs in the two cases. But they are still proportioned, or similar. We can view this pair of relationships as a proportional comparison:

wine : taste : : ballplayer : his function

For this reason, the many-to-many analogy is usually called "the analogy of proportionality."[5]

After this analysis we can examine the analogy of being to see where and how it can best be expressed.

27. Analogy of individual beings

Being is never presented by any two beings as *exactly* the same. In other words, *being*, as presented by one existent, is always and necessarily and intrinsically different from the being presented by another. From one existent I derive one definite in-

---

to the animal, not to the intrinsic qualities of the complexion considered in itself. So the "health" example remains a valid one.

It is not amiss to point out that it does have two defects. As we have noted above, the act or perfection, health, is found only in one of the analogates, and so the analogy is improper or extrinsic. Secondly, health is first of all a univocal term in relation to a number of individuals, the healthy animals, and is only afterwards applied analogously; we can call it a "secondarily analogous term." But being is analogous from the start; it has no original univocal sense. We can therefore, by contrast, call it a "primarily analogous term." This is a very important difference.

[5] A "relation of relationships" or "a proportion of proportions" can just as well be univocal as analogous. Take the proportionality, 2 : 4 :: 3 : 6; here the relation "double" is obviously univocal. Or, if this seems too simple, consider this one: 2 : 4 :: 3 : 12 :: 4 : 32 :: 5 : 80; the rule of this progression is absolutely univocal.

telligibility; from another, another; and so on.[6] So it is clear that we are not dealing with a univocal term but with a proportional predication; moreover, since each existent is by its own intrinsic perfection a being, the predication is proper or intrinsic. Hence, there must be some sort of relation between beings.

Our predicating of being must, of course, be based upon what we find in the real order. The question, then, is, Which of the three patterns is verified on the basis of what we have already found? for we do so predicate being on the basis of what we have found. Is there a direct relation of an individual being, as such, to another individual being? Obviously there are all sorts of relationships in our world: father and son, twins, builder and building, equally big automobiles, better rockets. But these are not relationships *of* and *in* being. My next door neighbor is another being, and it makes no difference to his character of being another being that he be my brother or a total stranger. Thus, we cannot find a one-to-one relationship between the beings of our experience simply as beings.

In fact, the individuals of our experience seem to be so unrelated directly that we might well be inclined to think that the many-to-many relationship is most likely to be the one. But is it? Remember that we are now considering two beings, explicitly taking into account only this, that they are *two beings*. We might think this way: a thing is a being inasmuch as it has an act of existing; one being is to its own act of existing as the second is to its own act, and so on; hence, individual beings are analogous with the analogy of proper proportionality. The only difficulty is this: if we only know that we are confronted with two beings, we cannot determine the meaning of the "similarity" expressed by the word "as" in our proportionality above.[7] We cannot

---

[6] See above, n. 3, and below, sec. 75.

[7] See above, n. 5. The fact that proportionalities *can* be univocal as well as analogous is clear from the mathematical examples given in note 5. It is the common teaching of Thomists that every proportionality in being is analogous. But consider a proportionality like this one: this man : his act of existing :: that man : his act of existing. In what sense can we say that this man is differently related to his own esse than that man is? He has exactly the same kind of nature, and nature (or essence) is just the capacity for existing in a certain way. Hence, we cannot at the same time assert the analogy of proper proportionality between two individuals of the same

determine *how* a given being is related to its act of existing unless we know what kind of being it is. So we must rule out the possibility of a many-to-many relationship as relevant in *all* cases of the analogy of individual beings among themselves.

What about the many-to-one relationship? We can find some help by comparing this predication with univocal predication. Let us take the relationship of *man* to Peter, James, and John. *Man* as absolute nature is in the mind, and so not identical with the three men; it is therefore a many-to-one pattern. But because *man* arises by abstraction, it is a single concept, with exactly the same relationship to each of the three, so we have, not analogy, but univocation. Now, take three beings, *x*, *y*, and *z*, of which we only know that they are actually existing things, three in number; therefore, they are related to the common conception of being as it is in the mind. But, unlike the case of the univocal term, being is not predicated in the same way, for it is predicated proportionally to the subject. Moreover, being is not a single concept but is at most a kind of ideal unity, which, in developing, transcends any individual being we may find. There is then, a kind of communication of *x*, *y*, and *z* as individuals in the ideal unity, which fits into the many-to-one pattern of relationship. We will call this the "analogy of individual communication."

This answers our immediate question, but at the price of raising a new one: How is it that individuals are thus understood? Can beings which are not directly related be truthfully understood in reference to one conception? To say that they *are* so understood is true enough but insufficient. The question cannot be answered with what we have already discovered; it can only be answered when we are ready to examine some of the real relations between beings, in Chapters VII, VIII, and IX.

28. Person and thing as beings

From the very start, we have recognized two very different sorts of beings: persons and things. We have noted that whenever we know a thing, we also necessarily know ourselves as beings

species and the univocation of the term that denotes their nature. For a fuller discussion, see G. P. Klubertanz, S.J., *St. Thomas Aquinas on Analogy* (Chicago, Loyola Univ. Press, 1960), pp. 136–140.

and precisely as the subject or agent of knowledge. Conversely, we cannot know another person without contacting a thing-aspect of him, namely, his body. In ordinary experience, we do not even experience ourselves as pure subjectivity. My body is myself, in some way, and yet ordinarily it is simultaneously perceived as thing (object, facticity), even if only by kinaesthetic (internal) touch. In this sense, subjectivity and thinghood are equally immediate (that is, one is not in terms of the other), and both are independently known as beings of two different kinds. (To prevent misunderstanding, it is necessary to point out that all reflective analysis of subjectivity and personality must take place through analogies with things as sensibly experienced, so that being as sensible retains a priority in the order of objective intelligibility; in the causal order, our mind is first actuated by the intelligibility received through the senses before [not in time, but in causality] it can be conscious of its own activity, and so it is first conscious of itself as understanding a sensible thing.)

Being as thing and being as subject each has its own intelligibility. These intelligibilities are alike only inasmuch as each is proportionally similar to the other. That is to say, we can and do recognize that as a thing is to its act of existing, so a person is to his.[8] But this comparison is not an equality. For a thing *has* an act of existing, in the sense that it has received it, and is now actuated by it; its act is in it, and in no other. On the other hand, a person has an act of existing, in the sense that he possesses it through the self-consciousness of intelligence and the self-determination of freedom. A thing is present only to some other than itself; a person is present to himself. A thing is self-identical only in a very imperfect way, in that its actuality is dispersed both in space and in time. A person's self-identity is only partially spatialized and temporalized and in its peak of self-consciousness is both aspatial and atemporal.

Yet these similarities and differences cannot be parceled out into two groups, one group containing univocally common perfections, the other listing simply diverse ones. The possession, presence, actuation of the being by its esse is just that which is both similar and unlike. Not only is the essence of a person not

[8] This "relation" is not a predicamental but a "transcendental" relation.

the same as the essence of a thing, nor a person's act of existing not a thing's act; the very way (mode, manner) the being is related to its own proper act is different. Hence, in this case, there is an analogy of proportionality, properly so called. (After we learn that there are more that just these two levels or "grades" of being, then we shall see that the analogy of proper proportionality applies to these grades also.)

In both of these analogies, the analogates are the things of our real world as they are presented to us in our experience. Each analogate is a whole individual existent, formally understood as a being. These analogies of being are therefore primarily and basically analogies between *beings*—between two or more real beings each having its own act of existing.[9]

Later on, we shall see that there are relationships and analogies within beings, that is, between the various internal principles of being. We shall also discover still other analogies among beings, especially between some effects and their causes, and finally a different kind of analogy between God and all other beings.

In summary, then, *being* is analogous. It cannot be applied to any two beings with exactly the same meaning. It is not a univocal intelligibility, for every being, inasmuch as it is a being, is unique. Being is not obtained by any kind of abstraction, properly so called. On the other hand, the term "being" is not equivocal. One being is simply diverse from any and every other being, but it is also similar to any and every other being of our experience. Between beings as individuals we find the analogy of individual communication. In addition, we find that persons and things are similar as beings, but also different, in that each possesses its own act of existing in its own way, as intrinsically proportioned to the kind of nature it has. Beings, as persons

[9] At this point it is traditional to treat of metaphor, and it is frequently said that metaphor is "the analogy of extrinsic proportionality." Thomists point to texts like *Summa Theologiae*, Pt. I, q. 13, art. 6. It should be noted that *metaphora* is a Greek term, translated into Latin as *translatio*, and means nothing more than "figure of speech" (as a proof of this, note that St. Thomas instances causal attribution as well as what is commonly recognized as metaphor in the passage cited). At the first level of analysis, metaphor is the extrinsic attribution of an alien nature; see Robert R. Boyle, S.J., "The Nature of Metaphor," *The Modern Schoolman*, XXXI (1954), 267-280.

and things, are therefore analogous by an analogy of proper proportionality.

29. Definitions

A *univocal* term (and knowledge) is one that is applied to many individuals in wholly the same sense.

An equivocal term is a term that has the same external sign (same in sound or spelling) but entirely different meanings.

An *analogous* term (and knowledge) is one whose meaning is is not exactly the same; nor is it entirely different; it is not merely a combination of a univocal and an equivocal element but that which is the same is somehow also different.

Analogy of proportionality is a many-to-many relationship, consisting in a similarity (proportion) of proportions between pairs of diverse parts, principles, and so forth, though the analogates which are constituted by these principles have no direct relationship to each other.

Analogy of individual communication is a many-to-one relationship, consisting in a similarity of the relationship of each of the analogates to a "one" which is distinct from the analogates singly as well as taken together; the analogates have no direct relationship to each other.

An analogue, or analogate, is one of the things, terms, principles, and so forth, to which an analogous term is applied or of which an analogous knowledge is true.

30. Summary

A. Only individuals exist.

Nonindividuals are either formal universals or absolute natures (simple, or direct, universals).

But: neither formal universals nor absolute natures exist (*a*) because formal universals must be *one* in order to be what they are, and that which is one is not-many and therefore not-common, yet an existing formal universal should also be common to many; and (*b*) because absolute natures, which *can* be either singular or universal, cannot simultaneously be fully actual. Absolute natures cannot exist as such in singulars, because a real thing cannot be composed of elements each of which is indifferent to reality.

Therefore: no nonindividuals exist, or only individuals exist.

B. Being is not a universal.

A universal is an abstract and univocal term.

But: being is not abstract, for it includes the whole real thing; nor is it univocal, for it includes all real differences.

Therefore: being is not a universal.

C. Particular beings are analogous with the analogy of individual communication.

The analogy of individual communication is found whenever there are many analogates which are not directly related to each other, but are similarly related to a "one" which is distinct from the analogates singly as well as taken together.

But: particular beings, considered merely as individual beings, are *as such* not directly related to each other, but are similarly related to "being," and "being" itself is neither one of these analogates nor their sum.

Therefore; particular beings, as individuals, are analogous with the analogy of individual communication.

D. Some beings are analogous with the analogy of proportionality.

The analogy of proportionality is found wherever there are similar wholes, which, although they are simply and really different, have a similar relationship of diverse parts.

But: some beings, although simply different, have a similar relationship of diverse parts because each of them is something having its own proper act of existing, not in the same way, but only in similar ways.

Therefore: some beings are analogous with the analogy of proportionality.

31. Readings

St. Thomas Aquinas, *Summa Theologiae*, Pt. I, q. 13, arts. 1, 2, 3, 4, 5 (a penetrating, detailed discussion of analogy and our knowledge of God); Pt. I, q. 30, art. 4 (on common terms); *On the Power of God*, q. 7, art. 7 (analogy between God and Creatures); *Contra Gentiles*, Bk. I, chap. 34 (same point).

Etienne Gilson, *The Spirit of Mediaeval Philosophy* (New York, Scribner's, 1940), pp. 477–448, n. 14; an excellent presentation of the role of analogy.

George P. Klubertanz, S.J., *Saint Thomas Aquinas on Analogy* (Chicago, Loyola Univ. Press, 1960), pp. 111–155.

Joseph Owens, C.SS.R., "Diversity and Community of Being in St. Thomas Aquinas," *Mediaeval Studies*, vol. XXII (1960), 257–302.

Kenneth Schmitz, "Toward a Metaphysical Restoration of Natural Things," *An Etienne Gilson Tribute*, ed. Charles J. O'Neil (Milwaukee, Marquette Univ. Press, 1959), 245–262; analogy as found in sensible things.

Paul Tournier, *The Meaning of Persons*, trans. Edwin Hudson (New York, Harper and Bros., 1957); differences between persons and things.

SELECTED PASSAGES FROM ST. THOMAS AQUINAS

8. Kinds of Common Terms

Something can be applied to many things in different senses, and this can happen in two ways. In one way, something can be said about many things according to intelligibilities which are entirely different and do not have any relationship to unity. These are called "purely equivocal" terms, for by chance it happens that one man names a thing by one name, and another a different thing by the same name; this is particularly evident in different men who have the same name. In another way, one name can be given to many things according to intelligibilities which do not differ totally, but agree to some extent. . . . Sometimes this agreement . . . is according to one proportion of different subjects. For sight has the same proportion to the body as the intellect has to the soul. Hence, as sight is a power of a corporeal organ, so also the intellect is a power of the soul alone without a body.

> *Commentary on Aristotle's* Ethics, Bk. I, lect. 7 (ed. Pirotta, No. 95).

9. Examples and Kinds of Analogy

Things are one by proportion or analogy which are alike in this, that this has itself to that as another to another. Such a relation can be taken in two ways: either some two things have diverse relations to one thing, as "healthy" applied to urine means a "sign of health," and to medicine, means "the relationship of cause with respect to the same health." Or, there is the same proportion of two things to different objects, as tranquillity to the sea and serenity to the air; for tranquillity is the quiet of the sea, and serenity, the quiet of the air.

Commentary on Aristotle's
Metaphysics, Bk. V, lect. 8
(ed. Cathala, No. 879).

The act of existing of a man and a horse is not the same, nor of this man and that man.

Summa Theologiae,
Pt. I, q. 3, art. 5.

IV

Becoming—Change—Motion

32. The problem of change

We have just engaged in a detailed consideration of the fact that things are. That things change is a fact which is also directly known, and the investigation of what change is will occupy us for the next three chapters. This chapter is introductory. We do not intend to prove any particular changes, nor whether there are different kinds of change. There is a prior problem of what we mean by change in general. Therefore we will begin with the ordinary idea of change, which admittedly is a rather vague one, and only gradually arrive at more accurate notions.

Some philosophers have found difficulty in admitting both being and change at one and the same time. Some of the essentialists, in defining reality as that-which-is-*what*-it-is, have combined permanence with this self-identity so much so that they consider the changing to be unreal. Some have even gone so far as to assert that all change is an illusion. We can take as a simple example of this kind of position the argument of Parmenides, an Italo-Greek who flourished in the early fifth century before Christ. According to this Greek philosopher, the real or being is that-which-is-what-it-is. If the real were to change, it would have to be what-it-is (by definition) and at the same time what-it-is-not (on the supposition that it changes). But this consequence is a contradiction, and so the supposition is false. Again, we can consider this position from another point of view. To change is to become other than what one was. Now, the real is what-

80

it-is, and that which is other than (or opposite to) the real is nothing. So, change would be possible only if the opposite of the real were also real; but this is false, and so change is impossible. This is a very simple position, but more elaborate forms of it have been held at various times.

A position which is almost the direct contrary of Parmenides' view is that of Heraclitus, an Ionian Greek of about the end of the sixth century B.C. He was impressed by the unity of the universe and by its ceaseless activity and change. It seemed to him that if change is real, then everything which is real is change. And so Heraclitus not only asserted that change is real, he denied that anything is permanent in being. Everything is in flux, in process; he found the best example of his notion in the restless, ever changing fire. An elaborated form of this opinion has been held at various times and is relatively popular at the present time. Many modern philosophers express their notion of it by saying that there is no substance, no *thing* which acts; there is only activity without an agent. They deny the reality of the things and persons which we immediately perceive, not because their perception is any different than ours but because they cannot see how they can admit the reality of both change and being.

Are we really forced to choose between change and being? It is easy to see that those who chose being and denied change did so because for them "to be" was "to be an essence"; to be real was to be *what* a thing is. But the strange thing is the same faulty understanding of being led others to the opposite position of denying being in favor of change. Accepting the notion that "to be" is "to be unchangeably and permanently what a thing is," they have also accepted the immediate evidence that the things of our experience are in constant, more or less perceptible change. Because they are empiricists, they prefer facts to theories. In their minds, the fact is that change is going on; the theory is the notion of being as "that which remains what it is." Rightly questioning this notion of being, they have failed to ask a more fundamental question: "What is it to be real?"

Hence, since we have seen that to be is to exercise an act of existing, and since we have direct and undeniable evidence that change is going on, it is necessary to ask whether change is incompatible with being when being is understood as that-which-is.

By change, we understand "becoming different." We must therefore investigate what is meant by "sameness" and "difference."

33. Identity, distinction, and difference

Identity is sameness, oneness of a thing with itself. We say that a thing is identical with itself when it is the same at two points of time, or under several considerations, and so forth. Identity is absolute when all the characteristics, traits, and so forth of a thing are the same. Identity is partial, limited, or qualified, if some of the characteristics, traits, and so forth are the same, and others are not the same. Several types of limited identity may be pointed out as examples. Numerical identity is the basic sameness of one and the same individual along with various minor changes; we speak, for example, of the numerical (personal) identity of one and the same person throughout his life. We speak of specific identity when we have two individuals which belong to exactly the same *kind* of reality; for example, in geometry we speak of identical triangles. We speak of the material or real identity of a thing which we are thinking of in several ways; for example, John Doe as father of a family is materially identical with the same John Doe as a business man, but he is being considered now with one set of relations, now with another.

Distinction is lack of identity. It always implies plurality and division of some sort or other, for wherever there is a distinction, there must be more than one thing or part or aspect. Distinctions are basically of two types: real and of reason. A real distinction is found wherever there are really several things, parts, elements, and the like, independently of any act of the mind. A real distinction and a real identity are opposed as contradictories: that is, a real identity denies a real distinction, and vice versa. A common sign of a real distinction is separability: wherever two things or parts can be separated, such that one can exist without the other, those things or parts are really distinct. But not every real distinction implies the separability of those things or parts which are distinct. When the distinction is between complete things or beings, we speak of a major real distinction. When the distinction is between the parts (elements, principles) of one thing, we call it a minor real distinction (for example, the distinction between a man's hand and his foot; or the distinction between his color and his shape).

A distinction of reason is not a distinction within the thing itself but a lack of identity between two ways of understanding one and the same real thing. A typical example of the distinction of reason can be found in the parts of a definition: "rational animal," which is the essential definition of man, is composed of two parts. What we understand when we say "animal" is different from what we understand when we say "rational"; but the thing we understand in these two incomplete ways is one and the same. When at least one of the two concepts (between which there is a distinction of reason) does not imply the other, the distinction of reason is a major one. For example, though "rational" does imply "animal," yet "animal" does not imply "rational," and this we can find as well from an inspection of these two concepts as from the fact that there are animals which are not rational. On the other hand, when both concepts imply each other, we speak of a minor distinction of reason; an example of such a distinction we will find later on is the distinction between "one" and "being."

Difference can mean the same as distinction in some of its uses, but often the term "difference" is used to express the reason for a distinction. In our usage, the term "distinction" will more commonly be used to indicate that one thing (part, element) is not another; the term "difference" will be used to indicate the way in which things differ or, sometimes, that by which things differ. Of the differences between things two will be mentioned frequently in the material which will be considered next. A "numerical difference" is that between two individuals which belong to the same species or kind; for example, there is a numerical difference between Peter and Paul, between two shepherd dogs, two trees, two chairs. An "essential difference" is the difference between two things, which, in addition to being individually different, also are of different kinds or species. In logic, we learn that a defini-

tion is composed of a genus and a difference and that things are
said to be specifically different when, having a common genus,
each has some attribute proper to itself by which it differs from
the others (this proper attribute is called the "difference").[1] But
in logic any common notion suffices for a genus, and any less
common one for a difference. In metaphysics and the philosophy
of nature we do not work with such arbitrary classifications.
Rather, we try to determine as accurately as possible *what* things
are according to their intrinsic constituents. When this has been
done, and we find that the intrinsic constituents of one are different from those of another thing, then we say that the things
differ essentially. These steps necessary for the determination of
an essential difference cannot be omitted, and there is no short-
cut.[2] The finding of essential differences is not so important
directly in the philosophy of being, but it is of major significance
in the philosophy of human nature.

Now, it is obvious from our own past experience that we
cannot simply look at a thing and know at once, immediately,
what it essentially is. We have to learn what things are, and we
discover this by seeing directly what they do. Thus, we often
cannot tell by looking at a thing whether it is alive or dead. But
we watch it act, and so we learn what it is. Briefly, we learn the

---

[1] Sometimes the "differences" are opposed as contradictories, as "sensitive"
and "nonsensitive" are the differences of the common genus, "living." This
essential difference is sometimes said to be "according to possession and
privation" (*secundum habitum et privationem*); it is the easiest to discover;
it is a greater difference than the one to be mentioned next. Sometimes the
"differences" are two (or more) positive, diverse attributes, as "sensitive
in the mode of touch alone" and "sensitive in the mode of many external
senses." It is usually hard to prove that such positive, differing attributes
are really essentially diverse in themselves, and it is often equally hard to
prove that they are the differences of some real things.

[2] Note that essential definitions and essential differences can be known
only if we have some knowledge of things as they are in themselves. This
knowledge includes two points: (1) a theory of knowledge in general which
allows us to say that we know things which exist independently of our
knowledge and (2) a method of knowledge which enables us to know at
least some things in distinct detail. Obviously there are very many things of
which we cannot give a *specific* essential definition, and which therefore we
cannot distinguish specifically. In these cases we can still give a *generic*
definition (perhaps only according to a remote genus), and then we could
still find some essential differences, that is, according to generic differences.

essence or specific nature of a thing from its activities or operations.

This must also be the method by which we discover specific
or essential differences. For example, two things are known to be
essentially different if one of them has some operations which
the other does not have. Thus, living things have some activities
(nutrition, growth, reproduction) which other material things
simply do not have. Hence, living things are essentially different
from nonliving things.

34. The correct way to talk about change

We began this chapter with a problem urged by many philosophers that there is some kind of incompatibilitiy between being
and change. For clarity's sake, we decided to obtain a clear
understanding of the terms involved in considering change. We
saw that change means "to become other than something was."
So we undertook an examination of difference, distinction, and
identity. Now we are ready to look at change as it actually happens, and our purpose is ultimately to discover the relation
between change and being. In order to keep our discussion concrete and in touch with reality, we shall use as an example the
change of a seed into a tree.

What do we mean when we say that a seed changes into a
tree? We mean that there was first an initial stage in which
there was a seed with a definite size, shape, and structure;
secondly that there was some kind of process; and thirdly that
there is a terminal stage at which the process arrives, in which
the tree has a quite different size, shape, and structure.[3] (Note
that the initial and terminal stages are not absolutely initial and
terminal but are such relatively to each other and the process.)
Moreover, there must be some continuity between initial stage,
process, and terminal stage. If, after the seed was planted, some
one came, replaced the seed with a seedling, then with a very
small tree, then with a larger tree, and finally with a very large
one, we would not have an instance of real change in one and the
same tree (but an illusion of change if we did not know the
difference, and a mere succession of different things if we did).

[3] For the relation of succession to change, see Selected Passages, No. 11.

Let us examine this analysis more closely. For something to change is to *become* other (different) than it was: the seed (*A*) becomes something different, a tree (*B*). To become is to come-to-be; in other words, becoming is a process which terminates in being—here, a tree (*B*). Because there must be a continuity throughout the process, and because the differences of the initial and terminal stages, which are not common to the whole process but precisely restricted to one stage, cannot themselves be the basis of that continuity, there must be something common in addition to the differences, namely, a subject which undergoes that process.[4] For convenience and brevity, we will make some use of the following symbols:

ac—the initial stage, the subject with its characteristics as it is before the change takes place (e.g., the seed *A*).

bc—the terminal stage, the subject with the characteristics it has after the change (e.g., the tree *B*).

P—the process itself

c—the common subject, not considered as determined by either the initial or the terminal differences

c is therefore both *ac* and *bc*, but this is not a contradiction, since it is not both of them simultaneously. Before *c* changes, it *can* be what it will be after the change is completed. Hence, at the point at which *c* is *ac*, *c* is said to be *in potency* to *bc*. After the process, when *c* has become *bc*, it actually has the trait, characteristic, or perfection to which the process was originally directed. Hence, after the change, *c* is now *bc in act*.[5] We can summarize this by saying, "*c* is both *ac* and *bc*; when *c* is *ac* in act, it is in potency to *bc*; when it is *bc* in act, it is no longer in potency to *bc*, but, if the process is reversible, when *c* is *bc* in act, it is in potency to *ac*." As an example of a reversible process, we can take heating and cooling; when a thing is hot

[4] On the common subject in change, see Selected Passages, No. 10.

[5] Note that we are here dealing with two conditions of a being: "to be in potency" and "to be in act." These two conditions are related to, but by no means identical with, the principles of potency and act which will be studied in Chap. VI. To discover the principles of act and potency is much more difficult than the analysis which is being made here. Moreover, an attempt to pass from the present consideration to the principles of act and potency will result in univocal concepts of act and potency—a consequence that will vitiate the whole understanding of metaphysics.

in act, it is in potency to being cold; when it is cold in act, it is in potency to being hot.

This distinction between "being in potency" and "being in act" enables us to see that change and being are not mutually exclusive as Heraclitus and Parmenides thought. It is not a profound distinction at all; it is primarily finding an accurate way to express the fact of change, and so it is a solution at the level of our language about a fact, just as, to some extent, the ancient Greek problem was at least partly a language confusion. Similarly, this distinction can give us a sharper, more accurate way to define what we mean by change: for a thing to change is for it to become in act what it was in potency.

35. A changing thing is composed

But the fact of change can be used to tell us something about the thing which changes. This will no longer be a linguistic analysis, but a real analysis of the thing itself, and of the conditions which must necessarily be true if change is even to be possible. Thus we will be able to relate change to the being of the changing thing.

We have seen that, first of all, a real change involves a subject which is present throughout the change, and this subject we have designated c. Second, after a real change has taken place, the thing which changed is different—ac is different from bc. Schematically:

$$ac\text{———}P\text{———}bc$$

to show more clearly how the common subject continues throughout the change, we can diagram it thus:

$$\frac{a}{c}\text{———}P\text{———}\frac{b}{c}$$

initial stage — process — terminal stage

This process involves two aspects which are present in every physical change, for after the change the special difference of the initial stage is no longer present, and the special difference of the terminal stage is present for the first time. We will call

the first aspect "passing-away" and the second, "coming-to-be."
All physical changes seem to contain both aspects, and to stress
the double aspect, we can call them "interchanges." (The gaining of knowledge seems to be a pure case of "coming-to-be"
without any passing-away; there does not seem to be any case
of a pure "passing-away."[6]) Schematically:

every interchange

$$\frac{a}{c} \text{---------} P \text{---------} \frac{b}{c}$$

involves both:

passing away   and   coming-to-be

$$\frac{a}{c} \text{--------} P \text{--------} \frac{\text{not-}a}{c} \quad \frac{\text{not-}b}{c} \text{--------} P \text{--------} \frac{b}{c}$$

The subject of change must ordinarily have *both* lost something
which it had in act at the beginning of the change and acquired
something which it did not have in act but only in potency.[7]

Can the (one or) two positive perfections which (are gained
or) interchanged be really identical with the common subject
which changes? Clearly, *a*, *b*, and *c* cannot be identical, and we
are here on the rock bottom basis of the principle of contradiction. If we suppose that they are really identical, then either there
is nothing really common (really no *c*)—and so there is no
change, but removal of one whole thing and the substitution of
another whole thing (Heraclitus)—or there is nothing really
gained or lost (really no *a* or *b*), if we choose to say that the

---

[6] We have *names* for processes which single out one or the other aspect;
for example, death is the loss of life (but this is not purely a loss, for
the soul is replaced by other form[s]); conception is the beginning of life
(but there is not purely a gain, for the soul replaces other form[s]); so,
too, amputation is not purely a loss, for a new figure is gained. The gain
sometimes outweighs the loss, sometimes is outweighed by it, and this
accounts for our emphasis of one or the other aspect. As for the special
case of coming-to-know as a coming-to-be without any passing-away, see
G. P. Klubertanz, S.J., *The Philosophy of Human Nature* (New York,
Appleton-Century-Crofts, 1953), pp. 72–77.

[7] There are some subtle difficulties of language involved when we want
to talk about the temporal interrelations of the elements of a change.
Selected Passages, No. 11, deals with these; for a fuller analysis, see G. P.
Klubertanz, S.J., "Causality in the Philosophy of Nature," *The Modern
Schoolman*, XIX (1942), 29–32.

common element which is identical in all its stages is the whole thing (Parmenides). Therefore, in a real change, at least one of the terms of the change must be composed of two really distinct components.

There are various types of components in a whole being. The term, "part" (although it sometimes is used to mean "any component or constituent") most often means "an equal constituent portion," and in this usual sense it is equivalent to an "integral part." Examples of integral parts are the parts of a human body, the parts into which a line can be divided. Integral parts usually are quantitative parts of an extended (and measurable) whole. There are other types of components which are not quantitative in character, which cannot be discovered by direct sense experience, and which are not capable of existing as distinct beings after the division of the whole. Such components we will call "principles," that is, intrinsic or constituent principles.

In a real change, the components must be really distinct; a distinction of reason cannot account for a real change. If the being which changes is one being, then the component principles will be distinct with a minor real distinction.

Now that we have developed, through an instance of real change, a pattern by which we can understand how change occurs, we are ready, in the following chapter, to look at various kinds of change.

36. Definitions

Change is the process of becoming different or other than something was. (This term stresses the difference between initial and terminal stages.)

Becoming is the transition or process from being in potency to being in act. (This is the technical, scientific definition; the term, "becoming," stresses the relation of process to being.)

Motion in the strict sense (local motion) is change of place or position.

Motion in the wide sense is any change which can be directly measured by time, any change which is continuous or gradual in character.

Motion in the widest (or transferred sense) is any change.

Identity is the sameness of a thing with itself.

Distinction is lack of identity.

Real distinction is a lack of identity independent of any act of the mind.

Distinction of reason is a lack of identity dependent upon an act of the mind.

Being in act is the condition of really possessing some perfection or modification.

Being in potency is the condition of not really having, but being able to acquire, some perfection.

37. Summary

A. Change and being are not incompatible.

Change involves an initial stage, an intermediate process, and a terminal stage. The subject of the change at the beginning is in potency to the determinations which it will have in act at the end.

Hence, change and being are not mutually exclusive or completely incompatible; rather, because change is directed toward being in act, it implies being. Yet, they are not identical either but are related as process and term of the process, as motion and the point of arrival of the motion.

B. Things which change are composite.

Whatever undergoes a real, intrinsic change must be different in its terminal stage from what it was in the initial stage, and yet there must also be a common subject.

But: that by which the initial stage differs from the terminal stage cannot be really identical with the common subject (and this subject is necessary for the continuity of the two terms).

Therefore: that which changes must be composed of a common principle which is in potency and (at least in one of the stages) a principle by which the stages differ.

38. Readings

Aristotle, *Metaphysics*, Bk. IV, chaps. 5, 6 (1010a15 ff. 1011b34), Bk. VIII, chap. 1 (1042a32); *Physics*, Bk. I, chaps. 7-9 (190a32–192b2), on change; Bk. III, chaps. 1-3 (200b12–202b29), on motion.

Jacques Maritain, *Introduction to Philosophy*, trans. E. I. Watkin (New York, Sheed and Ward, 1933), pp. 50–51, 60–63, 239–246.

John Wild, *Introduction to Realistic Philosophy* (New York, Harper, 1948), pp. 277–295, on change.

SELECTED PASSAGES FROM ST. THOMAS AQUINAS

10. A Common Subject in Change

Because every change is from one contrary to another, it is necessary that a subject underlie them, which subject can be changed from contrary to contrary. This the Philosopher proves in two ways. First, because one contrary does not change into another: for blackness itself does not become whiteness. Therefore, if there is to be a change from black to white, there must be something besides blackness which can become white.

The same thing he proves in another way, from this consideration that in every change something remains. For example, in a change from black to white a body remains, but the other thing, namely, one of the contraries—black, for example—does not remain.

Commentary on Aristotle's
Metaphysics, Bk. XII, lect.
2 (ed. Cathala, Nos. 2429-
2430).

Everything which is changed remains with regard to some element of it and with regard to some other element ceases to be. For example, that which is changed from whiteness to blackness remains with regard to its substance. Thus, in everything which is changed, some composition is to be found.

Summa Theologiae, Pt. I, q. 9,
art. 1.

11. Change Implies Succession

Since every change has two terms which cannot be together . . . in every change or motion there must be succession, for this reason that the two terms cannot be together. Hence, there must also be time, which is the measure of that which is before and after, and this latter is the essential note of succession. But succession occurs differently in different cases. For sometimes the end of the motion is remote from its beginning. Between beginning and end there may be the medium of dimensive quantity, as in the local motion of bodies, or in the motion of growth and shrinking. There may be the medium of virtual quantity, whose division is related to the intensity and remission of some form, as in the alteration of sensible qualities. In both of these cases, time directly measures the motion itself, because there is a successive progress to the term, for it is divisible.

Sometimes, however, the term of the change is not remote from the beginning, as in those changes which are from a privation to a form or vice versa, as in generation and corruption, and illumination, and all things of a like nature. Even in these changes, time is involved, since it is evident that matter is not simultaneously under a form and the privation of that form, nor is the air at once subject to darkness and light. However, time is not involved, in the sense that the going forth or passage from one extreme to the other takes place in time. But to one of the extremes (that one, namely, which is first lost in the change) there is joined a motion or alteration (as in generation and corruption), or the local motion of the sun (as in illumination), and at the term of that motion there is also the term of the change. Yet that change is said to be sudden, or in an instant, for this reason that in the last instant of the time which measured the preceding motion, there is acquired that form or privation of which formerly nothing was present. And in that instant we say that something has been generated, but not properly that it is being generated. . . . Consequently, all such instantaneous changes are the terms of some motion.

Commentary on the First Book of the Sentences, dis. 37, q. 4, art. 3.
Cf. *S.T.* I–II, q. 113, art. 7 ad 5

V

The Intrinsic Principles
of Change and Being:
I. In Particular

39. Accidental change and the substance-accident composition of being

GENERAL CONSIDERATION OF THE EVIDENCE

We must now take up the study of change more in particular. The first thing that we will need to reflect on is that, at least descriptively speaking, there are different kinds of change. For example, there is the kind of change that is typified by the various changes that one and the same person goes through in the course of his life. There are changes in size, in bodily appearance, in knowledge and character acquired, in activity, in relations with others. Then there is another type of change most strikingly exemplified in the death of living things; a dead dog, for example, is just not a dog any more.

CLARIFICATION AND DEFINITION

In our general discussion of change in the preceding chapter, we noticed that in every change there must be a *common subject,* and this means that the subject must be the same subject throughout the change, that is, it must keep some kind of identity.[1] But

[1] See above, sec. 33.

there are several kinds of identity. Total, or complete, identity would not allow for any change at all. Numerical, specific, and generic identity are all partial identities which allow for some change.

Unity, on the other hand, is similar to identity, but does not imply a comparison of the thing with itself (as at some other time, and so on).[2] By unity we mean the actual undividedness of something. A thing may be of such a kind as not to have any parts at all; such a thing, which we call *simple*, is not only undivided, but indivisible. All other things which are unified are composed of parts and are therefore divisible. They are units if their parts are actually undivided, no matter how easy or difficult such division may be.

Unity may be intrinsic to the unified thing, or it may be extrinsic. It is intrinsic if the parts belong together of themselves; it is extrinsic if the unity is brought about by something else than the parts. For example, the unity of the parts of an animal is intrinsic; that of a bushel of apples is extrinsic, namely, that of the bushel basket.

But we also say that the parts of an animal naturally belong together. In this case, we mean that the parts of animals are such that when they are together in one unit, they make up a special kind of thing which has its own specific essence.[3] A thing has one essence if all the parts when undivided make up a distinct kind of reality, as all the members of a dog belong to the same kind of animal. Such an essence is also called a nature when we consider it as the source of activities. A natural individual is an actually undivided instance of a certain specific essence, complete in itself and able to carry on the activities of that nature.

But because we can define these notions and give some instance of what we mean by them does not mean of itself that they are legitimate concepts of the real things of the world, nor that we

[2] On unity, see below, sec. 78.

It is also useful to recall that we could not observe change unless we could remember the thing as it was before the change.

[3] On the meaning of species, see above, sec. 33. See also G. P. Klubertanz, S.J., *The Philosophy of Human Nature* (New York: Appleton-Century-Crofts, 1953), pp. 417–420.

know how to use them. So we need to consider these problems also.

Are there natural individuals in the real world, and if so, what are they? The first and most obvious instance is that of one's own self: I am aware of myself as an actually undivided unit. And I know that I am the same individual, with the same specific essence capable of carrying out the same activities, throughout a number of changes which I can remember. Similarly, I know that other people are natural individuals. Most animals and plants can be distinguished as independent and complete sources of activity, but not all. Nonliving individuals are quite difficult to distinguish. Is a piece of iron one individual (as one man is one individual) or many similar individuals having the same sort of nature (like a line of men forming a "living chain" to pull a drowning person out of a lake)? For our present purposes, we can say that it makes no difference: if a piece of iron is not one individual, then it is many, but whatever the last actually undivided whole is, it will be an individual.

A similar problem concerns the kinds of change mentioned above. True enough, we can tell the difference between catching a cold and dying. But we said that a nature is the principle of a certain sort of activity. We know, for example, that living things can generate offspring of the same kind; suppose a man becomes sterile—has he undergone a change of nature? Or, to take a more striking case, suppose he "loses his mind"—does he still have the same nature? Here, we need to point out again that because we can tell some changes from others, it does not follow that we can correctly classify all of them. There have been people who wondered whether imbeciles are human beings, who thought that insanity proved the presence of a foreign nature—"spirit possession"; even people who get confused about their own identity. The difficulty is that often we do not know clearly what happened, and we cannot expect that simple day-to-day experience will reveal it without any effort on our part. In many cases, advanced scientific knowledge will enable us to tell what happened, and then the problem ceases. But there remain many instances which no one yet clearly understands.

If we were studying the philosophy of nature, where we would be concerned with natures for their own sake, then we would be obliged to find at least the principles of a solution. But in metaphysics we are interested in understanding how beings are, not in determining which one is which; in understanding how change takes place and how it is related to being; in getting to see the major sorts of change, not in determining all the fine points of difference. (This is somewhat like the problem of species; a biologist wants to know exactly how many species of plants there are; a philosopher of nature is more interested in seeing how species of plants are determined; the metaphysician finds the material for his reflection in this: that some individuals differ only individually within the same species, and others differ also specifically.)

DETAILED CONSIDERATION OF THE EVIDENCE AND ANALYSIS

We will take for our first consideration that sort of change in which we know that the same individual is the common subject of change, in the way in which I know that I am the same person even though I move around, talk, study, read, and so forth. We will begin with a number of examples. A baby frog has no legs, a full-grown frog has legs and has lost its tail. A scraggly tree may be trimmed into a regular shape. Birds fly from one tree to another. Some things change in size, particularly living things; a giant redwood, hundreds of feet tall and with a trunk many feet in diameter, was once a little seed. Some things change in activity; trees grow during spring and summer, and show no signs of such activity during winter; animals sleep, run, eat, and some hibernate during the winter months; men also change activities in much the same way as other animals (eating, sleeping, moving about), and they also change in their thoughts and desires, they grow in knowledge and acquire virtues or vices.

Now, each one of these beings undergoes a real change; the changes we have been speaking of are not like the changes of clothes on a show-window dummy; they are changes within being. The being, considered as a whole, is different after the change from what it was before. Yet there is also in some way an identity. The frog or tree that grows is the same frog or tree; the adult, mature man is the same human person that he was as a baby, a child, a young man. We know this because the changed thing does basically the same *kind* of activity before the change as after. We know what kind of thing a being is by seeing what kind of activities it has. We can sum up all these examples this way: in the kind of changes described above, the being that changes is the same *kind* of thing that it was before the change, and it is the same individual. In other words, there is a subject that at one time existed under one modification and then later on under another.

In the preceding chapter, we saw that there must be a real distinction between the subject of the change, the common element, and the determinations or qualifications which are gained or lost. But the components of a changing thing are not themselves whole beings but principles or parts. Hence, the distinction between these components is a minor real distinction.

What can we say about these various components and their relations to each other? First, in the kind of change we are considering here, the subject remains what it was, in the sense that it retains the same nature and individuality. But in itself this subject can, and often must, receive further determinations; for example, a man must be in *some* position, but he need not be sitting or standing or lying down in order to be a man. Because this subject remains the same "under" the change, and so "is under" ("sub-stands") the various determinations that it has, it is called a "substance."

Second, though a substance can receive further determinations, the substances which we experience as changing themselves exist, or are, in their own right, in themselves. As subjects of the determinations, they have various qualities, and so forth; substances possess their added and changing differences.

Third, the determinations which come and go "happen to" a substance; hence, they are called "accidents"[4] (*ac-cidens*, that which happens to). In "happening to" a substance, the accidents

---

[4] The term "accident" is also used in a logical sense, and in logic it means "that which is not necessarily connected with the essence of some thing." It is also used in a popular sense, "something (usually something harmful), which was unforeseen, unintended, and so on." We can call the meaning of *accident* used in the body of the text the "metaphysical accident."

further determine, or modify it. We can therefore think of them most accurately as modifiers.

Both substance and accident are principles of being, for they are found *within being;* they are components of a whole, not complete things in themselves. But the whole thing which is the modified substance (we could well say, the "accidentalized substance") is not a natural unit with only one specific essence, since the specific essence remains through the change. We will call it a "per accidens unit."[5] Moreover, substance and accident are not equal principles, for the nature of accident is to modify substance, and in this sense to be "in" a substance. Hence, philosophers often say that accidents *inhere* in substance.

How do we derive the distinct notions of substance and accident? Is "substance" an abstraction? If we look back at the way in which we arrived at substance and accident, it will be noticed that through an analysis of change we proved that one is not the other. But this is again a negative judgment. Substance is therefore a real principle, as real and concrete as the whole being of which it is a part; accidents, too, in their own way, are also real principles. (Substance and accident can also be treated for their own sake.

40. Substance and accident as beings by analogy

We have seen in the second chapter that the properly real thing, or the being, is the entire thing which is. In our analysis of accidental change we found substance and accident, as principles of being, each in its own way. Are substance and accident to be considered beings in the same sense as the individuals of our experience? They do not present themselves this way. Moreover, we could not legitimately conclude that they are beings simply and properly, for our original evidence begins with a single complete being. Now, granted that a changing being is composite, its components cannot themselves be complete beings, on the score that "one" cannot at the same time be "two." It is therefore impossible that a principle of being should itself be *something* which is.

Nevertheless, if substance and accident are the principles of

[5] On the kinds of unity, see below, sec. 78.

the real, they must also be real themselves in the real thing, since the real is not made up of unrealities. How then are they real? Since substance and its accidents together make up the whole real thing—and the whole real thing is that which properly is— they themselves are real with a many-to-one analogy. The "many" are the constitutive principles of substance and accident, and the "one" is the whole made up of them. This analogy of the constitutive principles to the whole composite which they make up we can call briefly the "analogy of composition."

In addition, substance and accident are directly related to each other: substance is the "basis" for accidents, and accidents are the modifiers of substance. Can this direct relationship be analyzed in terms of being? Substance is the (more or less) permanent nature of the thing and is that in the thing by which an existent has esse in itself; the act of existing pertains, within the being, most closely to substance. In other words, substance is not a being by itself; but the esse of the whole being is also the esse of all the principles of that being (many-to-one analogy); yet it is also true that this esse is not the esse of all the principles equally but in proportion to the way in which the principles constitute that being. Now, substance is the essential nature of that which is, and so we can properly and directly say that a substance exists. Hence, substance is directly ordered to the act of existing; we can say directly and without qualification, "A man, a cat, a dog, a tiger exists."

Accident, on the other hand, is related to that which is, not of itself, but through substance. The nature of an accident is to modify the substance in which it is. In other words, accident, according to its nature, is not in itself but in another.[6] Since accident naturally depends on substance for its being, we can say that accidents *are*, not directly but by inherence. For example, we can say, "Whiteness exists—in white things." Here then we have a one-to-one analogy of the constitutive principles of being, based on the relationship of these principles to each other. This relationship makes it possible for us, more or less properly, to

[6] See James S. Albertson, S.J., "The *Esse* of Accidents According to St. Thomas," *The Modern Schoolman*, XXX (1953), 265-278.

call both substance and accident beings.[7] Briefly, substance is being in its own right, since it is that in the being *by which* the being has an act of existing *in itself*. Accident is being by its proportion to substance in which it inheres, for when an accident modifies the substance of a being, the *whole* being *exists, by* that accident, *in a modified way;* so we will call this analogy an "analogy of proportion." For a concrete example, when we say, "A dog is," we mean, "Some individual existent is, having the nature of a dog as the principle by which it has esse-in-itself." When we say, "Whiteness is," we mean, "Some individual existent is, having in itself as one of its modifying principles the quality of whiteness," or, more simply, "Whiteness does truly modify the substance of some being," "Whiteness truly inheres in the substance of some being."

41. Substantial change and the matter-form composition of substance

EVIDENCE

In the discussion of accidental change, we considered those changes in which the changing being remained the same kind of thing and the same individual that it was. However, there are also other changes in which the thing after the change is of a different nature than the thing before the change. The clearest examples of essential change can be found in the death of living things. A live animal has a certain nature, which is shown by the fact that it can perform certain kinds of activities. When the animal dies, the dead body of the animal is simply incapable of vital activities, and so is essentially or specifically different from the living thing. A very similar example can be found in the nourishment of living things. In nourishment, some nonliving material is changed into and becomes a part of a single living thing. In this case, two beings of different kinds become one being.

Our experience shows us that there are some accidental changes which prepare for and are the means of bringing about the change of nature. And there are still other accidental changes

[7] See also, Selected Passages, No. 13.

which are necessarily consequent upon the specific change. To illustrate this from the examples given above, we know that whether death is violent or natural, in either case some dispositions or qualities are changed by force or disease or simply by the wearing out of the organism. And we know also that properties of a nature are necessarily connected with the nature, so that when the first nature is present, these properties are present, and they go with the nature, while the new nature which is the term of the change brings with it its own properties. But over and above these accidental changes, there is a change of the nature itself, which is made known to us from the kinds of activities that the two beings in question perform.[8] Hence, there is a change in the very substance of the thing changing.

ANALYSIS

By applying our analysis of change to these changes of substance from living to nonliving, we get the diagram:

(1) Living substance — changes to ⟶ nonliving substance

$$\frac{l}{c} \xrightarrow{\hspace{5cm}} \frac{n}{c}$$

(2) Living + nonliving — change to ⟶ one living substance

$$\frac{l}{c} + \frac{n}{c} \xrightarrow{\hspace{5cm}} \frac{l}{c}$$

Hence, all substances which undergo substantial change are composed of two intrinsic principles. One of these principles is that by which a substance is of a definite kind: living, nonliving, and so forth. This principle has received the name of "substantial form"—*substantial*, because it is the determining principle of substance; *form*, because it has the same relation to its coprinciple as shape or structure has to the materials used. Substantial form is the principle *by which* a substance is the kind of substance it is; therefore, it is not itself a substance, much less a being, and so it is not a reality which we could possibly find in our direct sense

---

[8] To establish this fact we are using knowledge at the subscientific level. In the philosophy of nature, substantial or specific changes and specific differences are considered and proved at the level of demonstrative knowledge.

experience or by any instrument. Note that in metaphysics we deal only with substantial form as a principle of substance and being without qualification; in the philosophy of nature we shall discover that there are different kinds of substantial form and that one kind of form (the human soul) is not only a substantial form but also a principle of operation and of being.

The second of the two coprinciples of substantial change and composition cannot of itself have any particular nature, since it is precisely the common element in the change of nature or kind. It is of itself merely a subject of change, and for this reason it is called "primary matter" or "first matter." It is called primary matter because it is the first principle of the most basic type of change and is determin*able* to any nature which material things can have. Since substantial form is not a thing or a being or a substance properly so called, much less is primary matter a thing or a being. Of itself, primary matter is not actually any kind of thing; nor does it have quantity or any kind of qualities or other accidents. Hence, primary matter cannot exist in itself; it cannot be found as such in direct or indirect sense experience; it cannot even be understood separately from substance or substantial form. It is an intelligible *co*principle and so is real as a principle of substance and can be understood only in the same way.[9]

Are primary matter and substantial form really distinct? Since the changes which are explained by these coprinciples are real changes, matter and form must be distinct with a minor real distinction. In a way, matter and form are like substance and accident, yet there are also many differences. One of these differences is that accidental change can be gradual because the subject of accidental change (namely, substance itself) is the actual principle by which an individual is in itself. But substantial change must be instantaneous since the subject of substantial change (namely, primary matter) is purely determinable. Substantial changes seem to take time because of the accidental changes which are the means of substantial change.[10]

[9] See also, Selected Passages, No. 12.
[10] That continuous change implies primary matter is established by St. Thomas in his *Commentary on Aristotle's* Metaphysics, Bk. VIII, lect. 1 (ed. Cathala, No. 1686). But this consideration seems to belong to the philosophy of nature rather than to metaphysics.

Another approach to the composition of sensible things is derived from a consideration of the various ways in which accidents are related to their subjects. On the one hand, we find that there are specific qualities and properties which indicate different kinds of things. What one thing is is different from what other things are; what each thing is is characterized by determination, actuality, and some kind of fixity. Hence, substance, which is the proper subject of accidents, must itself have these characteristics. On the other hand, we also find that some modifications are common to all material things—chief among them being quantity and the continuous way in which their contingent accidents vary. Thus, we find two sorts of modifications of substance: one characterized by being proper (that is, not common) and relatively fixed, the other by being common and fluid or relatively "formless." But this distinction of accidents cannot be based on a simple, indivisible substance, for a simple subject cannot be the source of contrary dispositions. Hence, material substances are composite, made up of two principles, one of which is determining and specific (substantial form), the other, common to all material things and in itself indeterminate (primary matter).

Primary matter and substantial form are not things or beings; they are not each, properly speaking, a substance. But they are principles of substance; *by them* a substance is respectively capable of substantial change, relatively indeterminate, and like other material substances, and, at the same time, actually of a given kind or species, determinate, and different from other kinds of material things. Hence, these two principles can be called substances—not in the primary sense of that term but by an analogy of proportion, inasmuch as they are proportioned to each other and to the substance which they constitute. They are reducible to the category of substance.

42. Individuals in a species and matter-form composition

So far we have been considering material substances with regard to their real changes and real internal constitution. There is another important consideration of material substances whose point of departure is our knowledge of them.

THE PROBLEM

We have already noted, as a fact, that in material things there are many individuals having one and the same specific nature. We have also noted that a specific identity is not a total identity, but a partial one. We have observed, as a fact, that we have universal knowledge, and that this universal knowledge is true of individuals, though each individual is distinct and different from each other. This fact of universal knowledge is indeed striking, and it is one of the perennial starting points of philosophical reflection from Plato's time on. As metaphysicians, we are interested in seeing whether these various facts show us anything about the structures of being and, to a lesser extent, anything about the structure of knowledge.

A simple parallel between our knowledge and the structure of reality might appear an appealing solution, and because the first of such solutions was attempted by Plato, similar efforts are usually dubbed "Platonic." The basic principle is that universals are real by themselves, and they are to be found either in a "world" all their own (Plato's version) or somehow in singulars, yet still not merely mentally distinct from singulars. Aristotle pointed out one difficulty with this solution: it creates a new problem of the relation of the universals to the sensible singulars. Moreover, the metaphysical status of these distinct universals is difficult indeed: we have seen above that universals canot exist, and if they do not, how can they account for the nature of the sensibles and for our knowledge?

A second solution eliminates the problem by denying universal knowledge, the "solution" offered by nominalism. Only words (and perhaps also concepts) are universal, but the universality of knowledge is just a fiction. To this attempted solution, we can first retort that universal knowledge cannot be just a fiction of the human mind.[11] That which we know in our universal knowl-

---

[11] We are here appealing to many evidences for a moderate realism. First of all, we do have true knowledge of a world of sensible beings distinct from ourselves, and we know the existence of these beings by our intellect but through sense perception. This evidence cannot be proved, first, because it is an evidence; secondly, because sense perception is a principle of all our knowledge, as will become clear from the philosophy of human nature.

edge is somehow found in the real order. Comparing our knowledge to reality we find the situation which can be diagrammed in this way:

The real being, Peter, who is individual throughout	*is known* *by means of*	{ man { Petreity

Therefore, if our knowledge is true, there must be some reason or foundation in things for our knowing them universally and particularly, and yet this foundation cannot be a common nature as common really distinguished from particularity.

THE SOLUTION

The solution has three steps. The first may be called the epistemological; it consists in clarifying the relation between the universals of knowledge and the singulars of sensation and being. First, it is not to be thought that universal knowledge is a complete and adequate knowledge; it is only partial. It may be a very important part, yet it does not substitute for the direct experience of singulars; it simply does not include in any way the real individuality of the singular things. Second, when we say that universal knowledge is a knowledge of singulars, we mean this with a distinction: it is true with regard to what it says and with regard to what things are; it is not true with regard either to the mode of the knowledge (its universality, abstractness, "timelessness," necessity) or to the mode of the singular (its singularity, concreteness, temporality, contingency).

The second step may be called the psychological, and consists in examining the origin of our universal knowledge. We will here

---

Secondly, there are many considerations which particularly concern universal knowledge. Pragmatically speaking, universal knowledge can be used as a means to deal with real singulars. More deeply, when we mentally construct fictions we are aware of our activity in that construction and can trace the process, but in knowing singulars by direct universal knowledge we do not find ourselves constructing a fiction. Ultimately, we can see that our universal knowledge is a knowledge of the thing which exists. It is not a complete knowledge but one which abstracts from singularity. However, to abstract is not to deny. It would be false to deny that things are singular; we have a true but incomplete knowledge when we know a singular thing without knowing its singularity. To develop these brief considerations is the task of an epistemology or theory of knowledge.

present only a sketch of what is found and proved in the philosophy of human nature. The human intellect receives its knowledge of reality through sense from sensible things. First, then, sensible things act on us; action arises from form (substantial and accidental), not from matter, and therefore does not principally bear the imprint of individuality but of nature and form. Second, sense knows according to formal intelligibilities (color, sound, and so on), even though it knows them only in a singular. The repeated fleeting experiences of sense are conserved in the imagination; the complex image thus developed is already partly disengaged from absolute singularity as found in external sense. Third, the absolute nature is received in the intellect; the intellect, as knowing subject, contributes no temporality or individual limitation of its own, and is affected only by the formal intelligible attributes of what is contained in the image. (The precise causalities of this process need not concern us here.)

The third step is the metaphysical, and consists in elaborating what we already know about material things, together with some additional reflection on these things.

We have in the immediately preceding section found that material things are composed of primary matter and substantial form. Substantial form is that principle by which a substance is *what* it is, that is, has such a nature or essence. Primary matter is that principle by which a thing is capable of substantial change and which therefore is the subject or recipient of substantial form. The possibilities opened up by this very composition are suggested by a simple comparison with accidental form and substance: accidental forms are multiplied (as in the mass production of artifacts) insofar as there are a number of substances to receive them (there are as many pins as there is metal to be cut into pieces). Similarly—and very much in general—primary matter is a recipient for substantial form, and as recipient is the ontological basis for the possibility of there being many individuals (for example, many men) in the same species, whereas the (abstract) unity of the substantial form is the basis of our knowledge of these many individuals in a single concept, the universal. But this parallel has only a heuristic value; we need to look at the things, not merely at some parallel from which we would attempt to deduce the structure of reality.

What then do we find in the real order? We find individuals differing a great deal. Among men, for example, there are both seven-foot Watusi and the five-foot Pygmy; the fragile Japanese dancer and the beetle-browed Neanderthal man.[12] We find some individuals whom we can easily describe by means of relatively distinctive qualities, and others who are alike as identical twins. But even though an individual has apparently unique qualities, these qualities alone do not, absolutely speaking, "identify" him; any quality or any combination of qualities can, at least in principle, be found in another individual. Consider, for example, how qualitatively "identical" two crystals can be. Things can still be two even if these two have no discoverable qualitative differences. But two material beings cannot be two beings unless their temporally determined locations are different.[13] In other words, we can always certainly identify an individual if we know where he is and when.

Now, qualitative differences are differences of accidental form, and so suppose the substantial individual already constituted. Moreover, qualities flow from substantial form—in various ways, as properties, as contingent attributes, as possibilities of modification by external agents.

The substantial individual, who is one of many in a species, is therefore exactly our problem. If all these individuals belong to the same species, then their forms as such cannot be the source of their differing as individuals. What about primary matter? Since primary matter is the subject or recipient of substantial

[12] It must be stated very emphatically that the notions of both "individual" and "species" are analogous. Moreover, such problems as the variability of species and the origin of particular species (speciation), the possibility of varieties and families within species, evolution, degeneration (as in parasitism), hybridization, isotopes—just samples of problems occurring in particular sciences and in the philosophy of nature—these are simply not capable of being treated by a metaphysician. As a wise philosopher remarked centuries ago: metaphysics bakes no bread.

[13] This is not meant to deny "compenetration" or the possibility of a subatomic particle "passing through a solid"; if such events do happen, they are nevertheless explained by means of differences in the "here" and "now."

form, it could, by division, account for the plurality of individuals. But this seems impossible. Primary matter cannot be divided in itself, since in itself it is purely indeterminate, and division implies distinction, difference, and so some kind of determination. True enough. But so far, we have not yet made use of the ultimate criterion of the individual—his being here and now. *Here* and *now* are functions of quantity, as we shall see more clearly later on. Quantity or extension is such that it has parts outside of itself and of itself is divisible. Hence, primary matter with quantity or dimensions[14] is that which is the principle of individuation[15] of a material thing. There are many individuals in a species inasmuch as the recipients of specifically the same substantial form are divided from each other in relation to tridimensional extension.

It will help us if we compare the order of logical composition (common nature + individuality) with the quite different order of real composition (substantial form + primary matter + quantity).

(1) *In the order of logical composition,*

Peter	James	John
$\left\{\begin{array}{c} \text{man} \\ + \\ \text{Petreity} \end{array}\right\}$	$\left\{\begin{array}{c} \text{man} \\ + \\ \text{Jamesness} \end{array}\right\}$	$\left\{\begin{array}{c} \text{man} \\ + \\ \text{Johnness} \end{array}\right\}$

[14] At any given moment, the dimensions in question are the actual three dimensions of the particular individual limited by the external surface; these are called "determinate dimensions." But because in some individuals (living things) the dimensions change—between limits—during their lives, we must consider their dimensions with their variable limits; these are called "indeterminate dimensions." By indeterminate dimensions we mean the tridirectional quantity of an individual, with variable limits, as it were, "at the center."

[15] The principle of individuation is that in the particular thing by which that thing has its particular part or share of the specific perfection and so is only one of many in the species. Distinguish this term from "individuality." Individuality is the sum total of positive perfections pertaining to this individual as *this* individual. Individuation is the quasi-negative, limiting principle; individuality is the correlative, positive perfection.

(2) *In the order of real composition,*[16]

Peter	James	John
$\left\{ \dfrac{f}{p_x + x} \right\}$	$\left\{ \dfrac{f}{p_y + y} \right\}$	$\left\{ \dfrac{f}{p_z + z} \right\}$

f = substantial form by which each individual is a man.
p = the primary matter.
x, y, z = the diverse quantities.
The subscript letters indicate the determination [designation] of matter by diverse quantities.

Once this has been understood, we can easily come to see how new individuals arise by the division of previously existing ones. This is basically the way in which new living beings arise; we can see it most simply in the origin of new unicellular organisms. Many of these organisms are multiplied by simple division (fission); one individual divides into two individuals which are numerically distinct from each other, and yet each of the new individuals has the undivided perfection of the species or kind of living thing. Diagrammatically:

$$\frac{\text{form}}{\text{matter}_{qu} + \text{quantity}} \longrightarrow \left\{ \begin{array}{l} \dfrac{\text{form}}{\text{matter}_{qu}^{1} + qu^{1}} \\[2ex] \dfrac{\text{form}}{\text{matter}_{qu}^{2} + qu^{2}} \end{array} \right.$$

From our consideration of individuation, we arrive at a fuller understanding of the relationship between matter and form. Form of itself as form is simply what-it-is; it is the principle of determination, actualization of specific or substantial perfection. But matter, as divided recipient or capacity, is the principle of multiplication and limitation as well as of substantial change. No individual has the full perfection of what-it-is-by-nature (that is, through its form), because each form is concretely limited by

[16] Because the diagram is somewhat complicated, here is how it should be read: "In the real order, Peter, as *this* man, is composed of a substantial form (principle of specific perfection) and of a primary matter distinguished in function of a particular quantity plus the quantity which has the function of designating primary matter as this (principle of individuation)."

the matter in which it is received.[17] Some of these perfections actually are mutually exclusive; if it belongs to a nature to have one of several colors, a given individual can have only one, and thereby cannot have the others. In many subtle ways similar alternative possibilities are found at the levels of the higher qualities of sense and intellect. Thus, no man has the full perfection of the human nature which he possesses through his form (his soul), because each man's soul is concretely limited by the body (in the sense of primary matter) in which that soul is received. As a result, we can derive some understanding of a species by coming to know one individual, for we will find in that individual (supposing it to be mature and otherwise capable of manifesting its nature) all the properties of that nature, at least in their minimal form. But only after knowing many individuals can we learn the full range of the possibility even of the properties, and much more of the contingent actualizations of that nature.

This relationship of form and matter may perhaps be better understood by a consideration of a kind of being about which various philosophers have spoken, namely, the separated substances, also called "angels," "pure spirits," "pure intelligences," and so forth. There are a number of very subtle and difficult arguments by which the existence of such beings is suggested and proved. Neither the time nor the background is available to us here, so we will speak of such beings hypothetically. If such

[17] Some students are bothered by the pseudo problem, What keeps a separated soul from either ballooning up to be a universal or being identified with all other human souls? All existents are singular; if the soul exists after death, it exists as a singular and with the singularity and existence it had before. Along these lines, there are only two reasonable questions that can be asked. (1) How can separated souls, which are singular forms, be known by universal knowledge? (2) In what sense can a separated soul be said to be the "soul of Peter"? The answer to both questions is the same: because each separated soul has been the soul of a given individual and permanently retains a relation to that individual's body.

Other students are confused because it seems to them that geometrical figures, though pure forms (abstract, it is true, instead of real), are multiplied by themselves without composition. Careful reflection will show that such abstract forms are not multiplied by themselves *qua* forms, but by "intelligible matter." In simpler terms, such abstract forms are multiplied positionally, that is, by reference to a hypostasized extension which serves as a receptive background. This substantialized quantity is quality-less, and therefore individuates only numerically, i.e., without other distinctions.

beings exist, their substance is not composite; they are not substantially determinable and so cannot undergo substantial change.[18] Furthermore, their substance is entirely determinate; they are entirely what they are. There is nothing else in their substance except their specific pefection. Hence this substance is entirely expressed in a single individual, and consequently there cannot be many of these beings in a single species. Each one differs specifically from every other (and so in a kind of way also "numerically"). Because they are pure forms, the formal perfection of such beings is incapable of multiplication; by a somewhat improper use of language, we could say that each individual pure form is its own species (for there are really no species among such beings).

43. That-which-is and the act of existing (esse)

THE PROBLEM

So far we have found composition and distinction of principles at the level of accident and activity and at the level of substance. Because we can know *what* is by simple apprehension (concept), but whether a thing *is* only in a judgment (affirmation or negation), we are led to inquire into the relations between what is and its act of existing (esse). It is quite clear that the questions, "What is it?" and, "Is it?" are two quite different questions. It is also clear that as far as all the things in our direct experience are concerned, the act of existing is not a specific perfection, not a further determination of what the thing is. As Kant said, a hundred real dollars are not a penny more than a hundred possible dollars.

If we attentively reflect upon an existent as it is given to us in immediate experience, we see first of all that the meanings of *to be* and *what-is* are different. As we progressively understand this difference between what-is and its act of existing, we form the primitive understanding of being, "some (sensible) thing which is"; then, on the level of the scientific knowledge of metaphysics, we are led to make the judgment of separation, and so come to understand being as *that which is*. Now, however, we need to study being still more closely.

[18] See also, Selected Passages, No. 14.

ANALYSIS

Let us consider a being, for example, a person, present to us in immediate experience. What that person is (namely, this concrete human nature with all his accidental modifications) can be grasped in a series of concepts and is analyzable into the principles of matter and form, substance and accident. These principles are principles of an existent, but their immediate role is that of constituting the essence.[19] These are the principles by which the being is what it is, is limited, is capable of change in various ways. But a being must *be* before[20] it is determined, limited, modified, capable of changes. *To be*, as we have seen, is the ultimate actuality of all principles—essence and form among them. To be limited and capable of change is thus the correlative opposite of being: a person is limited in the sense that he does not have some perfection; he is capable of change only if he does not yet have the perfection. The principles of limitation and change cannot as such also play the role of intrinsic actualization. What then makes a thing to *be?* Precisely, the act of existing (esse), that real principle in the thing that corresponds to the "is" of the judgment.

Again, the actuality of being is found in many things, each of which as an individual is different from all the others, many of which differ also specifically from some others. *If* being were an abstraction, a remote genus like "sensible substance," we could be tempted to think that the "generality" of being is merely an abstraction, merely the real conceived in the most vague and poten-

---

[19] On essence, see sec. 16, n. 18. Historically, the term "essence" is used in the strict sense to mean "the specific constitution of a thing." In this sense, *essence* is that "part" or "aspect" of the substance of a thing which constitutes it in its species. In the secondary sense, we can speak of the *essence* of an accident as "that specific intelligibility of the accident according to its kind, abstracting from its individual and contingent circumstances."

In a wide sense, the term "essence" has been used to mean "what a thing is." In this sense, we can speak of an individual essence. Nevertheless, in the direct phenomenological analysis of concrete being, we first find *essence* in the wide sense, as the *thing-principle* of that which is. On this broad sense of "essence," see *Summa Theologiae*, Pt. I, q. 29, art. 4 ad 2.

[20] "Before," in this sentence, does not mean a priority of time, but a priority of nature and intelligibility. In other words, determinations and so on presuppose an existent and depend on the act of existing of the existent in order to be real.

tial way. But, since being is not an abstraction; since, in fact, it is opposite to the vague potentiality of a common genus, because it expresses the ultimate actuality of the concrete real, the community of being must be based on a principle that is real and intrinsic in each being. This is the same reason that we considered above when we were forced to accept the *analogy* of being, though it is here used in a different context. In somewhat the same way as specific unity is accounted for by substantial form, and numerical individuality by primary matter, so the analogous unity of being must be referred to one real principle, and the multiple and limited individual beings must derive their multiplicity from another real principle, really distinct from its correlate.[21] It is clear that distinction and limitation are connected with the essence of things, by which each is *what* it is. The act of existing, then, which is common to all of these many things, must be really distinct from the essence, as a correlative constituent principle.

Thus, direct experience and analysis of the real show us that essence and the act of existing are really distinct. These principles, of course, are not spatial or integral parts (like the trunk and members of a living body) nor essential parts (like matter and form). They are purely intelligible principles, not observable as distinct but understood to be distinct with a minor real distinction. (It will be noted that essence-esse as a being is precisely that which is and is analogously.)

CONFIRMATION

The fact of change can be used to support the conclusion that essence and esse are really distinct.[22] We experience a thing com-

---

[21] This point is explained more fully in Selected Passages, Nos. 15 and 16. See, in addition, sec. 64, where the relation of essence and esse is still further clarified.

[22] There are some philosophers, and even some Thomists, who think that this proof is inadequate. They hold that (*a*) an explanation of change can be given by means of the principles of substance and accident, matter and form; (*b*) that the composition of these two principles is a sufficient basis for the proof of the existence of God. Both of these statements are true enough. One can give some explanation of change without going into the question of the distinction between essence and esse. But if one remains entirely on that plane, one is reasoning within the philosophy of nature, and therefore should not expect to find anything about being as the meta-

ing to be and ceasing to be. But neither essence nor form (which is the determining principle of essence) can change—*horse* cannot become cow or carrion. A horse can die; but what-it-is-to-be-horse cannot die or change in any way in itself. The unchange-ableness of an essence is simply a particular expression of the principle of contradiction: "horse is horse and cannot be not-horse." If what-a-thing-is and its act of existing were really identical, then the horse-which-is would exist as necessarily as horse-is-horse. But living things do die; things do change. Hence, what-a-thing-is and its act of existing are distinct, with a minor real distinction.

Hence, what-a-thing-is and its act of existing are two really distinct principles of a being. What-something-is, because it is immediately related to esse (the act of existing), is often called essence.[23] Sometimes also that principle is called quiddity (from the Latin *quid*, meaning "what").[24]

44. The agent and his activity

In our first approach to the intrinsic composition of beings, we discovered the two principles, substance and accident. At that point, we were looking at being from the point of view of change and what was necessary for change to take place. From this point of view, accidents include the activities of the thing. After dis-cussing matter and form, we turned to what is and the act of

---

physician considers being. The distinction between essence and esse is implied in any metaphysical solution of the problem of change. If this distinction remains only implicit (as it did in Aristotle), the solution is good as far as it goes, but it is incomplete. If, however, essence and esse are thought to be identical in the real order, then each one of the com-ponents of a thing, such as substance and accident, which are essences, must be identically also acts of existing. But that which is its act of existing can-not lose it. All that could happen would be to move the necessarily existing components around, and such an interpretation of change is the denial of all *intrinsic* change. But intrinsic change evidently happens, and therefore essence and the act of existing cannot be identical in the real order.

[23] "Essence" implies that we are considering what a thing is as a principle of its being. "Quiddity" implies rather an absolute consideration of what it is, as a pure intelligibility. Strictly speaking, therefore, metaphysics is in-terested in essences but not in quiddities.

[24] See also, Selected Passages, No. 17.

existing, and from this point of view, we saw that both substance and accident belong to what is. If we stopped here, we would have a static and formal notion of activity which could be very misleading, and at least would be very incomplete.

EVIDENCE

At least some activities are distinct from substance and the act of existing of a being, and this is clear from experience, without much analysis. For example, most living things have one or more activities[25] which are sometimes interrupted—by sleep, by climatic changes, by development from immature offspring to senility, and so on. For example, consider the conscious activities of a human being: he has certain kinds of activities like seeing and thinking, and these change from one act to another throughout the waking day; when he is sound asleep, these activities cease altogether. Here, obviously, the activity is distinct from the rest of the being, for it comes and goes and varies, although the being itself continues in existence.

In all the things of experience, we find activity. There is no existent which is absolutely deprived of all action. Even the most passive-looking, apparently inert being is also active, as the investigations of physicists have abundantly proved. Activity is a consequence, an overflowing into the order of action, of the dynamism of the act of existing.

ANALYSIS

What is the relation of activity (action, operation) to the thing which acts? First, a thing acts only if it exists; a nonbeing cannot do anything; a mere concept cannot perform real actions. Second, a thing acts according to its nature. In fact, we learn the nature of a thing first and foremost from its activities. Not only is this true in fact; it is necessarily true. For action comes from an agent; it is the fullness, the complement of that agent's being. The substance is that which receives the other accidents and at the

---

[25] How we distinguish one activity from another and one power of activity from another will be considered in another part of philosophy; cf. G. P. Klubertanz, *Philosophy of Human Nature* (New York, Appleton-Century-Crofts, Inc., 1953), pp. 86–102.

same time is the ultimate principle of activity. Now, as we have seen, a substance in our experience is what it is because of its substantial form, and, likewise, the same substantial form specifies the kind of activity which a given kind of being has. Hence, activity and nature must necessarily correspond.

Third, in the things of our experience, being is *for* its activity.[26] This is most obvious in the things we know best, persons and living things. Inactivity is felt as a loss and a restriction; successful activity as an expansion, a fulfillment of capacities and tendencies. These three relationships are all stated implicity in a common axiom, "Action follows being."

But these relationships, particularly the third, raise a question. There seems to be a double line of actuality: esse and activity. How can this be? How are they related to each other and to being? These questions cannot be answered here, because, though the evidence that raises them is direct enough, we have not yet elaborated the tools of analysis.

45. Definitions

Accident is that principle of being whose nature it is to be in another.

Substance is that principle of being which is modified or determined by accidents (nominal definition).

Substance is that principle of being whose nature it is to be directly ordered to esse in itself (real definition).

Essence in the strict sense is substance considered as being of a certain kind of species and being capable of receiving an act of existing.

Essence in the wide sense is what a thing is. It may include substance and accidents (together as subject of esse); it may be used of principles, of objects of knowledge, of operations, relations, and so forth.

Nature is substance or essence in relation to activities.

Analogy of composition is that many-to-one analogy in which the "one" is the whole made up of the "many," and the "many" are the constitutive principles of the whole, in such a way that

---

[26] One important distinction between two kinds of activity, immanent and transient, will be made from the viewpoint of teleology; see below, sec. 69.

they are not univocally of the same nature as the whole nor of a different kind.

Analogy of proportion is that one-to-one analogy which is based on definite direct relationships between two of the analogates.

Substantial form is the determining and specifying principle of essence or substance.

Primary (first) matter is the determinable and limiting principle of substance in material things and, thereby, is also the common subject of substantial change.[27]

Individuation is the limitation of a nature to a particular individual.

Individuality is the sum total of positive perfections, or the fundamental positive perfection, peculiar and proper to some individual.

That-which-is is the essence in the wide sense.

Act of existing (or, *esse*) is the principle by which ultimately a thing is or exists.

46. Summary of the argumentation

A. Beings that change accidentally are composed of substance and accidents.

It is a fact of experience that at least some beings change in some characteristics while remaining of the same nature as they were.

But: this change is not possible unless the accidentally changing being is composed of a principle which is of itself and others which are in the former as in a subject.

Therefore: accidentally changing being is composed of substance and accident.

---

[27] Aristotle gives two classic definitions of primary matter. It is "the primary substratum of each thing, from which it comes to be without qualification, and which persists in the result" (*Physics*, I, 192a31, tr. by Hardie and Gaye), and "By matter I mean that which in itself is neither a particular thing nor of a certain quantity nor assigned to any other of the categories by which being is determined" (*Metaphysics*, Bk. VI, 1029a20, trans. Ross).

B. Beings that change substantially are composed of primary matter and substantial form.

It is a fact of experience that one kind of thing changes into another.

But: this kind of change implies that each of the beings is composed of a principle by which it is specifically what it is and a principle which is common to both terms and receives the determining principles.

Therefore: things which undergo substantial change are composed of substantial form and primary matter.

C. Individuals in the same species are composed of matter and form.

It is a fact of experience that material things belong to a limited number of kinds of things yet differ among themselves.

But: identity and difference in nature cannot flow from one and the same principle but require two distinct principles.

Therefore: individuals in a species are composed of a principle of specific perfection (substantial form) and a principle of individuation (primary matter with quantity).

D. That which is and the act of existing are distinct in all limited beings.

The beings of our experience manifest themselves as subjects having or exercising an act of existing.

The beings of our experience manifest themselves as many, and as each limited in its being.

But: multiplicity and limitation cannot come from the same principle which constitutes the analogical unity of beings in their being.

Therefore: multiple and limited beings are composed of a principle in virtue of which they are what they are and a principle by which they are (act of existing, esse).

47. Readings

St. Thomas Aquinas, *On Being and Essence*, trans. Armand Maurer, chap. 2, pp. 30–34 (on essence, matter and form, on essence and individuation); *Summa Theologiae*, Pt. I, q. 3, art. 2 (no matter and form in God), art. 4 (no distinction of essence and esse in God), art. 6 (no accidents in God); q. 12, art. 4 ad 3 (on our knowledge of the act of existing); q. 14, art. 6 (the act of existing is not the only perfection); q. 50, art. 2 (angels are pure forms); q. 76, art. 1 (the human soul is the form of a body), art. 2 (and is individuated by the body); q. 77, art. 6 (on the relations between accident and substance); *On Spiritual Creatures*, art. 1 ad 9 (individuals in a species), art. 3 (is there a medium which joins form to matter?); *Commentary on the Metaphysics of Aristotle*, Bk. VIII, lesson 2, Nos. 1691–1702, pp. 627–630 (on form and matter).

Leonard J. Eslick, "The Real Distinction: Reply to Professor Reese [see below]," *The Modern Schoolman*, vol. 38 (1961), 149–160, excellent for understanding some of the more subtle difficulties.

Etienne Gilson, *Being and Some Philosophers* (Toronto, Pontifical Institute of Mediaeval Studies, 1949), pp. 169–170, 175, 184–185, on essence and the act of existing.

Etienne Gilson, *The Christian Philosophy of St. Thomas Aquinas* (New York, Random House, 1956), pp. 84–95, on the real distinction and the proper meaning of the act of existing.

J. Quentin Lauer, S.J., "Determination of Substance by Accidents in the Philosophy of St. Thomas," *The Modern Schoolman*, XVIII (1941), 31–35, on substance and accident.

Bernard J. Lonergan, S.J., "The Concept of *Verbum* in the Writings of St. Thomas Aquinas," Part III, "Procession and Related Notions," *Theological Studies*, vol. VIII (1947), pp. 408–413, esp. p. 412, activity is more than essence or form.

Jacques Maritain, *Introduction to Philosophy*, trans. E. I. Watkin (New York, Sheed and Ward, 1933), pp. 207–210, 217–227, on substance and accident, matter and form.

Armand Maurer, C.S.B., "Form and Essence in the Philosophy of St. Thomas," *Mediaeval Studies*, XIII (1951), 174–176; form, essence, and the act of existing.

William L. Reese, "Concerning the Real Distinction of Essence and Existence," *The Modern Schoolman*, vol. 38 (1961), 142–148, some difficulties with the real distinction.

William A. Van Roo, S.J., "Matter as a Principle of Being," *The Modern Schoolman*, XIX (1942), 47–50; the relation of matter to form and to the act of existing.

William M. Walton, "Being, Essence, and Existence," *Review of Metaphysics*, III (1950), 339–365.

SELECTED PASSAGES FROM ST. THOMAS AQUINAS

12. Change, Matter, and Form

He says that it is necessary to posit matter in sensible substances as substance and subject. For in every change there must be a subject common to the terms of the change in changes which involve contraries. For example, in change of place there is some common subject, which now is here, and then, there. And in growth, there is a common subject, which now has this quantity, and then a smaller one (if it is a decrease), or a larger one (if there is an increase). And in alteration there is a subject, which now is healthy, and then sick. And since there is also a change in substance (that is, generation and corruption), there must be a common subject, which lies under contrary changes of generation and corruption, and this involves the positing of terms, which are form and privation—in this way, namely, that at one time the matter is in act by the form, and at another time, it is the subject of the privation of that form.

From this reasoning of Aristotle's, it is clear that substantial generation and corruption are the principle of coming to a knowledge of primary matter. For if primary matter of itself had some proper form, by that form it would be something actual. Thus, when some other form were brought about in addition to the former, matter would not simply be by that form, but would become this or that modified being. And thus there would be some kind of generation, but not generation simply. Hence, all those who posited that the first subject was some body—as, air or water—held that generation was the same as alteration.

From this consideration it is clear how we must take the understanding of primary matter, for it is so related to all forms and the privations of them, as an alterable subject is to contrary qualities.

> Commentary on Aristotle's
> Metaphysics, Bk. VIII, lect.
> 1 (ed. Cathala, Nos. 1688–
> 1689).

13. Substance and Accident as Beings by Analogy

Those things which have one predicate in common, which is not univocal, but is predicated of them analogously, belong to the consideration of one demonstrative knowledge. But being is predicated in this way of all beings. Therefore, all beings belong to the consideration of one knowledge which considers being as being, namely, both substance and accidents. . . .

He says, first, that being, or, that which is, is predicated in many ways. But we must know that something is predicated of different things in many ways; sometimes, according to an intelligibility which is entirely the same, and then it is said to be univocally predicated of them, as animal of the horse and the ox. Sometimes the predicate is predicated according to entirely different intelligibilities, and then it is said to be predicated equivocally of them, as dog, of the star and the animal. Sometimes the predicate is predicated according to intelligibilities which are partly different and partly not different; different, that is, inasmuch as they imply different relationships; the same, inasmuch as these different relationships are referred to some one and the same thing. Then they are said to be predicated analogously, that is, proportionally, according as each one, by its own relationship, is referred to that one same thing.

Secondly, we must know that that one thing to which the different relationships are referred in analogates is one in number, and not merely in intelligibility. . . .

Every being is called being, in relation to one first thing. This "one first thing" . . . is the subject. For some things are called being, or are said to be, because of themselves they have *esse*, such as substances, which are principally and primarily called beings. But others are called beings, because they are the passions or properties of substance, such as the per se properties of any substance. Some others are called beings, because they are the way to substance, such as generation and motion. Still others are called beings, because they are the corruptions of substance, for corruption is a way to nonbeing, as generation is the way to substance. And because corruption ends at privation, as generation at form, it is suitable that even the privations of substantial form are said to be. And again, qualities or some other accidents are called beings, because they are active or generative principles of substance, or of such things as are related to substance according to one of the above mentioned relationships, or according to any other relationship. Likewise, the negations of those things which are referred to substance, or even of substance itself, are said to be. Hence, we say, "not-being is not-being." We would not say this, unless "to be" pertained in some way to negation.

Commentary on Aristotle's Metaphysics, Bk. IV, lect. 1 (ed. Cathala, Nos. 534–536, 539).

14. Essences: Simple and Composite

The intelligible nature of quiddity or essence does not require that it is composed or a composite. Consequently, there can be found and understood a simple quiddity, which is not a result of the composition of form and matter. But if we find a quiddity which is not composed of matter and form, that quiddity either is its esse, or it is not. If that quiddity is its esse, it will perforce be the essence of God himself, which is its esse, and it will be entirely simple. But if it is not its esse, it is necessary that it have an esse acquired from another, as is every created quiddity. And because this quiddity is by supposition not subsisting in matter, esse will not be acquired by it in another, as is the case with composite quiddities, but it will acquire esse in itself. And so, this quiddity will be that *which* is, and its esse will be that by which it is. And because everything which does not have a perfection of itself is possible with regard to that perfection, such a quiddity, since it has esse from another, will be possible with regard to that esse and with regard to that principle from which it has esse (in which principle no potency can be found). And thus in such a quiddity there will be found potency and act, inasmuch as the quiddity itself is possible, and its esse is its act. This is the way 1 understand composition of potency and act in Angels, and of that by which they are and that which they are, and likewise in the soul. Hence, an Angel or the soul can be called a quiddity, or a nature, or a simple form, inasmuch as their quiddity is not composed of diverse principles; and yet they have a composition of these two, that is, of quiddity and esse.

*Commentary on the First Book
of the* Sentences, dis. 8, q. 5,
art. 2.

15. Multiplicity in a Species

Whenever the essence of some thing is divided by the sharing [of many in it], the same essence is shared according to its intelligible constitution, but not according to the same act of existing. Therefore, it is impossible for that in which essence and esse do not differ to be divided or multiplied by an essential sharing.

*Commentary on the First Book
of the* Sentences, dis. 2, q. 1,
art. 1, arg. 4

16. Multiplicity and Composition vs. Unity

That which is simply the First can only be one, and this for three reasons. First, from the order of the universe, whose parts are discovered to be ordered to each other, somewhat like the parts of an animal in the whole animal, which parts help each other. There can be no such coordination of many things, unless they are striving for some one end. Therefore there must be one highest and ultimate good, which is striven for by all, and this is the principle. Secondly, this is evident from the very nature of things. For we find in all things the "nature" of being, in some of greater value, and in others of less. And yet the natures of these things are not the esse which they have. If they were, esse would belong to the understanding of any essence, and this is false, for the quiddity of any thing can be understood, without understanding that it is. Therefore, it is necessary that they have esse from some principle, and ultimately we must come to something whose very nature is his own esse, otherwise we would have an infinite regress. This is the principle which gives esse to all things, and it can be only one, since the "nature" of being has one intelligibility according to an analogy. For the unity of what is caused requires unity in its per se cause, and this is the proof of Avicenna. The third reason is the immateriality of God. For it is necessary that the cause which moves the heavens be a power which is not in matter, as is proved in the eighth book of the *Physics*. In those things which are without matter, there can be no diversity, except inasmuch as the nature of one is more complete and more in act than the nature of another. Therefore, it is necessary that that which is perfectly complete and entirely act, is only one, from which proceeds everything that contains potency. For act precedes potency, and the complete precedes the lessened, as is proved in the ninth book of the *Metaphysics*.

Commentary on the Second Book of the Sentences, dis. 1, q. 1, art. 1.

17. The Meaning of Being

Since in everything which is, it is possible to consider its quiddity, by which it subsists in a determinate nature, and its esse, by which it is said to be in act, the noun *thing* is given to it from its quiddity, according to Avicenna, but the name, *He Who is,* or *Being,* from the act of being. But since it is the case that in every creature its essence differs from its esse, such a thing is properly named from its quiddity, as "man" from "humanity." But in God his very act of existing in His quiddity, and so the name which is taken from the act of existing properly names Him, and is His proper name.

Commentary on the First Book of the Sentences, dis. 8, q. 1, art. 1.

Our intellect can consider in abstraction [in the broad sense] what it knows as concreted. For, although it knows things having a form in matter, nevertheless it analyzes the composite into the two [principles], and considers the form by itself. And, like our intellect, the intellect of an angel, though naturally it knows esse concreted in some nature, nevertheless separates esse by the intellect, inasmuch as it knows that it itself is one [really distinct principle] and its esse is another.

Since, therefore, the created intellect by its nature is able to apprehend the concreted form and the concreted esse abstractly by way of analysis, it is able to be elevated by grace to know [directly] a separated subsisting substance and a separated subsisting esse.

Summa Theologiae, Pt. I, q. 12, art. 4 ad 3.

VI

The Intrinsic Principles
of Being: II. As Analogously One

48. Comparison of the three sets of intrinsic principles

We have seen that the individual beings of our experience are composed of various sets of principles. To sum up the results of our preceding investigation, we can consider a being thus:

$$\text{being} \begin{cases} \text{act of existing} \\ \text{essence} \end{cases} \begin{cases} \text{accident} \\ \text{substance} \end{cases} \begin{cases} \text{form} \\ \text{matter} \end{cases}$$

If we look back at our arguments by which we discovered these principles, we find matter and substance are alike in this: that each is a common subject for a different type of change, and that essence is somewhat similar to matter and substance in that it is the source of possibility in being itself. Hence, we can link these principles in a proportionate series thus:

$$\frac{\text{accident}}{\text{substance}} \quad : \quad \frac{\text{form}}{\text{matter}} \quad : \quad \frac{\text{esse}}{\text{essence}}$$

Considering these principles in this relationship, we can find a corresponding similarity in accident, form, and esse, for each of them determines a subject, making its correlative subject to be respectively such, this kind or species of thing, or simply to exist. Yet there are also differences in the three sets of correlatives. For example, the subject of accidents is a being in itself, whereas the

124

subject of form is a mere possibility of being-determined-to-some-essence, and essence, in turn, receives all its reality in receiving the act of existing. Hence these three sets of principles, being both similar and different in their relationships to each other, are analogous to each other; and the analogy is an analogy of proper proportionality within a being.[1] But inasmuch as they are analogous, their relationships can be summed up in a single relationship, which is called "act and potency," or the "act-potency correlation."

We first discovered act and potency in the preliminary analysis of change,[2] and at that time we saw that that which changes is first *in potency* and later on *in act*. We saw at that time that the stages of being *in* potency and being *in* act exclude each other— that which is in potency is not yet in act, and that which is in act is no longer in potency. But a further analysis of change showed us that the thing which changes is composed, and the still more detailed analysis of change carried on in the preceding chapter (Chapter V) showed us that the changing things of our experience have at least a triple composition of essence and esse, substance and accident, and matter and form. We need therefore to learn a new and different meaning of "act" and "potency," a meaning which is to be developed from a much more advanced knowledge of change.[3]

What is meant by "act"? We need to go back to experience and consider what has been acquired when something has come to be in act. For example, actual knowledge of biology is what the biologist has when he is considering what he has previously learned. Act is, for example, seeing as compared with the inactivity of closed eyes; being awake as compared to the unconsciousness of sleep; what the carpenter does to a piece of wood when he is at work; the way in which a wax candle is molded as compared to the possibility of being thus molded when it was just a roundish lump; the billiard ball rolling as compared to its previous state of rest; the new tissue become human in the living

---

[1] Note that we do not say, "Accident is to its esse as substance is to its esse," and so forth.

[2] See above, Chap. IV.

[3] On the meaning of "act," see Selected Passages, No. 18.

body of a man as compared to the assimilability of the undigested food. Thus, act may mean any sort of activity, immanent or transient, any sort of actuality, determination, or perfection. Hence, act is an intrinsically analogous intelligibility;[4] with what analogy, we shall see later on.

So, too, with potency as a capacity for act. Potency in itself, it is true, is not act. But we must understand potency positively. Take, for example, the knowledge of biology (the information of a certain kind, and competence in using it). A baby, a puppy, and a doll are alike in this: that none of them know biology; they do not have or possess the actual knowledge. But from our experience with human beings we have found out that some adults know biology and that all (normal) adults can learn it. From this we infer that the baby also can learn biology. We also know that puppies and dolls cannot. There is therefore a real difference between them and the baby: the baby has a potency to know biology; the others do not have this potency. Now, such a potency is something real, but it is not something which can be discovered in itself *as potency*. (The potency we have been studying here is an operative potency, a potency to perform an operation or action. Some operative potencies can sometimes be without their acts, but we cannot apply this to other types of potency.)

Another type of potency is commonly called "passive potency." A passive potency is one which merely receives an act or perfection. For example, a piece of wood or wax is in potency to receive another shape than the one it has now. But its potency to receive a shape (which potency is the substance) is almost purely passive —that is, it depends almost entirely on something else outside it. A thing at rest is in potency to local motion, and this potency depends entirely on something outside itself to be actuated. A piece of steak is in potency to become part of a living thing, and in this case the potency is the primary matter. This steak can become living, not by itself but by the activity of a dog or a man, for example. Primary matter, in itself, is a pure potency; that is, of

---

[4] "Act," when used about the things of our immediate experience, is an intelligibility, not a being or even a principle of being. There is no being of our experience which is purely act; and each of the actuating principles of being is some *kind of act*: form, esse, accident, operation.

itself it has no act and cannot positively contribute to the acquiring of an act. Passive potencies other than primary matter and the capacity for local motion are passive only inasmuch as a subject is capable of receiving a perfection, or determination. Thus, the sense powers, the human intellect, and the will are primarily passive.[5] But they are not *purely* passive; they are also principles of operation. So too, essence is a potency for the act of existing. We never *find* essences in potency—this would be a contradiction—but always as actuated. And yet the facts of change, limitation, and multiplicity show that essence of itself *can* be and that the act of existing is precisely that by which an individual essence *is* in the real order.

49. Theorems of act and potency. I: Act and potency are distinct in their order

Thus it is clear that act and potency are first learned together, in relation to each other. As we find them in immediate experience, neither act nor potency are absolute designations, but correlative intelligibilities: act is the act of a potency, potency is the potency to some act. When we attempt to state the relations between act and potency accurately and inclusively, we state them in exact propositions or formulas which may be called "theorems." These theorems are not obviously self-evident upon casual inspection; neither are they deductively proved; rather, they are the products of an analysis of experiential evidence in the light of being as being.

The act and potency we have been talking about so far are real act and potency, and we have already seen—in the case of substance and accident, matter and form, essence and esse—that these principles are really distinct. By a real distinction, we mean a real absence of identity, independent of any one's consideration of them. Act and potency can also be found in the logical order: the subject of a proposition is potential to the predicate, the genus to the difference. But these are considerations of the mind and, consequently, are distinct with a distinction of reason.[6]

[5] It is important to note that "passivity" should be considered not merely in relation to form or esse or efficient cause but also—and this is a fundamental point often overlooked—in relation to telic cause (purpose, goal).

[6] On distinctions, see above, sec. 33.

We might wonder: granted that in fact, in the cases we have seen, act and potency are distinct in the order in which they are respectively act and potency, must they be distinct? What are act and potency? They are principles which stand in correlative opposition to each other. As intelligibilities of being, they must always have all the characteristics which belong to their own nature. Now, when we understand a *relation*, we understand that it consists in the way in which one (thing) *is* to another (thing), and this necessarily implies that the one is distinct from the other. It would be a contradiction to suppose that there is a relative opposition and that in the same order in which the opposition is found there is at the same time a lack of distinction. Hence, act and potency *must* be distinct in the order in which they are act and potency.

50. What is the potency for activity?

When, in the preceding chapter, we analyzed the various changes of beings, we found in the first three cases a paired set of correlates: substance and accident, matter and form, essence and the act of existing. We had originally included activity as one of the accidents, and thus it follows that in some way substance in changing beings is correlative to activity.[7] Yet, a further consideration of activity showed us that it stands in a special relation to being—action *follows* being, and is the perfection of being to which being is ordered. It seems therefore to be a special kind of act. Can we therefore think of substance and activity as standing in the correlative opposition of potency and act?

On the one hand, substance does seem to be able to have this relation. *Substance*, after all, is the same as *nature*, for nature is just the substance considered as the ultimate intrinsic source of activity. Substance, from one point of view, as essence, is the proper and correlative potency for the act of existing. The same substance, from another point of view, as subsisting subject, is the potency for the various accidents which are its formal modifiers. Why could not substance, from still a third point of view, be the potency for activity?

On the other hand, there are the special characteristics of activ-

[7] See above, sec. 44.

ity. We have already discovered and discussed several points about activity. First, the operation or activity of any limited thing is not and cannot be identical with the act of existing. For (a) transient action affects something distinct from the agent, whereas the esse of a thing is its own, and (b) immanent actions are interrupted, whereas the esse of the thing continues throughout interruptions and variations.[8] Second, other accidents are modifications or determinations of substance; they confer an added or secondary perfection to the essence-side of being rather than to the existence-principle. Third, activity is by no means the same as substance and certainly is not the substantial form of a being. Fourth, activity is on the side of existence; it presupposes existence. Yet, activity is not the act of the act of existing, for the act of existing cannot be considered as in any way at all a potency, so that the act of existing could be the potential principle which receives activity. To be is strictly an ultimate actuality. So, activity is somehow existential without being a further actuation of esse. Fifth, activity in some cases corresponds to inclination; we know that in some of our actions these actions are the realizations of tendencies. When we look at the natural activities, properly so called, of other things, we find that they are present if they are not impeded.[9] We find also that it requires a positive action to impede such activities, and therefore we conclude that there are similar tendencies in other cases and other beings.[10]

There is still another point of view to be taken on activity and

[8] This argument is sufficient for all the beings of our immediate experience. If we wish a complete argument which would include even the angels, who are not subject to such variations, we can take the argument of St. Thomas, *Summa Theologiae*, Pt. I, q. 54, art. 3, which is based on the intrinsic and necessary correlation of act to potency. Since activity is a distinct kind of act, its proper potency must be a distinct one, proportioned to the act, and this potency is precisely the accidental operative potency, or power.

[9] Recall that many "activities" of things, especially nonliving things, are not the *natural* activities of those things, but passions which happen to them from other causes. Thus, the movement of the rocket as it rises is not an action *of* the rocket, but rather a passion. In ordinary language we use these terms loosely, but here we must carefully distinguish between the action *of* a thing, and a passion, which is the action of something else *in* that thing.

[10] Tendency will be considered at greater length below, secs. 60 and 69.

the passivity that corresponds to it. The other principles which we have considered earlier are all *intrinsic* principles: they make a being in itself. Some of these principles indeed give grounds for various similarities and comparisons,[11] but just by themselves the relations that follow are purely formal and static. Only through activity and passivity does our world become, not only dynamic, but positively and dynamically interrelated. These dynamic inter-relations are constituted by or are the results of activity. Activity, therefore, in creatures, relates a being to other beings outside itself.[12] From this point of view, also, as outgoing and directed to other beings, activity is a different kind of act from all the other acts.

Must it then have a proper and distinct potency that corre-sponds to it? There are three considerations by which we can answer this question. (1) In some cases, the activity is a property of the nature (for example, reasoning in man). This activity is also sometimes not actually present. But: a property cannot be absent from a nature, since the formal connection between essence and property is necessary, as we know from logic; moreover, properties in creatures are really distinct from the essence. There-fore, if a proper activity is sometimes not actually present, it must be potentially present, formally as such a specific characteristic and as distinct from the essence. This formal, accidental property, which is the operation in potency, is the power of performing the proper operation. (2) The activities of any being are multiple and varied. It is very difficult to see how an essence that is actually one can simultaneously and immediately give rise to multiple and varied activities. But powers as sources of kinds of activities would be fewer in number and more easily ordered to each other and to the essence. Therefore, it would be easier to understand a being by means of powers as mediating between the unique essence and the multiple activities. (3) Potencies must differ from each other in the same way that acts differ, for potency and act are correlative

[11] On relation, see Clifford J. Kossel, S.J., "The *Esse* and *Ratio* of Rela-tion," *The Modern Schoolman*, XXIV (1946), 19-24, 30-36, 96-107.

[12] Activity can also be directed to the being which acts; for example, we can know not only things distinct from ourselves, but ourselves also. We are not saying, therefore, that *all* activity is directed to something distinct from the agent. We are saying that only through activity and passivity are beings dynamically interrelated.

and define each other. In every creature, however, as we have seen, activity is a distinctive kind of act, different both from the esse of the being and from its form. But, essence (and the formal principles associated with it) are potencies to esse, and conversely, esse is the act of the essence (substance primarily, formal accidents secondarily). Hence, there must be a distinctive and proper potency for activity, and since this potency must be distinct from the substance, it can only be one of the accidents. Therefore, the proper potential principle of activity is a qualitative accident inhering in the substance; this proper potency we will call "power."

51. Theorem II: Act and potency are not strictly beings but principles of being

If act and potency were each a being, they could not be found combined within a single being (1 being + 1 being = 2 beings). In every order, act is that *by which* a being is or is some kind of thing or exists according to some modification; and for its part potency is that *by which* a thing can be or can be some kind of a thing or can exist according to some modification. But because act and potency are precisely principles of being, we can correctly speak of them as being, by the analogies of composition and proportion.

This analogy, however, works out differently in the different analogues of act and potency. The most proper sense of *being* is that which is, or something having esse. The being, properly speaking, is the whole. And only the entire thing perfectly fulfills the intelligibility of "that which is." But, after the whole, and in a derived and less perfect sense, the various principles of a being can be called beings, to the extent and according to the way in which they pertain to being and share in the esse of the whole. Substance and accident are the constitutive principles by which an essence is this essence. Substance, as we saw, is that principle of essence by which an essence has being *in itself*. Within essence, therefore, substance is the more proper subject of the act of existing. Accident is, on the other hand, *by* being *in another* (that is, in substance) as in a subject. According to its nature, therefore, accident is called being inasmuch as it actually inheres in the substance which is in itself. Yet, accident is as act to substance, which is as potency. The substances of the things of our experience could not exist as stripped of their accidents, since in that condition they would be indeterminate within one whole order of essence and yet have their ultimate act, which is esse. Accident, on the contrary, is act in the order of essence, but its relation to esse is naturally indirect, that is, through substance.[13] Matter and form are not directly beings but rather principles of substance, which is being by proportion. By being the principles of substance, form and matter can be called beings by an indirect proportion—form, more properly, inasmuch as it is the actualizing principle of substance; matter, less properly, or more remotely, inasmuch as it is capable of being actualized by form and so made suitable to receive an act of existing. Esse, however, although it is most truly act among all the principles of being and is precisely that by which a being *is*, nevertheless, in the beings of our experience, is precisely distinguished from essence and so is *not* a *subject* of existing in those beings. Hence, in all such composite beings the act of existing cannot be called a being even by proportion. The act of existing—as a principle of being—is not that which shares in, or is proportioned to, an act, but is precisely the act which is shared, to which there is a proportion.

52. Theorem III: Act, in the order in which it is act, is unlimited in itself and limited by the potency in which it is received

All the beings of our immediate experience are limited, and the acts they have are likewise limited. Act, as we find it, is a principle of being. Acts are found as perfections of some being. They are all limited acts, correlates of some potency. Indeed, all acts of limited beings are necessarily limited. This holds true, whether the act in question is esse, substantial form, accidental form, or activity. Thus, the act of understanding as it really occurs is necessarily limited, as the act of this or that power, of this or that person. The knowledge of biology for instance, as it is to be found in any existing biologist, is limited by his particular capacity. The act of playing a violin by even the most skilled of

[13] See St. Thomas Aquinas, *On the Power of God*, qu. 7, art. 7, par. 1.

violinists is in fact limited and determinate. The accident of whiteness, as it is found in any white thing, is a particular grade of whiteness. The circularity of any round thing is just the kind of roundness that a material subject can have.

But none of these acts is a limitation of itself—not the act of understanding, not the act of playing the violin, not the substantial form of man, not the act of seeing. A limited act is this limited act precisely and only because it is received in the potency or proceeds from the potency. Any accident inhering in a substance is limited by the nature of the substance; thus, "roundness," as it really exists, is limited by the nature of the substance which is round. In the order of matter and form, we can also see the limitation of act by potency. For example, a man is a man by his substantial form, which is his soul; but human nature is never found in its complete fullness in any existing man because the soul, in being the act of a particular body, can actuate the potency only as it is in that particular body. Similarly, in the order of knowledge, the relationship between the absolute nature and the individual is a relationship of limitation. What is meant by "man" taken in itself is verified in "Peter" according to the limitations of Petreity. In the judgment, "Peter is a man," "man" is not found according to its full perfection as absolute nature but is limited and particularized by its reference to Peter.

In the orders of accident and substance, we have been speaking of the "limitation" of act by potency. To understand this more clearly, we must recall that some accidents are acts in one order and potencies in another. This situation is especially verified in the case of the powers which as accidental qualities are acts of substances, but as powers are potencies to activity or the undergoing of activity. Take, for example, the human power to see. The power of sight is a qualitative act and, as such, is limited by the potency which receives it: the substance of the person who possesses such a power. On the other hand, the power of sight is an operative potency which limits the act of seeing. When therefore we say, "Accidents are limited by the substances in which they are received," we must understand "accidents inasmuch as they are acts," because accidents, in the order in which they are potency (namely, in the order of operation), are themselves principles of limitation. There is a sense in which we can say that a potency is "unlimited"; for example, my potency to see is unlimited, in the sense that I *can* see all visible things, but my act of seeing is limited at any particular time, in the sense that I actually *see*, not all visible things but only some few. Here, the unlimitedness of potency is precisely an imperfection, for my being able to see is not the act of seeing at all. The unlimitedness of my ability to see is at the opposite pole from act, for the ability to see is no vision at all. This kind of unlimitedness we will call "indetermination." When, on the other hand, we speak of an act being unlimited as act, we mean an unlimitedness in the sense of completeness of perfection. For example, as an act of vision, seeing this white paper is entirely determinate and is completely perfect as act of vision, but *my* act of seeing is in fact limited by the capacity or ability of my eye.

DIFFICULTIES

There are several points which tend to interfere with the perfect understanding of the relationship between act and potency. One of them is that essences seem to be limited to what they are by being themselves and not by any potency. For example, a horse by being a horse is not a cow, and so horseness by being horseness is not cowness. It would thus seem that essence, which is an act, is limited by itself. But this is a confusion. Horseness is not *limited* by being horseness, for cowness is not a limitation of horseness at all in any sense. If cowness were unreal, impossible, and even unthinkable, horseness would not be the more perfect for that. If we stay strictly in the order of essence, then essence is precisely unlimited as essence; one essence is not limited by another or by itself; essence is limited by individuation (horse as horse is complete in itself; it is not lessened by "cow" but is limited in "Man of War"). The source of the confusion is that some philosophers have failed to distinguish between being and essence; they say, "A horse by being a horse is limited, for it is not also a cow." Do they mean, "is limited as a being" or "is limited as a horse"? It is true that a horse, by being a horse, *is* in a limited way; but this is not a limitation of essence by essence but of the act of existing by essence.

A second confusion which sometimes occurs to philosophers is the apparent limitation of a being by its efficient cause. For example, a pail has the potency of holding water, but how full it is seems to depend on how much someone pours into it, and this is a limitation by efficient cause. Two remarks are to be made about this and all similar examples. Firstly, what is limited in the example is not an act but a complete being (the water or whatever else is used as an example). Secondly, the potency in question is not a real potency (for example, an intrinsic potency of the pail), but it can be thought of as a property of the space (which is not a real being). Hence, this kind of example does not illustrate the relationship of potency and act, for it contains neither potency nor act but a number of beings which are composed of potency and act. Another sort of example sometimes used shows merely that an efficient cause is necessary for the production of a limited being. A line, for example, is divisible, but it is actually divided only when an efficient cause makes a division in it. How long a given line is to be depends on the cause which produces the line. but note that we are dealing either with an abstract line (which as abstract is a pure form, and so its precise length is a formal characteristic) or with a line in or on the surface of a real being. In the former case, the line is completely perfect as a line; that is, if it is a five-inch line, it is absolutely and completely perfect as five-inch line, and that it is not a six-inch line is by no means a limitation of a five-inch line. (Line, as genus, of course, is unlimited in the sense of being indeterminate; but in that sense, "five-inch line" doesn't *limit* "line," it determines it formally.) On the other hand, if we are speaking of a line on the surface of an existent being, the perfection of the line is limited by the nature of the surface on which it is, and this kind of limitation the efficient cause can do nothing about. All the examples drawn from quantity and quantified perfection are subject to the same confusion.

We can summarize this analysis thus: a form as form is limited *to* its order, but not limited within its order. A form is self-limited to its order, unlimited within it.

THE LIMITATION OF ESSE

The act of existing transcends all orders. As we have seen, esse is the actuality of all other principles, including forms and essences. But we do not find in our experience an unlimited esse, just as we do not find any other unlimited acts. All the beings of our experience are limited as beings; a being as we find it is always some *kind* of being. So, too, the acts of existing which pertain to limited beings are limited. For example, a tree exists according to the nature of a tree; it *is* by an act of existing proportioned to that nature. A man is, and he *is* in the way in which human nature proportionately has the act of existing. Human existence, the esse of a man, is different from the existence of any and every other kind of being. Is the act of existing limited in and by itself? If we were to say that it is, we would be implicitly contradicting the evidence that the act of existing is that-by-which-a-being exists, simply and absolutely. If the act of existing were limited as act, then things could be only in that one limited way, and other kinds of existents could not be. And so the act of existing, like all other acts, is limited by the potency in which it is received, namely, essence.

53. Theorem IV: Act can be known by itself, potency only through act

This proposition does not mean that in every single case we discover the potency through its act; it does mean that in the first instance of any kind, we can discover potency only through act. If we know something about explosives, we can calculate how strong a particular charge is without setting it off. If we already know something about biology and chemistry, we can sometimes predict what a particular new drug will do. But if we had never heard of radar and knew nothing about electronics, we could not even make an intelligent guess about what a radar set could do if it were turned on. So, too, with living things; to find out whether a grain of wheat is dead or alive we wait to see whether it actually grows or not.

Ultimately, the reason why this is true is that we derive our first knowledge of things from the things themselves. This means that in the first instance things must act upon us before we know them; things do not act inasmuch as they are in potency but in act.[14]

54. Theorem V: Act and potency divide being in general

The things of our experience are neither simply potency nor simply act but composed of potency and act, and that in many ways. In the order of existence, being is divided into potency and act; essence and the act of existing. In this order, potency cannot *be* without its act, for a thing is through its act of existing. Likewise, in this order, a thing either is or is not; there is no other alternative. In the order of essence, that-which-is is divided into substance and accident, and here, too, there is no third alternative; nor can either one of them naturally exist without the other. In the order of substance, material substance is divided into matter and form. Between matter and form there is no third alternative; matter cannot be without any act. In the order of operation, there is potency to act (power) and operation or activity itself. Here, however, some powers can be without their operation. We also find habits, which are acts by comparison with the power of operation itself, but potency in comparison with the operation.

55. Concluding remarks about act and potency

In connection with the order of operation or activity, there are ways of speaking with which we must have some acquaintance. There is, for instance, the term "active power." By an active power, we mean the power which an agent has of influencing something else. It is called "active" by comparison with the thing influenced, but it is called "power" because it is not identical with the action or operation.

Again, there is the term "virtual act," by which we mean that X has the power of producing Y and usually imply that X itself does not have the perfection of Y. For example, in logic it is said that the premises of an argument "virtually" contain the conclusion; this means that the premises bring about the conclusion, but they do not have identically the same perfection.

[14] On the priority of potency to act, and act to potency, see Selected Passages, No. 19.

Finally, there are the expressions "first act" and "second act." For example, if a thing has the nature or essence of man, we say it is human in first act; when it performs the activities proper to man, we say it is human in second act. In general, if we line up the following factors thus:

form	esse	accidents	activity	causality
(*first act*)				(*second act*)

we may lay down this general rule for the use of the terms "first act" and "second act": of any two terms in the above line, the term to the left is first act relatively to the term on the right.[15]

In reflecting on the act-potency correlation and its various analogates, we must be careful to keep in mind our order of approach. First, we found the distinction between substance and accident, matter and form, essence and the act of existing. The arguments for the distinction of substance and accident and of matter and form are very similar and are very closely connected; nevertheless, they are, strictly speaking, independent arguments. The distinction between essence and the act of existing is found without any direct logical dependence upon the previous two arguments. It is only after these sets of principles are each distinctly known that we can see their similarity and formulate this similarity as "the act-potency correlation."

There are two consequences of this approach to act and potency. The first is that we cannot simply *deduce* the existence or distinction of these principles from any of the theorems of act and potency. Nevertheless, we can learn a great deal about each set of principles from our reflections on them as analogously act and potency. One clear case is the discovery of power as an accidental principle of operation in limited beings, which we cannot clearly

[15] That which is pure potency is primary matter. "Form" is very often defined as "the first act of matter," for matter cannot receive any other act until it is informed; once informed, it can be, be modified, act, and cause. Of course, this sequence of acts is not a sequence in time. Moreover, we need not take the next term in the series for our comparison of first and second. Thus, when form is called "first act," authors most often are thinking of accident or activity as "second." The series as it is presented above is not something which should be memorized; it is given as a key to help us read St. Thomas and other authors who use the expressions "first act" and "second act."

understand except by reflecting upon activity as an act and reasoning to its corresponding potency. Again, although each set of constitutive principles has its own unique, independent characteristics, the discovery of the analogical unity of these principles as act and potency helps us to see the unity, the internal consistency, and the harmony of being.

Secondly, act and potency are analogous conceptions. The pairs of correlatives—matter and form, substance and accident, essence and esse, the power and activity—are analogous to each other with the analogy of proper proportionality. But, esse, activity, accident, and substantial form are analogously act. Esse is the one principle which is act without qualification, for it is the actuality of any and all principles and the actuality of being. The other acts are acts by proportion,[16] inasmuch as they are similar to, and yet not the same kind of act as, esse. Similarly, but in inverse order, primary matter is pure potency without qualification. All other potencies are potencies by the analogy of proportion, inasmuch as, in relation to their acts, they are determinable and actuable in a way similar to the potency which is primary matter.

In every one of the analogates of potency and act, we find a mutual correlation. Act, as we find it, is always the act of a potency, and potency is that which receives, possesses, and is actuated by act. But potency is always for the sake of act; potency is ordered to act. We can by no means say that every act is ordered to its potency. Hence, act and potency are not equal principles. Potency is an absence of act, yet at the same time it is suited to

[16] The analogy of proportion here is somewhat different from the other analogies of proportion we have found to hold between the intrinsic constitutive principles of being, essence, and substance. The previously found instances could be called "intrinsic," since the analogues are directly related to each other and are denominated from the whole which they intrinsically constitute. In the analogy of proportion by which esse, activity, and form are all called "act," we find an extrinsic similarity; none of the principles are principles of one whole inasmuch as they are acts. Yet there is a proportion and a dependence of all other acts upon esse, so that esse is the primary analogue of act. Hence, we would call this an *extrinsic* analogy of proportion. However, in the order of discovery and knowledge, activity is found first, and all other acts are discovered through activity; see Selected Passages, No. 18.

the act which is its perfection and complement. Perhaps the interlocking of act and potency can be symbolized in the following diagram:

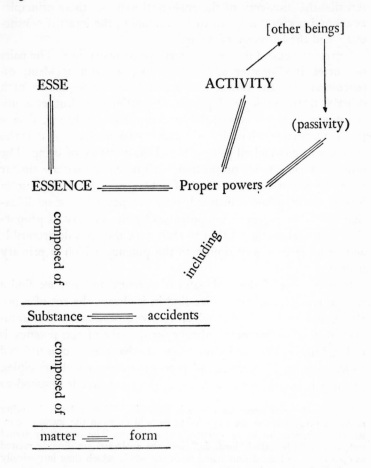

In all these cases, the order of potency to act can be expressed in several ways. "Order" means specification, intelligibility—potency is known and defined by its act; "order" means suitability or conformability—potency and act "fit" each other, though with obvious differences in the various cases.

In the case of power and activity, a very important, special kind of order is to be found. A striking instance of this can be seen in beings which have knowledge. We find that men, for example, can be in three different states with regard to some activity. (1) They can be simply not acting in this particular way. (2) They can be actually engaged in that activity. (3) They can be wanting to act but not doing so for one reason or another. This situation shows us the factor of desire or tendency. Animals likewise have likes, desires, and so on. Plants are not only *able* to grow but tend to; we truly say, for example, that their roots "push" their way—who has not seen a cement sidewalk broken by a tree root seeking water? We even personify nonliving things and say that they "want" this and that, indicating that we discover in them active tendencies. Every power of operation is thus a tendency to that operation.[17] This is so much the case that in nonfree agents that do not undergo structural changes, if the power is present and not externally impeded, the activity is also necessarily there. The very notion of "violence," with its corresponding notions of "active resistance," "reluctance," and so on, testifies to the reality of tendency in things. The tendencies of things flow from the proper nature (substance) and are determined in various ways, depending on the kind of nature and the kind of power. We will have to consider power as active tendency again in the two following chapters.

56. Exercise

Take the three major analogues of act and potency (matter and form, substance and accident, essence and esse), and apply to them the five theorems of the act-potency correlation, pointing out both likenesses and differences between the theorems as stated generally and the particular analogate in question.

57. Readings

St. Thomas Aquinas, *Contra Gentiles*, Bk. I, chap. 22 (the identity of essence and esse in God); Bk. II, chap. 54 (compendious summary

[17] In the philosophy of human nature, we find that over and above the tendencies identified with powers of operation (called "natural tendencies" or "natural appetites"), beings with knowledge also have *conscious* tendencies which are distinct powers (sometimes called "animal appetites").

of act and potency in relation to the various analogues); *Summa Theologiae*, Pt. I, q. 84, art. 2 (limitation of form by matter); q. 87, art. 3 (act is known before potency); *Compendium of Theology*, chap. 18, par. 1 (limitation of act by potency); *On Spiritual Creatures*, art. 1 (on the nature of pure forms); *Commentary on the Metaphysics of Aristotle*, Bk. IX, lessons 1, 4, 5, 7, 8, Nos. 1768–1785, 1815–1831, 1844–1866, pp. 654–658, 671–677, 683–689 (on act and potency).

Bernard J. Lonergan, S.J., "The Concept of *Verbum* in the Writings of St. Thomas Aquinas," Part III, "Procession and Related Notions," *Theological Studies*, VIII (1947), pp. 408–413, a striking expression of the distinctive nature of acting, esp. p. 412.

Jacques Maritain, *Introduction to Philosophy*, trans. E. I. Watkin (New York, Sheed and Ward, 1933), pp. 239–256.

A. D. Sertillanges, O.P., *Foundations of Thomistic Philosophy* (St. Louis, B. Herder, 1931), pp. 25–44.

William A. Van Roo, S.J., "Act and Potency," *The Modern Schoolman*, XVIII (1940), 1–5.

John Wild, "Tendency: The Ontological Ground of Ethics," *Journal of Philosophy*, XLIX (1952), 468–472; an excellent presentation of tendency.

SELECTED PASSAGES FROM ST. THOMAS AQUINAS

18. Origin and Meaning of the Term "Act"

He shows what it is to be in act, and he says, that this word *act*—which is used to signify the entelechy and perfection (that is, the form), and other things of a like nature, as any operations whatsoever—is derived mainly from motion, as far as the origin of the term is concerned. Since names are the signs of intellectual conceptions, we first impose names on those things which we first understand, even though they may be later according to the order of nature. But among all the acts, motion is the best known and evident, for it is sensibly experienced by us. And so it first of all was given the name of act, and from motion, the term was applied to other things.

Hence, motion is not applied to things which do not exist, although other predicates are applied to non-existents; for we say that non-beings are intelligible, or objects of opinion, or even desirable, but we do not say that they are moved. Since "to be moved" means "to be in act," it would follow that actual non-beings would actually be, and this is evidently false.

> *Commentary on Aristotle's*
> Metaphysics, Bk. IX, lect. 3
> (ed. Cathala, Nos. 1805–
> 1806).

Not only that pertains to perfection in which all creatures communicate, namely, esse itself, but also all those [things] by which creatures are distinguished from each other, as to live, to understand, and so forth. . . . For the proper nature of every thing consists in this that it shares in the divine perfection in some way.

Summa Theologiae,
Pt. I, q. 14, art. 6.

19. Priority of Act over Potency

Act is naturally prior to potency. And, simply speaking, it is prior in time, for potency is not moved to act except by a being in act, although in one and the same subject which is at one time in potency, at another in act, potency temporally precedes act. Hence, it is clear that form is prior rather than matter, and is also being more than matter is, because "that by reason of which something is such, is itself more such." But matter does not become a being in act except by form. Hence, it is necessary that form is being more than matter is.

Commentary on Aristotle's
Metaphysics, Bk. VII, lect. 2
(ed. Cathala, No. 1278).

First, act is prior to potency in intelligibility. . . . That by which another is necessarily defined, is prior to it in intelligbility, as "animal" is prior to "man," and "subject" to "accident." But potency cannot be defined except by act. For the first intelligibility of the possible consists in this, that it is suitable for it to act or to be in act, as "a builder" is "he who can build," and "a speculator" "one who can speculate," and "the visible" is "that which can be seen," and so on. Therefore it is necessary that the intelligibility of act precede the intelligibility of potency, and the knowledge of act the knowledge of potency. Hence, Aristotle earlier manifested potency, defining it by act; but act he could not define by anything else, but only manifested it inductively.

[Secondly] he shows how act is prior to potency in time, and how not prior. . . . Therefore, he says first that act is prior to potency in time, in this sense that in the same species, the agent, or the being in act, is prior to the being in potency; but one and the same numerical subject is in potency temporally before it is in act. . . .

After the Philosopher has shown that act is prior to potency in intelligibility, and in some sense in time, he shows that it is prior in "substance" . . . that is, in perfection. . . . If perfection and end did not consist in act, there would not seem to be any difference between a wise man . . . and a fool.

Commentary on Aristotle's
Metaphysics, Bk. IX, lects. 7,
8 (ed. Cathala, Nos. 1846–
1847, 1856, 1861).

VII

The Extrinsic Principles
of Being: I. The Agent

58. Principles of change

Change has already been considered from the point of view of the principles within (intrinsic to) the thing which changes. These principles we have found to be either matter and form or substance and accident. Are these principles sufficient to bring about a change? Or is there something outside the thing to produce the change?

In our experience, we not only find things changing but, in very many instances, we find within direct experience factors external to the changing thing which accomplish the change. For example, we experience a match lighting a cigarette, ourselves pushing an object to make it move, hitting things and being hit by them, and so forth.

Sometimes we make mistakes in determining which agent is the source of a particular change; for example, little children may think that when they turn on the light switch, they are the agent which brings about the light. The child is an agent, not directly of the light but of the local motion of the switch. His action closes a circuit, removes an impediment to the activity of the dynamo. Such an agent which removes an impediment for another agent is called an *active condition*[1] of the effect of the second

[1] The English word "condition" more commonly means a "passive condition," or disposition, which is in the line of material causality. The verb,

agent. At other times, with regard to causes and effects outside ourselves, we may even confuse an occasion with a cause. By an *occasion* we mean a factor that provides an opportunity for an agent to act. In some cases, we may not be able to distinguish which of the factors present before an effect is the cause, and which are the conditions and occasions; sometimes our failure to distinguish arises from negligence or inattention on our part. There are also many situations in which we do not immediately perceive the change as coming from an agent. For example, before the discovery that lightning is an electrical discharge, it was popularly thought that the damage was caused by the thunder (hence the expression "thunderbolt"). (In O. Henry's classic story, "The Ransom of Red Chief," the kidnaped boy asks his captors, "Do the trees moving make the wind blow?")

But even if we sometimes make mistakes in determining the agent or are unable directly to perceive the agent or sometimes confuse an agent with a condition or even an occasion, it remains true that sometimes we do perceive an agent bringing about a change in some other thing. Hence, a child's perception of his causality can be erroneous to some extent, but his error does not invalidate his perception and direct experience of himself causing something.

Our immediate experience of causality, either as children in the first instance or later on, is a direct and concrete knowledge that a cause is working. We do not have a clear and distinct, abstractive concept of cause, for cause and causality are not essences, nor are they found in the order of essences. Causes are concrete beings which we can experience. That is why even on the level of spontaneous knowledge we have a true and certain (judgmental) knowledge of causes. In the present chapter, we are trying to obtain a scientific knowledge of causality.

As far as terms are concerned, when we use the word "agent," we mean "that which brings about a change in some other thing"; an agent is also called an "efficient cause." The thing which is changed by some agent is called a "patient"; that which is brought about in the patient is called an "effect."

"to condition," is used both in the active sense (bring about a disposition or qualification) and in the intransitive sense (be a disposition).

59. Causal factors

In Chapter V we discussed the intrinsic principles of change (substance and accident, matter and form). Inasmuch as these principles not only are necessary for the explanation of change but also join in the coming-to-be of the effect, we can consider these principles to be intrinsic causal factors. Substance and matter, which are both potency to change, are called the "material factors" or "material causes"; accident and substantial form, which are the acts by which the being is what it is and such as it is, are called the "formal factors" or "formal causes." How and in what sense can these intrinsic principles be called *causal factors?* Because each in its own way concurs in the coming-to-be of the effect. The material cause has its influence in the effect by being the subject and determinable factor in the patient, in other words, by its self-communication to the effect as fully constituted. The formal cause has its influence in the effect by being the act by which the effect is actually what it is, in other words, by its self-communication as the determining and specifying factor.[2]

The agent is distinguished from the intrinsic principles, first, because it is extrinsic to the patient, that is, is not a part of the patient precisely as such, and secondly, because the precise way in which it influences the effect is by its activity, by acting.

There is also a fourth causal factor, the goal (telic cause) which influences the effect by determining the agent to act; we will consider this factor in the next chapter.

[2] Since the intrinsic components of a being are causal factors, and since the act of existing (esse) is an intrinsic principle or component, one might wonder whether it should be included among the causal factors. Most strictly speaking, esse is the very actuality by which the thing is a being, and so is not strictly a causal factor, but rather the very "being made" of the effect. However, in a broader sense of "causal factor," we can say that esse is the principle by which a thing is, and so could be called a causal factor of the being's actuality. What sort of causality would it then have? We could legitimately say that it is somewhat like a formal cause (except that it is not a form in any sense of the word); thus, St. Thomas says that esse is "as it were, the most formal principle in the thing." Or we could say that it is a fifth sort of causal factor. (Or, if we consider the exemplar cause [see below, sec. 63] the fifth kind, then esse would be the sixth. But this whole discussion is more a matter of the propriety of words; what is important is that esse is a distinct internal principle or component of being.)

What precisely does a cause do? In general, it influences the actual being of something; it makes something to be in act. A cause influences the act of existing of some thing. This influence is what we directly designate when we speak of "causality."

60. The causality of the agent or efficient cause

Only a being-in-act can be an efficient cause. A potency, as such, can only be a material cause; that is, it is a cause inasmuch as by receiving the action of a cause according to its capacity it influences the coming-to-be of an effect. From the viewpoint of action, a potency is a principle by which beings can be acted on. We have seen that various principles of being can be considered as "acts." Can we identify the activity of causing with any of the other acts of a being? A careful comparison of each of these acts to causing will not only help to answer this question but will greatly increase our understanding of causality. First, a being is in act when it possesses substantial form, and so substantial form is an act (correlated with primary matter). Is substantial form the act by which immediately a being is an agent? This act is not sufficient to make a being a cause. It is true that an efficient cause actually must be of a certain kind or species and must be a being in itself, but (a) substantial form is of itself the act of a matter, and its direction is toward the internal constitution of a being, and (b) a patient must likewise be of a certain kind and be in itself, so that it can receive an influence. Second, the act of existing is certainly an act—in a sense, it is the ultimate act even of substances, accidents, and forms. And we can go so far as to say that the esse of a thing is the root of all its agency—esse is the dynamism of a thing. Is esse in a limited thing the same as its causality? No, for the actuality of dynamism which is esse is first and foremost an actuation of a being's *own* essence. Third, the formal accidents (quality and quantity) are also acts in relation to substance, and these accidents, too, are necessary for an agent, but as such they are not activity or operation itself. Tridirectionality, expanse, shape, structure, and so on, are indeed related to the activity of material things, as we have seen; they condition and even determine it. These accidents, however, are formal causes of activity rather than acting itself.

The acting of a thing is to all the other acts of that thing as seeing is to the eye, growing to the plant cell, running to the race-horse, thinking to the intellect, and so on. "Acting" is the full internal actuation of a thing; it is the activity in its full concrete actuality as in the agent itself. As such, it not only pre-supposes but in a sense includes the being's actual existence. Hence, "acting" is an analogous perfection, not only because there are different kinds of actions but more directly and immediately because it is an act in the order of existence.[3]

Acting is the actuation of an existing agent *and its power* inas-much as that actuation is in the agent. What is the relation be-tween this act and causality? As a help in making this analysis we can take an example of an artifact, provided we remember that an artifact is not one natural agent, but a number of natural agents grouped together. Let us take the example of a flashlight. It must be a certain kind of substance; it must be structured in a certain way; it must not be worn out; and so on. But merely from the possession of all these acts it does not yet have the full actuality of a flashlight. It exists, it has a formal structure, but as *flashlight* it is still in potency. When the switch is closed, a new act occurs. The flashlight is now *shining*. Is it necessarily *illuminating* any-thing? Suppose the light ray is beamed into a vacuum. The light continues to shine, but nothing happens to any other being. Now, suppose an opaque object is moved into the path of the beam. Immediately that object is illuminated; it is actually visible, and this visibility is caused by the light.

Now, let us see how a natural agent compares with this example. Let us take a man who wants to be a builder (we will not con-sider now that his freedom will come into play, since, in order to carry out his free choice the man will have to make use of his ex-ternal powers). In order to do this work he needs certain abilities and perfections. He must know what a house looks like and how to go about building one. He must decide what he wants to do and, finally, he must carry out his decision by appropriate external activity. That activity is complex, but in the last stages it is a

---

[3] Note how St. Thomas explains the very notion of act itself through activity; the text is quoted above (see Selected Passages, No. 18).

question of something happening to the bricks, mortar, wood, and so on, of the house that is being built.

In these examples, and others like them, we can mentally distinguish a series of steps in efficient causality (this sequence need not be verified in the form of *really distinct* steps). These distinctions will help us to understand what causality is. First of all, the agent must be in first act. A flashlight without a bulb or with worn-out batteries is still lacking part of its structural perfection, and so there is no activity. Secondly, the agent must not only be complete as a being (first act), it must be in full act as an agent. The flashlight must be actually shining, the builder actually building, and so on. Thirdly, the patient must be actually receiving the action—an opaque object being-illuminated, movable and formable objects being-built, and so on. Thus, there are three steps: a being with its tendencies, its acting, and the reception of its influence. The same three steps can be found in other cases of efficient causality. In the production of a marble statue there are (1) the sculptor with his hammer and chisel; (2) the movements of arm, hammer, and chisel; (3) the being-shaped of the marble. Hence, the causality or influence or action of the agent, considered precisely as such, is in the patient (and not in the agent).

In the patient there is a becoming, motion, or change. Considered as received *in* a subject (from an agent) which changes, the change itself is called a *passion*[4] (that is, an undergoing or being-

---

[4] Let us recall again that potency is by its nature ordered to act. But this by no means implies that every potency is a passive potency, for, as we have seen in sec. 55, there are active potencies. Moreover, it is easily possible to fall into univocation in two ways. One is to imagine that all act is form and that all potency is the capability of being informed by the reception of a specifying form (the basic error of historical essentialistic Aristotelianism). The second is to think that the only cause is the efficient cause and that all passivity is toward an efficient cause (medieval nominalism made this mistake). There is the passivity of matter toward form (and this passivity is reception of a determination); there is the passivity of a passive power toward its corresponding agent (and this passivity is the reception of an influence from an agent); there is the passivity of a tendency toward its goal (and this passivity is not a reception at all—either of a form or of an influence). These remarks are merely a warning against univocation; they cannot be explained at this point. They will be explained partly in the next two chapters and partly in the treatment of the appetites in the philosophy of human nature.

affected; the abstract term is derived from the same root as the term *patient*). Identically the same change, considered as coming to the patient *from* the agent or cause, is the action or causality.

Distinguish efficient causality in the strict sense, as we have been treating it here, from immanent activity. Immanent acting is the kind of acting or operating that we find in living things; living itself, sensing, thinking, and the like. Immanent acting is the perfection of the being which acts, whereas transient activity or causality as such is the perfection of the patient. Immanent acting will be treated in great detail in the philosophy of human nature; it will be considered only incidentally in this course.[5]

Moreover, a cause, in causing, does not *necessarily lose* anything. For example, a teacher does not lose any knowledge when he teaches someone. An engineer, an inventor, a business executive, and a statesman do not lose that which they contribute; although they expend energy, the energy is not the essential part of the causality. It is true that an agent which is a purely material being, in causing a purely material effect, does lose what it gives. But that is because of the *type* of causality involved. If a man gives money, he no longer has it; if he gives intelligent direction, he does not lose any knowledge or intelligence.

From these two considerations, a very important conclusion follows. (*a*) That which is already in full act does not intrinsically change in becoming a cause, for the action and the change are in the patient. (*b*) An agent as agent does not necessarily lose anything in causing. Hence, an agent, as agent, does not undergo change. If an agent, in our experience, does change, it does so because it is material, because it is dependent upon other causes, and so forth.

From the consideration of what is necessary in order that a being actually be a cause, another important conclusion can be drawn. We have seen in Chapters V and VI that power and activity are related to each other as potency and act. Hence, it follows that causality, which is transient action received from an agent in a patient, and passion are identical with each other as

[5] In metaphysics, the distinction between transient and immanent activity is important mainly from the viewpoint of teleology; see below, sec. 70.

well as with action. Hence, the passion, which is the effect in the narrowest sense of that term, is related to the operative power of the agent as act to potency. Now, we also saw that potency and act are proportioned to each other—a potency is specified by its act; an act is precisely the act *of* some potency. Hence, between the agent as agent and the patient as patient there is necessarily a proportion or similarity. Every agent causes something like itself.

A DIFFICULTY

An unreflectively materialistic conception of the origin of our universe offers an opposed view: the cause does not contain the perfection of its effect, and so does not cause something like itself. Many people imagine the story after this fashion. In the beginning, they think, there was a large amount of matter with a huge amount of energy; the matter was either one giant molecule or an undifferentiated mass of elemental particles, depending on the particular theory taken. Simple interactions produced gradually increasing differentiation, with a corresponding loss of energy. After enormous periods of time, the originally undifferentiated cause(s) produced matter in differing structures, though these structures were not precontained in the originating condition. In other words, the laws present-day chemicals obey were themselves produced along with these substances. (This "explanation" contains all sorts of ambiguities; matter and its energy are simply accepted as given; "cause" is probably used in the modern sense of "antecedent"; no distinction is made between partial and total causes; what might be meant by the notion that undifferentiated energy evolves into differentiation with specific laws is rhetorically glossed over. In addition; the explanation is materialistic, and therefore already inadequate, as we have already seen; it denies, usually, all telic causality, which we will consider in the next chapter.)

We can use this difficulty to clarify the theorem that every agent causes something like itself. We will therefore state the supposition in formal, abstract terms, so that its opposition to our theorem is sharp: an effect, as such, is simply unlike the agent as agent, that is, neither univocally the same nor even similar in any way. It would then follow that the agent would not be in act in this particular way at all. But then it further would follow that the active power of the agent would not be proportioned to the act of the patient—which is the same as saying that it is not the power of producing this effect.

From this we can also see that in our universe we have (*a*) agents, with active powers, ordered to, and tending toward, (*b*) patients, with corresponding passive capacities to be acted on and modified. Hence, every such agent capable of transient activity is radically (virtually) related to, or ordered to, any and all other beings which have the capacities to receive such activity.

61. Types of agents: univocal and equivocal causes

The kinds of agents we find in our experience depend upon other agents for both their being and their causality. When we want to express the dependence of an agent upon other agents, we call it a *secondary* cause. In contrast, an agent which does not depend upon other agents is called a first cause.[6] One special aspect of the dependence of a secondary cause upon other causes is that it presupposes a pre-existing patient; in our experience, there must be something for a secondary cause to work on before causality can take place. Consequently, the causal influence of a secondary cause upon the act of existing of another being (patient) does not consist in making something to be where nothing was before (in causing a transition from not-being simply to being) but in bringing about a transition from one kind of thing to another. Hence, we say that a secondary cause does not cause being simply but causes some kind of being. There is a further consequence of this: no thing in our experience is totally dependent upon a single agent. For an effect is dependent upon a cause only in so far as the cause is a cause. For example, a builder is the cause of the coming-to-be of a house, and, conversely, the house is dependent upon the builder for its becoming. But when this coming-to-be has reached its term, and the house is (exists) as a finished thing, it does not depend upon the builder for its

---

[6] As we shall see later, there is only one First Cause, which is God.

being. The builder therefore is not the cause of the being of the house except indirectly as the cause of its becoming.[7]

A second and rather easy distinction to make is based on the kind of similarity between the cause and effect.[8] Some causes and effects are exactly of the same nature. We can see this very clearly in the ordinary generation of living things: parent and offspring are of the same species. Similarly, the heat in the heater and in the thing heated are exactly the same kind of perfection. Any cause which has strictly the same kind of perfection as the effect is called a "univocal" cause. Sometimes, however, the perfection in the cause is not of the same kind as the perfection it brings about. At times, the cause is only a mediate cause. For examples, we can take the remote general causes of particular effects, such as atmospheric pressure, gravitation, sunlight in relation to growth, and so on. Here, the unlikeness between the (remote) cause and its effect is largely due to the proximate causes which are between the remote cause and the ultimate effect. Such causes, which are not univocal because they are not the immediate causes of their effects, we shall call "equivocal causes."[9] Similarly, when the efficient cause of a thing is actually a collection of partial causes, one of these partial causes, considered separately from the others, could well be an equivocal cause. But generally we are more interested in the efficient cause which is adequate in its own order to account for the effect, whether that cause be a collection of distinct things or a numerically single entity. Some causes, on the other hand, are somewhat unlike their effects because they act through knowledge: the bird is not identical in nature with its nest, the man is not of the same nature as the machine or the art work which he produces. A cause, which is somewhat unlike its effect because it causes through knowledge and not simply through nature, we shall call an analogous cause.

[7] As a completed being, the house depends on other causes for its being: the substances out of which it is made, its structure, the earth, and so on.
[8] See Selected Passages, No. 20.
[9] Most authors use the terms, "equivocal," "analogical," and "analogous," as equivalent terms when they speak of causes. St. Thomas uses the various terms indifferently. We have chosen to make a distinction in order to handle the cases more clearly.

The kind of analogy which is in question between an analogous cause and its effect shall be investigated below.

62. Types of agents: principal and instrumental causes

If I write *abc*, the fact that these are letters is due to me and not the pen. The power of the pen is to make ink marks when applied to paper, but the power to make letters is in me and not in the pen. Thus, we can distinguish two powers in the instrumental cause which are really distinct; the *natural* power which the instrument has of itself (a saw has power to cut, a typewriter to type, and so on), and the *instrumental* power which the instrument has from the principal agent.

There are two powers, but not two actions. In the working-together of principal and instrumental causes, for example, the writing of a letter, there is only one action and only one effect which is due to two causal factors. We can make a distinction of reason between the natural action of the instrument and the instrumental action; or, in the effect, we can make a distinction of reason between what is due to the instrument as a natural being and what is due to the instrument as instrument.

We can consider the relation of principal cause to the instrument from the part of each one of them. The instrument limits and particularizes the action of the principal cause; thus I get different effects with a pen, a pencil, a brush. On the other hand, the instrument as such is not active of itself; it is caused to be a cause, it is "moved" by the principal cause to produce an effect.

N.B. Distinguish between an instrument in the strict sense which is moved to cause by the principal cause and the instrumental use or application of a natural cause. Compare the instrumentality of an engraver in using a tool and in using an acid to engrave a name on a piece of metal. A chemist, in producing synthetics, uses some instruments and also makes instrumental applications of the proper natural effects of chemicals.

There can be wide variation in the principal-instrumental relation. Compare the relationship of a man with a pen to the work produced and that of a man to the electrical calculator he uses. Many modern machines are extremely elaborate, and the nature of the effect is largely determined by the natural materials and the artificial structure of the machine: for example, the push-button machine which turns out automobile frames.

There is a similarity between the conception, "instrumental cause," and the conception, "secondary cause."[10] In both there is a dependence upon another cause (or causes). The instrument, to the extent that it is merely an instrument, is a cause only inasmuch as it receives and transmits the causality of the principal cause. The only evident example of such a purely passive instrument is in the area of local motion. For example, when a person uses a stick to push a stone, the causality of the stick is purely received; it moves the stone only to the extent that it itself is caused to move the stone. In the relationship of the principal to the instrumental cause we find this distinguishing trait: that the very causing of the instrument is received, not as a nature, not as a permanent possession (that is, by way of an inherent form), but as an essentially transient influence. The secondary cause, on the contrary, although it does depend on other causes so that without them it cannot cause, has a causality all its own and has a proper and positive influence. A secondary cause may need the co-operation of other causes; it may be moved to action by some other cause. But when it is moved to action, its causality is at least partly its own, an active expression of its own nature—although not exclusively so.

63. The exemplar cause

An intelligent agent engaged in the production of something has a more or less perfect knowledge of the thing he intends to make and directs his activity according to that knowledge. The object as known, according to which he directs activity, is called an "exemplar." (A man may use an external model, as when a painter has a bowl of fruit in front of him which he is copying, but the external model is not directly a cause; it has influence only in so far as it is known.) An exemplar is a true cause because it does have an influence upon the being of the effect—not immediately but through the agent.

[10] See Selected Passages, No. 21.

The type of causality of an exemplar is like that of *form;* that is, it specifies the effect. But instead of being the form of the effect directly and of itself, it is the form of the (intelligent) efficient cause. For this reason, the exemplar cause is sometimes called an "extrinsic formal cause."

64. The theorem of causality[11]

So far we have been considering the causality which we directly experience, that is, where we experience both the coming-to-be of the patient and the activity of the agent. In still other words, we understand that some things as a matter of fact come to be in dependence upon an agent. Or again, we understand that some things pass from potency to act under the influence of an agent which is in act.

Now the question arises: Is this necessarily so? In other words, can something come-to-be, pass from potency to act, without the influence of any agent in act? As far as our everyday knowledge is concerned, we know that every case of coming-to-be has an efficient cause somewhere or other—things don't just happen. So, too, the whole of science proceeds on the implicit understanding that events and things have causes which determine them to be and that with sufficient patience, skill, and instruments, these causes can be discovered. But our question is: Is this implicit knowledge correct?

DIGRESSION ON NECESSITY

In general, that is necessary which cannot not-be. What does it mean to say that something cannot not-be? It is relatively easy to understand this in the logical order, in the connections between concepts and between propositions. Examples of necessary con-

[11] Most authors call this the "principle of causality." Most of them then proceed to say that it is "self-evident" from the very analysis of the concepts or that it is deduced from the principle of sufficient reason, and so forth. These implications are historically attached to the term, "the principle of causality," and so this text avoids using it. What we are talking about is a proposition of a very general and inclusive character, whose truth can be established beyond doubt. Such a proposition is called a "principle," "law," or "theorem." On the nature and treatment of causality in its general formulations, see Joseph Owens, C.Ss.R., "The Causal Proposition," *The Modern Schoolman,* XXXII (1955), 159–171, 257–270, 323–339.

nection are: "If there is 'red,' there is 'color' "; "If Socrates is sitting, he is sitting." In the sense of these examples, that is necessary which must be granted if something else has been granted. Most logicians try to show that such relations are based on identity, and with this they are content. We can concede that anything which is called necessary can be expressed in a proposition or a set of propositions.

But we have noted earlier that the principles of knowledge, though by no means identical with being, are nevertheless based on being. So the question arises, Is there any necessity in being itself? We must be quite careful in handling this question, for logical relations based merely on identity are not real relations. Thus, the inclusion of the genus in the species ("red" includes "color") is not a case of the necessity of being, since the distinction between genus and species is a result of the mind's activity.

We can begin to consider this question by still understanding necessity as a connection between terms. Are there connections between things, such that if one thing is, another also is and cannot not-be? We know that there are causes which are not free but act by nature, and often they are adequate to produce their effect. If there is a natural adequate cause and a sufficiently disposed patient, then the effect necessarily follows, that is, the cause makes the effect to be, and its producing of the effect is the necessity itself. When the effect is being caused to be, it is not able not to be. We can truly call such a necessity a necessity of and in being.

What about the corresponding relation of the effect to the cause? We say that if something is being produced, there *must be* an adequate cause to produce it. But this is not properly a necessity in being; it is more accurately a necessity between two propositions: that is, if we grant that something is being produced, we must grant that a cause is producing it.

However, the notion of necessity is broader than that of a necessary connection between two terms. We began our consideration by saying that that is necessary which cannot not-be. We can therefore also legitimately consider necessity as the absence of potency. For example, a material thing has within its nature a real potency to become something else, and thus to cease to be itself; this potency is primary matter. But an angel is a pure form without an intrinsic potency to become something else. Therefore an angel is essentially speaking a necessary being. There is, indeed, a potency in an angel in the order of existence, namely, its essence. Now, essence is a potency to be, but it is not, properly speaking, a potency to nonbeing. Hence, we can even say that an angel is hypothetically necessary even in the order of existence. Why hypothetically? Because we must suppose that an angel is caused, and so on the hypothesis that its cause is operating, then the angel exists necessarily. As far as it is concerned, it cannot not-be; though it depends on its cause (see the next part of this section), it is possible that an existing angel not-exist only if that cause is a free cause. Only a being that is entirely without potency can be called a necessary being without qualification—a being that is entirely act ("pure act") cannot not-be simply.

From this broader and at the same time more profound metaphysical consideration, we can see the basis even for logical necessities. For all logical necessities are based on the principle of contradiction, and that principle is ultimately based on the correlative opposition between act and potency. Only in the difference between act and potency is it finally clear that whatever is, to the extent and in the sense that it *is*, cannot not-be—for esse is the correlative opposite of all potencies and all other perfections, as we have seen.

For convenience's sake, we will list some of the types of necessity, trying to point out the bases on which the various divisions are made. Necessities are:

(1) based on the source of the necessity, intrinsic (for example, acid necessarily reacts with certain metals) or extrinsic (a pencil moves necessarily as long as I, an efficient cause, am moving it).

(2) based on the scope of the necessity, absolute (under all conditions, a triangle must have three sides) or relative (exercise is necessary for a growing boy, but he can live without it).

(3) based on temporal or causal priority or posteriority in relation to the thing which is necessary, antecedent, or de jure (the actions of nonfree agents are antecedently necessary because they flow from the nature which is causally prior to action) or con-

sequent, or de facto (once Socrates is sitting, he sits necessarily [in virtue of the principle of contradiction]).

(4) based on the object of the necessity, logical (if the premises are true and correct, the conclusion must follow) or real (this event must come about if its necessary causes are actual).

(5) based on the objects of real necessity, essential (the essence of man necessarily makes him rational) or existential (God, Whose essence is identical with His act of existing, exists necessarily) or operational (any nonfree agent, like a dog or a chemical, necessarily performs its operations).

(6) based on the kind of causality, formal, telic (the necessity [or utility] of means in relation to goals), and efficient (sometimes called the necessity of coaction or violence).

The opposite of necessity is *contingence*, the possibility of undergoing change, of being and not-being, and so forth. Note that necessity and contingence are not so opposed that a thing is either completely necessary or completely contingent. No thing is so completely contingent that there are no necessities about it—the most contingent of beings and events has at least consequent necessity (now that it is, it cannot not-have-been) and some essential necessities (being what it is, while it is, it cannot not-be). On the other hand, though necessity as necessity is not contingent, there are some particular contingent necessities. For example, the necessity by which a nonfree agent acts is contingent upon its continued existence, the co-operation of other causes, and the like; something which is necessary with consequent necessity is contingent with regard to its antecedents. The essential (formal) necessities (e.g., if a man is to be, he *must* be rational, he *must* possess an intellect and will) of limited beings are existentially contingent (e.g., if man did not exist, there would be no one who must be rational, and man does not necessarily exist).[12] The concrete copresence of both necessity and contingence in the

---

[12] But one may say, "It is eternally true that man must be rational." Of course, but what does the verb "to be" mean in the dependent clause? Pure essences (which are not of real things) are negatively eternal and necessary: that is, if they are thought of, they can only be thought of in a certain way. Essences either are in things or are objects of thought, and this is the only being they have. See below, sec. 76, on the possibles.

same being is a point of great importance for this reason among others, that it shows how we can arrive at a knowledge of something which is necessary from beings which are contingent.

BECOMING, CONTINGENCE, AND LIMITATION IN RELATION TO CAUSALTY

Now, our question is: "Can something come-to-be without any agent?" Note that something which comes-to-be does not have before its becoming the perfection which it later acquires but is only in potency to it. Potency is ordered to act, but it is also and by its very nature distinct from act. It is not-act. To suppose that a being in potency can of itself acquire the act corresponding to that potency[13] is implicity to deny any significant difference between potency and act; it is to suppose that potency is a kind of *hidden* act. But this is not true and not even really intelligible; it is an implicit contradiction. If potency is not the same as act, then any transition from potency to act takes place under the influence of an agent in act. From these considerations we derive our first general statement about causality: Anything which comes-to-be—which passes *from* potency to act—does so under the influence of an agent. This statement of causal dependence is first discovered in immediate experience and is known to be true without exception by an analysis of the beings themselves and their intrinsic constitution. Such a proposition, which depends on no outside evidence except on the intrinsic intelligibility of the being about which it is said, can be called "self-evident," or "per se known."[14]

[13] Living things are said to "move themselves" (that is, from potency to act). This is by no means contrary to the causal dependence of things which change; for the living thing is not entirely in potency—it has its substantial act and its operative powers; moreover, many distinct causes (moisture, food, sunlight, and so forth) are necessary so that the living thing can continue to live and grow. See also, Selected Passages, No. 20, par. 1.

[14] Please note how the term, "self-evident," has been defined. Students sometimes think that "self-evident" means "evident to itself"; sometimes they think that a self-evident proposition is one that is explicitly known and admitted by all men—babies, barbarians, people who have never thought about it, and so on.

Philosophers have historically used the term "self-evident" in other senses; often, they have said that a self-evident proposition is known to be certain

Every thing which comes to be is existentially contingent; that is, of its nature or essence it is such that it can exist or not-exist. But contingent existence is more inclusive than the conception, "a thing which comes to be"; hence, at least as far as our knowledge of a thing is concerned, there may be some things whose temporal origin we know, but others about which we know first that they are contingent, and as yet know nothing about their origin. Hence, we can extend our question about causality to include those things about whose temporal origin we are ignorant. Let us suppose a being about which all we know is (*a*) that it does exist (for example, a pure spirit, or angel), and (*b*) that it is a limited being. A limited being is a limited actuality. We have seen that an act is not limited of itself as act but can only be limited by a potency distinct from it by which it is limited. Hence, that which is limited as a being is composed of two really distinct principles in the order of being itself, namely, essence and the act of existing.

We can make some definite statements about the relation between essence and the act of existing in a being in which these principles are really distinct. First of all, since the act of existing is not a quiddity or form, it can never be a *part* of an essence. Secondly, esse cannot be the property of any essence. A property is an accident which inheres in a substance, is necessarily connected with that substance, and is a natural and necessary consequence thereof, as risibility is a natural and necessary consequence of the essence of man. Now, that which is a consequence of an essence is caused by that essence and is posterior to it in nature. For to be a cause, a thing must first exist in itself. An essence which is really distinct from its act of existing exists only by the possession of that act of existing. And the act of existing, inasmuch as it is an act, is prior in nature to its correlative potency. To suppose that esse is the property of an essence really distinct from it therefore involves a contradiction. Such an essence would be both prior and posterior to its own esse and would have to exist before it existed—it would have to exist in order to

_____

from an analysis of the concepts (and even of the terms!). There are some propositions which are known from an analysis of their concepts; the causal proposition is not one of them.

be a cause of esse; and this would be before it existed, since it is by its act of existing that a thing is. Therefore, in a limited being, esse cannot be a property of the essence. Esse is contingently had; it is never possessed by such an essence de jure.

Two statements can therefore be made about the esse of a limited thing. First, esse is not the essence or a part of the essence of a limited thing. Second, esse is not a property of the essence of a limited thing.[15] But esse is related to such an essence; this relation is one of non-necessary, or contingent, possession. Esse is possessed as an act and, therefore, as prior to its receptive subject. Yet it is prior in such a way as not to be a thing in itself, nor to have the essence as its property or possession. The essence, although it is posterior to the esse, is necessarily the subject of that act. Hence, the esse, even as prior and as act, cannot be independent. It depends on something other than itself. The "something other" cannot be the essence of the limited thing itself, as we have just seen. Hence, in order that a *limited being* can be, it must depend on a cause. Hence, every limited being is existentially contingent, and every existentially contingent being depends on a cause.

This statement of causal dependence is a very inclusive statement. It includes and goes beyond the first statement of causal dependence, and it is proved true by a reasoning process based on act and potency and the analysis of an essence really distinct from its act of existing. Hence, this proposition may appropriately be called a "theorem."

65. The analogy of causality

In considering the types of efficient causality, we noted that there are both univocal and nonunivocal causes. Univocal causes belong to the same species as their affects, whereas nonunivocal causes do not. Nonunivocal causes are in some way unlike their effects.

But we have also seen that an adequate cause of a thing must be

---

[15] Compare the statement of Bertrand Russell: "There does not even seem any logical necessity why there should be even one individual—why, in fact, there should be any world at all" (*Introduction to Mathematical Philosophy* [London, 1924], p. 203).

in some way like its effect. Since such a cause does not possess the caused perfection univocally, it must posses either a different but equivalent perfection[16] or a perfection which somehow includes the caused perfection though it is greater. In the former case, the analogy will be said to be "extrinsic"; in the latter, "intrinsic." For example, the food which conserves the health of an animal is truly called "healthy." But health, properly speaking, is a quality of a living thing; it can be the intrinsic modification only of a living thing. Therefore, the food—for example, a broiled steak—is not intrinsically healthy; yet it does have a relation to the health of a living man. For an example of intrinsic analogy, consider a bird building a nest. The bird does not have as its own intrinsic perfection the shape and structure which it gives to its effect, and so it must have some other perfection. We know that birds are beings capable of knowledge, and so we can see that the perfection, "having sensitive knowledge of a nest," is intrinsic to the bird. A man, inventing a marvelously complicated machine, and not being such a machine by nature, must possess a similar perfection through which he can bring about the perfection in the patient upon which he acts. This perfection is intellectual knowledge, which includes in some way the perfection of what is known. Hence, we can truly and intrinsically speak of a "powerful idea," a "mighty conception," and so on. Conversely, we can call the effect by the perfection of the cause, and this is usually an extrinsic analogy; for example, we speak of a "clever gadget."

The nonunivocal cause is either greater than or equivalent in perfection to the effect. Sometimes the relation is a definitely known proportion, and so we can correctly speak of an analogy of proportion between the nonunivocal cause and its effect. At

[16] Electrical energy is equivalent to local motion, and an electric motor is precisely a machine for converting one kind of energy into another. Again, photosynthesis in plants turns solar energy into the locked-up energy of chemical combination. For another example—good meat contains such a mixture of chemical compounds that the animal which feeds on it can maintain itself in good health. For still another example: the two parents of a plant hybrid together contain the equivalent of the perfection of the hybrid offspring; polyploidy in plants can be brought about by the normal processes of cell division interfered with by high energy rays; the rays together with the normal processes of the parent cell are equivalent to the peculiar structure of the new cell.

other times, we may find a nonunivocal cause whose nature we do not definitely know, at least so as to be able to state a definite proportion between it and its effect.[17] This causal analogy we will call "the analogy of eminence."

We have seen earlier[18] that there are two kinds of nonunivocal causes: analogous and equivocal. If we now recall that the analogy of causality can be either intrinsic or extrinsic, we can see a correspondence between the kinds of causes and the kinds of causality. An analogous cause acts through knowledge and so need not have a nature univocally the same as its effect; nevertheless the knowledge is intrinsic to the cause and shows a nature more perfect than the nature of the effect. An equivocal cause acts by nature; it is a remote or a partial cause, and so its effect need not be of the same nature, since the nature of the effect may be determined by a proximate cause or by one of the other partial causes (or by the concurrence of the causes, as in chance effects[19]). The equivocal cause truly causes and so can truly be denominated from the effect, but the denominated nature is extrinsic to the cause.

We can distinguish intrinsic analogies of causality from the extrinsic by seeing whether the perfection of the cause is different and equivalent or similar and inclusive and therefore greater and intrinsic. Note that this distinction rests on some kind of knowledge of the cause in itself and its intrinsic perfections. If we merely know that X is the cause of some perfection and is a nonunivocal cause, we are unable to tell whether it is an equivocal or an analogous cause, nor do we know that there is a definite proportion; consequently, we do not know whether the analogy is intrinsic or extrinsic, and the perfection must be predicated as indefinitely greater. This is the analogy of eminence, used indeterminately—a very useful analogy at the beginning of an investigation.

66. Definitions

Active condition is that which removes a hindrance that prevents another agent from acting. (For example, an agent who

---

[17] See Selected Passages, No. 22.
[18] See above, sec. 61.
[19] On chance, see below, sec. 71.

opens a shutter is a condition of the sun's illumination of the room.)

Passive condition, or disposition, is a state or modification of a patient influencing an activity after the manner of a material cause. (For example, the general run-down condition of a sick person can influence the way in which the action of a medicine is received.)

Occasion is that which provides an opportunity for an agent's action without acting itself. (For example, an anniversary celebration may be the occasion of a man's getting drunk.)

Cause is that which influences the act of existing of some thing.

Agent (or efficient cause) is that which by its activity influences the being of another. (For example, a sculptor)

Patient is that which is affected or being changed by another. (For example, marble)

Effect is that which is brought about by a cause. (For example, the statue)

Acting is the full intrinsic actuality of an operative power. (It is therefore a concrete, existential, and analogous act.)

Action (in the strict sense) is the change produced in a patient, considered as received from the agent. (For example, the taking-shape of the statue as brought about by the sculptor.)

Transient action is a more explicit term for action in the strict sense.

Passion is the change received from an agent, considered as taking place in the patient. (For example, the taking-shape of a statue under the influence of a sculptor, considered as a modification of the statue.)

Causality is the influence of the cause upon the effect.

Formal cause is the intrinsic principle of being which influences the being of the effect by communication of itself to the effect as the determining or specifying act. (For example, the soul of a living thing.)

Material cause is the intrinsic principle of being which influences the being of the effect by communication of itself to the effect as the subject and determinable, limiting factor. (For example, the body of a living thing.)

Efficient cause (or agent) is the extrinsic principle of being which influences the being of the effect by its activity. (This is a more formal definition.)

A secondary cause is one which depends upon one or more causes for its being and its activity.

First cause is one which does not depend on other causes for its being or its activity.

Principal cause is a cause which acts by its own power and is a source of causality. (N.B. This does not exclude the possibility that a principal cause may be previously caused by another.)

Instrumental cause or instrument is a cause which acts by the power of the principal cause and only to the extent that it is moved by the principal cause.

An exemplar is an object known by an intelligent cause, according to which that intelligent cause directs his activity.

Necessity is that condition or qualification of a being by which it is (or is what it is) and cannot not-be.

Existential necessity is the necessity by which a being which is cannot not-be.

Essential necessity is the necessity by which a being is *what* it is.

Absolute essential necessity is the necessity by which it is simply impossible that a being be otherwise than it is, and is based on the real identity of an essence with itself.

Relative essential necessity (physical or natural necessity) is the necessity by which distinct properties or activities are linked to the essence from which they flow and is based an formal causality.

Contingence is the condition or qualification of a being by which it can be otherwise than it is.

Univocal cause is one which belongs to the same species as its effect. (For example, a heater and the thing heated)

Analogous cause (in the strict sense) is one which does not belong to the same species as its effect but intrinsically possesses a perfection which includes and goes beyond the perfection of its effect. (For example, a man, possessing intellectual knowledge [the greater and more inclusive perfection] causes a structure in a collection of material things [a perfection of a different kind]). (In the wide sense, analogous cause and equivocal cause are used interchangeably.)

Equivocal cause (in the strict sense) is one which does not belong to the same species as its effect but possesses a different and equivalent perfection. (Healthy food, as cause of the health of an animal)

Analogy of eminence in causality is an analogy based on causal dependence of an effect on its nonunivocal cause, involving a true attribution of the perfection of the effect to the cause, in an indeterminately higher, greater, or "eminent" sense. The analogy is intrinsic if the cause is strictly analogous; extrinsic, if the cause is equivocal. (Conversely, the perfection of the cause can be truly attributed to the effect in an imperfect or lesser sense, and this perfection, too, can be either intrinsic or extrinsic.)

67. Proofs (to be developed)

A. Whatever comes to be has a cause.

B. Whatever exists contingently has a cause.

C. No effect can be greater than its total cause.

68. Readings

St. Thomas Aquinas, *Contra Gentiles,* Bk. II, chap. 21 (proportion between cause and effect); Bk. III, chap. 21 (tendency), chap. 69 (that creatures are truly causes of esse); *Summa Theologiae,* Pt. III, q. 19, art. 1, par. 2 (distinction between instrument and instrumental use of a natural cause), q. 62, art. 1, last par. (distinction between principal and instrumental causes); Pt. I, q. 46, art. 1 ad 6 (on the conditions under which a particular cause acts), q. 48, art. 1 ad 4 (on types of causing), q. 54, arts. 1–3 (a very important series of texts on being, substance, esse, acting, and power), q. 104, art. 1 (a difficult but very important text on the difference between the cause of coming-to-be and the cause of being); Pt. I–II, q. 72, art. 3 (the difference of causality of the four kinds of causes); *Commentary on the Metaphysics of Aristotle,* Bk. V, lesson 2, Nos. 736–776, pp. 305–308) (on the kinds of causes).

Aristotle, *Metaphysics,* Bk. IV, chaps. 1–2, 1013a–1014a24 (on principles and causes).

Etienne Gilson, *The Christian Philosophy of St. Thomas Aquinas* (New York, Random House, 1956), pp. 174–186; on causality.

Francis L. Harmon, *Principles of Psychology,* rev. ed. (Milwaukee, Bruce, 1951), pp. 202–204; a brief summary of the work of Michotte on the perception of causality.

Robert O. Johann, S.J., "A Comment on Secondary Causality," *The Modern Schoolman,* XXV (1947), 19–25.

Arthur A. Vogel, "Efficient Causation and the Categories," *The Modern Schoolman*, vol. XXXII (1955), 243–256; that causation is a reality that does not fit into the categories.

John Wild, "A Realistic Defense of Causal Efficacy," *Review of Metaphysics*, II (1949), 1–14.

SELECTED PASSAGES FROM ST. THOMAS AQUINAS

20. Kinds of Agents and Patients

Those artifacts which have such a nature [that is, one to be produced by art], as stones are the matter of a house, cannot be changed by themselves, for it is impossible that they be changed except by another. And this principle is true, not only in artifacts, but in natural things. For in this way the matter of fire cannot be changed to fire except by another. And hence it is that the form of fire is not generated except by another. . . .

Hence, it must be said that only living things are found to move themselves locally, but other things are moved by an exterior principle, either that which generates them, or that which removes a preventing condition, as is said in the eighth book of the *Physics;* so, too, only living things are found to change themselves according to the other kinds of change. This is because they are found to have different parts, one of which can be the agent, and the other the patient, and this is the situation which obtains in everything which moves itself, as is proved in the eighth book of the *Physics.* . . .

It is about such matter having in itself an active principle that the Philosopher is speaking here, and not about inanimate things. This is clear from the fact that he compares the matter of fire to the matter of a house in this regard, that both are moved to the form by an extrinsic agent. Yet it does not follow that the generation of inanimate things is not natural. For it is not necessary for natural change, that the principle of motion in that which is moved be an active and formal principle; sometimes it is passive and material. . . .

He had said above that everything which is generated is generated by something like it in species. But this is not the same in all cases, and so he intends here to show how this is found in different cases. . . . Everything which is generated from something, is generated from it per se, or per accidens. But what is generated from another per accidens, is not generated from it according as it is such as it is, and so it is not necessary that in the generator there is the likeness of that which is generated. Thus, the finding of a treasure has no likeness in him who, digging in order to plant, finds the treasure accidentally. But the per se generator, generates such as it itself is, as a generator. And so it is necessary that in a per se generator the likeness of the generated must be in some way.

But this comes about in three ways. In one way, the form of the generated pre-exists in the generator according to the same way of being, and in similar matter, as fire generates fire, or man generates a man. This is wholly univocal generation.

In another way, the form of the generated pre-exists in the generator, not according to the same way of being, nor in a substance of the same kind. Thus, the form of the house pre-exists in the builder, not according to its material mode of being, but according to an immaterial mode of being, which it has in the mind of the builder, but not in the stones and wood. This generation is partly univocal, as far as the form is concerned, partly equivocal, as far as the mode of being of the form in the subject is concerned.

In the third way, the whole form of the generated does not pre-exist in the generator, but some "part" of it, or some part of a part, as in hot medicine there pre-exists the warmth which is a part of health, or is something leading to a part of health. And this generation is in no way univocal.

> *Commentary on Aristotle's* Metaphysics, Bk. VII, lect. 8 (ed. Cathala, Nos. 1440, 1442e, 1442z, 1444–1446).

21. Difference between Principal and Instrumental Causes

For a principal agent acts according to the requirements of its own form, and so the active power in it is some form or quality having complete reality according to its own nature. But an instrument acts inasmuch as it is moved by another. Hence, it has a power proportioned to this motion. But motion is not a complete being, but it is a way to being, as it were something between pure potency and pure act, as is said in the third book of the *Physics*. And so the power of an instrument inasmuch as it is an instrument, according as it acts to produce an effect beyond that which is proportioned to it according to its nature, is not a complete reality having a fixed being in its nature, but an incomplete reality (like the power of affecting sight which is in the air inasmuch as it is an instrument moved by an exterior visible thing).

> *Commentary on the Fourth Book of the* Sentences, dis. 1, q. 1, art. 4, qa. 1.

22. Analogy of Composition Compared to the Analogy of Eminence in Causality

The creator and the creature are reduced to one, with a community, not of univocation, but of analogy. This latter community can be of two kinds. It can consist in this, that several things share in one thing according to priority and posteriority, as potency and act share in being, and, similarly, substance and accident. Or this community can consist in this, that one receives its esse and its essence from the other, and this is the analogy of the creature to the creator. For the creature does not have an act of existing except inasmuch as it has come from the First Being; consequently, it is not called being except inasmuch as it imitates the First Being.

Commentary on the First Book of the Sentences, prologue, q. 1, art. 2, ad 2.

VIII

The Extrinsic Principles
of Being: II. The Goal of Action

69. The goal of action

So far, in our analysis of change and being, we have considered the material, formal, and efficient causes of becoming and being. Are these three causal factors sufficient? Or, at least in some cases, is it still possible and meaningful to ask, "Why?" For example, when we know who did this, what he did, and to whom he did it, are we satisfied that we fully understand the action? When we ask "Why?" do we not want to find out the *reason* or cause, which is, in the context, the purpose or motive of the action? In other words, when we have found material, formal, and efficient causes, we still have not discovered the full intelligibility of action and causality.

An inspection of various kinds of beings shows us that they have various kinds of activity; they are either conscious beings or beings without knowledge. We will consider each kind in turn.

A. ACTIONS WHOSE RESULTS ARE FORESEEN AND DESIRED

In the case of our own activities, we find that we often know, or at least think we know, the results of our transient actions. What is more important, we find ourselves wanting, desiring, choosing these results either for themselves or as a means to something else, and so we go on to perform those actions. For example, a man may want the money he can earn by his work, or he may want the product itself. In the former case, we speak of "the goal of the agent"; in the latter, of "the goal of the activity (or work)"—though the latter is also desired as a goal by the agent. In both cases, the goal is foreseen and desired by the agent.

We also often foresee and want our own vital activities for their own sake. For example, a student may want to know something, and the knowledge itself is the goal which he foresees and desires. Again, a man may travel in order to *see* and *experience* for himself the scenes or the customs of different countries. In these cases, the action itself is a goal which is foreseen and desired.

A goal which is foreseen and desired is called a "purpose." A purpose is a real cause of action, for it influences the coming-to-be of something, either a product or an immanent activity. A purpose is by no means an efficient cause. People sometimes think that an efficient cause pushes an object, and a purpose "attracts" or "pulls" it. Pulling is as much an efficiency as pushing, but we have to use some words to express the causality of a purpose, and these words are applied to purpose by an analogy with efficient causes. So, when we say that "A purpose moves an agent, or directs or influences him," we are understanding this of an influence which is not an efficiency. A purpose, then, causes by directing an agent to make actual that which is preconceived and desired. This direction to a goal we can call "goal orientation"; the goal as causing we can call "telic cause." An intellectually knowing agent is oriented by the knowledge it has of a goal to be made or gained.[1]

In the activities of brute animals, there is also indirect evidence of some foreknowledge and desire of goals. Certainly, we do not have the same evidence that we find in ourselves. But there is some; a hungry dog, for example, goes hunting for food. The dog does not know that it has a *purpose* as such; it only knows that it is hungry, that food will satisfy that hunger, and that food can

---

[1] A goal that is to be made is, for example, a picture to be painted, a house to be built. A goal that is to be gained is, for example, a house or a field or an automobile to be acquired. In the second case, the goal already exists, but not *as possessed by* the agent, and it is as a goal *to be possessed* that it moves the agent to act.

We use the words "goal" and "purpose" to translate the Latin *finis*, instead of the more common but misleading word "end." We use "telic cause" to translate *causa finalis*, rather than "final cause"; "teleology," rather than "finality"; "goal orientation" or "goal-directedness" rather than "finalization"; and "to orient," rather than "to finalize."

be found by looking for it. When we want to know why a particular dog is hunting, we are satisfied when we know that it is *looking for food*. (In saying this, we are intellectualizing the brute's activity; the brute doesn't think of a goal; it imagines and desires food, and we understand that this foreknowledge of food is as a matter of fact a knowledge of a goal.) The brute's activity of hunting is oriented by its knowledge of the sensible object. This sensible object is not known precisely *as a goal*, but it is known concretely and in the particular as something to be gained or avoided. Hence, we can speak also of the purposive activity of animals. A sensitively knowing agent is oriented by the knowledge it has of a sensible object (which is a goal) to be gained or avoided.

What exactly is the function of a purpose, that is, a consciously held goal? We want to know this, because from an analysis of our own purposive activity we can understand what is meant by the terms "goal," "telic cause." A purpose is obviously not one of the intrinsic causes or principles of our being, like matter and form or essence and the act of existing. First and foremost, a purpose is concerned with activity. How does purpose function in connection with activity? It is clearly not another efficient cause, for a known goal, as such, is not a real being and so has no activity in the strict sense of that word. We can see still more clearly the function of a purpose if we compare it with an exemplar. An exemplar causes by way of specifying some type of activity, but only conditionally; that is, if there is to be activity, it will be of such-and-such kind, as specified by the exemplar. But a purpose, as such, "moves" the agent to act; it is a determinant of *action* simply, and only secondarily of action of this or that *kind*. It functions as the correlative object of tendency (that is, of desiring, wanting and so forth). From this analysis, the conclusion emerges: a goal is that principle which influences the coming-to-be of an effect inasmuch as by being the object of tendency it influences the agent.

B. NATURAL ACTIVITY

There is not much difficulty in establishing the goal orientation of activity which flows from knowledge. But are other activities so oriented? There are many activities which do not flow from knowledge: the activities of nonliving things and of plants, and those actions in men and animals which are below the conscious level (such as digestion, growth, regeneration of tissue, reflex actions, sleep).[2] All such activities are called "natural activities." Clearly we cannot say that such actions are purposive in the sense that they proceed from the agent's own conscious knowledge. But can we in any sense speak of the goal orientation of these natural activities?

To help us see that this is a good question we can reflect that in some fields of natural activity we distinguish between a normal or natural result and a defective result. This is particularly the case in the generation of living things: plants, animals, and men are sometimes born defective in one way or another. The natural processes of generation tend to normal results; if we did not at least vaguely apprehend this tendency, we would never talk of monsters or of healthy, full-formed births. A somewhat similar indication can be found in some extremely complicated processes of nonliving things, for example, in the formation of crystals. Sometimes there are "defective" crystals which occur when the natural processes do not altogether succeed in reaching their goal.

This vague indication of goal-directedness needs to be carefully explored and analyzed. Suppose we begin with the activities of living things without knowledge (and with similar activities performed by agents which possess knowledge, but not as guides of these activities). For example, a tree's roots push through the ground to find water. A tree growing in wet ground will have a relatively shallow root system, whereas the same variety of tree growing in a dry spot will send its roots much deeper. The sprouting seed pushes through even hard ground to get to sunlight. The tendrils of a vine wind around supports to hold the vine upright. Certain plants turn their flowers or leaves with the apparent mo-

[2] Note that orientation is properly a characteristic of *action*. In the classic example of the archer and the arrow, the arrow in flight has a direction temporarily imposed on it—by the archer. Strictly, the arrow has no intrinsic orientation for the target, nor even for any local motion. Modern thinkers point out that local motion has no goal of itself—and that is true, for they are considering the thing which moves locally (that is, the thing which *is moved*). But orientation is to be looked for in the *agent*, not in the patient. This caution must be kept in mind throughout. Cf. *Summa Theologiae*, Pt. I, q. 103, art. 1 ad 3.

tion of the sun to get more sunlight. What do these various activities show us? First of all, we see that a distinct result *is reached:* some new being or some new effect is attained. Secondly, we see in living things a tendency, an impulse, a dynamism *toward these* results. Even before the results are reached, there is an orientation of the activity toward them. Vital activity is in fact goal-directed.

The analysis of the activity of nonliving things is more difficult than that of living things, and so our investigation will have to proceed more slowly. In the first place, nonvital activities do reach results. This fact is so obvious as not to need further explanation. Secondly, the results of nonvital activities are consistent results. Of course, there is not an absolute invariability of action and result. But there is a definite *constancy*, within limits, so much so that physicists and chemists can construct mathematical formulas for these activities, and so much so that in the past two generations entire industries have been built on the exact, universal knowledge acquired by scientists. Now, what does the constancy of nonvital activities show us? It shows us that nonliving things are, in a real sense, sources of activity. They are not independent sources, it is true; other surrounding things are necessary and frequently energy must be supplied. Nonliving things, therefore, are real, secondary causes. Furthermore, these nonliving things are intrinsically determined to their activities. If this were not so, they would be determined entirely by circumstances, and constancy would vanish. Therefore, nonliving things have some intrinsic principle of determination to their proper activities. Proximately, this principle is the power by which they act; ultimately, the determination is from the substantial form, by which each one of these things has its own given nature.

The result of this investigation can be summarized briefly: nonliving things, as agents, are intrinsically determined to some definite activities that have constant results. Now, we must ask a further question: "Are nonliving things determined to act, as well as to the kind of action? Or are they, on the contrary, pure instruments which cause only as long as they are being made-to-cause by another cause?" It must be admitted at once that there is much passivity in nonliving things. It was suggested above that local motion is a passion of the thing which moves rather than an action. It should also be admitted that in some cases we do not know very much about the activity of nonliving things. But there seem to be some clear cases of real activity. When energy is released through chemical action—for example, when phosphorus combines with oxygen—the material things themselves seem to be active, not merely to be moved like instruments. At some time in the past, energy was put in; but this merely means that such agents are caused causes, or, in other words, secondary causes. Again, there are activities like those of radium, which are quite clearly cases of activity that is not merely instrumental. By carrying this induction further, enough examples could be found to enable us to conclude that nonliving things are truly agents and of themselves tend to act, even if their agency or efficiency is a very limited one.[3]

If there were no agents, there would be no need for goals of action. For example, from the "point of view" of the lumber, the coming-to-be of a table is in no sense a goal. This is because the lumber is wholly passive in regard to the becoming of the table. But an agent is precisely in some sense or other *active*, and that means having a tendency and an impetus toward something. Since there cannot be an impetus which is not an impetus toward something, every action has a goal. Similarly, material things as such are purely passive in regard to their own local motion. As such, they are indifferent or "free" to move in any direction, and so there is no goal-orientation in local motion if we consider only that which moves. But from the point of view of that which moves it, that is, the agent (whether the agent moves by contact or gravitation), local motion does have a direction and, consequently, is oriented.

[3] Another way of discovering the goal-directedness of nonvital activity is by examining the activity itself. Many complex natural activities take time and occur in a series of distinguishable steps, which have an intrinsic relation to the results which they bring about. Modern chemistry finds it quite practical to determine, from a consideration of the product that is wanted (for example, a plastic of a certain hardness or resilience), the required materials and the various stages and order of production. The order of natural process is more strikingly evident when the activity of one agent is interfered with by that of another, although it can perhaps be found even in simpler activities.

We can now summarize the results of our investigation of the activity of nonliving things. Nonliving things, to the extent that they are agents, are intrinsically determined to some definite activities which have constant results and also intrinsically tend to perform these activities.

C. THE CAUSAL ANALYSIS OF ACTIVITY

In studying activity, we must try to see it as a whole and try to account for all its aspects. It is possible, and legitimate for certain purposes, to consider activity abstractly. But, in the philosophy of being, an abstract consideration is seen to be only a partial one. Just as being is considered concretely and as a whole, so, too, activity must be considered concretely and as a whole.

In Chapter V, we studied the intrinsic principles by which being is constituted and by which change is possible. The intrinsic principles of being are concerned with the being itself. As causal factors, they bring about the being in which they are. They determine, specify, or structure a being in relation to itself. For example, the form is that by which a being is what *it* is substantially, and the form brings with it certain properties (namely, accidents) which perfect that being *itself*. So, too, the act of existing is that by which a being *itself* exists. By understanding these principles, we can understand how change is possible. But, so far, we cannot say *that* change is actually taking place; nor can we exactly decide *what* the effect will be.

Hence, in Chapter VII, we discovered that change demands an extrinsic principle, the agent, by which the passive potencies of beings are actualized. Given that there is an agent with its tendencies (active powers), we can understand (1) that change actually occurs,[4] and (2) what the effect will concretely be;[5] and so we can have a full understanding of the coming-to-be of contingent things. "Given that there is an agent," we can understand activity. But why should any being be an agent? Why should any being be endowed with active and operative powers that are tendencies toward new actuality?

Here, the analysis of human purposive activity shows us a

[4] See above, Chap. VI, sec. 55.
[5] See above, Chap. VII, sec. 60.

fourth causal factor, the goal, on account of which an agent acts. We need to investigate this factor further, both in transient and in immanent activity.

In transient activity, the direction of efficient causality is toward the patient which, as such, is distinct from the agent. Transient activity is an impulse toward a new being which does not yet exist but is to come into being through that activity.[6] The fact that causality is directed toward the esse of another, namely, of the effect, requires a causal factor over and above the principles by which a being is constituted. And since the production of a distinct effect is found in all transient activity, we can truly say that every agent, as principle of transient activity, acts for a goal.

Living things have immanent activities, and immanent activity is, as such, the perfection of the agent which acts immanently. Plants bring themselves to their perfection by the immanent activities of growth and nourishment and the immanent aspect of generative activity. Animals and men perfect themselves by exercising their powers of knowledge and appetition. These activities are either desired for what they bring to the agent (and so are oriented to a further goal), or they are sought and valued for themselves, in other words, are themselves goals (for example, games, which are "for" nothing else, the contemplation of truth, the exercise of sympathy, love, and so forth).

Sometimes, it is true, we speak of "aimless activities"; what we mean is that where we expect a conscious purpose there is none. For example, semiautomatic actions, like scratching one's head or drumming one's fingers, are said to be aimless because they are activities which ordinarily flow from a conscious purpose. But here the purpose is not conscious, or perhaps the goal is not a humanly desirable one—but there is a goal nonetheless. In the explanation of immanent activity, therefore, the intrinsic principles explain what a thing is, and how it is possible for it to acquire further perfections. The thing in its substantial perfection itself is the agent which brings about the accidental perfection of immanent activity; but that the agent should act at

---

[6] Hence, the nature of a being which has only transient activity is profoundly different from one which has properly immanent action; see sec. 70.

all is precisely the function of the goal (telic cause).[7] Consequently, for both immanent and transient activity, the goal is the reason (cause) why the agent acts. In a word, every agent, no matter what its type of activity, acts for a goal.[8]

How is an agent oriented to its goal?[9] An agent which has knowledge (sensory or rational) is oriented by the object known, toward which it tends to by its conscious appetite. An agent which does not have knowledge is oriented by its nature (ultimately by its substantial form, proximately by the active powers which are the properties of that form; by these powers the agent is adapted to its goals). How can a substantial form be a formal cause and, at the same time, a principle of goal-directedness? This is an important question which cannot be answered at this point.[10]

70. Orientation in being

In the very intelligibility of the act-potency correlation we have a manifestation of goal orientation, for a being in potency is a being ordered to an act or perfection. For example, essence is ordered to the act of existing by its very nature, and so is intrinsically oriented. The same is true of the other instances of the act-potency correlation; matter is ordered to form, is "for" form; substance is "for" accidents. And all the beings which we directly know exist for their operations. In other words, not only is it true that all the agents we directly know act for goals, but also, because there are goals,[11] these agents act necessarily (with different kinds of necessity depending on their natures).

But as we have seen before, there are two basic types of operation, immanent and transient activity. Immanent activity, as we

[7] For a clear analysis of the causality of the goal and the mutual influence of the four causes on each other, see Selected Passages, No. 23.

[8] This proposition is often called "the principle of teleology" ("finality").

[9] Previously it has been mentioned that the passivity of a potency is not necessarily always passivity to the reception of an influence from an efficient cause (see sec. 48, n. 2, and sec. 60, n. 3). The fallacy of univocity in the explanation of the passivity of tendencies is as misleading as any other mistaken univocity. This remark concerns chiefly the theory of powers in the philosophy of human nature and the theory of premotion in natural theology.

[10] See below, the Fifth Way of Proving the Existence of God.

[11] Recall that as was explained in n. 1 of this chapter, some goals already exist and need only to be obtained; other goals must be produced.

have also seen, is the perfection of the agent, and so an agent with immanent activity has an internal goal: it acts for its own good, in some sense at least, and so, to that same extent, exists proximately for its own sake. This is least perfectly true of merely vegetative living things, for their highest operation, generation, is ultimately ordered to the production of a distinct living thing. It is more perfectly verified in animals, which have sensitive knowledge; but sensitive knowledge is very limited, as we shall see in the philosophy of human nature. It is most perfectly verified in intellectual beings, whose immediate goal is their own perfection, to be attained by the possession of the good which is the completion of their nature.[12]

On the contrary, beings which have only transient activities cannot be said to be for themselves. Their being is for the sake of their effects; in other words, their goals are wholly external. They share in activity only to the extent that they bring other things to perfection. That is why some philosophers have found only an extrinsic or instrumental teleology in nonliving things; for example, that they serve the goals and purposes of men, animals, and plants. But this is a confusion. Nonliving things have an intrinsic principle of goal-directedness, their nature, but their goals are always external.

71. Chance

The term "chance" is often used loosely to indicate that we do not know the efficient causes or agents of a particular event (coming-to-be). But if someone is ignorant of the causes of an event, or even if the event cannot be foreseen (foreknown), there is no philosophical problem about reality involved. For example, ignorance may keep a person from knowing what a gun is, but when such an ignorant person pulls the trigger and the gun fires, the firing of the bullet is not chance. Again, we may not be able to tell which way the dice will fall, but the *chance* we take is our ignorance, not the absence of causes for the event.

Some philosophers have taken the position that some events

---

[12] As we shall see in moral philosophy, the ultimate goal of man is the possession of the subsistent truth (for knowledge) and goodness (for appetite), which is God.

happen without efficient causes. Of course, they admit that within our immediate experience causes are always to be found and to be expected. But for various reasons,[13] these philosophers maintain that some events remote in time or space occur without efficient causes, and they state this supposed situation by saying that these events happen "by chance." Note that this is no explanation. If, with these philosophers we would say, "Chance is the coming-to-be of some event without an efficient cause," then the statement, "An event has happened by chance," means, "An event has happened by the coming-to-be of that event without an efficient cause." This is the same as saying that something comes to be without a cause. And, as we have seen in the preceding chapter, every being which comes to be has a cause.

However, there is another meaning of the term "chance" which does offer a philosophical problem. We call that chance which happens without design or expectation. For example, a man in spading his garden comes upon a hidden treasure: we say he found it by chance. The miser who hid the treasure had the purpose of concealing or safeguarding it, not the purpose of having it found. The man who was spading his garden had no purpose of finding a treasure. Or another case: a man on his way to the store met a robber at an alley; the meeting of the two men was chance. What happens in such a case? There is a meeting of two lines of causality, each of which is purposive in itself, but the meeting of the two lines is not included in the purpose of either agent. In this sense of chance, all accidents are chance. In this sense also, we can correctly speak of chance even in the world below man. The stone on top of the mountain is pulled by gravity, which is a goal-directed activity, toward the bottom. A plant halfway up is engaged in the goal-directed activity of growing and nourishing itself. But the destruction of the plant by the descending stone is not due either to the causes which pull the stone down or to the activity of the plant; it is a chance result due to the interference of two lines of activity. For another example, we know that when molten iron cools without interference, it takes a crystalline structure which is relatively brittle.

[13] See below, objections to the First and Second Ways of proving the existence of God.

When it is violently pounded while cooling, it becomes tough and malleable. From the point of view of either the iron itself or the forge, the malleability of the iron is a chance result due to the interference of two unconnected lines of activity. Hence, we can define chance as "the concurrence or interference of several causal chains,[14] such that the concurrence is outside the goal of any of the causes taken singly."

Chance, considered from the viewpoint of the agents immediately involved, is certainly something real. Because this consideration is restricted to the immediate or proximate agents, we will call chance taken in this way "relative chance." But this is not the only way in which we can consider chance, as is clear from the example of the iron and the forge, for what is chance from the viewpoint of either of those causes is intended by the operator of the forge. If, then, we take into account all the causes involved in an event, both proximate and remote (or mediate) secondary[15] causes, we would have a complete consideration of all the causes in the universe, so that, if an event were a chance event with regard to all these causes, we could speak of "absolute chance."

Can there be an event which would be a chance occurrence with regard to absolutely all causes, even a cause outside the entire universe of limited beings—"total chance"? To answer this question we must first distinguish between a positive chance and a merely destructive one. Most chance events are less perfect (less actual, and so on) than the effects which the causes would have produced if they had not been interfered with. With such an event there is really no problem of causality and goal orientation.[16] But what about positive chance results? Let us suppose an effect arising from an interference of distinct causal lines,

---

[14] Recall that natural goal-directedness or deliberate purpose will be orienting each one of these lines of causality in itself.

[15] On the meaning of the term, "secondary cause," see above, sec. 61.

[16] Imperfection, or lack of act, does not need an efficient cause, since as such it *is* not. Supposing that God exists (which we have not yet considered philosophically): such a destructive result would indeed fall under His foreknowledge and providence and could not happen unless He permitted it; yet He would not be its cause.

which is more perfect than any single one of its proximate causes.[17] When we were considering efficient causality, we saw that an effect may possibly be more perfect, more actual, of a higher degree of being than any one of its proximate causes, but not more so than all of its causes taken together, else it would be really uncaused. The situation with regard to telic causes is not altogether the same. A positive effect may well escape the goal orientation of any of the proximate and particular causes and so be a relatively chance effect. Moreover, granted a real plurality of contingent beings, and granted especially the real internal freedom of some finite agents, a positive chance effect may escape the goal orientation of any and all secondary causes.[18] Is this a sufficient and complete analysis? If we were to say that an event or a being in its coming-to-be has escaped the goal orientation of every cause without any qualification at all, would we not, first, have separated two of the causal factors (agent and telic cause) and, second, have left the determinate nature of the effect without any cause, thus also separating the intrinsic principles of the effect from each other? And does this not violate both the nature of cause and of being as we have found them? This problem brings us to the topic of the next chapter.

72. Definitions

Goal, or telic cause, is that to which an activity is directed. It is that for the sake of which something exists or is done. It is the cause which influences the being of an effect by being the object of an agent's tendency. It is sometimes called "end," or "final cause."

[17] To the extent that more perfect living things were born of less perfect ones their origin would be ascribed to chance. How a nature can arise in this way will be considered more specifically in the philosophy of nature; see G. P. Klubertanz, *Philosophy of Human Nature* (New York, Appleton-Century-Crofts, 1953), pp. 405–407; 422–425; "Chance and Equivocal Causality," *Proceedings of the XIth International Congress of Philosophy,* VI (1935), 203–208. This article also shows how the statistical character of some scientific laws is to be related to both efficiency and teleology.

[18] To suppose the opposite is to admit mechanical predetermination. Such a system of thought would hold that a sufficiently powerful intellect (for example, Laplace's demon), given an adequate knowledge of any moment of world history, could discover all the events which led up to it and predict all subsequent events.

Purpose is a *consciously held* goal.

Goal orientation is the being-directed toward a goal.

Teleology is the being-ordered or directed toward something which is a good or perfection in some sense.

The "principle of teleology" is the universal statement of the goal-directedness of every agent—"Every agent acts for a goal." This principle is also called the "principle of finality."

Chance is the concurrence or interference of several causal chains, such that the concurrence is outside the goal of any of the causes taken singly.

Relative chance is the concurrence of several causal chains which is outside the orientation of the proximate causes involved.

Absolute chance is the concurrence of several causal chains which is outside the orientation of all secondary causes.

Total chance would be a concurrence of several causal chains which would be totally uncaused.

73. Proof

Action is either immanent or transient.

But: immanent action is itself a perfection of the agent and so a goal; transient action flows either from a conscious purpose or from a nature so structured as to act toward constant and determined results.

Therefore: every agent acts for a goal.

74. Readings

St. Thomas Aquinas, *Contra Gentiles*, Bk. III, chaps. 2 and 3 (every agents acts for a goal which is a good), chap. 16 (every limited being has a goal); *Summa Theologiae*, Pt. I, q. 5, art. 4 (how the causes are related), q. 44, art. 4 (God is the goal of all beings); Pt. I–II. q. 1, arts. 1 and 2 (teleology in human activity), q. 26, art. 1 (love and the good).

Etienne Gilson, *The Spirit of Mediaeval Philosophy*, trans. A. H. C. Downes (New York, Scribner, 1936), pp. 102–107.

A. D. Sertillanges, *Foundations of Thomistic Philosophy*, trans. Godfrey Anstruther (St. Louis, Herder, 1931), pp. 148–158.

George P. Klubertanz, S.J., "St. Thomas's Treatment of the Axiom, 'Omne Agens Agit Propter Finem,'" in *An Etienne Gilson Tribute* (Milwaukee, Marquette Univ. Press, 1960), 101–117.

Leo R. Ward, C.S.C., *God and the World Order* (St. Louis, B. Herder, 1961).

Selected Passages from St. Thomas Aquinas

23. That the Goal Is a Cause

The fourth kind of cause is the goal (end). This is that for the sake of which something happens, as health is the cause of walking. Because it is less evident that the end is a cause, since it is the last to come to be, therefore also was it omitted from consideration by earlier philosophers, as is noted in the first book. Hence [Aristotle] proves in a special manner that the end is a cause. For the question, "Why?" or "On what account?" is a question about a cause. For when someone asks us, "Why, or for what reason, is someone walking?" we give a suitable answer when we say, "For his health." And in answering this way, we think we are giving the cause. Hence it is clear that the end is a cause. Not only the ultimate end for which the agent acts is a cause with regard to those things which precede it, but all the intermediate steps between the first agent and the ultimate end are called ends with regard to what precedes them. In the same way, the intermediaries are called the agent cause and source of motion with regard to what follows them. . . .

Since the term *cause* has many meanings, it happens that there are many causes of one thing, not accidentally, but properly. . . . For the cause of the statue, in itself and not accidentally, is the sculptor and the brass, but not in the same way. . . .

He says that it also happens that two things are causes with regard to each other—but this is impossible in the same kind of causality. This indeed becomes clear if we consider that causes are of many kinds. For example, the pain from a wound is a cause of health, as efficient cause or the principle of change; but health is a cause of that pain, as end. For according to one and the same kind of causality it is impossible that one thing be both cause and caused. . . .

We ought to understand that, of the four kinds of causes previously mentioned, two of them correspond to each other, and the other two also. For the efficient cause and the end correspond to each other, in that the efficient cause is the principle of change, and the end is its term. Similarly, matter and form correspond to each other, for the form gives esse, but the matter receives it. Therefore, the efficient cause is the cause of the end, and the end is the cause of the efficient cause. The efficient cause is the cause of the end, inasmuch as it makes it to be, because by bringing about change, the efficient cause makes the end exist. But the end is a cause of the efficient cause, not indeed of its being, but with regard to its causality. For the efficient cause is a cause inasmuch as it acts, and it does not act except for the sake of an end. Therefore, the efficient cause has its causality from the end.

Form and matter are causes of being with regard to each other. Form is the cause of matter, inasmuch as it makes the latter to be in act; but matter is the cause of form, inasmuch as it sustains it. But I say that both of these are causes of being for each other, either simply or in some regard. For the substantial form gives being to matter simply. But the accidental form does so in a qualified manner, inasmuch as it too is a form. Furthermore, the matter does not always sustain the form in being simply, but inasmuch as the form is the form of this matter, having its being in it, as the human body is related to the human soul.

Commentary on Aristotle's Metaphysics, Bk. V, lect. 2 (ed. Cathala, Nos. 771, 773, 774–775).

IX

The Transcendentals

75. Being is a transcendental

Some predicates[1] can be said only of particular classes or kinds of things, and these predicates are usually univocal ones; for example, "white" (which can only be said of things that are extended); "square" (which can only be said of things that have a surface). These predicates will be considered in Chapters XI, XII, and XIII. But the predicates to be treated here are common to many kinds of things, and so their community must be one of analogy, as we have already seen with regard to *being* and *substance*. A predicate which is not restricted to any category, type, or class of reality, but goes beyond, or "transcends," all limited areas of reality and all distinctions within reality is called a "transcendental." The transcendentals are predicates.

We have seen that *is* can be said or predicated of *all* real things. From our study of being, which we know is common by way of analogical inclusion, we can see that being is not a genus, not even the widest possible genus. For genus is always abstract; and the wider and more universal the genus, the more abstract and potential it is. For example, *material substance* is a predicate that can be applied to every thing in our material universe; it is also a very abstract concept and is in potency to all the specific

---

[1] The term "predicate" is here taken in a very wide sense to include verb-predicates (such as "runs," "is") as well as nouns and adjectives. For a discussion of those "metaphysicians" and logicians who wish to reduce all two-element propositions (*de secundo adjacente*) to three-element ones (*de tertio adjacente*), see Etienne Gilson, *Being and Some Philosophers*, 2d ed. (Toronto, Pontifical Institute of Mediaeval Studies, 1952), pp. 190–205.

determinations—merely material, living, sensitive, rational. But *being* as it is understood in its first and proper metaphysical sense is named from that which is most actual and concrete, namely, the act of existing. Being is *not* the "widest in extension and the least in comprehension," because the logical rule of the inverse variation of extension and comprehension holds only for universals. Being is at once the widest in extension—for *is* can be said of all things—and the fullest in (implicit) comprehension—for any real act or perfection *is*. Being includes all reality; indeed, all the reality of any and all individuals. Therefore, *being* (understood as "the being of metaphysics") is a transcendental.

This conclusion is simple and obvious. A series of problems, however, remains. We have seen that *is* has many meanings and that in addition to its strictly metaphysical meaning, it is also used of things which are real only in the wide sense, and even of purely mental objects. We must therefore also consider how these meanings are related to the metaphysical sense. Moreover, there are some terms which are used more or less in the same sense as *being,* and so we should give a brief consideration to these terms. Finally, some philosophers have raised a question about the sense in which being is *a* transcendental. We will take up these topics in inverse order.

The question, "In what sense is being *a* transcendental?" is a question about the unity of being.[2] The question, "Is being one?" has many meanings. It may mean, "Is there only one being?" and immediate experience shows us many distinct individuals. The question may mean, "Is being univocal?" The reflection which we have made in Chapter III (and the following chapters) shows us that being is analogous. The question may mean, "Is there only one 'kind' of being, for example, material being or limited being?" and a study of the being of metaphysics and of the proof for the existence of God leads us to the conclusion that there are many kinds of beings, which are analogous with several kinds of analogy (analogy of eminince in causality, analogy of proportion, analogy of participation). The question may mean, "Granted

[2] See above, Chap. II, sec. 17, nn. 17 and 21, and Chap. III, sec. 24, n. 3. St. Thomas explicitly says, "There is no single intelligibility in the things which are said analogously" (*Summa Theologiae,* Pt. I, q. 13, art. 5).

that beings as they are are many and analogous, can they be correctly understood as beings by one concept?" An attentive reflection on our knowledge of being has shown us that it is impossible to have a *concept* of being in its first and proper sense, and so the unity of being is not even of one concept.[3] The community of the act of existing is only an analogical one, and so being is *one* transcendental only by the unity of analogy (according to all the kinds of analogy which we found in being).

Finally, the question about the unity of being may mean, "Is there at least an indirect way in which some, if not all, the analogates can be understood in one act of understanding?" Now, concepts are formed by abstraction, and in the first instance directly from the things which we wish to grasp. Conceptions, however, are formed from judgments; they can be formed either by abstraction (from an attributive judgment, from which we derive a composite essence, e.g., gold mountain) or by a negative judgment. Can we form a conception of being? We can if it is possible to make a series of judgments from which the same conception can be derived. Now, we have noticed that among the analogies of being there are some in which one analogate is prior and the other is posterior, and that in such analogies, the secondary analogate (as far as our *knowledge* of the two is concerned) is defined through the first, whereas the first does not include the secondary analogates. Thus, substance is prior to accident and to the other intrinsic principles of being, and sensible creatures are prior in our knowledge to God. Thus, we can form a common conception of being, so that, when we say, without any further qualification, "Something is," or name an object, "something which is," we are understood to mean, "A sensible subsistent exists," "an individual sensible subsistent which is." In this derivative and limited sense we can truly speak of a single conception of being.

We can now take up the consideration of the terms which have somewhat the same meaning as *being*. One of these terms which we have already used is "reality," or "the real." As we have seen,

[3] Much more can be said about our knowledge of being; see, for example, Stanislas Breton, *Approaches phénoménologiques de l'idée de l'être* (Paris, Vitte, 1959).

this is a term which belongs to the level of everyday, spontaneous knowledge; hence, it is often used in a loose or less precise sense than the term "being." "Thing" as a term from the level of everyday knowledge is like "reality." As used on the level of demonstrative knowledge, "thing" stresses the essence or quiddity and connotes the act of existing (whereas "being" includes the act of existing more directly). "Something," as a technical term on the level of demonstrative knowledge, means the same as "thing," but connotes, in addition, the division of that which is named "something" from other things. In other words, "something" is a term which implies that there are other things in addition to the one we call "something." Hence, it implies the unity of the thing (it is *a* thing) as well as the diversity or multiplicity of things.

76. Possibles

As we have already noted, the properly real is being, that which has an act of existing. Nevertheless, we understand that some things *can* be in the real order which here and now actually are not. We understand this from the contingent real things which we experience. For these beings manifest themselves as contingently existing. They are composed in the order of being itself—namely, of an essence and an act of existing—and consequently we can consider things in relation to existence even though they are not.

When we consider a thing inasmuch as it is able *to be*, we call it a possible.[4] A thing which is not, whether it be possible or a mere fiction, is simply nothing in the real order. Such a thing, under the aspect that it simply is not, is not the subject of any form of knowledge at all. If we consider a thing as simply an object of the mind, we are not thinking of a possible; we may be thinking of a logical entity; we may be studying the content of dreams as a psychologist might do. If we investigate an essence down to the last detail, but only from the point of view of *what* it is, we are not dealing with a possible as possible and so are not

[4] By a "pure possible," we mean something which does not exist, but is an object of knowledge with a reference to what could be extramental. We can also, however, consider the possibility of a being which exists; in this case we are not thinking about a possible in the strict sense of the word (sometimes called a "mixed possible").

dealing with it from the point of view of the philosophy of being
—we may be engaged in mathematics or one of the sciences. But
when we consider an essence (a thing) inasmuch as some properly real thing can or could correspond to it, then we are considering the possible as possible, that is, in relation to being. A
possible considered in this way belongs to the subject of metaphysics.

The intelligibility of a possible, therefore, lies in its relation to
being. As a possible thing, an essence has the possibility of having an act of existing; in other words, it is known as that to which
in the real order there could correspond a contingently existing
thing.

Now, to understand an essence with a relation to an act of
existing there must be a foundation. This foundation is twofold:
(a) in essence, and this consists in the noncontradictoriness of
the constituent elements of that essence; (b) in an act of existing
—not its own, of course, because a possible has no act of existing
—the act of existing of some actual cause, past, present, or future.
Hence, the intelligibility of a possible depends on its essence (understood with reference to an act of existing which a corresponding real being might have); its possibility of *being* depends on
the act of existing of some cause (or causes) adequate to produce
an actually existing (real) being corresponding to the knowledge
we have.

Possibility, therefore, can readily be divided into two parts:
essential possibility (the noncontradictoriness or consistency of
its constituent intelligible notes, understood with reference to a
being which might exist), and existential possibility, for only
that can truly exist which exists necessarily of itself or is produced by an existing cause.

Because the possibility of being depends on a cause, and causes
can be proximate or remote and variously disposed to act, possibility itself can have degrees. Moreover, because that which is
possible depends for its possibility on an actual being, a possible
can be said to be by an analogy of proportion—although the relationship of a possible to an act of existing is mediate and indirect—namely, through the esse of a distinct real being which is
its cause.

77. Beings of reason and pure intelligibilities

Whenever we think of something, that "something" can be either a being in the proper sense of that term or some principle of being or something pertaining to a being or sometimes not a being in itself at all (for example, a fiction).[5] All of these "things," however, can be considered *as known*, and as such they can be called intelligible objects or intelligibilities[6] (in the wide sense). These intelligibilities, from the viewpoint of being, can be classed into three groups: real beings, beings of reason, and pure intelligibilities (*rationes*), that is, intelligibilities in the strict sense. So far in this book we have been considering mainly real beings, although there have been occasional references to the other two groups.

A being of reason is an object which can be thought of but which does not and *cannot* exist in itself. Consequently, in the proper sense of being, such objects are simply not beings. Nevertheless, they are understood *after the manner of beings*. They are objects conceived or mentally constructed with reference to the real order; yet they have no direct correspondent in that order.[7]

Beings of reason are of three kinds. (1) Negations and privations (for example, "nobody," "a hole"; "blindness," "ignorance") obviously do not correspond to any real existent or to any real principle of being. A negative or privative proposition may be true or false, yet the truth of a negative proposition does not imply the existence of a negation. (2) Relations of reason are beings of reason, either because they join together objects which exist only in a mind (for example, the relations of genus, property, subject and predicate) or because they are mentally applied to real beings without a direct and a real foundation in the real, for example, the "right" side of a table (transferred to tables from the distinction between the sides of an animal body), the "top" of a box whose top and bottom are constructed the same, and so forth. (3) There are also mental constructs which are beings of reason, because as such they cannot exist, and are only indirectly related to the real, that is, through some other real being from

---

[5] See Selected Passages, No. 25.

[6] See Selected Passages, No. 26, especially par. 1, where intelligible objects are divided into three classes.

[7] See Selected Passages, No. 24.

which the construct is derived. Among such constructs there are
to be found some second-level abstractions (for example, "humanity," which, although it is understood after the manner of the
substantial form of a being, is rather the abstracted formal intelligibility of "man," which is the product of a total abstraction) and
some transferred intelligibilities.[8]

Beings of reason are beings *because* that is the way we think
of them. They are understood as having the nature of being. Because beings of reason are correlative with the real on which they
are modeled, the predication is by proportion; because beings of
reason are not intrinsic constitutive principles of being but are
understood after the manner of beings, the analogy is not intrinsic
but extrinsic. Hence, we may say that beings of reason are by an
extrinsic analogy of proportion.

Why do men produce or invent beings of reason? For the purpose of a better understanding of, and a more efficient dealing
with, real beings. For example, consider how awkward it would
be to think and talk of "digging a hole," "curing an illness," "being
in debt," without making use of any beings of reason. Again,
consider the poverty of our literature if all metaphors were removed from it. Thirdly, our direct (or ontological) understanding
of beings is frequently very limited. There are many things which
we cannot directly understand in themselves, particularly as soon
as we get beyond immediate experience into science. (To say that
science makes use of constructs is by no means derogatory to the
dignity of science; in a way it is a glorification of the human
mind, for although the human intellect is limited by being the
intellect of a rational animal, it can at least to some extent transcend its limitations by means of the products of its own activity.)[9]

[8] For example, many metaphors like "John Doe is a pig," where we understand John Doe's greediness in terms of the understood nature of a pig. In
such metaphors, we attribute an alien nature to the subject. The "pig" we
are speaking of is not an existent individual (for such a predication would
be false); nor is it a being of reason (for beings of reason cannot be
directly predicated of existents like John). See above, Chap. III, n. 8, and
the article there cited.

[9] For a fuller discussion of the nature of constructural knowledge and its
difference from ontological knowledge, see Jacques Maritain, "On Human
Knowledge," *Thought*, XXIV (1949), 225-43.

Besides real beings and beings of reason, there is a third class of intelligibilities, the pure intelligibilities.[10] Universals, for example, are pure intelligibilities: they are neither merely constructed mental objects nor real beings. With regard to universals, we must distinguish between that which is known and the manner in which the known is in the mind. "Man," for example, can be truly said to be the knowledge of a real being, because that which we know when we know "man" is wholly and entirely real. But the manner in which we know "man"—namely, as abstract and universal—is unlike the manner in which a man exists—namely, as concrete and singular. Similarly, many of the objects which we speak of in metaphysics are pure intelligibilities. To see the difference between a pure intelligibility and a being of reason it may help to compare two conceptions. As an example of a pure intelligibility we will take the act of existing of a being with respect to what is known when we know it. This act is real (for it is that principle in a being by which it *is*); but with respect to the manner in which it is known, it is not immediately real (since it is known as if it were a subject). As an example of a being of reason, we will take the concept of existence,[11] namely, "the form by which a real being is." Existence is a positive formalization, to which no being or principle in the real order directly corresponds. In the real order, there is the esse of some being. This esse is referred to indirectly by the concept "existence." The mind constructs and conceives, after the manner of a form, a substitute representation of a real intelligible which in itself is not essential or formal. In other words, the mind essentializes and formalizes by way of a construct (derived from a real principle) what it recognizes in the real as belonging to the existential order.

78. The transcendental "one"

The term "one" is used in two quite different senses. The numerical "one" is used in counting and, at the level of demonstra-

[10] See also, Selected Passages, No. 26, for a very full explanation of what an intelligibility is.

[11] For the difference between the "concept of existence," which is a constructural concept, and the "conception of the act of existing," which is a direct intelligibility, see above, sec. 17 (n. 17, 21), sec. 24 (n. 3; see also, G. P. Klubertanz, *The Philosophy of Human Nature* (New York, Appleton-Century-Crofts, Inc., 1953), pp. 179–180.

tive knowledge, in arithmetic. At present we are not going to deal with the numerical "one" at all. The transcendental "one" means "actually undivided"—for example, in the expression, "in one piece." The transcendental "one" is an absolute adjective; it does not in any sense imply that there are other things. In form, it is a positive term; but as far as its meaning is concerned, it is negative, for it means "not actually divided." Terms related to "one" are "unique," which means "one and only one"; "whole," which implies that the thing which is actually undivided is capable of division into parts; and "simple," which means "not only undivided but indivisible, having no parts."[12]

"One" is the first "property"[13] or attribute of being. It is the *first* property, because it refers to being absolutely, considered in itself (and so is prior by nature to the other transcendentals which belong to being relatively, as we shall see). "One" does not add anything positive to being; it is the being in itself which is undivided. However, we understand this absence of division after the manner of an added qualification.

Every being is one. For a being is either simple, that is, indivisible and so, of course, actually undivided, or it is composed. But parts do not make up a being unless they are *united* in some way or other. And there are a number of kinds of unity.

ONE

per se	{ according to one act of existing[14] { according to one essence (nature)
per accidens	{ by composition of substance and accident (or two accidents, according to their inherence in the same substance)
accidental	{ of many substances according to some accident: dynamic: joined in operation (activity) static: joined in place, structure, and so forth

[12] See also, Selected Passages, No. 27.

[13] From the Latin, *proprietas* or *passio entis*.

[14] Ordinarily, both these types of per se unity are found together, for the undividedness of essence and of the act of existing are naturally proportioned to each other. Hence, for many purposes, that can be said to be "per se one" which has one essence or nature. But it is still the undividedness of the act of existing which is the most basic reason for denominating a being *one* being.

"One" and "being" are clearly not synonyms. On the other hand, they clearly do not refer to really distinct principles. Hence, there is a distinction of reason between "one" and "being." Moreover, since "that which is actually undivided" is a being, and *a* being is actually undivided, the distinction between "one" and "being" must be a minor distinction of reason.[15]

The opposite of "one" is "many" or "the divided" or "the distinct" or "the different" or "the diverse." Which one will be precisely the opposite of "one" in any given case depends upon the precise connotations in the particular usage of "one."

79. Being-in-itself and being-for-another

In most of metaphysics—up to this point in our present study— the being that we consider is the being which a thing has in itself. However, in most of our prior experience and probably much of the experience we will have in the future, the being which a thing has *for us* is more significant.[16] In the practical order, our world for us is a biocultural world. The biological world is the world of immediate vital utility. The cultural world, which in the last century has become very profoundly a technological world, is the world in which we spend most of our time. Thus, our ordinary world is a world in which things have a meaning as food, shelter, tools, artifacts, and symbols. But, when we are looking at our surroundings in terms of food, shelter, tables, roads, traffic signals, pianos, books, and on the persons surrounding us as parents, friends, enemies, strangers, we are not considering them according to the reality which they have in themselves, but rather according to the being which they have for us. A thing has being-for-us to the extent that it is known, is the object of some tendency (love, hatred, and so on), or is the object of our transient activity.

As far as noncognitive things are concerned, their being-for-us is not part of their intrinsic reality, except that things must have in themselves the possibility of entering into relations with us.

[15] See above, sec. 33.

[16] It is not metaphysics alone that considers being-in-itself; it is a mark of all purely intellectual knowledge and especially of all the kinds of speculative (theoretical) scientific knowledge to be directed to the object as it is in itself.

The being-for-man for such a thing is therefore principally a fact about man. The anthropologist is the one who is interested in knowing that an oddly shaped piece of stone is an arrowhead, not the geologist.

Persons, however, not only have being-for-another, but in turn are aware of this being. As a result, their being-for-another intrinsically affects them. A child, for example, first sees his own value as a reflection of the value which he thinks others put on him. Similarly, he reacts to his surroundings primarily in terms of their being-for-him, and habitual reactions structure his personality. However important such relations are for our practical life as well as for psychologists, artists, educators, and the like, the contingent forms which they take have little meaning for speculative science of any kind.[17]

Nevertheless, the basic fact that persons and things have being-for-us, and that we have being-for-other persons needs to be investigated further.

80. The transcendental "true"

The first kind of being-for-another is being-known. We can begin our investigation by considering the relationships between knowledge and the things which are known.

In logic and theory of knowledge there are many references to "truth." There, "truth" means the "conformity of the mind to things" and, when we are speaking accurately, should always be called *logical* truth. So, too, when we ask whether something is true, we are ordinarily speaking of logical truth. And we use "falsehood" or "falsity" in the same kind of way. However, even in our ordinary speech, we occasionally use the term "true" and especially "false" in a related but quite different sense, as in the expressions "false teeth," "true love," "a true albino." In this sense, we are talking about the conformity of the thing to its definition, essence, and so forth, or, more generally, to knowledge or a mind. (Compare the meaning of the verb "to true.") This is the sense in which we speak of the true in metaphysics, namely, the conformity or conformability of a thing to a mind.

---

[17] This is another reason why a universally valid metaphysics can hardly be begun starting with "subjective," personal experience of "our world."

The true is not a negation or a negative attribute, for it expresses something positive, namely, conformability with intellect. But "true" does not add anything really distinct to "being," for "true" is simply "being" expressed in its relation to intellect. Hence, the distinction between "being" and "the true" is a minor distinction of reason.

When we say, "The true is being in relation to intellect," we must determine explicitly which intellect we are referring to. In order to make our exposition complete, we shall include the relation of finite beings to the creative intellect of God; both the fact of His existence and the nature of the world's relation to Him will be proved in the second part of this book. Since the beings of our experience, by their very participation in being, are related to the First Being, it is to the Divine Intellect that the true has an essential relation. Because the beings of our experience exist by creation and God creates through intellect and will, all created beings are actually conformed in their being to the Divine Intellect. The predicate *true*, therefore, when applied to creatures, means "made so as to conform to the Divine Intellect." When applied to God Himself, however, the predicate *true* means essentially that God, Who is a subsistent intellect and act of understanding, knows Himself so perfectly that what He is and what He knows of Himself are entirely and completely identical.

But in addition to the Divine Intellect there are also other, contingently existing intelligent beings; and, of these, we are especially concerned with man. Note that only those beings are necessarily conformed to the human intellect which come into being in dependence upon a human agent. In the case of artifacts, *true* means "made so as to conform to the artist's mind." In the case of all other finite things, however, there is no necessary relation of actual conformity to the human intellect. Some things are in fact known by man. With regard to the nature and existence of these things, it is extrinsic and accidental to them that they be in fact known by some man. Therefore, *true* in the sense of "actually conformed to a human mind," when applied to artifacts, is an essential predicate; when applied to natural beings, it is an accidental and extrinsic predicate.

The relation between being and the human intellect can be considered in terms of conformability rather than conformity. By this we mean that whether such things are known or not, they can be known, they are knowable. The relationship of conformability to some created intellect is a necessary one, given the existence of these things and of an intellect, but it is secondary (the primary essential relation is to the Divine Intellect). The relationship of conformability to any given individual created intellect or to any kind of created intellect—for example, that of man—is contingent or accidental, for it is not necessary that men exist. Applied to creatures, therefore, the term "true" in the sense of conformability means that they are such as can be known by man. Some things, of course, are here and now not actually knowable by man—things hidden from man's experience within the earth or at the far reaches of the stellar universe or among the multitude of angels. But the reason these things cannot be known at present is some hindrance external to the nature of the things—their lack of contact with us, for example. Hence, we can state what is sometimes called the "principle of intelligibility"— "All things are intelligible."

We can also ask whether the predicate *true* in the sense of conformability to the human intellect can be applied to God. Prior to our knowledge that God exists we cannot, of course, say that He is true. But after we know that He exists, it is evident that He can be known by man.

True, in the sense of conformability to some created intellect, is a necessary but secondary predicate of all things. In the sense of conformability to some particular created intellect or to some kind of created intellect, *true* is an accidental and extrinsic predicate.

Being-true is, then, being-knowable and (sometimes) being-known by another. When the being which is knowable and known is a person, then this being-for-another which is (ontological) truth is the foundation for truthfulness in communication, which in turn is one of the foundations of society. Being-true is also the foundation for particular relationships, such as that of fidelity to promises, or of the knowledge aspect of friendship.

According to the various meanings of *true* which we have been considering, it is a relative attribute: it describes a thing as related to something else (namely, an intellect). In other words, it denominates a thing from something distinct from it (an intellect), to which it has a relation.[18] Does *true* have any absolute signification? In other words, does it say anything about the being in itself? Yes, because a being to be conformed and conformable to intellect must be of a certain kind. Intelligibility supposes that being has a certain structure. We have previously seen that potency, as such, is not knowable in itself but through act and in relation to act.[19] We have also seen that the first and primary of all acts is the act of existing. Hence, the primary one among the absolute meanings of *true* is the one which designates the act of existing of a thing:[20] "The *true* is the esse of things." On this basis we can see why every being is true. For being is "that-which-is," "something having an act of existing." The act of existing is intelligible, even if we cannot have a simple apprehension or direct abstractive concept of it. At the very least, we can know in a judgment that a being is. This does not imply that every being is perfectly or completely intelligible to man; it only means that no being is completely unintelligible to man. Therefore, *true*, in its first absolute meaning, designates the basic internal actuality of a being, its act of existing.

Moreover, act is also form, especially substantial form. Hence, a second absolute meaning of transcendental truth is the actual possession of a form and, consequently, of a nature. Again, inasmuch as act is intelligible, the being which possesses an act— that is, a form—is thereby intelligible. Here, however, not all beings are equally true, that is, equally conformable to the human intellect. Sensible things can be directly known by us. But pure forms—the angels and God—cannot be directly known in themselves to the human mind, because it is impossible for us to have an abstractive concept of such forms. Therefore, *true*, in the secondary, absolute sense of the possession of a form or nature, can

[18] Recall what was said above, that the relation in question is not something added to being; it is only rationally distinct.

[19] See above, sec. 53.

[20] St. Thomas most often gives among the "absolute" meanings of the *true* the esse of things; but there are also other meanings; cf. for example, "*veritas humanae naturae,*" in *Summa Theologiae*, Pt. III, q. 5, arts. 1 and 2.

be predicated of all beings, but in different ways of sensible things, separate substances, and God.

The transcendental true is related to knowledge as that which can be grasped and that which is to be grasped. As goal of knowledge, it is a telic cause of knowledge. Two consequences follow from this. One is that we meet again a reason for rejecting materialism, since even the sensible, as being, is intrinsically ordered to knowledge. Thus, the very material being, as true, implies the existence of a knower. Secondly, we mentioned in the beginning of this course that metaphysics can start from the fact of knowledge. The transcendental true is the reason why such a procedure is possible; for, if being as being is true, then from the fact of true knowledge we can work back to the necessary conditions of being and of knowledge.[21] For one example of this in metaphysics, we could work from the experienced fact of universal concepts to the composition of matter and form in things. For another example, we could work from the coexistence of a being which is both knower and known and another being which is only known but not a knower, to the role of act (esse and form) as source of intelligibility, and the contrary role of (primary) matter as that principle in a being which impedes full intelligibility.

Hence, we can sum up the entire discussion of transcendental truth in this way. The transcendental true is analogous. First— supposing we have proved the existence of God, as we shall do later—there is the subsistent truth of God Who is pure act, perfectly known to Himself. Then there are the participated truths, which are primarily true inasmuch as beings by participation are conformed to the creative intellect, and secondarily true, as such beings are conformable to some created intellect. In a derived sense, *true* designates the absolute (that is, nonrelative) perfection of a being, and here, too, there are degrees of truth. That is most true which is pure, subsistent act. That is more or less true which has more or less of act—primarily the act of existing, secondarily other acts, especially substantial form and essence.

The opposite of the true is the false. Being is not, absolutely

---

[21] This method is quite popular; it is sometimes called the "method of transcendental deduction," sometimes, of "reduction."

speaking, false, for that which has, absolutely speaking, no act of existing in any sense is not a being. However, a being may be called false from some limited point of view. For example, when we speak of "false teeth," we mean "some things which are not really teeth, but have something of the appearance of teeth and perform some of their functions."

81. The transcendental "good"

The second kind of being-for-another is being-loved or being the object of some activity. We have already seen, in our discussion of telic causality, that the correlative of tendency and action is "the good."

THE PROPER GOOD

The predicate "good" is used in many ways. In its unqualified sense (for example, "John is a good man"), it means "that which is perfect according to its kind." In this sense of the term "good," the goodness of a thing is proper to it; and the goodness of one kind of thing is different from the goodness of another kind. For example, a pen is good when it writes well; a race horse is good when it runs fast; a man is good when he has the virtues and other qualities which human nature ought to have. The unqualified "good" is therefore also called the "proper good." The proper good is clearly not possessed by every thing, for there are bad men, bad bargains, bad food. Moreover, in the beings of our experience, their proper good is a perfection distinct from their substance and so is an accidental perfection. (The proper good of man is studied in ethics or moral philosophy.)

The opposite of the proper good is the evil. Taken concretely, "evil" or "bad" designates some thing which is without (deprived of) some particular good which it should have according to its kind. Taken abstractly, "evil" or "badness" is the privation[22] itself; and privation itself is not a real being (just as blindness is not a being) but a being of reason. An evil thing, of course—"evil" taken concretely—is a real being, real with the reality of the

---

[22] Distinguish between privation and the simple absence of something. Privation means "the absence of something which is due, or suitable, or necessary." On evil as a privation, see Selected Passages, No. 29.

thing that lacks a good which is due to it according to its nature.

But goodness and evil are not simply absolute predicates, like perfect and imperfect. In the full sense of the term "good," a thing is good when it is not only perfect in its kind but is at the same time an object of appetite, or tendency. Good food, for example, is not merely a material substance with all the accidents suitable to its nature but also one which corresponds to a particular appetite, namely, the biological tendency of a living thing toward that which nourishes it. Similarly, a good race horse is not merely one which exercises the particular activity of running rapidly; that activity is also desired by someone. Again, a good man is not merely one who has certain virtues; he has the virtues he *ought* to have—and *ought* expresses the basic natural tendency of man to be in the condition of possessing such virtues. These examples—similar ones can easily be found—show us that *good* is a perfection for which there is an appetite (tendency) either in the thing itself which possesses or is capable of possessing the perfection or in something else.

Thus, the proper good is always a goal for that whose good it is. Conversely, all goals are objects of striving or tending, and are (or are thought to be) proportioned to the needs or capacities of the agent and its powers. Hence, every goal is also good. So we can say not only that every agent acts for a goal, but also that every agent acts for a good.

But men commit sins, that is, seek things that are evil; and the effects of natural causes are often evil. Quite so, and the understanding of how these facts are related to the statement that every agent acts for a good will be an advantage. First then as to sin. Sin involves a double aspect: that man does not will the good which he should be willing and that he wills something which is not, properly speaking, good for him. But the fact that a man does not accept as the actual goal of his activity that good to which he should be tending does not change the fact that that good is his proper good and that he should be striving for it, and this aversion from his proper good is not the primary object of his will, but rather something else which he wants which is incompatible with that good. On the other hand, what the sinner does actually take is considered by him at that point to be the good which he wants, and it is viewed as a good for him under some limited aspect or for a particular power (for example, sense pleasure, even against reasonable use, is a good for the senses considered in themselves; being responsible to no one could be considered good if a man forgets that he is a limited and dependent being; and so on). That is why we said above that every goal is a good or is thought to be a good. Second, as to evil effects from the operation of natural causes. Here we must remember two things that we have seen. First, that every physical change necessarily involves the passing-away of something, else the new thing could not come to be; so some evil (loss) is necessarily included in every change. But change is for the sake of what comes to be. Second, we must also remember that causal changes can interfere with each other; this chance result is not intended by either of the causes, but rather is accidental. But since the physical evil that results from the action of natural causes is accidental, it remains true that every agent acts for a good.

The proper good is not always able to be obtained immediately; sometimes we must make use of other things, or engage in a series of actions, which are necessary in order that finally we may obtain the good that is desired. Objects or actions that are necessary or useful to obtain a proper good are called "means." By a *pure* means, we mean one that is not desirable for its own sake, but only for the good which it leads to; thus, an unpleasant medicine is sometimes good for a sick man—not that it is desired for itself, but because it is a means to recovering good health. Other things and actions not only are means to something else which is good, but are desirable also in themselves, such as a well-prepared meal. Means which are also good in themselves are often called "intermediate goals."

Since proper goods are proportioned to natures, and so differ as the natures differ, *good* in its unqualified sense will be predicated relationally and proportionally. Is it univocal or analogous? Natures not only differ, but what it means for one to have the perfection which is suited to it is quite different from what it means for another kind of nature. For example, a nature which has knowledge derives from the possession of its proper good pleasure or joy, whereas a nature without knowledge cannot be said to enjoy its goods; again, for man, the perfecting of his sensory nature is quite different from that of his rational nature. Hence, *good* is analogous, and so it will be analogous with the analogy of proper proportionality. Means are proportioned to the goals; hence, they are analogously good by the analogy of proportion.

THE TRANSCENDENTAL GOOD

The purpose of this analysis of the proper, or unqualified, good, has been to help to clarify the question, Is being good? Obviously, this question cannot be asked about the proper good, since it is a fact of immediate experience that there are evils. We must therefore mean something different by *good*, and yet not simply and entirely different, or there would be no point in using the same term. What then have we found in analyzing the unqualified good? There are three parts to the description of this good: (1) There is some real, intrinsic perfection which is (2) suited, or proportioned to, (3) a tendency. In order that we can call something a proper good we must know something of the proper nature of the perfection and of the tendency. What happens to this understanding of *good* if we substitute "being" for "nature"? We recall that a thing is properly a *being* if it has the act of existing: being is that which is. Now, the act of existing, as an act, is a perfection. Hence, every being, as being, possesses at least this perfection: the act of existing. Moreover, we have also seen that the act of existing is the act of its own proper potency, namely, essence, and that every potency is ordered to, and proportioned to, its act. From this we can conclude that the act of existing is a good and that every being, as being, *has* a good.

Is this enough to enable us to say that every being, as being, is good?[23] Here we must recall what we saw earlier about the nature of agency and goal-directedness. Some beings have only transient activity; that is, their goals are all outside themselves; in other words, they do not act *for themselves*. But action follows being, as we also saw. Such beings, then, do not have any self-directed tendencies, and thus are not good as beings if they are considered by themselves in isolation from all other beings. Other

[23] On the transcendental good, see Selected Passages, No. 28.

kinds of being, living and cognitive beings, do have themselves and their own perfection among the goals which they act for; hence, they act for themselves, and thus can also be said to *be for themselves*. Living beings, even considered in an isolated way, are truly goods for themselves as beings. Cognitive beings, and especially intellectual beings, are for themselves—not for themselves as absolute goals, as we shall see, but still truly for themselves.

One of the ways in which this truth is made clearer is in the tendency of living things to continue in being. Plants and animals resist death in ways proportioned to their nature and will work very hard to keep themselves alive for their normal life span (whether this be a few hours or hundreds of years). Men resist death and try to avoid it; one's own death is feared and disliked; even those who commit suicide voluntarily do so under the impression that life for them is so joined with evils that they seem greater than the evil of death.

We have already seen that the material things we know form an interconnected dynamic whole; they act for the good of the universe as an on-going process. In this limited sense, these material beings are good, not in themselves as isolated, but in relation to the other material things. They are the objects of tendency with respect to each other. Moreover, in a general way, merely material things serve the needs and tendencies of the living and the cognitive beings, and this is another sense in which we can say that these beings are good.

But can we from this analysis say that *every* being is good? Could there not be somewhere a material thing, not a part of our universe nor a part of any other universe, which would not be the object of any tendency, have no transient action, and not be the object of any transient action? This is very difficult to show from the argument as we have so far seen it, and the easiest way to approach it is indirectly.

We will assume here some of the conclusions of the proofs to be given in the second part, namely that God is by His essence; He is the pure and subsistent actuality of being. So it follows that He is absolutely perfect as being. Because He is an intelligent being, He also has an intellectual tendency, a will. It is only

natural that His own infinite perfection should be an object of
this intellectual tendency, since He is a living being, and, therefore, the infinite perfection of God is also infinite goodness.[24]
"Infinite" goodness means goodness without limit, without flaw.

We will see that God is the cause of the world by creation,
through intellect and will. Because the things He makes are willed
by Him, it follows that creatures can be named good through
the analogy of eminence (and deficiency). Is the goodness of
creatures as such merely an extrinsic denomination?[25] or is it
also an intrinsic perfection? Recall that the relation in being
between God and creatures is proved to be an *intrinsic* analogy
of eminence in causality and, therefore, also the analogy of participation. Since God is good inasmuch as He is by His nature,
whatever participates in being also and to that same degree participates in goodness. And since every being is either being by
essence or being by participation, every being is good.

This answer to the question, "Is every being good?" has been a
priori.[26] But it enables us to come back to the question we left
unanswered: Could there be a being, purely material in its own
nature and not part of any universe? We now see that this supposition is impossible, since creatures must be willed as *good* by
their Creator; a material thing cannot be good unless it enters
into activity, as we have seen;[27] and merely material things have
only transient activity. Conversely, every being which is part of
the universe, as part, is good.

Since all beings are good, persons also are (ontologically) good

[24] Since the nature of God is identically the act of existing, the transcendental goodness of God is identically His proper goodness. And since God
is an intelligent being, His proper goodness is also moral goodness. This
identity of perfection is not found in any other being.

[25] Here, it will suffice to define *extrinsic denomination* as "a name
and a conception truly applied to one being because of another." Hence,
it is evident that an extrinsic denomination is not a real being: it does not
designate an intrinsic or inherent perfection or act. It is an intelligibility.

[26] The a priori approach to transcendental goodness is not in conflict with
the truth previously stated that we have no direct, immediate knowledge of
God, that we know Him only through creatures. For in the a priori approach as it is used here, we do begin with an immediate experience; namely,
the experience of proper goodness. From this, by way of analogy and
negation, we proceed to find transcendental goodness in the fullness of being,
which is also an object of tendency.

[27] See above, sec. 44.

as beings. Being-lovable, being-loved, and being-perfective-of-others is the foundation for that mutual love which is friendship. It is likewise the basis for justice, especially for those parts of justice which are often overlooked, such as respect, allowing the other person freedom and equality of opportunity, and the like. Thus it is also the remote basis for society, as well as for the duty of giving good example.

What is the relation of the transcendental good to being? The transcendental good is being inasmuch as it is in act. Consequently, good is not something really distinct from being and added to being, but in the real order is identical with being itself. But the conception, *good*, is not identical with the conception, *being*, for the very intelligibility of *good* adds to being the relation to some tendency or appetite. Therefore, the transcendental good adds to being the relation to appetite and so is distinct from being by a minor distinction of reason.

The beautiful is similar to the good.[28] Among the many definitions of beauty that have been offered, the most useful preliminary one is the one which declares beauty to be the capacity of some being to satisfy (please) in being known. Because man has different powers of knowledge and different tendencies, there will be, descriptively, different kinds of beauty: sensible beauty (especially visual and auditory[29]), intellectual beauty, moral beauty. In all cases, it is the very knowing of the being which causes the pleasure, and thus it can be said that beauty includes both truth and goodness.

Just as the first good we come to know is the proper good, so the first beauty we recognize is proper beauty. And, as the proper good has an opposite, the evil, so proper beauty has an opposite, the ugly. Yet beauty is not a univocal quality: the beauty of a

---

[28] In an introductory book, the study of the beautiful must necessarily be brief. But as proper truth is studied in a special discipline, logic, and proper good, in ethics, so beauty is studied in aesthetics. For those students who wish to do further reading in the philosophical analysis of beauty, two books can be recommended: Jacques Maritain, *Creative Intuition in Art and Poetry* (New York, Meridian Books, 1960) and Etienne Gilson, *Painting and Reality* (New York, Pantheon Books, 1957).

[29] Sight and hearing are the two senses that can be used for the sake of knowing alone. The other senses tend to be subordinated to biological utility, and thus to prevent the perception of beauty.

sunset is not that of a tree; the beauty of a sun-drenched landscape is not that of a statue; the beauty of a poem is not that of a symphony. It appears, therefore, that the beautiful is analogous with the analogy of proper proportionality. Since it is analogous, we cannot give a definition that is both adequate and fully determinate; we must be content with a vague and general one. If we look at the various objects which we call beautiful, we find these elements: an ordered multiplicity and a certain excellence of form and cognoscibility.

Is there also transcendental beauty? Is every being beautiful inasmuch as it is? Every being, inasmuch as it is a being, possesses actuality; all finite beings are made up of an ordered multiplicity of "parts" or principles—whereas God, Who is the simple actuality of existing, with regard to our knowledge of Him is a virtual ordered multiplicity of unified perfections; every being has at least some splendor of actuality, be it only the act of existing; and every being can be related to both knowledge and appetite, and in some way we can take pleasure in the knowledge of it. This is the a posteriori approach to transcendental beauty.

The a priori approach to transcendental beauty is richer and fuller. We find beauty in created things, and in them beauty is a perfection without any intrinsic limitation or imperfection. Hence, God, the creative cause of all being, must also be beautiful. And any perfection predicated of God must be predicated infinitely, without any limitation, and as identical with His essence and act of existing. Hence, God is subsistent beauty, beauty by essence, infinite beauty inasmuch as He is. Therefore, all His creatures, which are beings by participation, also possess transcendental beauty by participation. Therefore, every being is beautiful inasmuch as it is, either essentially or by participation.[30]

---

[30] There are also some analogous perfections (like life, knowledge, understanding, willing), which are similar to the transcendentals. These perfections are not strictly transcendental, for they are not found in all beings, and are not "properties" of being as being. Their similarity lies in their analogy. In its analogous sense, "life" is a special way of existing; knowledge, understanding, and willing are special ways of acting immanently. Note, however, that life, understanding, and willing are also used in univocal senses. These differences are explained in the philosophy of human nature.

82. Definitions

A transcendental is a "predicate" and a perfection which transcends all genera and differences.

Thing (as a scientific term in metaphysics) is that which has an essence or quiddity, and, only by implication, an act of existing.

Something is a thing which is distinct from other things.

A possible is something which could be or could have been.

A being of reason is an object (an essence or form) whose actuality is the act of being-understood, which, as such, cannot have an act of existing (in the proper sense of that term) but which is understood after the manner of a being.

An *intelligibility* (in Latin, *ratio*) is that which the intellect understands of the meaning of some term. (This is a purely descriptive definition.) In the strict sense, an intelligibility is neither a being of reason (for *what* is understood exists), nor a real being (for it does not exist in the way in which it is known).

The transcendental *one* is that which is actually undivided.

Simple is that which is undivided and undivisible, that which has no parts.

Whole or composite is that which is actually undivided but can be divided, that which has real parts.

Per se one is that which is one of itself, not by an external principle.

Per accidens one is that which is one by inherence.

Accidental one is that which is substantially many and is one by some distinct accident.

Logical truth is the conformity of the mind to the object.

Transcendental truth (ontological truth) is the conformity or the conformability of being to knowledge.

The *good* is that which is desirable. (This is the preliminary, descriptive definition.)

The proper good is some actuality or perfection in relation to the appetite of a certain *kind* of being.

Transcendental goodness is the actuality or perfection of a thing inasmuch as it is the object of some tendency.

Evil, taken concretely, is a being deprived of some particular good.

Evil, taken abstractly, is the privation of a particular good in a subject apt to have that good.

83. Proofs (to be completed)

A. Every being is one.
B. Every being is true.
C. Every being is good.

84. Readings

St. Thomas Aquinas, *Summa Theologiae*, Pt. I, q. 11, arts. 1 and 2 (on the meaning of transcendental unity and its relation to multiplicity), q. 76, art. 3 (on per se unity), q. 16, arts. 1–6 (on the various meanings of truth, its relation to being and to God), q. 17, arts. 1 and 4 (on falsity and its relation to truth), q. 5, arts. 1–5, q. 6, arts. 1-4 (on goodness, its relation to being; the goodness of God and of creatures), q. 37, art. 2 (on "quasi-forms"); Pt. I–II, q. 94, art. 2 (on the relationship of the various transcendentals, and the analytical [logical] priority of being); *On the Power of God*, q. 7, art. 11, ad 2 (on the order of the transcendentals to each other); *Truth*, q. 1, art. 1 (the meaning of truth), q. 21, arts. 1 and 2 (the meaning of good and its relation to being); *Contra Gentiles*, Bk. III, chaps. 18, 19, 20, and 24 (good and the will; relation between good and final cause); *Commentary on the Metaphysics of Aristotle*, Bk. X, lesson 1, Nos. 1920–1936, pp. 708–711 (on unity).

St. Augustine, *Confessions*, Bk. 10, chaps. 27, 33–34 (some passages on beauty).

Etienne Gilson, *Elements of Christian Philosophy* (New York, Doubleday, 1960), pp. 145–163.

Clifford G. Kossell, S.J., "Principles of St. Thomas's Distinction between the *Esse* and *Ratio* of Relation," *The Modern Schoolman*, XXIV (1946), 28–36; an excellent exposition of what is meant by an "intelligibility."

Jacques Maritain, *Art and Scholasticism*, trans. J. F. Scanlan (New York, Scribner's, 1930), pp. 23–38, 167–172, 161–166; the first two selections deal with beauty and its characteristics; the third with the perception of the beautiful.

Anton C. Pegis, "The Dilemma of Being and Unity," *Essays in Thomism* (New York, Sheed and Ward, 1942), 151–183; 379–382.

Gerald B. Phelan, "Verum Sequitur Esse Rerum," *Mediaeval Studies*, vol. I (1939), 11–22.

24. Substance and Accident Contrasted with Beings of Reason

. . . the quasi-definition of "being" is "something having esse." But substance alone is that which subsists. Accidents, however, are called beings, not because they are, but rather because by them something is; as "whiteness" is said to be, because its subject is white. Hence, [Aristotle] says that accidents are not simply called beings, but beings of being, such as quality and motion.

Nor is it to be wondered at, that accidents are called beings though they are not beings simply, because even privations and negations are said to be somehow beings, as "not-white is," not because not-white has an act of existing, but because a subject is deprived of whiteness. This, therefore, is common to accidents and privations, that being is applied to them by reason of their subject. But they differ in this, that the subject has esse to some extent according to accidents, but according to privations it does not have esse in any sense, but rather is deficient in esse.

> Commentary on Aristotle's
> Metaphysics, Bk. XII, lect.
> 1 (ed. Cathala, Nos. 2419–
> 2420).

25. The Difference Between Being and Being-known

It is clear to anyone who carefully considers the arguments of Plato, that he arrived at his erroneous positions, because he believed that the manner of being of the thing understood is like the manner of understanding the thing . . . But this is not necessary. For even if the intellect understands things by this, that it is like to them as far as the intelligible species (by which it is put into act) is concerned; yet it is not necessary that this species be in the intellect according to the way in which it is in the thing understood. For everything which is in a subject, is, according to the manner of the subject in which it is. Therefore, on account of the very nature of the intellect, which is different from the nature of the thing understood, it is necessary that the mode of understanding by which the intellect understands be different from the mode of being by which the thing exists. For, though that which the intellect understands must be in the thing, it need not be there in the same way.

> Commentary on Aristotle's
> Metaphysics, Bk. I, lect. 10
> (ed. Cathala, No. 158).

26. The Meaning of "Intelligibility"

There are three ways in which things are signified by words. For there are some things which according to their entire and complete being are outside the mind, and these are complete beings, like "man" and "stone." There are other things which in no way are outside the mind, like dream-objects and the image of a chimera. There are still other things which have a foundation in reality outside the mind, but the completion of their intelligibility, with regard to what is formal in them, is by the operation of the mind, as is clear in the universals. For "humanity" is something in reality, but does not have the nature of a universal, since there is no humanity common to many outside the mind. But in the way "humanity" is present in the intellect, there is joined to it an intention ["intention" here means "a note or characteristic added to the understood form 'humanity' because of the latter's relation to many things"], according to which it is called a species. Similarly, "time" has a foundation in motion—namely, what is before and after in the motion itself—but with regard to what is formal in time—namely, the measuring [of duration or motion]—it is completed by the operation of the intellect which measures. I make the same distinction with regard to truth. Truth has a foundation in the thing, but its intelligibility is completed by the action of the intellect—when, that is, the thing is apprehended in the way it is. Therefore, the Philosopher says [*Metaphysics*, Bk. VI, 1027b26] that the true and the false are in the mind, but good and evil are in things. Now, in the thing there are its essence and its esse; truth is founded rather on the esse of the thing than on the essence. As the name "being" is given to something from the act of existing, so in the operation of the intellect which takes the esse of the thing as it is (by becoming like to it), the relation of equality is completed, and the intelligibility of truth consists in this relation. Therefore, I assert that the very esse of the thing (as it is in the knowledge of the intellect) is the cause of truth.

> *Commentary on the First Book of the* Sentences, dis. 19, q. 5, art. 1.

An intelligibility (*ratio*), as it is taken here, is nothing other than that which the intellect understands of the meaning of some name. In those things which have a definition, the intelligibility is the definition itself, as the Philosopher says, "The intelligibility signified by the name is the definition" (*Metaphysics*, Bk. IV, 1012a25). But some things have an intelligibility in the present meaning of the term, which have no definition, as (for example) quantity and quality and similar things, which are not defined, because they are the most general genera. Yet, the intelligibility of quality is that which is signified by the name "quality," and this is that by which quality is quality. Hence, it makes no difference whether the things which are said to have an intelligibility have or do not have a definition. Thus, it is clear that the intelligibility of wisdom which is predicated of God, is that which is conceived as the meaning of this noun, although the Divine wisdom itself cannot be defined. Yet the noun *intelligibility* does not mean the conception itself, for this latter is signified by the noun "wisdom," or by some other name of a thing, but it signifies the intention of this conception, just as the noun *definition* signifies an intention, and so also other nouns of second imposition.

From this it is clear . . . how an intelligibility is said to be in reality. For this does not mean that the intention which we signify by the noun *intelligibility*, is in reality, nor even that the conception to which this intention applies is in reality outside the mind—since it is in the mind as in its subject—but it is said to be in the thing, inasmuch as in the thing outside the mind, there is something which corresponds to the conception of the mind, in the way in which that which is signified corresponds to its sign.

> *Commentary on the First Book of the* Sentences, dis. 2, q. 1, art. 3.
> Cf. *Responsio ad F. Joann. Vercellens. de art. 108*, a. 1.

27. The Transcendental "One"

"One" . . . is used in two senses. In one way, inasmuch as it is convertible with being, and thus, every thing is one by its essence . . . and "one" does not add anything to being except only the intelligibility of "being undivided." In the second way, "one" is used, inasmuch as it signifies the intelligibility of the first measure, either simply, or in some genus.

> *Commentary on Aristotle's* Metaphysics, Bk. III, lect. 12 (ed. Cathala, No. 501).

For "one" which is convertible with being designates being itself, adding the intelligibility of indivision, which, since it is a negation or a privation, does not posit any nature added to being. And thus "one" in no way differs from being in reality, but only in intelligibility. For negation and privation are not beings in the real order, but beings of reason.

> *Commentary on Aristotle's* Metaphysics, Bk. IV, lect. 2 (ed. Cathala, No. 560).

He says, therefore, that "one" is said to be per se and per accidens. And he shows that we must consider the per accidens one primarily in singular terms, and this in two ways. In one way, there is a per accidens one, according as an accident is compared with a subject; in the other way, according as one accident is compared with another. In both cases, there are three things to consider: one composite, and two simple principles. For if we take the one per accidens according to the comparison of an accident to a subject, we have, for example: first, Coriscus, second, "musically-inclined," third, "the musically-inclined Coriscus." And these three are one per accidens, for "Coriscus" and "musically-inclined" are one in subject. Similarly, when we compare an accident to an accident, there are three things: of which the first is "musically-inclined," the second "just," the third, the "musically-inclined, just Coriscus." And these examples are said to be one per accidens, but in different ways.

For "just" and "musically-inclined," which are the two simple principles in the second way, are called "one per accidens," because they happen to one subject. But "musically-inclined" and "Coriscus," which are the two simple principles in the first way, are called one per accidens, because "one of them," that is, "musically-inclined," happens to the other, that is, Coriscus.

> Commentary on Aristotle's
> Metaphysics, Bk. V, lect. 7
> (ed. Cathala, Nos. 843–844).

28. The Transcendental "Good"

The good according to its proper intelligibility is a cause, in the way in which a goal is a cause. This is clear, because the good is that which all seek after. But that, to which an appetite [tendency] tends, is the end. Therefore, good, according to its proper intelligibility, is a cause after the manner of causing of an end.

> Commentary on Aristotle's
> Metaphysics, Bk. I, lect. 11
> (ed. Cathala, No. 179).

29. Evil Is a Privation

"Evil," like "white," can be said in two ways. For, in one way, when we say "white," we can understand "that which is the subject of whiteness"; in a second way, "white" is "that which is white inasmuch as it is white," that is, the accident itself. In like manner, "evil" can be understood in one way as "that which is the subject of evil," and this is something. In another way, we can understand "evil itself"; this is not anything, but is the privation of something good.

To see this, we must realize that good, properly speaking, is "something inasmuch as it is appetible"; for, according to the Philosopher (Ethics, Book I), those philosophers gave an excellent definition of *good* who said, "Good is that which all seek"; *evil*, however, is said to be "that which is opposed to good." Therefore, it is necessary that evil is that which is opposed to the appetible as such. That which is opposed to the appetible as such cannot be something, for three reasons: First, because the appetible is an end, and the order of ends is like the order of agents. For, if an agent is higher and more universal, the end for which it acts is a more universal good, for every agent acts for an end and for a good. . . . Since in efficient causes there is no infinite regress—for we must arrive at one first agent which is the universal cause of being—it is necessary that there is some universal good to which all other goods are ordered. The reason is that, since the appetible moves the appetite, and the first mover must be unmoved, the first and universal appetible must necessarily be the first and universal good, which does all things because of its love of itself. Consequently, as whatever there is in the real order must derive from the first and universal cause of being, so, whatever there is in the real order must derive from the first and universal good. But that which comes from the first and universal good can only be a particular good, just as what comes from the first and universal cause of being is some particular being. Therefore, whatever is something in the real order must necessarily be some particular good. But that which is good cannot, inasmuch as it is, be opposed to good. Hence, finally, evil, inasmuch as it is evil, cannot be something in the real order, but is the privation of some particular good, inhering in some particular good.

The second reason demonstrates the same truth. Whatever is in the real order has some inclination and tendency toward that which is suited to it. But that which is appetible is thereby good. Therefore, whatever is in the real order is proportioned to some good. Evil, however, as such is not proportioned to good but rather is opposed to it. Therefore, evil is not something in the real order. But even if evil were some thing, it would have no tendency, nor be the object of any tendency; hence, it would have no action or change, because nothing acts or is moved except on account of the appetite for some good.

The third reason leads to the same truth. Being itself most especially is that which is desired. That is why we find that every thing naturally tends to conserve its being, and avoids what destroys it, and resists destruction as it is able. Therefore, being itself, inasmuch as it is appetible, is good. Therefore, it is necessary that evil which is entirely opposed to good is also opposed to the very act of being. But that which is opposed to the act of being cannot be something. Hence, I conclude that that which is evil itself is not something; that to which evil happens is something, inasmuch as evil deprives its subject only of some particular good (just as blindness itself is not something, but that to which blindness happens is something).

De Malo, q. 1, art. 1.

PART TWO

NATURAL
THEOLOGY

X

The Existence of God

A. The nature and characteristics of natural theology

Having established the intrinsic structure of an existent or being, together with its general characteristics, and having seen what are its extrinsic proximate causes, we are ready to ask ourselves these final questions: does each being have an absolutely *first* or *uncaused* cause of its existing? How does a philosophical analysis of the beings of our experience establish such a cause, and what are its characteristics, and how is it related to man and the world?

It is with the asking of these questions that metaphysics becomes natural theology.

Natural theology, which is essentially the same science as metaphysics, treats of the existence and nature of God, insofar as these can be known through an understanding of created things.

A. STATE OF THE QUESTION

Before we begin our study of the existence and nature of God, it will be of great help to have some understanding of the nature of the science we want to acquire. What is natural theology? How does it differ from the other sciences? What are its peculiar characteristics? How, finally, does it proceed in its investigation of God? These are questions we will briefly answer in this section.

B. EXPLANATION OF TERMS

1) *"Natural theology . . ."* A "natural study of God" proceeds through the natural light of reason alone. In this science our un-

aided reason, through the understanding of material and sensible things to which it is naturally ordered and proportioned, is led to the understanding of a Being that is immaterial and supra-sensible, that is, the Infinite Being of God. Thus, natural theology is different entirely from revealed or sacred theology, where God himself reveals himself to man. Natural theology, beginning with creatures and our understanding of creatures, *ascends* to some understanding of God insofar as God is revealed in creatures. Thus, in natural theology God is treated only as the first cause of things, so that our knowledge of him is relative to our knowledge of creatures. Whereas in sacred theology we begin with God, and from an understanding of God for his own sake, we then *descend* to creatures and study them insofar as they have some relationship to God. And so in sacred theology God is studied absolutely and for himself, and creatures are studied relatively, that is, as ordered to God.

2) "*. . . is essentially the same science as metaphysics . . .*" This becomes clear once we realize that metaphysics, the science of being *as being*, can be considered in two ways. We can consider, for example, the *subject* of the science, which is *being as being*, and from this aspect of its subject matter, the science is properly called by its general name, *metaphysics*. Or this science can be considered from the point of view of the *principles or causes of its subject*. And from this point of view metaphysics has two names, since there are two kinds of principles or causes of its subject matter that are considered in this science: *incomplete* principles and *complete* principles. And insofar as metaphysics treats the incomplete principles of being, such as essence, *esse*, act, potency, substance, accident, and so forth, the science is aptly called *first philosophy*, since these principles are first principles or causes of being.

But in this science we also demonstrate the first *complete* principle of being as being, whose causality extends to all beings. And this first complete principle, entirely perfect and completely in act, is something separate in itself and divine. And therefore metaphysics, insofar as it demonstrates the existence and nature of this first complete principle is aptly called a *divine* science, or natural *theology*. And we conclude that since it belongs to one and the same science to treat of its subject matter and the causes or principles of that subject matter, it must follow that metaphysics and natural theology are essentially one and the same science.

3) *"Natural theology . . . treats of the existence and nature of God . . ."* These words tell us not only the difference between natural and sacred theology, but also give us the *formal subject* of natural theology. In sacred or revealed theology God *himself* is the subject of the science, the material subject being God and the formal subject *"as revealing himself to man."* But God cannot be the subject matter of any natural science, that is, something that is *directly given in nature* to be investigated and known. For God is not directly offered to our intellect (as he is through faith in sacred theology) as an object of understanding about which we can make predications and draw conclusions. Rather in the natural order, God is offered to our intellect as some *term* whose existence must be demonstrated through reason. Thus he is offered to our intellect only indirectly and mediately, not through himself but through creatures. So strictly speaking, God cannot be the subject of any natural science, but only a principle or cause of the subject.

God, therefore, is the subject of supernatural or revealed theology inasmuch as he is immediately and directly offered to our intellect through faith; but the subject of metaphysics is *being as being*, and God as the first complete principle of being as being is a principle of the subject of metaphysics. Nevertheless, once we have demonstrated the existence of this first cause, seeing this cause as Pure Act and Subsistent Being, we can treat God so considered as a sort of subject for a part of metaphysics, namely, natural theology. About God so considered, as an intelligibilty gained through creatures but properly refined by negation, analogy and eminence, we can make certain predications and further conclusions.

In this sense God is the material subject of our science of natural theology, and God as *first cause* is the formal subject of natural theology, that is, God insofar as he is revealed to us in his effects. The material *object* of natural theology are all those conclusions that our intellect is able to reach concerning such a cause. And, finally, the *formal* object are the premises or reasons why the intellect is able to make the conclusions; for example, such principles of demonstration as the principle of causality, finality, eminence, negation, analogy, and so forth; all of which principles arise from the evidence of being.

C. THE PROOF

1) *First part: Natural theology is a science:* (*a*) Because it proceeds from principles or premises to conclusions known through these principles. For example, from the principle of causality or finality we can conclude to the existence of God; from principles of negation and eminence, we can conclude to the simplicity and eternity of God; from the principle of causality and analogy, we can conclude to the fact that God has an intellect, a will, and so forth. (*b*) Because natural theology gives *certain* and *necessary* knowledge of God, and not merely probable knowledge or contingent knowledge. And the reason for this is that natural theology proceeds from principles or premises that are themselves necessary and certain, and so because of them we can conclude to truths about God that are necessary and certain. Further, the reason why these principles or premises are themselves certain and necessary is that they arise from our consideration of being *as being*, and not from being as *this being* or *that being*, or as *sensible* or *material*, but simply insofar as something is or exists—as it shares in the act of existence. Hence, insofar as these principles of demonstration arise from what is common to all existents, they can give science or scientific knowledge, knowledge that is certain and necessary.

2) *Second part: Natural theology is essentially the same science as metaphysics.* This is clear from the following argument: It is the nature of a science not only to treat of its subject matter but also of the causes or principles of its subject matter; because a science does not reach its perfection except through a knowledge of the causes or principles of its subject. For all scientific knowledge is a knowledge through causes. For example, the *philosophy of nature* does not merely treat of changeable being as changeable, which is the subject matter of the philosophy of nature. It also considers primary matter and substantial form, which are the causes or principles of changeable being. So, in like manner, *meta-*

physics does not merely treat of being as being, which is its subject matter, but also of act and potency, substance and accidents, essence and *esse*, and so forth, which are the causes or principles of being as being.

But as we have seen, causes or principles of a subject may be of two kinds: some that are merely incomplete causes, like *esse*, essence, and so on, and others which are in themselves complete natures and beings subsisting in their own right and in their own proper natures. For example, a father is a complete being in his own right as well as the cause of the being of his son. And just as it belongs to a science to treat of the incomplete principles of its subject matter, so too it belongs to that same science to treat the complete principles of its subject matter. For example, the philosophy of nature does not merely treat of the primary matter and substantial form of bodies here on earth, which are the incomplete principles of its changeable being, but also of such complete causes as the sun or stars, insofar as these influence or cause change in bodies here on earth. So, in like manner, metaphysics does not only consider *esse*, essence, substance, accidents, and so forth, but also God himself, who is the first complete principle of being as being. Therefore it is clear that metaphysics and natural theology are essentially the same science.

But that natural theology and metaphysics are in a certain sense, or accidentally, different is also obvious. Because only the first *complete* principle of being as being is divine. And the reason for this is that this principle is the most complete and most perfect act, removed from all matter and separate from all motion. Therefore, it belongs to such an act that it can in no way exist in matter or in motion. But the incomplete principles of being are sometimes found in matter and motion and sometimes not. And therefore it does not belong to them that they *must be* in matter or motion. Thus in themselves they are not divine things. Whence it follows that only in its demonstration of the existence and nature of the first complete principle is metaphysics a truly divine science, and not in its demonstration of the first incomplete principles. Thus there is an accidental difference between metaphysics and natural theology, although natural theology is an *essential* part of metaphysics.

3) *Third part: Natural theology treats of God in his existence
and nature insofar as these can be known from an understanding
of created things.* Because this science is a natural science, it proceeds from the natural light alone of human reason. Our human
intellect according to its nature is a power or faculty of our soul,
and this soul is the *natural form of our body.* And therefore just
as the soul itself is naturally ordered to the body, so this power
of our soul—our intellect—is naturally ordered to the understanding of *bodily* or material things. And our intellect understands these material things by abstracting their essences from
phantasms through the natural light of our agent intellect. Therefore our intellect cannot understand *immaterial* things, such as
God, except insofar as its understanding of material things can
lead it so such knowledge. So in natural theology God cannot be
known except from our understanding of created things, by
which understanding our intellect is lead to a *mediate* and *analogous* knowledge of God.

READINGS

St. Thomas, *The Division and Method of the Sciences,* translated
by Armand Maurer, O.S.B. (Toronto, Pontifical Institute of Medieval Studies, 1953), pp. 17–23, 46–66. *On the Truth of the Catholic
Faith,* translated by A. C. Pegis (New York, Hanover House, 1955),
Book One, pp. 59–78.

Etienne Gilson, *God and Philosophy* (New Haven, Yale University
Press, 1941), pp. 109–144. *The Christian Philosophy of St. Thomas
Aquinas* (New York, Random House, 1956), pp. 7–25.

Jacques Maritain, *The Philosophy of Nature* (New York, The Philosophical Library, 1951), pp. 73–89.

Joseph Owens, C.Ss.R., "Theodicy, Natural Theology, and Metaphysics," *The Modern Schoolman,* 30 (1951), 126–137.

SELECTED PASSAGE FROM ST. THOMAS AQUINAS

Since the notion of science consists in this, that from certain things
that are known other unknown things are understood, and since this
takes place concerning divine things, it is clear that there can be a
science concerning divine things. But the understanding of divine
things can be considered in two ways. First, from our side, and in
this way divine things are not knowable to us except through
creatures, for we receive their understanding through the senses.

The second way is from the nature of the divine things themselves. And thus taken in themselves they are the most knowable of all things. And although according to their own mode of being divine things are not known by us, nevertheless they are known by God and the blessed in heaven. Thus there is a twofold knowledge or science of divine things. One according to our way of knowing, which is to receive from sensible things principles with which to understand divine things, and in this way have the philosophers handed down to us the knowledge of divine things, calling first philosophy the divine science.

"The other is according to the manner of the divine things themselves, namely, that divine things themselves be grasped according to themselves; which indeed is impossible for us to do perfectly in this life. But there does take place in us in this life a certain participation in this knowledge, and a certain assimilation to God's knowledge, insofar, that is, as through faith that is infused in us, we adhere to the first truth itself for itself. And just as God, by the very fact that he knows himself, knows also other things in a manner peculiar to himself, that is, by a simple intuition and not by any discursive reasoning, so to, from the things which we know by faith by adhering to the first truth, we arrive at the knowledge of other things in a manner peculiar to ourselves, namely, by going from principles to conclusions. Whence those things which we hold by faith are for us as the first principles of this science, and the other things we know from them are as the conclusions of this science. From which it is clear that this science is of a higher nature than that divine science which the philosophers have studied, since it proceeds from higher principles."

Commentary on Boethius'
De Trinitate, qu. 2, a.2.

B. The nature and validity of *a posteriori* demonstration

The only valid demonstration for the existence of God is one that proceeds by way of *a posteriori* reasoning, beginning with the actual existence of the things of our experience.

A. STATEMENT OF THE QUESTION

In this section we will briefly point out how one must proceed in order to establish a valid proof for the existence of God. Only *a posteriori* reasoning is valid.

B. EXPLANATION OF TERMS

1) "... *a posteriori reasoning* ..." A valid argument for the existence of God must begin with the *existence* of things. The

demonstration itself consists in showing, through an analysis of their nature and operations, that these things are so many *effects* which immediately and necessarily demand the existence of a supreme Being as the only proper cause of their existence. And because our knowledge of these things is *prior* to our knowledge of the existence of God, this knowledge of things can be a true means or *medium* for demonstrating the existence of God. Therefore, this demonstration is rightly called *a posteriori*, because our knowledge of God's existence is *posterior* to our knowledge of the existence of things. The demonstration proceeds from things in the world known *as effects*, to God as their necessary *cause*. Therefore, the first step in the demonstration consists in understanding things in the world precisely as effects, and the second step consists in understanding that only a necessary Being, one here and now existing through his essence, can be the proper cause of the existence of these effects.

In the following section, the different *a posteriori* arguments themselves will be studied in detail. Here we wish to give a general description of any *a posteriori* argument. When the things existing in the world are understood to be changeable, imperfect, limited, and contingent in their existence, at that moment they are precisely understood as effects. That is to say, they are understood as having received their existence from another. This other is their cause, and their proper cause. Through a power proportioned to its own nature, it necessarily and immediately produces existence as its proper effect.

2) "... *only a posteriori reasoning is valid* ..." (*a*) Because the conclusion is only virtually and not actually in the premises. For we do not begin with the things in the world *as effects*, but only *as existing things*. They become known as effects through an analysis of their nature and operations. And once seen as effects, the intellect sees that they have a necessary relation to a cause.

(*b*) Because the knowledge of the conclusion follows the knowledge of the premises. Here the logical order, or order of demonstration, is just the reverse of the ontological order, or order of being. Ontologically, God is prior to creatures, since creatures receive their being from him. But in our demonstration, which takes place in the logical order, our knowledge of creatures is prior to our knowledge of God. Hence, our demonstration is valid, for God is *known* through creatures, and not through himself, although God *exists* through himself, and all creatures exist through God.

(*c*) Because we necessarily conclude to a necessary Being. Although we reason from contingent things (creatures), their very contingency necessarily relates them to a Being that is not contingent.

3) *The nature of this demonstration of God's existence.* The movement of our reason from the existence of the things in this world to the affirmation of the existence of God, is a complex one and demands at least some explanation.

First, the intellect grasps some self-evident fact, for example, "this thing is moving," or "this thing is more perfect than that." This self-evident fact constitutes the point of departure for further reasoning.

Secondly, the intellect understands something new about this thing it has grasped, for example, that "that which is moving is being moved by another," or that "the being which is more perfect than the other, is really 'approaching' a most perfect Being." This new knowledge constitutes a true *conclusion* for our intellect, and is grounded in evidence found in the "moving being itself," in the "more perfect being itself." This point will be made clearer when we study the different arguments.

Having made this second judgment (for example, whatever is moved is moved by another), the intellect now proceeds to a new conclusion (third step). This conclusion is made in the light of the principle of non-contradiction, as was also the second judgment. This new (third) conclusion is that one cannot proceed indefinitely (*ad infinitum*) in beings that are moved by another. For the intellect positively sees that such a procedure is self-contradicting. Because in such a procedure there is no *first* mover, and hence no intermediary movers (moved movers) that have received their motion. And in understanding that we cannot proceed "into infinity" is moved movers, we see that there must be a first unmoved mover. We see that God must exist.

This process of arriving at the existence of God can be called

intellective induction, because the necessity of the truth so affirmed is really *seen* by the intellect. But also in the process *strict
reasoning* is involved, since one or more middle terms are used
in arriving at our conclusion. Finally, and obviously, this process
is *inductive* throughout, for we do not proceed from a more universal truth to a less universal one (as is done in deduction), but
rather from a particular existent to a necessary truth.

<h4 style="text-align:center">READINGS</h4>

Etienne Gilson, *The Christian Philosophy of St. Thomas Aquinas*
(New York, Random House, 1956), "Existence and Reality," pp.
29–45. These pages are practically indispensable for an understand-
ing of St. Thomas's doctrine of being. *Being and Some Philosophers*
(Toronto, Pontifical Institute of Mediaeval Studies, 1949), Chapter
V, "Being and Existence," pp. 154–189.

Joseph Owens, "A Note on the Approach to Thomistic Metaphysics," *New Scholasticism*, 28 (1954), 454–476. "A Note on the
Intelligibility of Being," *Gregorianum*, 36 (1955), 169–193.

Norris Clarke, "What Is the Really Real?" in *Progress in Philosophy* (Milwaukee, Bruce Publishing Company, 1955), pp. 61–90.

XI

Proofs for the Existence of God

A. The first way: proof from the existence of motion

1. STATEMENT OF THE PROBLEM

In this first way we begin with an evident fact of both internal and external experience: the fact that there is motion in the world, that the things of our experience undergo change. For example, the youth becomes the man, the seed blossoms into flower and the flower into fruit; things change their size, their colors, their shape. Motion or change, the losing of one perfection and the gaining of another, is a simple, undeniable fact of human experience and knowledge. The problem of the First Way, therefore, can be stated as follows: Given this fact that here and now something is undergoing motion or change, can the human reason conclude to the existence of something that is here and now the first cause of this motion or change, but which itself undergoes no change whatsoever, a first unmoved mover that is God?

2. THE SOLUTION

The first step in our solution is to understand what we mean by motion. By motion or change we understand a transition from potency to act, the acquiring of any new perfection in any way. Hence we include the following kinds of motion or change. First of all, local motion. This is the most obvious of motions, but by no means the only kind. Secondly, we include here accidental changes in both qualities and quantity; for example, when an object becomes hotter or redder, or bigger or smaller. Thirdly, we include substantial change, the motion or mutation of one substance into another; for example, the changing of food into living human tissues. Fourthly, we include the immanent activities of cognition and appetition, like seeing, understanding, willing, and so forth. While the act of understanding or the act of willing are not in themselves motion, the intellect or the will cannot acquire these perfections without undergoing some change. In reaching their respective terms, the intellect in knowing truth and the will in desiring good go from potency to act. In this sense, these acts are real changes for man. But in themselves, as understanding and willing, they are the act of a being in act, and thus are not motion, which is the act of a being in potency insofar as it is in potency.

3. WHATEVER IS CHANGED IS CHANGED BY ANOTHER

Granted the fact of change in the world, we are now ready to argue from this fact as follows: things change. But nothing changes itself. Therefore, whatever is changed must be changed by another. Let us see now why this is so.

Change or motion is a transition from potency to act. A piece of marble takes the shape of a statue beneath the strokes of the sculptor. My hand, which was cold, feels itself becoming warm beneath the rays of the sun. And so I say the sculptor produces the statue, the sun warms my hand. In the face of the myriad changes that take place around us, the intellect makes this affirmation concerning them: they are brought into being by an agent that is distinct from the change. Why? Because nothing is moved from potency to act except by a being already in act. And this is true because no being can give to another or to itself a perfection it does not possess.

Take a very simple example. I have a glass of cold water. It is actually cold, but potentially hot, since it can become hot. Now if the glass of water is heated, it must be heated by something besides itself, for it must be heated by something that actually possesses heat. To say that cold water can make itself hot is to deny the principle of contradiction. [1] For at one and the same time the water would have to be actually hot, since nothing gives what it does not have, and actually cold, since it is being moved from cold to hot. But to say that a glass of water is at one and the same time actually hot and actually cold is to say that it is cold and is not cold, that this perfection exists and does not exist at the same time. And this is an evident contradiction in being.

Therefore, we see that it is impossible for any being to move itself from potency to act. For this would mean that at one and the same time it has and has not the perfection involved. Thus anything that is moved from potency to act, as takes place in every change, must be moved or changed by another, by some being already in act.

We can formulate our direct experience of change into a proposition that has the force and validity of a universal principle: nothing is moved from potency to act except by a being already in act. To act means to be in act. To be acted upon (to be changed) means to be in potency. And since nothing can be in act and in potency at the same time, as regards the same perfection, it follows that nothing can move itself from potency to act. Nothing can be the cause of its own change. If it is changed, it is changed by another.

4. IN THINGS THAT ARE CHANGED BY ANOTHER AN INFINITE REGRESS IS IMPOSSIBLE

This brings us to our third step. In this step we argue as follows: If something is being moved here and now by something else, and this something else that moves is itself being moved by a third mover and the third by a fourth, and so on, either we must come to a first mover that is itself entirely unmoved, or the motion here and now existing is unintelligible. That is to say, there cannot be an infinite regress in an ordered series of moved movers. Why this is so is easy to understand. In such a series, each thing that is moved is moved by another. For example, the chisel is moved

[1] Our example of hot and cold water is taken from St. Thomas who thought that cold, as well as heat, was a positive quality. We know that cold is only the absence of heat. Thus water can lose its heat (i.e., become cold) "of itself." But the point of the example is that water cannot heat itself.

by the hand, the hand by the nerves, the nerves by the will, the will by the soul, the soul by that being from which it has received its nature, and which is keeping that nature in existence. Now in such an ordered series, if any one of the movers is removed, the motion of the chisel immediately stops. If the soul or the will or the nerves or the hand stops moving, the motion of the chisel ceases at once.

It is clear, then, that such a series cannot be infinite. For then, by supposition, there would be no first mover, and hence no motion here and now. An infinite series would render the existing motion unintelligible. All these infinite moved movers would have received their motion, but since there is no first mover, the *whole series* is one of received motion. And this is   contradiction. For such a motion would at one and the same time be received, since it has come from some other, and not received, since there is no first from which it originated. There would be no reason why any motion would be here and now existing. But since motion or change does so exist, we must conclude that there is a first unmoved mover, a mover that gives motion, but in no way receives it, a Being, therefore, that is in no way in potency to change, but is simply in act. Here is how St. Thomas puts the matter:

> In movers and moved things that are ordered, where one, namely, is moved in order by another, it is necessary that if the first mover is removed or ceases from moving, none of the others will either move or be moved. And this is so because the first is the cause of the moving for all the others. But if there are ordered movers and moved things into infinity, there will not be any first mover, but all will be as intermediate movers. And so none of them will be able to be moved. And thus nothing will be moved in the world.[2]

And so we can conclude that in an ordered series of moved movers, that is to say, in a series where each mover receives its power to move from another, either the series must be finite, or if it is infinite, there must be some mover outside this series, upon which mover the movement of the whole series depends. An infinite series of movers, all of which have received their motion, is unintelligible without a first from whom they have received it.

[2] *Contra Gentiles*, Bk. 1, Ch. 13.

5. This first unmoved mover is pure act or God

Once the mind has seen the necessity of positing a first unmoved mover, it has already concluded to the existence of God. For such a mover must needs be a pure act of subsistent Being, a Being in which there is no potency whatsover. For we have seen that in the order of being, something moves or acts insofar as it is in act, and something is moved or acted upon insofar as it is in potency. Now insofar as the first mover moves another, it is in act. But if this Being were any way in potency, to that extent it would not be in act, but able to receive act. Thus it would be movable, able to receive motion or perfection, and to that extent it would not be first, but would be ordered to something higher or more perfect than itself. Thus the first unmoved mover is in no way movable, exists in no way in potency, but is the pure acuality of subsistent Being. And this is God. In our proof we have considered motion as any change in being. In this unmoved mover there is, therefore, no potency for any change in being. Thus the Being of this first mover has not been received. It is by its very nature. Its nature is Being.

6. Answering the objections

This "first way" of St. Thomas has been strongly objected to by philosophers of all kinds. It is to the answering of these objections that we must now turn our attention. First of all, living things move themselves, and so are the cause of their own motion. Thus a living thing would be itself a first unmoved mover. But since such things are obviously not God, the first way is clearly inconclusive. Again, according to modern physics, a moving body tends to remain in motion unless impeded by some other body. Thus such a body needs no cause of its motion, but rather of its cessation of motion. Finally, reciprocal causality would seem sufficient to explain the changes we experience. For example, I desire to paint a picture. The good of the object desired, that is, the picture to be painted, is enough to move my will. And my will, so moved, can move my hands to actually paint the picture. In none of these cases does it seem either necessary or possible to conclude to the existence of a first unmoved mover because of the existence of motion or change in the world.

To the objection that a living thing moves itself, we answer that it does so only because it is moved by another. A little reflection will make this clear. I get up and walk across the room. I am moving myself. Before "I exerted myself," I was not moving, I did not actually have the perfection I have now. Thus, even a living being cannot be in act and potency at the same time regarding the same perfection. A living being like man is a composite being, consisting of many principles or "parts" of being, so that one part can move another part, but no part can move itself, no part can give to itself a perfection it does not have.

And so I conclude that before I walked across the room, as a living being I had the active power or potency to walk across, not merely the passive potency to be moved across the room, like a stone. One part of me moved another. My will moved the nerves in my legs and they moved my legs, and my legs moved the rest of my body. But what moved my will? In the order of final causality, it was my desire to open the window and let in some fresh air. But in this first way we are interested in the adequate efficient causality of a given motion. And so I must repeat my question: Whence comes the efficacy of the will to move my locomotive faculties? From itself, in the sense that being a free will, it has power to "move itself"; but also from another, in the sense that this power to move itself it has received from another. And independently of this other it cannot move either itself or anything else. The will, being an accident, is immediately and directly dependent upon the substantial being of the soul, because of which being the will itself is and acts, and without which the will could neither inexist nor act.

But the soul of man itself has "come into being," it has received its existence from another. And just as the soul has received a share in being, it has also received a share in the activity that follows upon being.[3] Hence the soul has not of itself either the source of its being or of its activity; it has received its power to be and its power to act from another. So we concluded that, just

[3] See St. Thomas, *Summa Theologiae*, I, 115, 1. "For according as something is participated, it is also necessary that that, too, is participated which is proper to this thing; for example, just as that which participates in light, also participates in the perfection of being visible. Now to act, which is nothing else than to put something in act, is *per se* proper to act as act."

as the soul itself must be here and now existing and "holding in being" its powers of will and intellect, so, too, there must be here and now existing in the soul and "holding it in being," the first unmoved mover, "moving" the soul to its being and to its being-a-mover.[4]

St. Thomas answers this objection about living beings moving themselves as follows:

When it is said that something moves itself, the same being is considered as both moving and moved. When, however, it is said that something is moved by another, one thing is considered as mover and another thing as being moved. Now it is clear that when something moves another, the fact that it is moving another does not mean that it is the first mover. Whence to say that something moves another does not exclude the fact that it itself may be moved by another and have from this other the fact that it is a mover. So, in like manner, when something moves itself, this does not exclude the fact that it may be moved by another and have from this other the power to move itself.[5]

Our second objection concerned the principle of inertia and the First Newtonian Law of Motion: "Every body continues in a state of rest, or of uniform motion in a straight line, unless it is compelled to change that state by forces impressed upon it." And the objection was as follows: Since a body in motion, if unimpeded, remains indefinitely in motion, the philosophical principle that governs the first way, "Whatever is moved is moved by another," is false.

Our answer is that this law of inertia, even granted its complete validity as a principle of physics, in no way contravenes the metaphysical principle that whatever is moved from potency to act is moved by a being already in act. For physics is here treating motion and rest as two states. The body is considered as already in motion, or already at rest, and not as a body that begins to move or comes to a rest. Whereas the philosopher wants to know, why did this body begin to move? Whence came its power to move in the first place? And even while the body is in a state of motion, if that motion is accelerated, the law of inertia itself demands that this acceleration come from some extrinsic force. Thus

[4] See St. Thomas, *In I Sent.*, d. 36, q. 1, a. 1; *C.G.*, Bk. III, Ch. 66 and 67; *De Pot.*, qu. 3, a. 7.

[5] *De Malo*, qu. 3, a. 2, ad 4m.

our principle, "Whatever is moved is moved by another," remains a true assertion and is even, at the level of the phenomenon of local motion, verified in a certain sense by the law of inertia.[6]

Our third objection stated that the fact of reciprocal causality is sufficient to explain adequately the existence of any given motion. One object is the final cause of the motion, and then the mover, thus "finalized," exercises its efficient causality. Our answer to this is that in any transition from potency to act, final causes are indeed involved, and even material and formal causes. Moreover, as we shall see in the second way, there cannot be an infinite regress in these kinds of causality either. But the only cause of motion we are directly concerned with in the first way is the efficient cause. Even as inclined to act, even when I desire, for example, to kick a stone, I must exercise my power of moving. Whence comes this power? From myself or from another? That is the question. Our philosophical problem of moved movers here is explicitly one of a series of efficient causes alone. Final causes might indeed explain why the agent acts in this way rather than that, or even why the agent acts at all, rather than not acts. But a final cause cannot explain the efficiency itself of the agent.

7. SUMMARY OF THE FIRST WAY

"From the existence of motion in the world, the existence of God can be demonstrated under the aspect of a first unmoved mover."

A. PRENOTE

This first way of St. Thomas proceeds from the following fact of both internal and external experience: that things are changing

---

[6] Notice, too, that the atomic theory which states that within the atom the particles called electrons are continually revolving around the nucleus, no matter how this theory is understood to express the mass-energy aspects of material reality, it in no way contradicts the philosophical truth that whatever is moved must be moved by another. Again, the scientist finds matter in motion; but it hardly follows from this that therefore matter puts itself in motion. No more than to find something existing means that this thing has caused its own existence. Matter needs to be conserved in motion just as much as it needs to be conserved in being. If matter is in motion it is because it has been created in motion and the first unmoved mover is here and now the ultimate cause of that motion. See Jacques Maritain, *Approaches to God* (New York, Harper & Brothers, 1954), pp. 26–29.

and moving in the world about us. For example, I see bodies moving from one place to another, I see living things growing, changing their color, their shapes, and so on. Now the intellect, understanding that things are being changed or moved, looks for the source of this motion. This source cannot be the being itself that is being moved. For then this being would be the mover and the thing moved at the same time and as regarding the same perfection. Thus this being that is moved must be moved by another. But what about this other? Is it the source of its own motion, or is it being moved by another in order to move something else? Reflecting on such a series of moved movers, the intellect sees that there must be a first unmoved mover, or else the efficiency of the moved movers and, therefore, the actuality of the motion itself, is unintelligible. In this way the intellect sees the necessity of positing a first unmoved mover to explain the actuality of any given motion it experiences. And this first unmoved mover is God.

B. EXPLANATION OF TERMS

1) *"From the existence of motion . . ."* Thus, in this first way, we proceed from the existence, not the nature, of motion. We consider motion as a passage from one state of being to another, and we consider that passage insofar as it shares in some way in the actuality of existence. That is to say, we consider a being changing (in some way) in its existence, and insofar as it is so changing.

2) *". . . motion . . ."* Any passage from being in potency to being in act. Thus, motion here includes: (*a*) all accidental changes: a change in a being according to place, or quantity, or quality, and so forth; (*b*) all substantial changes, as when, for example, non-living being becomes living being, and vice versa; (*c*) the acquirement of any new perfection, like willing or understanding, even though these are not the act of a being in potency, but the act of a being in act.

3) *". . . the existence of God is demonstrated . . ."* Insofar as the very actuality of this change could not exist, unless there also existed some first unmoved mover as the only adequate existential source of the change, and from whom all moved movers receive the power of moving others.

4) *". . . under the aspect of a first unmoved mover . . ."* In this

first way the existence of God is affirmed as a necessary term for the understanding of the existence of motion in the world. Hence God in this way is seen precisely as the first cause of change, as a Being that can move others, but is himself incapable of undergoing any change.

C. OPINIONS DENYING OUR POSITION

1) *The Eleatics*—for example, Parmenides and Zeno. This school of philosophy denied the very reality of change, calling it an illusion. The real was immobile, unchanging being. That change is an illusion is easy to prove. For a being to change means that it becomes other than it is. A man is ignorant; then he becomes a philosopher. He is now other than he was before the change. But where does the change come from? Either the change was already there or it was not. If it was already there, there has been no change. If it was not there, then change has come from non-being. But from non-being, nothing comes. Hence the obvious conclusion: all change is impossible. Change is simply an illusion of the senses. The only thing that exists is being, unchanging and immobile.

The answer to the Eleatics and their dilemma was first given by Aristotle. What becomes does not become from non-being nor from being in act, but from being in potency. When water becomes hot, the change is not from hot water (for then there would be no change), nor from the water as cold, but from the water as capable of becoming hot—given, of course, the actual heat of an extrinsic agent.

2) *The Ionians*—for example, Heraclitus; also Bergson and others. This school goes to the opposite extreme and says that the only reality is motion or becoming itself. It is being that is the illusion. Reality is a mighty river of flux, and just as a man cannot step twice into the same river (for the waters have already passed downstream), so the mind cannot enter into the flux of becoming. For by the time it has grasped a thing in order to judge it, that thing has already changed. Being is the stabilizing and solidifying (and thus falsifying) work of the intellect. So there can be no first unmoved mover, since immobile being is an impossibility.

This position goes against our experience of motion. For man, with his senses and intellect, never grasps motion as such, but always something that moves. We do not experience change, we experience something changing. Motion is always the motion of something. A ball is moved; water is heated. Motion without a subject that is moved is as unintelligible as thought without someone who thinks, or existence without something that exists.

D. PROOF

It is certain and evident to our senses, that in the world some things are in motion. Now whatever is moved is moved by another, for nothing can be moved except it is in potentiality to that towards which it is moved; whereas a thing moves inasmuch as it is in act. For motion is nothing else than the reduction of something from potentiality to actuality. But nothing can be reduced from potentiality to actuality, except by something in the state of actuality. Thus that which is actually hot, as fire, makes wood, which is potentially hot, to be actually hot, and thereby moves and changes it. Now it is not possible that the same thing should be at once in actuality and potentiality in the same respect, but only in different respects. For what is actually hot cannot simultaneously be potentially hot; but it is simultaneously potentially cold. It is therefore impossible that in the same respect and in the same way a thing should be both moved and mover, i.e., that it should move itself. Therefore, whatever is moved must be moved by another, and that by another again. But this cannot go on into infinity, because then there would be no first mover, and, consequently, no other mover, seeing that subsequent movers move only inasmuch as they are moved by the first mover, as the staff moves only because it is moved by the hand. Therefore it is necessary to arrive at a first mover, moved by no other; and this everyone understands to be God.[7]

B. The second way: proof from the existence of efficient causes

1. STATEMENT OF THE PROBLEM

The problem of the second way can be stated as follows. Granted that it is evident through internal and external experience that there does exist in the activity of beings ordered efficient causes, can the mind conclude from this fact to a first uncaused cause, which as first and as uncaused would be God?

[7] St. Thomas, *Summa Theologiae*, I, 2, 3. Translated by A. Pegis, *The Basic Writings of St. Thomas* (New York, Random House, 1945), p. 22.

2. The solution

A. STEP ONE: EFFICIENT CAUSES ESSENTIALLY AND ACCIDENTALLY ORDERED

Having already established in Chapter 3 the nature and the origin of the principle of causality, the first step in our solution consists in knowing precisely what is meant by a series of *per se* subordinated efficient causes, and how such a series differs from that of a *per accidens* ordered series.[8]

Causes can be ordered in two ways. One way is *per se,* or essentially, and the other *per accidens,* or accidentally. Causes are ordered *per se* whenever the virtue of the first cause influences the ultimate effect produced through the intermediary causes; when the causal influx of the first cause reaches to the ultimate effect through the other causes. For example, the art of a craftsman moves his hands, and his hands move the hammer, and the hammer moves the chisel, and the chisel moves (that is to say, forms) the statue, which is the ultimate effect. In this series of causes, the causal influx of the art-skill reaches the ultimate effect (the statue) through the other causes (the hands, the hammer, the chisel, and so forth). Here is the explanation of St. Thomas:

. . . two things may be considered in every agent, namely, the thing itself that acts, and the power whereby it acts. Thus fire by its heat makes a thing hot. Now the power of the lower agent depends upon the power of the higher agent, in so far as the higher agent gives the lower agent the power whereby it acts, or preserves that power, or applies it to action. Thus the craftsman applies the instrument to its proper effect, although sometimes he does not give the instrument the form whereby it acts, nor preserves that form, but merely puts it into motion. Consequently, the action of the lower agent must not only proceed from the lower agent through the agent's own power, but also through the power of all the higher agents, for it acts by the power of them all. Now just as the lowest agent is found to be immediately active, so the power of the first agent is found to be immediate in the production of the effect; because the power of the lowest agent does not of itself produce this effect, but by the power of the proximate higher agent, and this by the power of a yet higher

---

[8] Here we shall follow the doctrine of St. Thomas as set forth in his commentary on the *Liber de Causis,* lecture one.

agent, so that the power of the supreme agent is found to produce its effect of itself, as though it were the immediate cause.[9]

On the other hand, in a series of *per accidens* ordered causes, the causal influx reaches down not to the ultimate effect, but only to the proximate effect. The fact that this proximate effect itself causes some other effect is not due to the causal influx of the first cause in this series. As St. Thomas says, it is *praeter intentionem*,[10] outside the influence of the first efficient cause. Let us take a simple example of *per accidens* order causes to bring out this point. Suppose I light a candle with a match. The fact that this candle is then used to light another candle, and this second candle a third candle, and so on, is obviously outside the influx of the first efficient cause, that is, the match that lit the first candle. In this series of one candle lighting another, the influence of the first cause extends only to the proximate effect (the first candle as lit) but not to the ultimate effect (the last candle as lit). Since this last effect is outside the influence of the first cause, this series of causes is ordered only accidentally, for what is beyond the virtue of a cause is *per accidens*.

B. STEP TWO: GENERAL CHARACTERISTICS OF A PER SE ORDERED SERIES OF EFFICIENT CAUSES

The essential note of a series of *per se* ordered efficient causes is that the influx of the first cause extends to the production of the ultimate effect, through the instrumentality of intermediate causes. Let us now reflect upon some of the other features of such a series of causes.

First of all, whenever a new effect is produced in the material universe, all four causes, material, formal, efficient, and final, are simultaneously and actually exercising their proper causality. For example, an agent of itself may be indifferently disposed to any number of particular effects. If it is to act, it must act in a particular way, which means that the action is directed toward a particular end or effect. Just as a final cause is not actually causing unless it is actually influencing the agent to a particular end, so

[9] *Contra Gentiles*, Bk. III, Ch. 70.
[10] "*Intentio*" here is not the English "intention," but rather "influx" or "influence."

the agent is not exercising its causality unless it is actually influenced by the final cause. There is no efficiency without finality,
and there is no finality without efficiency. The final cause is not
a cause in act unless it is actually being desired by the agent.
Hence there is an essential ordering between these two causes,
final and efficient, so that if the causality of the one ceases, the
causality of the other also and simultaneously ceases.

What is true of final and efficient causes, holds also for formal
and material causes. Every new production of being involves an
eduction of some form, accidental or substantial. If any perfection is to be, it must be the perfection of something. Hence the
activity of the agent consists directly in educing a form from
matter. Obviously, the causality of form cannot be present without the simultaneous causality of matter; forms are educed from
matter.[11] That both matter and form are simultaneously required
for the existence of any finite material thing is evident from the
fact that they constitute the very intrinsic composition of the
effect itself. Hence, in any given production of an effect, in any
new coming into being, these four causes are simultaneously, actually, and in a *per se* order, exercising their proper causality.

Another thing to notice in any essentially (*per se*) ordered
causes is this: not only is the causality of the four causes properly
and simultaneously exercised in the production of the effect, but
it is also exercised in the conservation of the effect—in keeping
the effect in existence. A being cannot remain in existence unless
its matter and form be continually actualized, unless the *esse* of
the form and of the matter perdures. But this *esse* itself was
produced, either substantially or accidentally, through the eduction of a form from matter, and this eduction was achieved
through the efficiency of the agent. The *esse* or existence of the
effect is a produced or caused *esse*. As such it continually needs
the presence and influx of its proper cause.

Let us take a simple example to bring out this important fact.
A sculptor like Michelangelo, through his art, his hands, his
hammer and chisel—a whole series of *per se* ordered efficient
causes—brings into being the form of a statue, for example, the
statue of Moses. But Michelangelo has been dead for four hun-

[11] Or, as is the case with the human soul, created in matter.

dred years and the statue continues in existence. Why? The existence of the accidental form of the statue (the figure of Moses) perdures because of the continued existence of the marble. And the existence of the marble perdures because of the continued existence of the ultimate constituents of marble, whatever they may be.

But what about these constituents themselves? They are not their own existence as we shall see in the third way. Their existence is limited by their form and their matter; hence it is a received and thus caused existence. Therefore, there must be continually present the proper efficient cause of their existence. Not just the material cause of their existence, which is prime matter; nor the limiting cause of their existence, which is their substantial form; but also the efficient cause of their existence, the continual influx of an activity that keeps outside nothingness the received "to be" that actuates the substantial principles of the being. There may indeed be instrumental conservative causes, even instrumental conservative efficient causes, of the existence of an effect, but these are all *per se* ordered to the all-pervading activity of the one unique proper cause of existence, namely, the activity of a Being who is its own existence and is the first efficient cause of all beings and the activity of beings.

C. STEP THREE: SPECIAL CHARACTERISTICS OF A SERIES OF PER SE
   ORDERED EFFICIENT CAUSES

There are four special characteristics of such a series:

1) *From the very nature of the series,* all the efficient causes are required here and now, and in act, for the production of the effect. If any one of the causes is removed, the activity of the whole series immediately ceases. This follows from the fact that the causal influx of the first uncaused cause reaches down to the ultimate effect through all the intermediary causes, and not just through some of them. There is an essentially subordinated co-operation in the production of the effect; even the intermediary causes are subordinated one to another.

2) *The second special characteristic* flows from the first; namely while all the causes involved are efficient causes, each one is of a different nature or species; for example, in writing, the chalk

is a different nature from the hand. If these causes were of the same nature, one could do what the other does, and so we would not have to have many causes to produce the same effect. If the hand could do precisely what the chalk does, we would not have to use the chalk.

3) *The third characteristic is this*: Not only must all these causes be in act, but they must be in simultaneous act. There is no succession in time but only a subordination in causality. Here and now, at the instant the effect is being produced or maintained in existence, we have the first uncaused cause actually producing the effect through the instrumentality of all the intermediary causes. And these intermediary causes act as one single cause, since they all share in one single operation.

4) *This brings us to our fourth special trait*: In the activity of *per se* ordered efficient causes, there is question of only one single operation, one single causal influx in which all the efficient causes share according to their nature, forming therefore one causal principle from which this activity proceeds and which terminates in the same ultimate effect. There is, for example, only one operation by which God moves the will, the will moves the hand, the hand moves the chalk, and the chalk produces the lines on the blackboard. If there were many operations there would be many terms, and the effect would not be one but many. Of course, in the operation by which God operates, moving a nature, nature does not share; for the operation by which God operates is the divine substance. But the very operation of the nature is also the operation of the power of the first cause. Here is the way St. Thomas puts it:

. . . in the operation by which God operates, moving a nature, the nature itself does not operate; but the operation itself of the nature is also the operation of the divine power, just as the operation of an instrument is through the power of the principal agent. Nor is there any difficulty in God and nature producing the same effect, and this because of the order that exists between God and nature.[12]

[12] *De Pot.*, qu. 3, a. 7, ad 3m. Later on, in our treatment of creation, we will discuss in detail the mysterious nature of divine causality. But here we can mention, briefly, three things: 1) the divine operation as formally immanent; 2) that same operation as virtually transient; and 3) the effect of this virtual transient operation of God. As formally immanent, the divine

To repeat: There is one single causal influx shared in or received by many agents, whether these agents are complete beings, or simply different potencies or powers of the same being. This influence is received from the higher cause by the lower and according to the nature of the lower. Two important facts follow from this: first, that the lower cause, for example, the piece of chalk, acts through the power of the higher cause, since it has received the action of the higher or principal cause; and secondly, the lower or instrumental cause gives something proper of its own in the production of the ultimate effect, since it receives the influence of the higher cause according to its (the instrument's) own nature, thus limiting and determining this influence according to its own nature. The writing of a piece of chalk is different, for example, from the writing of a pen. Here are two texts from St. Thomas explaining these points:

It is possible, however, for something to participate in the proper action of another, not by its own power, but instrumentally, inasmuch as it acts by the power of another; as air can heat and ignite by the power of fire. . . . (And) the secondary instrumental cause does not share in the action of the superior cause, except inasmuch as by something proper to itself it acts dispositively in relation to the effect of the principal agent. If therefore it produced nothing by means of what is proper to itself, it would be set to work in vain; nor would there be any need for us to use special instruments for special actions. Thus we see that a saw, in cutting wood, which it does by the property of its own form, produces the form of a bench, which is the proper effect of the principal agent.[13]

Every instrumental agent executes the action of the principal agent by some action proper and connatural to itself; just as the natural

---

operation is identified with the divine substance. Hence, it is eternal, immutable, transcendent. As virtually transient, this same operation is *intentional*. It is a power or influx productive of effects. Under this aspect, the power of God looks outward, and is considered as a certain intention that produces an effect. Finally, the effect produced is the created being itself, or its operation, or the effect of its operation. St. Thomas (*De Pot.*, qu. 3, a. 7 ad 7m) gives an example to illustrate this divine causality. The colors that I see on the wall are also in the air, else I could not see them. I say the colors have formal existence in the wall and intentional existence in the air. So, in an analogous fashion, the divine power is formally in God (and is God), but intentionally (as an influx) in the creature. We should remember that this is only an example, and all examples are necessarily defective when applied to God.

[13] *Summa Theologiae*, I, 45, 5.

heat of the body generates flesh by dissolving and digesting, and a saw produces the perfection of the bench by cutting.[14]

D. STEP FOUR: WHY THERE CANNOT BE AN INFINITE REGRESS IN PER SE ORDERED EFFICIENT CAUSES

From the very nature of *per se* ordered efficient causes, it is easy to see why there cannot be an infinite regress in such a series. For an infinite regress means, by supposition, not to have a first cause. But if there is no first efficient cause, then neither can there be any ultimate effect. And the reason why there can be no ultimate effect is that there would be no causal influx which produced the effect. Why this is so becomes clear when we recall two facts about such a series. First, all the causes of the series are in act, in simultaneous act, and here and now actually producing the effect, either bringing it into being or keeping it in being. Secondly, each cause is essentially ordered to the cause above it, because it is here and now receiving from the cause above it the power by which it operates as cause. Now if we were to proceed infinitely in causes that receive their causality from another, we would always be dealing with causes that are intermediate, causes that are moved to their causality. Hence to say there is no first cause is to affirm and deny being at the same time. For on the one hand we affirm that all these intermediate causes have received an influence from another, and on the other hand we say they have not received it, since we deny there is a first from which they have received it. Since, *de facto*, the ultimate effect does exist, then *de iure*, there must exist a first cause which does not receive influence from another but is the cause of the influence received in those intermediary causes. Hence the necessity of positing a first uncaused cause.[15]

3. ANSWERING THE OBJECTIONS

First objection. It seems impossible to conclude to the existence of God as the first uncaused cause. This conclusion is based upon

---

[14] *Contra Gentiles*, Bk. II, Ch. 21, par. 7.

[15] The following texts from St. Thomas clearly demonstrates the point we are trying to make:

    (1) *In II Metaph.*, lect. 3, nos. 302, 303, 304.

    (2) *Contra Gentiles*, I, Ch. 13, second paragraph from end.

    (3) *Summa Theologiae*, I, 46, 2, ad 7m.

the principle of causality, and the principle of causality flows from a particular contingent sensible fact—for example, the sun is heating my hand. Now it is quite impossible, as well as quite illogical, to use a principle based upon a particular, contingent, sensible fact, to conclude to a universal, necessary, suprasensible term. Contingency cannot give rise to necessity. A principle that flows from sensible phenomena is valid only when applied to sensible phenomena. Hence this second way of St. Thomas is quite impossible as well as completely illogical.

We answer: The principal of causality does not have its origin in sensible beings insofar as they are sensible, but insofar as they are or exist. Thus this principle is founded in being as such and its application is valid beyond mere sensible being. Moreover, although this principle originates from contingent beings, there is in these beings some necessity; namely, these contingent beings have a *necessary relation* to a cause. Therefore, by applying this principle of causality, we are able to posit God as a first cause.

Second objection. If the world is eternal, there is no reason why a series of efficient causes could not be infinite. But philosophy cannot prove with certitude that the world is not eternal. Therefore, neither can it prove with certitude that there exists a first efficient cause.

We answer that even if the world were eternal, an infinite series of essentially ordered efficient causes would still be a contradiction. Because in causes so ordered, the power of the first cause extends itself to the ultimate effect. And therefore without this power neither the ultimate effect can be produced, nor are the intermediary causes able to act. The question of the eternity or non-eternity of the world does not touch our argument, since it is not founded in any position concerning the duration of the world, but rather in the very nature of *per se* ordered efficient causes. However, as is clear, if the world were eternal, an infinite series of accidentally ordered causes (*ex parte ante*) would not be contradictory.

Third objection. Even in *per se* ordered causes, although a first cause might be required, it does not follow that this cause must be itself uncaused. For example, cause A could produce the power of causing in cause B, and cause B could produce the power of

causing in cause C, and cause C could produce the power of causing in cause A. In this way, the first cause, cause A, would not be
itself uncaused, and our proof would not conclude to the existence
of God.

We answer that the mutual causality which this objection presupposes is not possible except among different kinds of causes;
for example, between material and formal causes, or between efficient and final causes. But in our proof there is question of explaining the actuality of only one kind of series; namely, of
efficient causes. And, as is obvious, the same efficient cause could
not at the same time both give and receive the power of causing.

Fourth objection. Finally, as Descartes has pointed out, all that
this argument can conclude to is the imperfection of my intellect.
I am not able to comprehend how an infinity of such causes could
so proceed one from another from eternity without one of them
being first:

> I have not taken my argument (for the existence of God) from
> the fact that I see in sensible things a certain order or succession of
> efficient causes . . . because from such a succession of causes I do
> not see how I can conclude to any thing else except the imperfection
> of my intellect to understand; to understand, that is, how such a series
> of infinite causes could succeed one another from eternity without
> there being a first.[16]

And a little later on Descartes gives an example of what he understands by such a series of ordered causes: "When I understand that
I was generated by my father, I also understand that my father
was generated by my grandfather; and since I cannot go on *ad
infinitum* asking about the parents of parents, I simply and arbi-
trarily make an end of the inquiry by saying that there was a
first." In other words, Descartes argues this way: from the fact
that I cannot comprehend an infinite series of causes, it does not
necessarily follow that therefore there must be a first cause. And
then he gives us this example to prove his point: from the fact that
I cannot comprehend the infinite divisions in a finite quantity, it
does not follow that there is an ultimate division beyond which
I cannot divide.

We answer this objection of Descartes as follows: The reason

16 *Primae Responsiones,* t. VII, pp. 106–107. Author's translation.

our intellect cannot go into infinity in such a series of *per se* ordered causes is that this series in its existence is finite. And our intellect positively sees that it must be finite, and thus it also sees, from the very nature of the series, the necessity of positing a first cause; for our intellect positively sees that an actual infinite series of essentially ordered efficient causes would be a contradiction.[17]

Furthermore, the example that Descartes uses of an ordered series of efficient causes shows that he essentially misunderstands the second way of St. Thomas, which argues from a series of *per se* ordered causes. Descartes gives an example of only accidentally (*per accidens*) ordered causes, not essentially (*per se*) ordered causes. As we have already noted, there is no repugnance in an infinite regress of accidentally ordered causes, for they are not all essentially ordered, are not here and now needed, for the ultimate effect. A man generates a son precisely as father, and not as son of his own father, let alone as grandson of his grandfather.

Finally, when Descartes talks about the infinite divisibility of quantity, he again misses the point. The divisibility of quantity is potentially infinite; whereas in the second way, we argue from the impossibility of an actually infinite series of *per se* ordered efficient causes.

4. Summary of the Second Way

"From the existence of subordinated causes, the existence of God can be demonstrated under the aspect of a first efficient cause."

A. PRENOTE

This second way of St. Thomas's proceeds from an evident fact of both internal and external experience; namely, the causality of things which we know through experience. I perceive, for example, that I am moving my hand, which moves the stick, which moves the stone. Now my intellect understands that such a series of efficient causes are so ordered among themselves that one cause essentially, that is, as a cause, depends upon the other, receiving

[17] See St. Thomas, *Summa Theologiae*, I, 105, 5; *Contra Gentiles*, III, Ch. 67; *De Pot.*, qu. 3. a. 7.

from it the very power to cause. Thus the intellect understands the necessity of positing an efficient cause that is first and uncaused, in order to explain the very existence and actuality of the series. And this first cause, uncaused in its causality, is God.

B. EXPLANATION OF TERMS

1) *"From the existence . . ."* It is a question of causes actually in operation, whether as regards the coming into being of their effects or their conservation in being.

2) *". . . of subordinated causes . . ."* That is, this series of causes which are here and now, simultaneously and actually, required to produce one and the same effect, are so ordered that the causal influx of the first cause touches the ultimate effect. And therefore all the causes between the first cause and this ultimate effect have the character of an intermediary or *medium*. And since all these intermediate causes act in virtue of the first cause, participating as they do in one and the same power of causation, they can all be considered as only one intermediary cause.[18] Each, however, participates in this power according to its own proper nature and disposition.

3) *". . . the existence of God can be demonstrated . . ."*—inasmuch as the very actuality of this series is impossible unless there exists the first cause, by whose power the intermediate causes operate. The mind sees that the existence of God is the only explanation of this actuality which is received in these inferior causes.

4) *". . . under the aspect of a first efficient cause . . ."* God's existence can be understood as a term, which term can take on different aspects; for example, a first mover, causing movement to other things. In this second way, this term, which is God, is understood precisely as a first efficient cause, influencing the efficient causality in the causes ordered below it.

C. OPINIONS DENYING OUR POSITION

1) *Kant and the Kantians.* All of these reject the proof of the second way of St. Thomas because of their doctrine on being and

---

[18] See St. Thomas, *In Librum de Causis*, lect. 1; *Contra Gentiles*, Bk. III, Ch. 70.

our knowledge of being. For the Kantians teach that the principle of causality upon which our proof depends is valid only for the phenomena or manifestations of sensible things. Such a principle has no validity when applied to God. This position has been criticized in our answer to the objections.

2) *Descartes and the Cartesians.* Descartes held that our argument concludes only to the imperfection of the human intellect and does not positively nor necessarily conclude to the existence of God. We have also answered this difficulty in answering the objections.

D. THE PROOF

Essentially ordered causes are found in reality. But it is impossible to proceed into infinity in essentially ordered causes without destroying the actual effect. Therefore, there must be a first or uncaused efficient cause, which is God.

Our first statement is simply a fact of experience, both internal and external. Our second statement is demonstrated as follows: First, it is impossible for a thing to be its own efficient cause, for then it would have to exist before it existed, which is impossible. Secondly, it is impossible to proceed into infinity in caused causes, for in all essentially ordered efficient causes, the first cause is the cause of the intermediary, and the intermediary is the cause of the ultimate effect; and this is true whether the intermediary is one cause or many. But if the cause is removed, the effect is also removed. Therefore, if there were no "first" in efficient causes, there would be no first efficient cause, and thus there would be no ultimate effect, nor any intermediate efficient causes. Hence it is necessary to posit some first efficient cause, whom all call God.[19]

This same argument can be put a little differently as follows: If we proceed into infinity in *per se* ordered efficient causes, there would be no first efficient cause. And if there is no first, then all these ordered causes would have the characteristic of intermediate. But this is impossible; for at one and the same time they would be intermediate inasmuch as they have received their power to cause, and they would not be intermediate inasmuch as they have not received this power to cause from another. They would

[19] See St. Thomas, *Summa Theologiae*, I, 2, 3.

be and would not be causes, which is a contradiction. For since all intermediate causes participate in the same power of causing which they do not hold from themselves, they act as one single intermediate cause; thus they must receive this power from another that is not an intermediate cause, but the first cause. It is therefore clear that we must posit a first efficient cause.[20]

C. The third way: proof from the existence of corruptible beings

1. PRENOTE

Having seen how the existence of essentially ordered efficient causes leads the mind to the existence of a first uncaused efficient cause, we now wish to embark upon the third way that leads to God's existence. Besides our experience of the activity of existing things, there is another experience that calls for careful analysis and reflection: beings around us corrupt, "go out of" existence, cease to be. Is it possible to show from the fact that things corrupt that there must exist an absolutely necessary Being?

2. SOLUTION

1) *The fact of experience.* The fact from which our proof proceeds is that there are things around us that actually do corrupt; men, animals, plants die, and since they die or do corrupt, they are corruptible.

2) *This leads us to analyze the nature of corruptible beings.* Here the natural theologian takes the data of the philosopher of nature who proves that a being corrupts because it has within its essence the reason for its corruptibility; namely, primary matter. Thus when we speak of corruptible beings, we refer to those beings whose very essence is composed of matter and form, with matter being the source of the possibility of corruption. Notice, matter is the source of this corruptibility, it is not its cause. For, obviously, corruption as such has no cause. To corrupt means to go out of existence; corruption is non-being, and you do not need a cause to produce non-being. A new substantial form is educed from the primary matter, which eduction involves the simultane-

[20] See St. Thomas, *Contra Gentiles*, Bk. I, Ch. 13, near end; *Summa Theologiae*, I, 46, 2, ad 7m; *In II Metaphy.*, lect. 3.

ous corruption of the old substantial form. But matter is the source of the corruption in this sense, that since it remains in potency to all substantial forms even while possessing one in act, new substantial forms can be educed from it, and this entails the corruption of the old form.

3) *The nature of incorruptible being.* This brings us to the consideration of the nature of beings that are incorruptible, that cannot cease to be by way of the corruption of their natures. That being is incorruptible which does not have within its essence the power to corrupt, whose essence has no potency for non-being.[21] This would be true, for example, of any essence not composed of matter, as in the case of immaterial substances, like the angels. Form, or formal act, says of itself, only a possibility for being, a capacity for existence; it does not say, of itself, a possibility for non-being. Hence where we find in existence simple forms, we have a necessary being, possessing no possibility for non-being, and thus naturally incorruptible, immortal, sempiternal. Another case in point would be the rational soul. Once in existence, the rational soul is naturally immortal; when man corrupts the soul remains in existence, since existence or *esse* comes to the soul and is shared in by the body through the soul.

Finally, every form as such is incorruptible, because as form, it says only act in the order of essence, and potency for existence in the order of being. But in the case of non-spiritual forms, existence comes to the composite. Thus when such a composite corrupts, the form corrupts with it. Whereas a spiritual form, like the rational soul, can corrupt neither of itself nor by reason of the corruption of the composite. Not of itself, because it has in itself no potency for *non-esse*; nor by reason of the composite, since *esse* is given immediately to it and not to the composite.

4) *Whence comes the necessity of incorruptible beings?* Beings which necessarily exist may, or may not, have received this neces-

---

[21] Strictly speaking, it is false to talk of a "potency for non-being," in the sense of a passive principle within the essence. For potency is always ordered to act, and there is no act of "non-being." Primary matter is a potency for form. Hence, when it is said that a composed essence has a potency for non-being, what is meant is that, since primary matter is a potency for all forms, a corruptible being can lose the form it actually has, thus corrupting, or ceasing to exist.

sity from another. By supposition, beings that necessarily exist may hold this necessary existence from one of three sources: either from their essence, their act of existence, or from some other being. Notice that with this consideration we have left the plane of essence and are carrying on our analysis on the plane of existence. We are concerned now with the contingency of being, why these necessary beings are rather than are not.

If existence comes from the form or essence, then the being exists of its very essence. Its essence is existence. The being is pure act in the order of existence, subsistent existence, God. But if not, then the essence is actuated by something other than itself, by an act of existence that has come from without, and not from the essence itself.

Now we must direct our attention to this act of existence by which a necessary being exists. Whence comes this act of existence? Did it cause itself? But nothing can cause itself, for that would mean it existed before it existed, which is impossible. Is this act of existence its own reason for being? But then it would be an act of subsistent existence, not the actuation of an essence, but pure act, unreceived existence. And this, again, would be God. But if this existence is received, that is, if it comes neither from the essence nor itself, then it must be received from some other being. And since the necessary being is here and now existing, it follows that here and now it is receiving that existence from another. Hence that other must be here and now causing the existence, holding the necessary being in necessary existence.

Now we cannot go into infinity in necessary beings that receive their necessity from another. For if we did, there would be no first necessary Being. Thus we would be faced with the contradiction of beings that have received necessary existence from another, and yet no other (that is, a first) from which they have received it. For there is question here of essentially ordered effects —of beings that are here and now receiving, as from their efficient cause, their necessary existence. Hence, we must posit a first and absolutely necessary Being who holds its necessity from no one. It is the very nature of such a Being to exist. Such a Being contains no contingency whatsoever, either in the order of essence or existence, for its essence is to exist. Necessary beings which receive their necessity from another are necessary in the order of essence. For they are incorruptible and will never lose their being since they have no potency for non-being. Yet they are contingent in the order of being, since they have received their existence from another.

But have not these necessary beings also received their essences from God, and hence are not these essences also contingent? We answer that they have received from God necessary essences which are capacities only for existence, since they contain no matter and thus no potency for non-being. But they have not received from God subsistent existence, for this is impossible. Subsistent existence means unreceived existence: caused being cannot be infinite Being.

5) *Steps of our proof.* Let us look over the steps of our proof by which we have gone from the actual corruption of the beings of our experience to the existence of God.

(*a*) Beings corrupt; therefore they are corruptible.

(*b*) But if all beings were corruptible, there would be no beings in existence, not even corruptible beings. But this is obviously false.

(*c*) Therefore, there must exist some incorruptible, that is to say, necessary being.

(*d*) But this being will hold its necessity either from itself or from another.

(*e*) Since we cannot go into infinity in beings which hold their necessity from another, there must exist a necessary Being that has of itself its necessary existence.

(*f*) This being is God.

6) *Proof of the steps.* (*a*) That corruptible beings need a cause of their being is easily seen. Corruptible beings are beings that are composed in their very essence. But a composed essence is one containing two distinct components or principles of being, matter and form. But components that are of themselves distinct do not come together in composition unless some extrinsic cause unites them, unless some agent educes the form from the potency of matter, by which eduction the composite begins to exist. As St.

Thomas writes: "Every composite being has a cause; for those things which are distinct of themselves do not come together to form a unit unless through some cause that joins them."[22] "The existence of composite beings arises from the components."[23] "The existence of a thing that is composite results from the coming together of the principles (components) of that thing."[24]

(b) If all beings were corruptible, there would be no beings in existence. Therefore, it is impossible for all beings to be corruptible. This is easy to see from the nature of a corruptible being. Even while such a being is existing it is possible for it not to be. Therefore, such a nature is of itself equally indifferent to *esse* or to *non-esse*. Thus if it is to exist and to remain in existence, it must receive this esse or existence from some cause. But we cannot go into infinity in corruptible beings that hold their existence from another cause, for reasons already studied in the second way. Hence we must place some being that is necessary. Here is the way St. Thomas states the matter:

We see in the world certain things that are possible to be or not to be, namely, things that can be generated and corrupted. But everything that is able to be has a cause; and since of itself it holds itself equally to two things, namely, to be and not to be, it is necessary that if it should come to be that this should happen because of some cause. But we cannot proceed into infinity in such causes, as was proved above through the argument of Aristotle. Therefore, we must posit some being that is necessary in its being.[25]

(c) Therefore, there must exist some necessary being, which holds its necessity either from itself or another. And we cannot go into infinity in necessary beings that receive their necessity from another. A consideration from St. Thomas will demonstrate very clearly the truth of this last statement. Existence is predicated of everything that is. Now when a common perfection is predicated of two beings, it is impossible that it be predicated of neither by way of causality. One must be the cause of the other, as fire is the cause of heat in another body, or some third being must be the cause of the perfection in both, as, for example, fire is the cause of

[22] *Summa Theologiae*, I, 3, 7.
[23] *In IX Metaphy.*, lect. 11, no. 1903 (Cathala ed.).
[24] *In Boeth. de Trinitate*, qu. 5, a. 3c.
[25] *Contra Gentiles*, I, Ch. 15, par. 5.

the heat in two bodies. Hence it is impossible for two beings that are, that one of them should not have a cause of its existence: either both exist through a third cause or one is the cause of the other. Thus everything that is, to the extent that it is, must receive its being from that cause which has no cause of being. And this Being which has no cause of being is the absolutely necessary Being, God.[26]

There are other ways to show why we cannot go into infinity in beings that receive their necessity from another. The reason we use this proof is that it brings out a fact sometimes overlooked in the third way; namely, that there is no necessary connection between the existence of corruptible beings and beings which receive their necessity from another. The actual existence of the latter is not necessary to our proof. Even if there existed no simple substances, no spiritual beings like the angels, the existence of an absolutely necessary Being would be required for the existence of corruptible beings. The second step, however, is added to obviate an objection: perhaps a finite necessary being can adequately explain the existence of corruptible beings, and so from corruptible things we could not necessarily demonstrate the existence of God. But now we see that, as a matter of fact, since such necessary beings cannot explain the source of their own necessity, neither can they explain the source of the being of corruptible things. Since they are caused in their own being, they cannot be the first cause of the being of other things that are not necessary.

Thus we see that there are three kinds of beings:

(a) Those that are both intrinsically and extrinsically possible not to be; intrinsically, because they have within their essence a potency not to be, whose source is prime matter; and extrinsically, because they depend upon an extrinsic agent both for their coming into being (their generation) and for their duration in being. These are corruptible beings.

(b) Those that are intrinsically necessary, since they possess within their essence no potency for non-being. But extrinsically they are contingent or possible not to be, in the sense that they depend upon an extrinsic agent both for the reception of their existence and its conservation. And these are subsistent forms, like

[26] *Contra Gentiles*, II, Ch. 15, par. 2.

angelic essences, and the human soul. These forms can never cease to exist because they have no potency for *non-esse*. St. Thomas writes:

For if there is some form which has existence, it is necessary that such a form be incorruptible. Because existence (esse) cannot be separated from something having existence, unless the form be separated from this thing; and so if that which has existence is the form itself, it is quite impossible that existence be separated from this thing.[27]

Existence follows upon form, since form is the ultimate complement of substance, making substance a subject capable of receiving existence. If something is to be, it must be something. In beings that are composed in their essence, form can be separated from existence, because form can be separated from matter. But in beings where form is subsistent and where there is no matter in the essence, form can no more be separated from existence than it can be separated from itself. A subsistent form could no more lose its existence than the number two could cease being an even number. Of course, the existence is not the same as the form, no more than "even" is the same as the number two. But just as "to be even" inseparably follows the nature of "two," so does existence inseparably follow subsistent forms. Of course, the existence is a received existence, and hence is continually and extrinsically dependent upon an agent from which it has been received.

(*c*) A third kind of being would be one that is both intrinsically and extrinsically necessary; one that not only possesses in itself no potency for non-being, but whose existence itself is unreceived, and hence is not subsistent form but subsistent Being. Such a Being is infinite and necessary in the order of existence. God is such a Being.

There remains now only to mention how this third way of St. Thomas's differs from the preceding way. Here we are interested in the nature of the things around us rather than in their activity, although we arrive at a knowledge of these natures through a phenomenon produced through activity; namely, the generation and corruption of beings. The third way, then, is concerned with the intimate being of things. Since existence is an actuation of es-

[27] *Quaest. Disp. de Anima*, a. 14c.

sence, existence is limited by the essence it actuates. Thus composed essences have a corruptible existence. Simple essences have an incorruptible, albeit a received, existence. The third way, then, is the way of contingent being. Through an analysis of beings that have received their existence from another, we necessarily arrive at a term which is its own existence. The third way grasps its term, God, under the aspect of necessary Being, and thus more directly and more explicitly than the other ways sees this term as the necessary and proper cause of existence as such.[28]

3. Answering the Objections

Some philosophers have denied the validity of this third way of St. Thomas. Let us see what their objections are and whether we can answer them.

1) Kant rejects our argument for the following reason. When the mind is confronted with contingent beings, there is a natural tendency to conclude to a necessary Being. But this is due to the passion the human mind has for unity, and not to the existence of a necessary Being. For from the existence of contingent beings all we can legitimately conclude to is the existence of other contingent beings, unless we want to go beyond the evidence—a common fallacy of the human mind.

We answer that the human mind naturally tends toward its own proper perfection, which is to know truth. The reason the human mind demands the existence of a necessary Being from the analysis of contingent beings is due to the truth of the matter, insofar as the intelligibility of contingent being requires a Being completely necessary. Otherwise a contingent being is not intelligible. Our intellect in a positive way sees this necessity of positing a necessary Being.

2) But Kant insists that our argument makes the existence of an absolutely necessary Being quite impossible. A necessary Being who is the cause of the existence of contingent beings, is by that very fact related to the contingent beings it causes. For between cause and effect there must needs be a mutual and real relation, since the necessary Being is the real cause of the existence of the

---

[28] See *De Pot.*, qu. 5, a. 3c.

contingent beings. But a necessary Being possessing a relation to other beings, is by that very fact not absolutely necessary, but in some sense relative, since it has a real relation to other beings.

We reply that if the necessary Being changes in causing the existence of contingent beings, it would have a real relation to contingent being. But in God his operation is his Being, which is unchangeable. The whole change is in the creature. Therefore in the creature there is a real relation to God, but in God there is only a relation of reason to the creature. This point will be treated more thoroughly in the section on creation and the divine will.

3) There is a statement in St. Thomas regarding corruptible bodies that can be misunderstood and has caused some thinkers to reject this proof.

> We find that some things are generated and corrupted, and conse-quently, are possible to be or not to be. But it is impossible that every-thing which is of such a nature would always be, for that which is able not to be at some time is not. If therefore all things were able not to be, at some time there would be nothing in existence. But if this is true, then there would be nothing in existence now . . . which is obviously false.[29]

To many these simple words contain a twofold fallacy. First, be-cause a thing is possible not to be, it does not follow, as St. Thomas explicitly states here, that therefore it must at some time not be. Such a being may not be allowed to corrupt because of other causes. We answer that this is true: corruptible things need never corrupt. For example, as we know from revelation, this would have been the case with man's body had he not sinned originally, and it will be the case with his glorified body in heaven after the resur-rection. But this requires something beyond the nature of the cor-ruptible being, and we would have to analyze the cause of this incorruption and see whether this cause is a contingent being or not. The second alleged fallacy is this: To say that things that are possible not to be must some time not be, and therefore if only cor-ruptible beings existed, there was a time when there were no beings in existence, and hence there would be no beings now, is not *prima facie* obvious. For maybe some of the corruptible beings that

[29] *Summa Theologiae*, I, 2, 3.

do exist have been around from the beginning; or if not, at least this statement of St. Thomas's would not be true when the world was still young and in its infancy.

What has happened is that these writers have missed the meaning of St. Thomas's statement. First of all, a corruptible being that is actually existing, must sooner or later cease to exist. For if, of itself, it never ceases to exist, never corrupts, that can only be because it is possible for it not to corrupt; but a being that is able not to corrupt is by that very fact incorruptible. Here are St. Thomas's words from his commentary on Aristotle's *De Coelo et Mundo:* "It is impossible that that which is corruptible should not at some time corrupt because if it at some time does not corrupt, it is able not to corrupt, and so it would be incorruptible."[30] Thus we can see how corruptible things must sooner or later of themselves cease to exist, else they are not corruptible. But what does St. Thomas mean by the second part of his statement; namely, that if only corruptible things existed, there would have been a time when no corruptible things existed?

His reasoning seems to be this: On the hypothesis that the world is eternal, generation and corruption have been taking place in an infinite duration of time. Now if all things were corruptible, that is to say, if all of them have in their essence the potency to go out of existence, then this potency, if it has any intelligibility at all, if it is a real objective potency, must sooner or later be realized. Certainly it would be realized in the course of infinite time.

If this potency were not realized during the course of an infinite time, this could only be because the beings were able not to corrupt, that is to say, were *incorruptible.* Hence during the course of an *infinite* time, the potency to corrupt would be realized. And if it were realized in the case of one such corruptible being, it would *also* be realized in the case of all of them, for there is question here of an *infinite* duration of time. Thus by now all beings would have gone out of existence and there would be nothing. But there is something; hence, there must be in existence now some incorruptible being.

Moses Maimonides, from whom St. Thomas borrows this proof,

[30] Bk. I, lesson 29, paragraph 6.

gives an example to prove his point. Supposing, he says, that we know that men have the power to write. If during an infinite duration of time, no man writes, we can only conclude that this is because there is no such potency in man. But we know from actual experience that some beings do corrupt and so possess the potency to do so. Thus this potency must sooner or later be realized.

If this is St. Thomas's reasoning, then it does seem inconclusive. A potency to write is one thing; a potency for non-being is quite another. For potency as such is always a relation or order to act. And apart from the act to which it is ordered, potency as such has no meaning, or intelligibility.

Now non-being is not act, but the denial of act. And so there can be no such thing as a real, objective potency for non-being. Matter is a real, objective potency for *form*. A being is generated *per se*, it corrupts *per accidens*. That is to say, it is because a new form is educed that the old form is reduced to the potency of matter. Corruption is not annihilation, it is only substantial change.

And so even on the supposition that the world is eternal, there would still be an eternal generation and corruption of individuals within a species and of individuals of different species. Thus beings would never go out of existence, since the potency that is in it for non-being is achieved only through the generation of another being. Of course, it is impossible (as we have seen) that there should be in existence only corruptible beings, but not, it would seem, for the reason given by Maimonides, and repeated here by St. Thomas. What St. Thomas may mean is that no corruptible things would be existing, not because they had all gone out of existence, but because they could never have existed in the first place. If we suppose a moment at which only corruptible things existed, at that very moment nothing would be existing. In other words, the supposition is quite impossible. For by supposition we would have beings which *qua* corruptible need a cause why they do not corrupt and at the same time do not have that cause, since by supposition only corruptible beings are existing. But since *de facto* corruptible beings do exist, it follows that here and now there must also be existing other beings that are incorruptible.[31]

[31] See *Contra Gentiles*, Bk. II, Ch. 30.

4. SUMMARY OF THE THIRD WAY

"From corruptible and contingent beings, the existence of God as an absolutely necessary Being can be demonstrated."

A. STATEMENT OF THE QUESTION

In the third way of St. Thomas, this is the problem: from the fact of experience that things in the world are generated and corrupted, is it possible to demonstrate the existence of an absolutely necessary Being? From an inspection of the innermost nature of contingent beings, is the existence of a Being in no way contingent demanded, as the only sufficient explanation of the act of existing in these contingent beings?

B. EXPLANATION OF TERMS

1) " . . *Corruptible Being* . . ."—That being whose essence is composed of matter and form. On account of its matter, such a being is intrinsically able not-to-be. Such a being can by its essence not-be.

2) *Incorruptible Being*—That being whose essence does not include matter, whether it is a simple subsisting form, like an angel, or the form of a body which has its own act of existing, like the human soul. (Text: *De Pot.*, qu. 5, a. 3c.)

3) ". . . *Contingent Being* . . ."—That which can not-be in the order in which it is contingent; for example, a corruptible being can not-be by reason of its essence; and *a fortiori* by an extrinsic reason, namely, by reason of an external agent. An incorruptible being can not-be only in the order of being; that is, it needs an external agent both for its beginning and duration in being.

4) *Necessary Being*—That which cannot not-be in the order in which it is necessary, for example:

(*a*) necessary by a necessity of consequence: while he sits, Socrates necessarily sits.

(*b*) necessary by a necessity of *matter*: if material things exist, they are necessarily corruptible.

(*c*) necessary by a necessity of form: forms which are not in matter, or which subsist in matter, *have a necessity of being.*

(*d*) necessary by a necessity of the *very act of existing:* what cannot not-be because it is the very act of Being. Such a Being does not *have* the necessity of being, it *is* the necessary Being itself. (Text: *C.G.*, Bk. II, Ch. 30.)

5) "*. . . existence of God can be demonstrated . . .*" From the fact of the corruptibility of material things, and from the fact of the contingency in the order of being of incorruptible things which have their necessity from another, we conclude to the existence of a Being which does not have its necessity of Being from another, but has it of itself. This Being is God.

6) "*. . . as a . . . necessary Being . . .*" That is, in this third way, God terminates our investigation not as the ultimate reason for the existence of motion, nor as the ultimate reason for causality in things, but as the ultimate reason for the act of existing in all things.

C. ADVERSARIES

Kant rejected our argument for many reasons. (1) Because more is contained in the conclusion (necessary Being) than in the premises (contingent beings). (2) Because by applying the principle of causality to God (by saying that God is the cause of things), we make God a relative being (since a cause has a real relation to its effect). We have seen the answer to these difficulties.

Spinoza: Beings in the world only seem to be contingent; for contingency itself is a mode, and contingent beings are different appearances of the same necessary substance. Therefore there does not exist a necessary Being really distinct from contingent beings. Such a position as Spinoza's is Pantheism, "which is listed among those positions of philosophy that are fundamentally erroneous since not only is it contrary to faith, but it undermines all the principles of moral philosophy," destroying our freedom, and so on (See *De Malo*, qu. 6, a *unic.*).

Geny, Chambat, Descoqs: What can be corrupted of itself may not corrupt accidentally, and therefore at least that part of the argument which says that if all things were corruptible, nothing would exist, is a fallacy. We have seen the answer to this also.

D. THE PROOF

The argument begins with a fact: things corrupt and are generated; for example, men and animals die and are born. From this fact we argue thus:

1) *First step*. What corrupts can corrupt. But what can corrupt can either be or not-be. And what can either be or not-be is indifferent to both. But what is indifferent to existence and non-existence, if it actually exists, must exist through some cause. Now it is impossible to proceed to infinity in corruptible things that have their being from another. This impossibility is based on the notion of essentially ordered causes which we considered in the second way. Hence there must be some incorruptible or necessary being. (Text: *C.G.*, I, Ch. 15.)

Another argument that starts from corruptible things can be stated in this way: Diverse things because they are diverse, must have a cause of their union or composition. And corruptible things are composed of matter and form which are really diverse. Therefore they must have an extrinsic cause of their composition. But we cannot proceed to infinity in things having their composition from another. Therefore, there exists some uncomposed and incorruptible or necessary being. (Text: *S.T.*, I, 3, 7.)

2) *Second step*. This necessary being either has its necessity of being of itself or through another. But we cannot proceed to infinity in beings which have their necessity from another. The reason for this is that all beings which have their necessity of being from another, whether considered as many or as one caused being, do not have in themselves the explanation why they necessarily exist. Therefore there must be a Being necessary of itself. This is what men call God. (Text: *C.G.*, II, Ch. 15; *S.T.*, I, 2, 3.)

D. The fourth way: Proof of God's existence from grades of perfection in beings

1. STATEMENT OF THE PROBLEM

Having demonstrated the necessity for an absolutely necessary Being as the only complete explanation of the existence of contingent beings, we wish now to consider a new question. Is there yet another way that can lead the mind to the existence of God? St.

Thomas tells us there is. Among the beings of our experience we find common perfections possessed by these beings in different degrees. Is it possible that these different degrees of perfections demand for their intelligibility as differing degrees the existence of a maximum degree of this perfection, and therefore the existence of a being who possesses this perfection in its maximum degree? This is the problem of the fourth way. We maintain that these different degrees of the same perfections do exist in beings; and, secondly, that they derive their intelligibility and their very existence from the maximum degree of the perfection. And this maximum is God. But in order to understand how this is so, an exact and careful understanding of the elements of our solution is required.

2. SOLUTION

1) First of all, what do we mean here by "grades of perfection"? We mean that in several existing things the mind recognizes the presence of the same perfection, but sees it as belonging more to one being than to another. For example, men, animals, and plants all share in the perfection of life. All are living beings; but life is seen to be more perfect in man than in the animal and more perfect in the animal than in the plant. Again, we see that some beings are nobler than others; the being of man is more noble than the being of a dog; and the being of a dog is more noble (of greater ontological value) than the being of a rock, and so forth. Thus there are different grades or degrees of the same perfection, for example, life, goodness, beauty, truth, nobility, in the different beings that exist around us.

2) Secondly, what kind of perfections are capable of existing in different degrees? Perfections which constitute the essences of things are incapable of different degrees. One cannot be more or less man, more or less dog. If the essence of man or the essence of dog changes, we have a different essence. We have non-man or non-dog. And this holds true for all essences, whether they be material essences like man or dog, or immaterial essences like the subsistent forms of the angels.

Two things about essential perfections are to be noted. Although incapable of existing according to different degrees (since "more or less essence" is a contradiction in terms: all men are equally men, else they are simply not men), an essence can exist in different individuals. But the fact that the perfection of man is found in Peter only "happens" (is incidental) to this perfection. That by which Peter is a man and that by which Paul is a man is the same specific or essential perfection: both possess a human soul and sensible matter. But that by which Peter is Peter and that by which Paul is Paul is different; namely, different individual sensible matters which are the principles of the individuation of the essence. Thus although all men are equally men, all men are not equal men, because of their accidental differences and their different individual sensible matters.

The second thing to be noted about material essences is that they cannot subsist. For an essential perfection to subsist means that it is able to exist apart from matter. But since matter belongs to the very essence of material perfections, such perfections can neither have existence nor intelligibility apart from matter. To be in matter means to be in individual sensible matter, for a universal as such cannot exist, since at one and the same time it would be common to many and yet be this existing thing—a clear contradiction. But this individual material essence can be considered by the intellect apart from its individual sensible matter, as happens when we abstract the universal from the particular. But the universal consideration of a material essence still includes common sensible matter.

To sum up: Essential perfections like humanity, rationality, animality, and so forth, since they cannot exist in varying degrees, are not numbered among those perfections considered in this fourth way. Moreover, these essential perfections if they are material cannot subsist. There is no subsistent man, no subsistent dog, since in order to exist, these perfections must exist in matter. What exists is this man or this dog, matter being the principle of thisness or individuation. Finally, since matter enters into their very essences, humanity, animality, rationality, and so forth, are not perfections of being as being but of being as limited being, for matter is the principle of limitation. Finally, even perfections of essence that are subsistent forms (such as the essence of an angel or the human soul), are limited perfections and not perfections of being as being. For any essence is potency in the order of being, since it receives and limits the act of being, which is existence.

3) There is a second class of perfections, which although capable of existing in different degrees in different beings, do not belong to that group of perfections by which the fourth way mounts up to God. These are the accidental perfections of material beings that depend upon matter both for their being and for their being intelligible. For example, the perfection of heat is found in fire, in hot water, in hot potatoes, and so on. This perfection can be found in material substances in different degrees, because this form can more or less intensely inform the substance. Now obviously there can be no such thing as subsistent heat; first of all, because heat as an accident cannot exist apart from substance. But even if heat were a substance, in order to be it would still have to be in matter, for sensible qualities demand sensible matter both for their being and for their being intelligible. Thus accidental perfections that depend upon matter also have no part in our proof; they are not perfections of being as being, but of material, limited being.

4) What kind of perfections then, when found existing in different beings in different degrees, demand for their being and for their intelligibility the actual existence of this perfection in its highest and most perfect degree? It must be those perfections in whose intelligibility no note of imperfection or limitation is present. If limitation is present, it will be there not because of the perfection itself, but because of the being that possesses the perfection.

There are two principles of limitation in beings. In the order of essence, there is matter which limits form; and in the order of being, there is essence which limits existence. Material perfections as such are limited and hence can never exist as a maximum or unlimited perfection; and essences as such are not gradated and do not vary in beings. Hence neither can lead us to a maximum or unlimited perfection. Only those perfections that follow being as being, which follow being insofar as it exercises its act, which is "to be," demand a maximum for their intelligibility and for their existence. *Hence only those perfections that flow*

*from the act of existing as such enter into the proof of the fourth
way.*

5) Precisely what is meant by a perfection that flows from
being *insofar as it is in act through its existence or "to be"?* We
mean a perfection that is a perfection because of the *actuality* of
the being and is a *limited* perfection not of itself, but because of
the *limitation of this actuality* by reason of the essence that is
actuated. A simple example will bring out our meaning. A flower,
because it is a *flower,* possesses *vegetative* life; a dog, because it
is a *dog,* possesses *sensitive* life; a man, because he is a *man,*
possesses *rational life.* Thus in each instance, the *kind* of life the
being possesses depends upon the *kind* of being it is, upon the
being's essence. But the *actuality* of this perfection depends upon
the actuality of the being. All are *living beings.* The perfection of
life in each case is both actual and limited; but it is limited not
because it is life, but because it is the life of a flower, or of a dog,
or of a man. Hence, apart from the principle that limits it, life
is an unlimited perfection of *being.* There can, therefore, exist a
being that is unlimited life, for the limitation is not from the side
of the perfection, but from the side of the particular essence that
receives the perfection. Of course, rational life is more perfect
than animal life, and animal life is more perfect than plant life,
because the essence of man is less limiting of the act of existence
than is the essence of an animal, and that of an animal less limiting
than that of a plant. But since essence is always potency in the
order of existence, it will always exercise some limitation on the
act of existing, and hence on those perfections given by the act
of existing. If no limit is placed on the act of existing, it will be all-
perfect and contain all the perfections of being.

The perfections of the fourth way, then, are perfections in
whose notion and in whose being there is contained no imperfection. In creatures, such perfections can be perfections like
being itself and the truth and goodness that are convertible with
being; or like life, which is a perfection of being for living things,
and so forth. These perfections are possessed by creatures by way
of participation and not by way of essence. Or these perfections
of the fourth way may be accidental perfections, like wisdom and
knowledge, which are acquired habits or qualities inhering in the

intellect. Hence their mode of being in the creature is both accidental, since these perfections inhere in a subject, and limited or
participated, since it is human knowledge and human wisdom.
But since "to know" and "to be wise" involve as such no imperfection, there can exist unlimited wisdom and unlimited knowledge.

A final characteristic of these perfections is implicit in what has
already been said. These perfections are analogous and transcendent. First of all, to possess a perfection by way of participation
and possess an analogous perfection does not always nor necessarily mean the same thing. For example, all existing men can be
said to participate in the perfection of humanity, but they participate in this perfection univocally, for it is the same in all men.
And this is so because humanity is a perfection of essence.

But to possess an analogous perfection is to possess a perfection
that is found in greater or lesser degrees in different beings. And
the reason why this participation is according to greater or lesser
(that is, analogous participation) is that these perfections are due
to the existence of the thing rather than to its essence. The act
of existing, as actuating the whole being, is at once "different"
for each being and absolutely incommunicable. It is possessed
analogously by each being and it cannot be abstracted from the
being the way a form is abstracted from matter. Existence cannot
be abstracted from existing beings, or life cannot be abstracted
from living beings, in the same sense that man can be abstracted
from human beings and dog from canine beings. When we talk
about existence and life, we formalize these perfections for purposes of communication and explanation, but they are not
abstracted forms.

Such perfections are also transcendent. They transcend the predicaments and belong to none of them. Not in the sense that all
beings possess these perfections (not all beings are living or have
knowledge), but in the sense that in those beings that do possess
them these perfections flow from the act of existing, which act
transcends all the predicaments and belongs to none of them. And
like the act of existing which they follow, these perfections cannot
be abstracted in the way we abstract an essence or form. They
are not common natures that we predicate univocally of existing
things.

3. The proof of the fourth way

Why does the intelligibility of "more or less" of the same perfection in different beings demand the existence of a maximum degree of that perfection? It seems clear that a rose possesses more being than a stone, and that a lion possesses more being than a rose, and that a man possesses more being than a lion. And by such a progression we would seem to be approaching a nature which possesses being in its highest perfection. But the point of the proof is to show that it is this highest perfection, unlimited being, that is the source of the intelligibility of the lesser degrees of the same perfection existing in these different natures. St. Thomas tells us that different degrees of the same perfection mean that these are participated perfections and hence are completely intelligible only on the supposition that there exists an unparticipated perfection, a highest degree. He demonstrates this fact in many places. We will analyze his proof from the *Summa Contra Gentiles*, Book II, Chapter 15.

The chapter itself is concerned with giving different reasons why God is the cause of being for all things. St. Thomas begins by saying that what belongs to a thing because of its own nature and not because of some other cause, cannot be found deficiently in that thing. For if something essential to a nature is substracted from or added to that nature, it becomes a different nature. Just as, for example, when a number is added to or substracted from, we have a different number. If on the other hand, while the nature remains unchanged, something in it is found lessened, then it is obvious that what is found lessened does not depend simply on the nature, but on something else. And its lessening is due to a greater removal from the thing upon which it depends.

Therefore what is shared in less by, or belongs less to, one thing than another, does not belong to this thing because of its nature only, but because of some other cause. And this cause will be responsible for these gradated perfections wherever they are found. Just as that which is hottest we see to be the cause of heat in all hot things, and that which is most perfectly light, the cause of light in all lighted things, so God is most perfect being and therefore the cause of all things of which we can predicate being.

Notice there are two phases here in the movement of St. Thomas's thought. The first consists in showing that degrees of more or less of the same perfection depend for their intelligibility upon the maximum degree of that perfection. The second makes more explicit what was only implicit in the first; namely, that the maximum grade is also the cause of the existence of the other grades of the perfections. The proof of the fourth way is formally complete with the end of the first phase, with the positing of the maximum degree as the only explanation of the intelligibility of the lesser degrees. Here we are concerned directly and explicitly with exemplary causality or the cause of the intelligibility of these degrees of perfection. The second step, which is outside the essential movement of the fourth way, consists in seeing explicitly what was present only implicitly in the first step; namely, that this maximum degree of the perfection is also the *efficient* cause of the very existence of the other degrees of this perfection.

Let us see whether we can grasp the cogency of the fourth way.[32] The fact from which we argue is the actual existence of different degrees of the same perfection. This existential experience is a composite and an intelligible one: the existence of many beings possessing the same perfection according to more and less. Reflecting upon this fact, we conclude that these grades would be unintelligible if there did not exist a maximum grade. Why is this so? Because perfections that are found in a deficient state are not in themselves adequately intelligible. They are intelligible only because they are more or less like that which is perfectly this perfection. Such perfections hold their intelligibility to the exact degree to which they approach or recede from the unlimited perfection in which they share. A thing is intelligible to the degree that it is and in the way that it is. We have seen that these perfections are not intelligible because of the nature in which they are found. For here the nature or essence is related

---

[32] Besides the basic text in the *Summa* (I, 2, 3), here are some other places where St. Thomas refers to and uses the argument from degrees of perfection to establish some truth about God: *Summa Theologiae*, I, 44, 1; *De Pot.*, qu. 3, a. 5c; *De Subst. Separ.*, Ch. 9 (explains how perfections like life, understanding, etc., are the act of *esse* for living, intellective, etc., beings); *Comp. Theol.*, Ch. 68.

to the perfection as receiver to thing received, as potency to act. And act neither is, nor is intelligible, through potency. It is the other way around: potency is and is intelligible through act. Hence, the intelligibility of the different degrees of the same perfection is not accounted for by the nature or essence that limits it. Rather, as act, the perfection renders intelligible the nature that limits it.

Nor can these more or less limited acts *of themselves* account for their intelligibility as limited. For of themselves *they should not be limited*. Here we are at the heart of the matter. Two things should be noted about each degree of the perfections. First, it is minorated (that is, it is not the highest degree since it is found in a limited condition), and, secondly, of itself it should not be limited (since, of itself, it says *only act* and in no way potency). As act, it accounts for the intelligibility of its limiting potency, for apart from its act, or its intrinsic order to its act, potency has no intelligibility. But what accounts for the actuality of the limited perfection? Only the fact that all these degrees participate in the same unlimited degree of the perfection. The conclusion is a simple but necessary one: unless there exists here and now the unlimited degree of this perfection, the limited degrees have no reason for being, and hence have no intelligibility as limited degrees of the same perfection. The source of the intelligibility of these minorated degrees of the same perfection cannot be the natures that limit them nor their own condition as act, but only the existence of the unlimited, unreceived, degree. This unlimited degree must, therefore, exist. In the fourth way we reach God under the aspect of unlimited Being.

Just as in the second way, the activity of finite beings is rendered intelligible only on the supposition that there exists an uncaused cause that is its own activity; and just as in the third way contingent beings are rendered intelligible only on the supposition that there exists an absolutely necessary Being who is its own necessary existence; so, here in the fourth way, the existence of different grades of perfection is rendered intelligible only on the supposition that there exists a Being who possesses these perfections in an ungraded or absolute degree. With the positing of this absolute degree the proof of the fourth way is completed.

But St. Thomas always goes on to show that this "Greatest Being" is the efficient cause of the participated perfections. God is not only the first exemplary cause why these grades of perfections are intelligible. He is also the first efficient cause why these grades of perfection exist. This addition to the proof is merely an explicitation in our knowledge of God's causality.

4. SOME ADDED CONSIDERATIONS

A. HOW THE DIFFERENT KINDS OF PERFECTIONS IN THE CREATURE PRE-EXIST IN GOD

In the course of our solution we analyzed three kinds of perfections: (1) perfections of essence, which do not allow of different grades; (2) accidental perfections which allow of grades but cannot subsist because matter is intrinsic to their nature; (3) substantial and accidental perfections which both allow of different degrees and in whose being and intelligibility there is no note of limitation or imperfection. Only this third class is validly used in our proof, because only these perfections allow of and demand the unlimited (subsistent) existence of the perfection. But God is not only the first cause of perfections that follow being as being. He is also the cause of prime matter and of perfections of essence. He is the cause of the existence of all perfections. Thus *all* perfections must somehow exist in God.

Later on we shall see in detail how different perfections found in creatures can be said to pre-exist in God as in their cause. It suffices here to say that those perfections in creatures that contain within themselves a necessary limitation, for example, humanity, are said to pre-exist in God's essence only virtually. That is to say, God possesses the power (*virtus*) to produce such perfections. But what this perfection properly signifies can in no way be predicted of God, not even by way of analogy.

However, perfections that follow being as being, in which there exists on the side of the perfection no limitation (like wisdom, truth, life, and so forth) pre-exist in God *properly*. This means that this perfection is in God not merely in the sense that he can cause it, but also in the sense that it belongs to him by reason of the perfection itself. This perfection, however, is said to be in God analogously, since God possesses it in an infinitely higher degree and according to an infinitely more perfect way than it is found in the creature. In fact, as found in God this perfection is identified with the divine Being, which is unreceived and subsistent, and thus the perfections are subsistent, unparticipated, one with the divine essence, which essence is subsistent existence.

B. HOW THE FOURTH WAY DIFFERS FROM THE THIRD WAY

It remains now to be seen how this fourth way of St. Thomas's differs from the third way, the way of contingent being. There are several differences:

1) The third way began with the existential fact that beings corrupt and are generated, a consideration based on the nature or essence of beings.

The fourth way began with the fact that different grades of the same perfection are found in different things, a consideration based on beings as gradated in their being. Thus the points of departure of the two ways are entirely different.

2) Secondly, the third way mounted from corruptible beings to incorruptible beings, and from incorruptible beings to that Being which is absolutely necessary. But corruptibility and holding one's necessity of being from another are characteristics that point to a dependence upon an extrinsic agent. The third way concludes directly and explicitly to a necessary Being as to a Being who is such a cause or agent.

In the fourth way, on the other hand, we mounted from different grades of the same perfection to the supreme grade of this perfection. Here we grasped the perfection, not as contingent or as necessary, but precisely as gradated, as approaching a supreme grade, as pointing to a term which would make these different grades intelligible as grades. The fourth way concludes directly and explicitly to the existence of the supreme grade of the perfection as the cause of the intelligibility of the other grades, and hence to exemplary causality. Our approach was by way of the *intelligibility* of the grades.

5. ANSWERING THE OBJECTIONS

First objection. If the different degrees of the same perfection depend upon the supreme degree of that perfection for their intelligibility, then the intellect must first know this supreme degree before it can know the lesser degrees. Hence, the fourth way does not prove, but supposes, the existence of God.

This objection is answered by a simple distinction. If one means that degrees of perfection are not intelligible to us unless we first know the supreme degree, this must be denied. But if one means that these degrees of perfection are not intelligible in themselves unless some supreme degree exists, the statement is true. It is a fact that we have knowledge of these degrees of perfection; hence, they are intelligible to us. And the intellect also understands that in themselves these degrees would not be intelligible unless there existed some supreme degree. Hence, for our intellect, the knowledge of this supreme degree constitutes a necessary *term*. But in itself this supreme degree is the first cause of the intelligibility of the other degrees and, indeed, of the very being of the graded perfections.

Second objection. The fourth way argues that the supreme degree is the cause of the perfections in which other beings participate. Thus the fourth way seems to be no different from the third, which argues from the contingency of beings.

Reply. Strictly speaking, the fourth way is formally complete once we have posited a supreme degree as cause of the intelligibility of the other degrees. What is then added, namely, that this supreme Being must be also the efficient cause of the perfections, is not essential to the proof.

Third objection. If this is true, then the fourth way does not seem to be based on the principle of causality. Hence the difficulty remains.

Reply. The fourth way is directly and explicitly based upon exemplary causality, but only implicitly on efficient causality. Efficient causality implicitly accompanies the whole of our proof, for from it flows the very existence of the perfections which are found in varying degrees in beings.

Fourth objection. Among things that are heated, we find various degrees of heat; hence there should exist some supreme degree of heat which is the cause of the heat in all hot things. And since this is clearly false, so is the parallel procedure of the fourth way of St. Thomas.

This objection is answered by showing that the perfection of heat is a perfection proper to being as material, not to being as being. And in the fourth way we do not argue from such perfections. St. Thomas's statement that fire is supremely hot and the cause of heat in all heated things, is used merely as a clarifying example. And he thought it was a good one, since in Aristotelian physics fire was considered (falsely) as one of the substantial elements. The error is in the faulty example, not in the principle exemplified.

Fifth objection. One does not understand a perfection as greater or less because it is approaching a maximum, but rather because of the order that is perceived to exist among the different things possessing this graded perfection. Thus "more and less" are intelligible independently of a maximum, and so the fourth way proves nothing.

We answer that this order itself, which is seen to exist among different things because of their greater or less participation in the same perfection of being, would not be intelligible unless there existed the supreme degree of this perfection. The very order itself, taken as a whole, implies reference to another; for *all* the degrees are minorated, since all the perfections are participated. And so our intellect sees that as such they are unintelligible without the existence of the maximum to which they are all ordered.

6. Summary of the Fourth Way

"The existence of God as the supreme and perfect Being can be demonstrated through the existence of degrees of perfection."

A. STATEMENT OF THE PROBLEM

It is clear that there exist among beings different degrees of the same perfection. One being is better, nobler, truer than another. How is this fact to be explained? We maintain that the different grades of the same perfection among various beings would have no intelligibility as degrees unless there existed a supreme degree of this perfection; and this supreme degree is also supreme Being, or God.

B. EXPLANATION OF TERMS

1) "*. . . degree . . .*" This word of its nature means something that is relative, that is, more or less. Different beings participate in the same perfection in different degrees.

2) "*. . . perfection . . .*"—that in a thing because of which it is or is said to be perfect (complete or finished) in some order of being.

(*a*) *Perfections of essence,* for example, the perfection of man, the perfection of animal, and so on: these perfections constitute the natures or essences of things and so are incapable of different degrees. There is no such thing as being more or less man; one is either a man or something else. Hence, there is no question of using this type of perfection in the fourth way.

(*b*) *Mixed perfections*—those in whose very perfection there is present some potentiality or limitation, and hence imperfection. Mixed perfections therefore do not follow from being as being, but from being as such a being. For example, in the perfection of reason there is necessarily some imperfection present; namely, a certain movement or passage from thought to thought. Furthermore, all perfections of essence are mixed perfections.

(*c*) *Perfections proper to a being as being.* These perfections contain no limitation or imperfection in their intelligibility. And if such a perfection is found limited, it is by reason of the subject which partakes of the perfection and not because of the perfection itself. For example, animality of itself is a limited perfection because it is material; but wisdom of itself is not limited, although human wisdom is. In the fourth way there is question only of these perfections. For all other perfections either do not admit of degrees, like the perfections of essence; or if they have degrees, these degrees are proper only to particular beings (for example, to material beings, like different degrees of heat in hot things). It is impossible that such perfections exist in a subsistent or unlimited degree. For to exist they must be in individual sensible matter. Perfections proper to beings as being follow upon the actuality of the act of existing itself. And for this reason they are perfections which are analogous and transcendent. Therefore, insofar as they are perfections actually being exercised, they cannot be known by any abstraction in the strict sense of the term.

3) *"The existence of God . . . can be demonstrated . . ."* By showing that the different degrees of the same perfection possess no intelligibility unless there exists a supreme degree of this perfection, we show that God exists, since he is this supreme degree.

C. THE PROOF

1) *General proof from the degrees of perfection in things.* (a) *The fact of experience:* in the existents of our experience different degrees of perfection are present. It is clear, for example, that a man is a more perfect being than a dog.

(b) *Metaphysical principle:* we do not predicate greater or less about different things except insofar as they approach some maximum.

(c) *Conclusion:* therefore, there must exist something that is the supreme good, supreme truth, supreme living being, and so on. And because that which is the supreme good, the supreme truth, and so on, is also the supreme Being, there must exist a supreme Being, or God himself.

(d) *Proof of the argument:* from the very notion of a graded perfection. Graded perfections, as graded, do not contain within themselves their complete intelligibility. Because there are many degrees of the same perfection, this perfection is participated and therefore incomplete and dependent upon something other than itself. Hence the very intelligibility of this order among these perfections which are participated in different degrees would have no meaning unless there exists at the same time a supreme degree of this perfection and unless that supreme perfection be in itself unparticipated, essentially such, and hence subsistent.

This supreme degree of perfection is both the cause of the intelligibility of the degrees and of the being of the perfections. In the fourth way it is the intelligibility of these perfections that is directly and explicitly considered. However, it is clear that the perfections hold their existence also from the supreme degree. But the formal and explicit argument of the fourth way is: Given the existence of the perfections, how explain the intelligibility or order of the differing degrees? That is why the fourth way is said to be grounded explicitly in exemplary causality and only implicitly in efficient causality, and why it is sometimes called a proof from truth rather than a proof from being. (Text: *Summa Contra Gentiles*, II, Ch. 15. Here the argument is expounded more completely.)

E. The fifth way: the proof of the existence of God from the finalized activity of natural beings

1. PRENOTE

The five ways of St. Thomas as they succeed one another become increasingly metaphysical. Each way exploits to a greater degree than the last the actuality of things. Motion, or an existent as changing, is for us the most obvious and manifest characteristic of sensible beings. Thus this evidence constitutes a good starting point; it is a good first way. But in itself such a characteristic of being is the least perfect and least stable manifestation of existential act. For here the very being of change is becoming, the reality of change consisting precisely in an ordering or movement to further being.

The second way is more actual than the first, for here our evidence is not the change itself that a being is undergoing in its existence, but the activity that is responsible for such a change.

The third way analyzes the natures from which such activity flows, which natures, as possessive of substantial being, are more perfect and stable than the accidental activity they exercise. But in the third way we analyzed these natures from the aspect of their corruptibility and contingency. We considered substantial being precisely as imperfect, namely, as corruptible and contingent.

In the fourth way our concern was an explicitly metaphysical one. For in this way we analyzed existents insofar as they manifested perfections that as such involved no imperfection, the minoration of these perfections being due to the limiting essence in which they were exercised. But the perfections themselves, as considered apart from their limiting principle, had nothing of contingency or imperfection about them.

The fifth way, the way of wisdom, is directly concerned with the existent as most actual. Here the transcendent property of being that this way considers is being as good, as perfect; hence, as desirable and therefore as finalizing the activity of natural agents. Thus the causality involved in the fifth way is final causality.

The student's knowledge of the general metaphysics of finality will be presupposed in our discussion of this fifth way. However, one or two statements about finality should be recalled here which bear more directly upon our demonstration. St. Thomas has described the final cause as the cause of causes and the cause of the causality in all causes.[33] It is both first and last; first in the order of intention and last in the order of execution. As actually exercising its causality, as actually "moving" or drawing the agent to its act, the end is in the intentional order, although what the agent desires because of this knowledge of the end is precisely the obtaining or effecting of the end in the real order.

A simple example will make these matters clear. If an artist desires to paint a picture, this desire must be founded in some knowledge, a knowledge of "a picture to be painted." Only if such knowledge is present can his efficiency be "finalized" toward its end. But what he wants to paint is a real picture. He desires the production of a real picture, but he is finalized to begin this production by his *knowledge* of a picture. The end as intended, as wanted, is the end as causing. This desire moves him to paint a picture; and the painted picture is the end as produced. Thus this end is last in the order of execution. For when the picture is finished, the desire of the artist is fulfilled, his efficiency ceases, and the total causal process comes to an end.

The importance of these considerations in the understanding of the fifth way will become clear as we proceed with the actual proof. But since the end as causing is the end as intended, and since the end as intended is the end as known, we can begin to understand how the presence of finality in the world demands the presence of an intellect that knows the ends for which things act and can thus direct such beings in their activity.

2. THE PROBLEM OF THE FIFTH WAY

In this fifth way, as in all the others, our starting point is an evident fact of experience; our everyday experience that natural

[33] See *Summa Theologiae*, I, 5, 4; I-II, 1, 2; *In V Metaphy.*, lect. 2, no. 775.

beings act for definite and determined ends. We experience that the activity of fire, for example, always produces heat, ice always produces cold; a cat will always generate kittens and a dog puppies, and so forth. When the mind understands that natural beings always act in the same way,[34] it sees upon reflection that the end produced by this action of the natural being must be somehow intended. It sees that the action must be directed toward this end.

But what is directing the action, and hence the agent, toward this end? To direct something toward an end presupposes that the one so directing wants or intends that end, and so must know it. The bowman, for example, can direct the arrow toward the target only because the bowman knows the target is there and wants to hit it. But knowledge of the end to be attained presupposes an intellect that possesses this knowledge, that knows this end. Now natural things like fire and ice and dogs and cats do not have an intellect. So on the one hand we have natural beings that have no intellect, and on the other we see them always acting for the same end, and thus really directed toward an end that is forseen and desired. Therefore the presence of some intelligence is necessarily involved. We say that this must be ultimately a divine or subsistent intelligence—the intellect of God.

Thus from the fact that natural things act for an end we can demonstrate the existence of God. The problem of the fifth way can be stated as follows: From the regular and uniform actions of natural beings does it follow that these beings are acting for an end? And if they are acting for an end, does this fact presuppose an intellect that is directing them to their end? And from this intellect directing them to an end, does it follow that there must exist an intellect that is its own end, and therefore an infinite and subsistent intelligence, which is God?

---

[34] Or almost always; for if an action of an agent is interfered with, it may not produce its proper effect. Fire, for example, may not burn the log if the latter is soaking wet. The water interferes with the action of the fire and prevents it from producing in the log its usual heat.

3. Solution

A. THE PROOF THAT THERE IS FINALITY IN THE UNIVERSE

It is a fact of evident experience that the natural beings[35] around us always act in a uniform and regular fashion. We see that things always act in the same way and produce the same effects. They are never defective in their natural activity unless interfered with or impeded by some outside influence. Thus, for example, grape vines always produce grapes, and fig trees figs; when grapes ferment, we get wine, not beer; when wine is distilled, brandy is formed, not water, and so forth.

Thus we can conclude from this regular and uniform activity of natural agents that these agents are ordered to these ends, to the production of these determined effects. A determined way of acting manifests a determined order or relation between the agent, its activity, and the effect produced by this activity. This definite order that obtains between the agent, its act, and the end or effect produced by the act we call finality. An agent is finalized or ordered to a certain act, and the act on its part is finalized or ordered to a certain term or effect that it produces.

Let us analyze this order a little more carefully. The determination that we find in the effect would not be present there unless that determination were already somehow contained in the action that produces the effect. Puppies would not be puppies unless they were produced by an action ordered to the production of puppies, and hence an action containing the determination that it produces in the effect. But let us go a step further: this action itself would not be ordered to the production of puppies (a determined effect) unless the agent in its turn was ordered to this kind of action. Thus the determination found in the effect is somehow pre-contained in the agent producing the effect. An agent can act in a determined manner only because the effect to be produced by the agent is already from the very beginning pre-contained in it.

If this is so, then it follows that the agent received the deter-

---

[35] Natural beings are the products of nature. They are opposed here to artifacts, the products of man through art.

mination of its activity from the effect or term that is to be produced. Thus the agent is ordered to its term. This is another way of saying that there is present a finality in the activity of natural things. If natural agents were not so finalized, the regularity and constancy of their activity would be unintelligible. If a natural agent were not determined to the production of a definite effect, there would be no reason why it should produce this effect rather than some other. If, for example, fire were not ordered to the production of heat, there would be no reason why fire should burn an object rather than cool it. If an agent produces a determined effect, it follows that it is ordered to that effect; the effect, therefore, has the aspect or characteristic of an end.[36]

The only explanation, therefore, of the constancy and regularity present in the activity of natural agents is the principle of finality. A determined effect would not be produced unless that effect was somehow already present in the agent before it acted. Now it is obvious that the effect to be produced is not pre-contained in its cause according to the *real* existence of that effect, since as an effect *to be produced* it has as yet *no* real existence. The effect to be produced must therefore pre-exist in the agent according to some *intentional existence*, and according to this existence it orders the agent to the production of a determined act, and thus influences or "moves" the agent. This influx or "motion" of the form of the term to be produced as influencing the production of the real or existential term is the causality of the end.

What we have said concerning the action of a single agent for a single end holds true also for the co-operation of many agents for a single end; for example, the constant recurrence of the seasons of the year, the action of the sun and the rain and the winds for the maintenance and growth of life upon the earth. It is also true of many actions of one agent acting for the good of the whole, as in the case of living beings. If all these agents, or if all these actions, work together for one determined end, that can only be because the end is somehow intended, somehow willed or desired of set purpose. Many different and diverse actions or agents cannot possibly act for a single determined and definite end unless they are ordered or directed toward that end. And they cannot

[36] See St. Thomas, *Summa Theologiae*, I-II, 1, 1.

be so ordered or directed toward that end unless the end be intended or willed of set purpose. But an end cannot be willed or
desired unless it be somehow known. This brings us to the second
step in our proof; namely, the fact that an agent acts for an end
presupposes the existence of an intellect that knows that end.

B. FINALITY DEMANDS AN INTELLECT THAT IS DISTINCT FROM THE
   WORLD

Why finality or the ordering of something to an end demands
an intellect is easy to understand. Between the agent, the action,
and the effect there is a certain proportion or relationship. The eye
is made for seeing, and so it is constructed accordingly. It is not
constructed like a foot or a hand, because its proper action is to
see, not to walk or to hold things. An examination of the eye shows
that it is correctly constructed for the reception of sense images
of colored objects; and because of this knowledge man can
make lenses and manufacture cameras to obtain somewhat the
same result. In a hundred ways man can imitate nature, because
he recognizes in natural things the presence of the correct means
for the desired end.

But this proportion of means to end indicates that among the
many possible means those were chosen that were apt and fitting
for the end; therefore, this fittingness and proportion was known.
This selection of means to end is the proper work of an intelligence. For to apprehend an object as an end is to know it as
something to which other things are ordered, and this means to
see the object under a certain universal aspect or condition. And
this is to abstract the object from its concrete material condition.
and see it simply as something to which other things are ordered.
But such abstraction from matter requires an intellect. It belongs
then to an intellect to contain within itself the forms of things and
their relations and proportions, even before the actual order of
natural things comes into existence. Here is how St. Thomas explains this:

It belongs to the wise man to order. For the ordering of things is
impossible unless there is known the relation and proportion that the
things to be ordered have to one another and the order they have to
the higher thing that is their end. [Just as in the case of the eye, there

is an ordering or a proportion of the various parts among themselves and then the further ordering of the whole eye to the higher end, which is the act of vision.] For the order of things to one another is because of their order to the end. Now to know the relationships and proportions of things to one another can be done only by one having an intellect.[37]

Thus we see that to order either oneself to an end or to order something else to an end can be done only by an agent that possesses an intellect. Natural beings that have no intellect tend by a natural inclination toward their end. Some of these, like brute animals, tend naturally (that is to say, by the inclination or orientation of their very nature) toward an end that they apprehend. But a brute animal does not apprehend the end as end, but simply as this concrete sensible thing. Other natural beings, that have no cognition whatsoever, tend naturally toward an end they in no wise apprehend. In all these cases the end is either not known or not known as end. Therefore, such beings do not order either themselves nor any other thing to their end. Instead, they are ordered, they are directed to their end.

If, therefore, this determinate ordering of an agent to its end is to be rendered intelligible, if this order is to have any reason for existing, we must arrive at some agent that has within itself the idea of the term to be produced. We must arrive at an agent that knows the end as such. This agent will be really distinct from these natural things that are ordered to their end, as one having an intellect is really distinct from that which does not have an intellect, or as the one who orders is distinct from the one who is ordered. St. Thomas puts the matter clearly:

The end is determined for an agent by some other principal agent; as is clear, for example, in the motion of an arrow, which is moved indeed to a determined end, but to an end that has been determined for the arrow by the bowman. So, likewise, in the motion or operation of a natural being; this, too, is toward a determined end; and this, too, presupposes an intellect, which establishes the end of the nature and orders the nature to that end.[38]

Natural things which are destitute of an intellect cannot possibly direct themselves to their end. These beings cannot establish for

[37] *Contra Gentiles*, II, Ch. 24. Words in brackets added.
[38] *De Veritate*, qu. 5, a. 2, ad 5m.

themselves their end since they do not know the end. Thus this end must be established for them by another; namely, by the one who has given them their natures. Nor could he establish this end for a nature unless he possessed understanding.

C. THE SUPREME ORDERER IS GOD

All that remains now is to show that this supreme orderer of the universe is God. To order or direct a nature to an end means that the end must be known and hence must pre-exist within an intellect. This intellect may either possess of itself this knowledge of the order, or it may have received this knowledge from another. If these ideas or forms of the ends to be produced are had by this intellect of itself, these ideas would be one with the nature of the intellect. As the first source of all order in other things, this intelligence would be its own end and ordered to nothing outside itself. And such an intellect would be infinite. But if this knowledge has been received from another, then such an intellect might know the order that is in the world, but it would not be the cause or source of this order. And that is why if the very order and finality that is in the material world is to be rendered intelligible, we must posit an intellect that is the very first cause and source of this order.

Here two things should be carefully noted. The first is that in going from an intellect that has received this knowledge of the order from another to that intellect that has this knowledge of itself, we have not left the order of final causality and taken up a new argument on the plane of contingency and efficient causality. For we are still looking "in the same direction"; namely, for the ultimate source of order in our material world.

The second point to note is this: it is quite impossible for any finite intellect to be the cause of the order that exists in natural beings. It would be metaphysically impossible for God to be the first cause of the nature of a being and for some finite intelligence below God to be the first cause that orders this nature to its end. For what the nature of a being is, is determined by the end to which it is ordered. The nature and the end of that nature are inseparable in their being. It is because God wished to create beings that could think that he endowed them with rational natures and the power of understanding.

It must necessarily be the creator of this universe that pre-established the end of the universe, as well as the particular ends of all the natures that people this universe. It is impossible for God, say, to cause fire, and then for some finite intellect to direct this nature to its end, which is to exercise the act of heating and by so doing to produce heat in other bodies. For it is of the nature of fire to exercise the act of heating and thus to generate heat in other bodies. It is because the creator wanted to produce a being that could exercise this act, that he has caused such a nature as fire to exist.

4. ANSWERING THE OBJECTIONS

1) *Materialists and determinists.* Our first objection against the fifth way comes from those philosophers who deny the very principle of finality in the activity of natural things. These are the materialists of all ages, from Epicurus and Democritus among the ancient Greeks, to Spencer, Darwin and Julian Huxley[39] among the moderns and contemporaries. The latter-named are also material evolutionists. All these deny that natural things act for an end or a purpose, and explain all the actions of beings by efficient causality alone. As summed up by Aristotle long ago, for these men, "rain does not fall from the sky that the grain might grow, but simply from necessity. For what is taken up to a great height must of necessity become cold, and becoming cold, it changes into water, and water being heavy must fall."[40] All of which proves for them that there is a necessity in the actions of natural things, not that there is any finality or purpose in these actions.

The trouble with these early materialists is that they did not go far enough in their analysis of this necessity. For a philosopher can still ask himself *why* fire *necessarily* burns and ice *necessarily* cools. Does not the very presence of necessary or determined ac-

---

[39] For some references and texts of Darwin and Spencer, see Descoqs, *Praelectiones Theologiae naturalis* (Paris, 1935), Vol. 2, pp. 327–331. For Julian Huxley, see "Rationalism and the Idea of God," in *Essays of a Biologist* (London, Pelican Books, 1939), Ch. 6, and Etiènne Gilson's comments in *God and Philosophy* (New Haven, Yale University Press, 1941), pp. 128 ff.

[40] *Physics*, Bk. II, Ch. 8 (198b18).

tions presuppose the presence of finality in this activity? If fire burns rather than cools, it must be because the nature of fire is ordered to burning rather than to cooling. Fire is ordered to its act; if there were no ordering there would be no acting, for there would be no reason in the being why this effect should proceed from it rather than some other or opposite effect. Either these things are ordered to their acts or they do not act. But we see that they do act; therefore, they are ordered to their acts. And if they are ordered to their acts, they must be ordered by something that knows the end or term to which they are so ordered. These early materialists simply did not go far enough in their reflections upon the activity of natural beings.

The modern materialists and the materialistic evolutionists have tried to remedy this *lacuna* in the thought of their predecessors. For this purpose they appeal to two pseudo-scientific surrogates for philosophical causes. For the efficient cause of the philosopher they have substituted time, and for the final cause of the philosopher they have substituted chance. And so they argue as follows: given a sufficient length of time, the present order we find in the world could well have been, and in fact is, the result of chance.

We can explain their position by a simple example. The Bible as we have it today is made up of a certain order or sequence of different letters. The various possible combinations of these letters, while mathematically overwhelming, are still finite in number. Therefore, given a sufficient length of time and trying one combination after another, there is no contradiction to say that sooner or later you would come up with the combination of letters that is our present Bible. So, too, with the order in this world. The universe is made up of particles of matter or energy existing in a certain combination or order. This combination, or order, could be merely the result of chance and a considerable length of time. Thus these scientists see no need for any principle of finality or for a God who is ordering things to an end.

What is our answer to all this? First of all, as far as possibilities go, if you throw into the air all the letters of the Bible they might come down the very first time just as they are found in the King James Version, even with all the footnotes nicely in place. So, too, the very first coming together of atoms could have resulted in the present order that exists in the world. But in the very first combination of the simplest of elements or gases, or whatever we call the primordial material being, there was activity. And being existential activity, it was a determined kind of activity. Why did this first particle act this way rather than that? Why did it act at all? If it acted at all, it acted in a determined way, and if it acted in a determined way, it was ordered to this act. And if it was ordered to this act, this order was intended.

A philosopher sees that the very activity of natural things presupposes finality and hence an intellect, just as the philosopher sees that the existence of natural things presupposes an efficient cause who is infinite and subsistent Being. Now a scientist, as a scientist, may not be expected to follow this reasoning, since it is philosophical rather than scientific; but it is not for that reason any less real or legitimate. The scientist as a philosopher, or maybe even as man, should be able to see it, provided he is willing to exercise his intelligence outside the limits of a strictly positive scientific method.

But someone may say: things can happen by chance, can they not? To which we answer, yes. And chance means that the action produces an effect that was not intended by the agent? Perfectly correct. Therefore, the present order in the world could have come about by chance, and since it is the only order we know, we cannot use it to show there is finality and hence a God who knows the order? This time the answer is no.

First of all, chance is intelligible only on the supposition that order exists. For example, if all truths were doubtful, you would not know they were doubtful, since you would not know they were not certain. Just as doubt presupposes certitude, so chance presupposes order. For chance is a privation of order, just as doubt is a privation of certitude; and so chance is intelligible only in terms of the order which it lacks. Therefore, chance can no more give rise to order than blindness can give rise to sight or doubt can give rise to certitude. A perfection cannot be caused by the very privation of that perfection. A thousand blind men will never add up to one man who can see, and a thousand chances will never add up to one instance of real order.

Recall from metaphysics how chance arises. Being "A" acts according to its nature, that is, for a determined end; being "B" also acts according to its nature; again, for a determined end. The two actions intervene and an effect is produced which is not the end of either of these agents or of either of their actions. We say the effect took place by chance. This effect or term is not ordered, at least not from the viewpoints of the immediate agents involved. But this term does presuppose order. So the occasional presence of chance events in our world, like monsters and floods and earthquakes, far from disproving finality actually proves it, for it presupposes it. It presupposes an order which in this particular instance is lacking.

2) *Kant*[41] *and the Kantians* see in the fifth way of St. Thomas a simple and naive anthropomorphism. Man sees that he acts for an end and has a purpose in what he does. He washes because he wants to clean his face; he studies because he wants to become a philosopher. And then man transfers this notion of purpose to non-human beings and asserts that they also, when they act, must be acting for an end or purpose. But it is highly arbitrary to transfer finality found in man to finality in the universe.

As is quite clear from our solution, St. Thomas in his fifth way makes no such transfer. We did not start with any analysis of human activity but with the regular and constant activity of things that have no intellect. And we did not conclude to the presence of an intellect ordering natural things by way of an analogy with our own human intellect, but by way of necessity, to explain the existence of the very order present in such activity. Furthermore, our own human intellect is itself a natural power that is ordered to its proper end. For man does not order his intellect to the truth; he finds that of its very nature it is already ordered to the truth. And man finds that his will is naturally finalized toward good. While man can order himself in many of his actions for ends that he sets up for himself, he nevertheless finds his powers initially

[41] The younger Kant, for example in his work *General Natural History and Theory of the Heavens* (1775), highly praised and commended the proof for God's existence from the order in the universe. But he criticizes this proof as anthropomorphic in the works of his maturity, for example, in both his *Critique of Pure Reason* (1781) and his *Critique of Judgment* (1790). He allowed to the principle of finality, at best, only a heuristic value for knowledge.

finalized toward ends that he has not established, but toward which these powers tend of their very nature.

But if natural things are ordered by their very nature to their proper end, such ordering is intrinsic and from within, and so they need not be ordered from without by an intellect distinct from these natural beings. The answer to such an objection should be obvious. A natural being is ordered to its proper end both by its nature and by an intellect. Immediately and intrinsically, it is ordered by its nature, but ultimately and extrinsically, it is so ordered by the divine intellect who has established the end and created the nature.

Finally, we should be careful not to confuse the fifth way of St. Thomas Aquinas, which argues from the existence of order in the universe to the existence of an infinite intelligence, with Paley's argument from design.[42] In the latter's argument the universe is seen as a complicated and intricate machine. And just as one who sees a complicated and intricate watch reasons to the existence of a watchmaker, so man, seeing the vast machine that is this world reasons, by way of analogy, to the existence of a divine watchmaker, or supreme architect of the universe.

This argument from design, as given by Paley and unfortunately repeated in many books on Christian apologetics, does not prove the existence of God. An architect of the universe would have to be a very clever being, but he would not have to be God; no more than a maker of watches would have to be God.[43] Also, like many a watchmaker, he may well have ceased to exist, as far as this proof is concerned, and his machine would be running quite smoothly without him. Many of the objections directed against what some writers believe is the fifth way of St. Thomas are really directed against the watchmaker of Paley. St. Thomas's proof is entirely different. It is grounded in the metaphysics of finality, namely, in the existence of order. And this order, which is a kind of being, demands as its cause the here and now existence of a supreme intelligence which is also supreme Being.

3) *The Creative Evolutionists*, such as Bergson and Le Roy, do

---

[42] See William (Bishop) Paley, *Natural Theology* (New York, Harper & Brothers, 1855), Vol. 1, pp. 37 and following.
[43] See E. Gilson, *God and Philosophy, op. cit.*, p. 142.

indeed admit finality, but it is not a pre-ordered or pre-determined finality. Things act for an end, but they do not find the end ready made for them; rather they create the end themselves. The end is immanent in the very thing that acts; it is nature in its most vital and existentially creative moment. What these philosophers want to avoid is a universe with a pre-ordained history. Finite being does not tend to some pre-existing exemplar or ideal which it strives to attain or imitate. If this were so, then the end of all things, at least in the intentional order, would already be a given fact. If the activity of natural things were governed by fixed and eternal laws, the future would simply be an endlessly repeated present. It is much more in keeping with the flux and rhythm of the universe to say that it progresses by creating its effects, which are not given beforehand as ends, let alone as foreseen and pre-ordained ends. To say otherwise would reduce the universe to a relative staticism; whereas it is a complete and perfect dynamism. So the end of the universe should not be considered as something foreseen and willed by a supreme and separate intellect.[44]

To this objection we answer: (1) to say that things create their own ends is to render all activity in the universe simply impossible; (2) the fact that the universe is governed by finality in no way subtracts either from its dynamism (which creative evolution destroys) or its history. The first point is easy to see. For something to create its own end is a contradiction, since the action which creates the end must itself be an action without an end, since the existence of the end depends upon the existence of the action. For Bergson, until the action is posited, no end exists, either in the real or intentional order. There is no reason, therefore, why the agent should act at all, or act in one way rather than another. On the supposition that agents create their own ends, all real activity is rendered impossible.

The second point deserves a fuller treatment than can be given here. We will have to content ourselves with two or three statements of fact. The Being of God is infinitely perfect and infinitely in act. The divine intellect knows the end of each being, the rela-

---

[44] See Father Descoqs, *op. cit.*, II, pp. 332-342; H. Bergson, *Creative Evolution*, translated by Arthur Mitchell (London, Macmillan, 1911), pp. 57 ff.

tions things have among themselves and their higher order to the good of the whole universe, whose end is God himself. The knowledge of this order by God constitutes, as we shall see later, divine providence. Now there is nothing static in a universe where things imitate and share in the being and activity of God. And since our universe is hierarchical, with one thing ordered to another, and all ordered to the good of the whole universe, there is room for endless progress and evolution in the universe.

And while God himself has no history, since his Being is measured by eternity and possessed by him wholly all at once, his universe unfolds in time and does have a history. The Being of God, since it is measured by eternity, physically and really co-exists with all times—past, present, and future. And when we recall that this divine Being is the proper cause of the being of all things, holding them in existence by his power and directing them by his providence, we see how God can bring things to ever higher and more perfect ends, in a dynamic and evolutionary sweep that knows no bounds, since its source and its end is infinite and perfect Being.

4) A wise orderer does not destroy what he makes; for this is useless and against the notion of wisdom. One who is wise takes care of what he has produced. But among things of nature some are contrary to others and destructive of others. There does not exist, therefore, a supreme orderer of the world.

We reply that a wise orderer not only attends to what is helpful for the individuals he has made but also to what is beneficial for the whole. Although the destruction of one thing in the universe is not good for that thing, it is, nevertheless, good for the perfection of the universe. By reason of the continual birth and destruction of individuals the perpetual being of the various species is preserved, in which the perfection of the universe necessarily consists.

5) At least moral evils, since they are especially repugnant to the divine orderer, must not be permitted in the world. Because moral evil is present in human acts, it seems that the supreme orderer of the world does not exist.

We reply that moral evil in no way comes from God, but solely from the free will of man; however, it is permitted by God on account of a greater good. St. Thomas writes:

God has a greater love for the greater good and therefore wishes the presence of the greater good than the absence of a lesser evil. Hence, for the purpose of bringing forth greater good, God permits some to do moral evil, which is in itself most repugnant, although one moral evil is more repugnant to God than another; thus to heal one evil he sometimes allows one to fall into another.[45]

It should be added, however, that the achieving by God of a greater good is not the final cause or reason for permitting the evil, but only the occasion for its being permitted. There will be more on this subject in the treatise on Divine Providence.

5. SUMMARY OF THE FIFTH WAY

"From the presence of order or finality in the world the existence of God is demonstrated under the intelligibility of supreme orderer."

A. STATE OF THE QUESTION

In the fourth way the intellect, considering the various degrees of perfections, attained to God as the supreme degree of these perfections. This way has been aptly designated the way of contemplation. By contemplating these grades of beings, the intellect comes to understand that there is in the world a kind of splendor arising from its order. In the fifth way, we consider this order. What is order? Does it exist in the world? If it exists, what consequences does this fact hold? From the presence of order in the world we can demonstrate the existence of God as the ultimate source of this order, or as the supreme orderer of all things. And since it is the office of the wise man to order, this way is correctly named the way of wisdom. As we progress along this way we see how all things have been ordered by God.

B. EXPLANATION OF TERMS

1) ". . . *order* . . ."—some proportion or relationship between two or more things. These things which are ordered are either distinct as complete beings or as principles of being. Thus, for example, matter is ordered to form, substance to accidents, essence to the act of existing, nature to operation, operation to its object, and so forth.

[45] *De Veritate,* qu. 5, a. 5 ad 3.

2) *"end"*—that on account of which something acts or that toward which something is ordered; for example, form is the end of matter, operation the end of a nature, the completed work is the end of the operation, and so forth. The end, moreover, perfects the thing because it is its good and the cause of the thing's activity. Everything seeks after good. Therefore, the end always contains the intelligibility of good and the good that of end.

3) *". . . finality . . ."*—the very order toward the end, or the ordination. This ordination is determined and definite for each nature.

4) *Final causality*—the influence of the end upon the operation of the agent. This influence, as such, is in the order of knowledge. For the end as the achieved effect does not yet exist in the real order. The causality of end lies in the attraction the end has as something to be accomplished or attained. Therefore, the causality which the end exerts always presupposes an intellect in which the term to be produced intentionally exists.

5) *". . . the existence of God is demonstrated . . ."*—that is, as supreme intellect in which there exists intentionally the term to be accomplished by each thing. We say the term exists in God intentionally because it exists there both as end and as thing known, or as an idea.

6) *". . . supreme orderer . . ."*—insofar as God possessing knowledge of the end of all things can direct them to their end.

C. ADVERSARIES

1) *The order in the world is the result of chance.* Epicurus, Democritus, Lucretius, and among the moderns, all the Materialistic Mechanists, most Positivists and many Evolutionists, deny that there is finality in the world: thus, for example, Buchner, Haeckel, Littre, Darwin, Spencer, the Marxists.

2) *The order in the world is the result of necessity*, that is, the result of blind fate and not of an intellect: Heraclitus, Empedocles, and others.

3) *Kant*, in his later years, having succumbed to the influence of Humean empiricism, said that this argument possessed no probative force, since the concept of finality was anthropomorphic and had sprung from an unwarranted application of the laws of

human activity to the activities of the things of nature. However, even if it is invalid in metaphysics, Kant said that the principle of finality does lead us to *believe* in God.

4) *Many idealists*, although they do not deny the finality in the world, admit only an immanent finality; there is no ordering cause really distinct from the things which are ordered. Thus Hegel, Renan, Richet, Goblot, and others.

5) *Bergson, Le Roy*, and other adherents of the Philosophy of Becoming assert that natural things do not act like an architect who by the use of certain means attains an end which he had previously set up for himself, but rather like an inventor, who continually searches and experiments until he finds an end. Therefore for these philosophers the end is more of a force which pushes rather than one which attracts; it is more a push from behind than an attraction from the front. Natural things give rise to their end by their own spontaneous activity.

D. THE ARGUMENT: THE FACT OF EXPERIENCE WITH WHICH THIS
   PROOF BEGINS

The things of nature always or almost always act in the same manner; therefore, their actions are determined and definite; for example, fire heats things, animals give birth to offspring of the same species, and so on. From this fact we argue in the following manner:

1) From the regularity of actions, there follows that there is an order between the agent, its operation, and the effect.

2) From this order it follows that all agents act for an end.

3) From the fact that the things of nature act for an end, it follows that this end must be foreknown.

4) But knowledge of an end presupposes an intellect which knows the end.

5) But natural things which act for a known end lack an intellect.

6) Therefore there must exist an intellect distinct from these things, in the manner that a thing not possessing an intellect is distinct from one having an intellect.

7) Moreover, this intellect which has knowledge of the ordina-

tion of things toward their end either has this knowledge of itself
or from another.

8) But there cannot be an infinite regress in intellects having this
knowledge from another. Therefore, there must exist a supreme
intellect which is the first cause of all things in the order of finality
and which guides them to their proper ends. And this is God.

E. THE PROOF FOR EACH STEP OF THE ARGUMENT

1) That which regularly and constantly produces the same effect is determined to that effect. For if the agent is not determined
to this effect, there is no reason why it should produce this effect
rather than some other. An agent which is not determined to some
effect would not attain any effect. But, as a matter of fact, it does.
Therefore, it is determined to an effect; and this is to act for an
end. (Conclusion of No. 2.)

3) That this end must pre-exist in the agent is clear. For the end
determines the agent in its action and, therefore, must be in the
agent in some way. But the end as effect does not yet exist. Thus
it must be intentionally present before it exists as effect.

4) That which is intended must be known because nothing is
desired unless it is known. But the end which is intended is an object of desire. Therefore, it must be known.

5) That many natural things have no intellect is clear. Brutes
act for an end apprehended in sense knowledge; therefore, the end
is not known as end but as something concretely pleasant or harmful. Plants and other natural things in no way apprehend an end.
But the end must be known as end; otherwise the thing cannot be
directed to it. Now the things of nature are directed to an end;
therefore, there must exist an intellect distinct from these things.
(Conclusion of No. 6.)

7) For an intellect to have this knowledge of itself or from another is a complete disjunction. If knowledge of the end is from
another, it is apparent that the intellect knows the order in our
world, but it cannot cause this order, because this knowledge is
from another.

8) If there were an infinite regress, the order in this world
would not be rendered intelligible because there would not be a
first cause to order things towards their end. There must exist an

intellect which possesses of itself and by itself the knowledge of the order in this world. In this intellect the ideas, or the forms of the terms to be produced, have not been received from another. Hence they are of the same nature as the intellect itself. Therefore this intellect is first truth, the establisher of natures and the ordainer of their ends. And this is God.

F. A general proof for God's existence

Having studied in detail the five ways of St. Thomas for establishing God's existence, let us turn our attention to a more general proof that underlies any Thomistic demonstration that proceeds from the being of our experience to the Being of God. Such a proof is drawn from a consideration of the act of existing and the proper cause of such an act. We will present this proof in a rather summary form, but with sufficient development so that it can be grasped by the student, provided he recalls carefully to mind what he learned in general metaphysics concerning the act of existing and the principles governing proper causality.

Our proof begins with a reflection upon the existing things around us. The purpose of this reflection is to see, in a general fashion, that within a being there is a difference between what the being is and the act of existing by which it is. Let us consider several different existing things: this red rose, this white horse, this newborn babe. Obviously, these are different kinds of being; a rose is not a horse, nor a horse a baby. And yet while they are different kinds of being, all these beings have something in common: they all are, they all exist. Therefore, at one and the same time they have something in common and they are different.

Why do they differ? Because each has a different essence, each is different in what it is. And what do they share in common? Existence; each one is, each possesses an act of existing proportioned to its essence. If I ask what each of these beings is, I get three different answers. But if I ask whether each being is, I get the same answer. Now, as is evident, when two beings differ and are alike at the same time, that principle in the being by which they are different, namely their essence, cannot at the same time be that by which they are alike, namely, their act of existing, which all have in common, although in varying degrees.

To the answer to the question, what a thing is, corresponds the essence of that existing thing. To the answer to the question, whether the thing is, corresponds the existence of the thing. And since we have seen that these two principles cannot be the same in the thing, it follows that there is a real distinction in the thing between the essence and the act of that essence—existence. Or to put it positively, there is in the thing an actual composition between essence and existence.[46]

Second step of proof. This step of the proof consists in showing that only a Being whose proper nature or essence is "to exist" can be the proper cause of the existence of other beings. Or to put it another way, the perfection of existence can never be the proper effect of any being in which there is an actual composition between its essence and its act of existing.

Existence (*esse*) is the common effect of all finite causes, for every cause influences in some way the existence of its effect, either substantially or accidentally. And since existence is the common effect of all finite causes, it can be the proper effect of no finite cause. But every effect must have its proper cause, something that produces the effect through an activity of its own nature, through an activity proper to itself. And since no finite being is the proper cause of existence, for existence is not the proper nature of any finite thing, the proper cause of existence will be infinite Being.

That uncreated Being is the first and only proper cause of existence (*esse*) is one of the most frequently established themes in the writings of St. Thomas.[47] To him nothing seemed more obvious or easier to prove than this fact. Where we have different causes producing many different effects, the diversity of these effects can only be due to the diversity of the natures involved:

[46] Notice, we are not saying here, in this general Thomistic proof for the existence of God, that any and every philosophical proof for God's existence is based on the actual distinction within a finite being of its essence and act of existing. But what we are saying is this: in our opinion every proof for the existence of God based upon *St. Thomas's* notion of being either presupposes this actual distinction or establishes it in the course of the demonstration. That the nature of such a distinction can be easily misunderstood goes without saying.

[47] See, for example, *Summa Theologiae*, I, 45, 5, ad 1m; *Contra Gentiles*, II, Ch. 15, par. 2; *De Pot.*, qu. 7, a. 2, *resp.*

every agent acts similar to the way it is. But if there is present in these different effects an element that is common to all of them, this common element cannot be reduced to anything that is proper to these natures. And since existence (*esse*) is the common element produced by every finite nature, existence cannot be the proper effect of any finite nature.

Let us take a simple example to prove this point. A builder causes a house to exist. Fire causes fire to exist. What is proper in the one case is the house, and in the other, the fire. Hence the builder is the proper cause of the *house* and fire is the proper cause of *fire*. But both made their effects exist. Hence, since existence is common to both effects, it is proper neither to the builder nor to the fire.[48]

Two important facts follow from this simple consideration. The first is this: if we are to find the proper cause of existence, we will not find it until we arrive at an agent whose own proper form is an act of existing. Causality is activity; to cause is to educe from potency to act. But eduction from potency to act can only be accomplished by a being in act. Every agent acts insofar as it is in act. And an agent is in act through its form. Now when we say that an agent is in act through its form, we do not mean to imply that it is the form that actuates a being. Form is act only in the essential order. What form actuates is matter, thereby giving to substance its final complement in the order of essence, rendering substance immediately capable of existential actuality. Through form, substance becomes a fit subject of existence. But it is existence that actuates substance in the order of being. Therefore, a being as being is in act through existence. But a being as agent, as producing this rather than that determinate effect, is in act through its form.

When we say, then, that every agent acts insofar as it is in act, and it is in act through its form, what precisely do we mean? We mean that the form, say the form of man or fire, limits the existence to the existence of a given particular nature. Hence, when a particular being acts, it will be limited in its activity by what it is, that is, by its form. When it acts, it must, therefore, produce

[48] *De Pot.*, qu. 7, a. 2c.

effects that are proportioned to this form. Its proper activity is confined to its proper nature.

Our conclusion, then, becomes clear. Existence as an effect can be proportioned or proper only to that being whose very nature is existence, where, therefore, existence is limited by nothing but itself, that is to say, where it has no limits whatsoever. Such a Being must be pure act, subsistent existence. And this Being we call God.

If only an agent whose very nature is existence can be the proper cause of created existence, then our second important fact becomes obvious. All other agents, insofar as they do produce existence, will do so only as instruments of this proper cause. All created beings do produce existence, because all created beings do participate in "the nature" of existence;[49] but the effect thus produced is not proper to them nor proportioned to them, but only to the Being whose nature is unparticipated, subsistent existence.

If God alone is the only proper cause of existence, then all created effects can remain in existence, only so long as God is continually present, causing and preserving this existence. For the removal of a proper cause automatically and immediately results in the removal of what it is properly causing. Thus if any creatures are even conservative causes of existence (*esse*), they will be so only as instruments of the first cause.[50]

Our general proof, then, for the existence of God can be summed up as follows: Every effect must have its own proper cause. A proper cause is one that produces its effect through an activity that is proportioned to its own proper nature. Fire is the proper cause of fire, man is the proper cause of man, since "fire" and "man" are the proper natures of these causes. The proper cause of existence, then, can only be a being whose proper nature is "to exist," where there is no distinction between what that being is and its existence. Hence, from a consideration of beings that share in existence, the mind is led to affirm a Being who is unparticipated existence, a Being who is by reason of his very essence, and who is, therefore, the proper cause of the existence of all other beings. And this necessary Being we call God.

[49] *Contra Gentiles*, II, Ch. 66, par. 7; *Summa Theologiae*, I, 45, 5, ad 1m; *Summa Theologiae*, I, 104, 1.
[50] See *Summa Theologiae*, I, 104, 2.

READINGS

Etienne Gilson, *The Christian Philosophy of St. Thomas Aquinas* (New York, Random House, 1956), Chapter III, "The Proofs for the Existence of God," pp. 59–83. Brief clear summaries of each of the five ways.

Jacques Maritain, *Approaches to God* (New York, Harper & Brothers, 1954), pp. 16–71. Discussion of some modern objections against the five ways.

Joseph Owens, "The Conclusion of the *Prima Via*," *The Modern Schoolman* (1952–1953), pp. 33–53.

XII

The Nature of God

A. Man's knowledge of the divine nature

1. THE PROBLEM OF KNOWING THE NATURE OF GOD

Having seen that the existence of God can be demonstrated, we are now ready to investigate a new and a different problem; for a philosopher is not only interested in the existence of things but also in investigating their nature or essence. Hence it is quite natural and in accordance with reason that having established the existence of the first cause of being as being, we should now want to understand the *nature* or essence of this first cause.[1] The essence of a thing is that by which a thing is what it is. Can the human mand know *what* this first cause of being is? Or can the mind of man simply arrive at the bare and unqualified fact that there *is* such a cause and no more? That is the precise problem we want to investigate in this present chapter.

One fact may be noted at the outset. It is quite impossible to have knowledge that something exists without by that very fact possessing some vague and confused knowledge of what that thing is. And this is so because the very causes that lead us to affirm the existence of this thing lead us also to affirm that existence in some qualified or determined way. Each of the five ways posited the same existing term, but each did so under a slightly different formality. I know that this term is immutable, necessary, unlimited, intelligent, and so forth. In other words, the five ways themselves give the mind some vague knowledge of the nature or essence of

[1] See *Summa Theologiae*, I, 12, 1.

the term to which they lead. Thus we have already achieved by means of these very investigations into God's existence more than the simple unqualified knowledge that when I say "God exists," all I know is that this proposition is a true proposition. The very truth of this proposition must include some other truths. If this proposition told me *absolutely nothing* about the subject "God" except *mere existence* it could not even tell me this; for I would have no way of distinguishing the existence of God from the existence of any other being. To know that God exists is to know that an unchangeable, necessary, unlimited, intelligent Being exists. And this is already some knowledge "about God's nature."

2. SOLUTION TO THE PROBLEM

Although God is supremely intelligible in himself, the human mind in its present condition is unable to know what God is, either through any intuition or through any abstracted form that could represent the divine essence. However, through God's effects in the world we are able to have some non-quidditative knowledge of God, by way of causality, excellence, and negation.

A. STATE OF THE QUESTION

Having established the existence of a Being completely immobile, wholly uncaused, absolutely necessary, supremely perfect, and the orderer of all things, we now wish to investigate a new problem. For the human intellect not only naturally desires to know the causes of things—even the ultimate causes—but it also desires to know the essences and natures of these causes. It therefore seeks to ascertain the essence of the first cause. (S.T., I, 12, 1)

An essence is that principle in a being by which it is what it is. Is it possible to know the essence of God? Or can the human mind in this life only ascertain the *fact*—and nothing further—of God's existence? In our position we see that the truth is found between two extremes. Although in this life the intellect can have no knowledge whatever of *what God is in himself*, it can, however, grasp more than the mere *fact* that God exists. And this knowledge of God (through the threefold way of causality, excellence and negation) can become for man more and more perfect. (*In Librum Boethii de Trinitate*, qu. 1, a. 2c.)

B. EXPLANATION OF TERMS

1) "... *intelligible* ..."—that which can be known in some way by the intellect.

2) "... *in its present condition* ..."—in this life, where our intellect is a power of the soul united to a body as the proper act of that body.

3) "... *what God is* ..."—the divine essence or quiddity as seen or known in itself; that by which God is God.

4) "... *intuition* ..."—that is, not merely immediate cognition, but knowledge of a thing according to that thing's mode of being, whether this intuition is effected without a *species* distinct from the thing known (as is the case in the beatific vision), or by means of such a distinct *species* (as in sense intuition). (S.T., I, 12, 2)

5) "... *through any abstracted form* ..." Although the intellect grasps, through a form or species an existing thing, it does not understand the nature according to its material mode of being. The material thing exists as sensible and individual, but it is understood as intelligible and universal. We say the nature is understood by abstraction, since it is considered apart from its individual sensible matter. Abstractive knowledge, moreover, may be had in two ways. (S.T., I, 12, 4):

(*a*) *immediately*—when a thing is known through its own proper form;

(*b*) *mediately*—when a thing is known through the form of another thing. (S.T., I, 56, 3) Here, in this context of knowledge, form and species are simply synonyms. Hence form here does *not* mean the substantial form of the thing, but rather it means that which the intellect abstracts from the thing. It is that because of which the thing is known. This form, as abstracted, is in the intellect; as known it is "in" the thing, that is to say, it *is* the thing as known.

6) "... *representing the divine essence* ..."—that is, giving us knowledge of *what God is* in himself.

7) "... *some non-quidditative knowledge of God* ..." This knowledge is:

(*a*) *proper*—that is, it is knowledge of God alone as distinct from every other being.

(*b*) But it is a proper knowledge obtained through other things; from the forms of God's effects and not from the divine form itself. In this sense the knowledge of God is opposed to proper knowledge derived from proper forms.

(*c*) *analogous knowledge*, that is, non-univocal, since the effects of God neither equal the power of their cause, nor are they in the same species or genus as this cause. Therefore, insofar as such knowledge that is gained about God can be applied only to him, it is called *proper*; insofar as it is based on other forms, it is *analogical*; and insofar as it is a knowledge from effects which do not adequate their cause, it is termed *analogous*.

8) ". . . *non-quidditative* . . ." In no way either perfectly or imperfectly, distinctly or confusedly, do we have any knowledge of the essence of God in itself. For in no way do the forms of his effects represent the divine essence as it is in itself. This non-quidditative knowledge *signifies* or points out God, but it does not *represent* his essence.

9) ". . . *through causality* . . ."—insofar as every cause, even an analogous one, produces effects similar to itself. The effects in the world are in some way similar to God. (*C.G.*, Bk. I, Ch. 29)

10) ". . . *through* . . . *excellence* . . ."—insofar as the divine agent, because he is his own act of existing, infinitely exceeds whatever is to be found in his effects. (*In Epistolam ad Romanos*, Ch. I, lect. 6)

11) ". . . *through negation* . . ." "Since God is a cause that exceeds his effects, nothing found in creatures can be compared to (the creator)." (*Ibid.*, cf. *C.G.*, Bk. I, Ch. 14) Through this "threefold way," which is not three independent ways, but rather one complete and adequate explication of the way of divine causality, the human mind more and more perfectly attains to knowledge of God. But this knowledge never tells us what God is, but only what he is not, or how he is, or how he is infinitely removed in his Being from creatures and infinitely transcends them.

C. ADVERSARIES

1) *Those who err through excess* say that God is the first thing known, or that the intellect in this life is able to have some sort of direct intuition of the divine essence. This is the position of the

Ontologists and *Illuminati.* For pertinent passages in St. Thomas, see *In Librum Boethii de Trinitate*, qu. 1, a. 1, and 3; *S.T.*, I, 88, 3.

2) *Those who err by defect.* (*a*) *Agnostics of ancient and medieval times:* as, for example, *Plotinus*, who taught that God was above being and therefore completely unknowable, and that men were united with God through love and not through knowledge. *Moses Maimonides*, who taught that men were unable to have any *positive* or *proper* knowledge of God. For example, when we say that God is wise, all we mean is that God causes wisdom, or that God is not stupid. As we shall see later, according to Maimonides names are predicated of God *equivocally*.

(*b*) *Modern agnostics:* such as *Kant*, who taught that God, as supra-sensible, in no way could be known through metaphysical principles. The existence of God is a postulate of the will, and his nature is entirely unknowable. The intellect can affirm nothing of God without contradiction. Others with the same views would include *Hamilton* and *Mansel. Modernists*, as *Loisy* and *Tyrrel*, hold that our knowledge of God has only an emotional and subjective value. It helps one to live a religious life if he thinks of God as personal, intelligent, and so forth. But such knowledge tells us nothing of God. The *Positivist* and *Empirical* view as put forth by *Hume, Mill, Spencer, Comte*, and others, has its philosophic foundation in the Kantian system: the principle of causality has no validity outside sensible things.

D. PROOFS FOR OUR POSITION

1) *God in himself is supremely intelligible.* (*a*) A thing is intelligible insofar as it is separated from matter, for matter, as pure potency, is the root of unintelligibility.

But God, as completely immobile, is separated from all matter. Therefore, in himself, he is supremely intelligible.

(*b*) A thing is knowable insofar as it is in act, for as in potency it can not act on the knowing subject.

But God is supremely *in act* (as first uncaused cause, completely necessary Being, perfect Being). Therefore, God is supremely knowable.

2) *The divine essence is not able to be known through sensible intuition.* God cannot be sensed, for there is no proportion be-

tween an actually intelligible object (God) and our sense power. (See *S.T.*, I, 12, 3.)

3) *The divine essence is not able to be known through intellectual intuition.* In this life the human intellect has no knowledge of essences unless they are abstracted from the phantasm. For the proper object of the intellect, as the power of a form in matter, is a quiddity which has existence in matter. But the essence of God does not exist in matter. Therefore, in no way can the divine essence be apprehended by the human intellect (See *S.T.*, I, 12, 4; 11)

4) *The divine essence cannot be known through any form representing it.* No created form can represent this essence, whether this form be abstracted from things or infused into the intellect by God. For any created form, since it is created, is not its own act of existing. But the divine essence is its own act of existing. Therefore, the created form cannot represent the divine essence as it is in itself. Note that the question here is about immediate (although abstract) knowledge. (See *S.T.*, I, 12, 2)

5) *However, we are able to have some knowledge about God through his created effects in the world.* (*a*) Every agent produces effects that are in some way like to itself; therefore, the effects of God in the world are in some way like God. (*C.G.*, Bk. I. Ch. 29)

(*b*) But God is not a *univocal* agent, and so the effects he produces are not of the same nature or essence as God. His effects do not equal the fullness of his power. Therefore, they are not adequate to give us a knowledge of God's essence in itself.

(*c*) Moreover, because the divine essence is its own act of existing, God cannot be put into any *genus*; and so we are unable, through his effects, to have any knowledge of his essence in itself, even the most generic and imperfect knowledge.

6) *By way of (a) causality, (b) excellence, and (c) negation:* (*a*) "... according as his power in producing things is more perfectly known; ... because a cause is more perfectly known through its effect in proportion as the relation of cause to effect is more and more perfectly seen in the effect." *In Lib. Boeth. de Trin.*, qu. I, a. 2.

(*b*) "... according as the cause of effects that are of higher degrees is known, for—since these effects bear a certain resemblance

to their cause—they more effectively manifest the superior perfection of the cause." *Ibid*. Moreover, since God is his own act
of existing and whatever is in God *is* God, it follows that all the
perfections of being are in God in an unsurpassed and eminently
perfect way.

(*c*) "Thirdly, insofar as God (the first cause) comes to be
known as more and more removed from all the qualities which
are manifest in the effects." *Ibid*.

Although St. Thomas does not always use the same terminology
in describing this threefold way, the following remarks can be
made concerning it.

(*a*) Since God can be put into no genus, we are unable, in our
advance toward a knowledge of God, to begin with a remote
genus and then add further differences. Instead of knowledge
by way of genus and difference, we must use the way of
removal, saying that God is not a body, not finite, and so forth.
One negation added to another makes more perfect our knowledge about God, until it becomes a distinct and proper knowledge;
that is, it can be said *only* of God and *distinguishes* him from
every other being.

(*b*) The material sensible beings of our experience are manifested to us chiefly through their accidents. God, of course, has
no accidents. But just as accidents are an external manifestation
of the inner nature of things, so God's effects (creatures) are in
some way an external manifestation of the divine nature. And so
we can use these effects to gain some knowledge of God. This is
done, *first*, by noting that these perfections in creatures are in
some way similar to God; *secondly*, by denying that these perfections are in God as they are in creatures. Since God is his own
act of existing, and since whatever is in God is God, these perfections as in God are identified with his own act of existing. And
so they are present in him in an infinitely more perfect manner.
Finally, since God infinitely exceeds and transcends all creatures,
none of the perfections in creatures are comparable to God. Our
investigation of God is always concluded by the use of the way of
negation. On this matter St. Thomas writes: "Whatever knowledge our intellect can have of God fails adequately to represent
him; and so the nature of God always remains hidden from us.

This, then, is the best knowledge we can have of God in this life: that he is above any thought we can have concerning him." (*De Verit.*, qu. 2, a. 1, ad 9m)

And again: "It is because human intelligence is not equal to the divine essence that this same divine essence surpasses our intelligence and is unknown to us; wherefore, man reaches the highest point of his knowledge about God when he knows that he knows him not, inasmuch as he knows that that which is God transcends whatsoever he conceives of him." (*De Pot.*, qu. 7, a. 5, ad 14m)

(*c*) For a better understanding of how our knowledge about God proceeds by means of this threefold way, let us consider how it works in the concrete, using as an example the perfection of "wisdom." We observe that some creatures are wise, and that wisdom is a perfection of being as being. So we affirm that God also is wise because he is the cause of wisdom in creatures (way of causality). We begin by affirming something of God.

But we see that wisdom in man is an accident and limited; so we deny that wisdom is in God as an accident or as limited. Here we deny something about God (way of negation). Finally, since wisdom in God is the same as his Being, we affirm that wisdom in God is infinitely more excellent than wisdom in creatures (way of excellence). By reason of the excellence that this perfection has in God, we end our investigation by stating that wisdom in God is infinitely removed from the wisdom of the creature, and that *what* this perfection is as in God is completely unknowable to the human intellect.

Even in its purified state this knowledge in no way represents the divine essence as it is in itself; neither as regards *that which is affirmed about God, nor the manner in which* it is affirmed. However, a more thorough treatment of this matter will be had later on, when we consider how this purified knowledge we have of God is predicated of him. For the present, we can say with St. Thomas:

There is a threefold application of terms to God. First, affirmatively: for instance, I can say *God is wise*, since there is in him a likeness to the wisdom that derives from him. But since that wisdom is not in God *as* we understand it and name it, we can truly deny this wisdom of

God, and say: *God is not wise.* Again, since wisdom is not denied of God as though he were lacking in wisdom, but because in him it transcends the wisdom we know and name, we must say that *God is super-wise.* Accordingly, Dionysius explains perfectly by these three ways of ascribing wisdom to God, how these expressions are to be applied to God.[2]

READINGS

St. Thomas, *Summa Theologiae,* in *Basic Writings of St. Thomas,* by A. Pegis (New York, Random House, 1945), Vol. 1, pp. 91–111. *The Division and Method of the Sciences,* translated by A. Maurer, C.S.B. (Toronto, Pontifical Institute of Mediaeval Studies, 1953), pp. 66–78.

Etienne Gilson, *The Christian Philosophy of St. Thomas Aquinas* (New York, Random House, 1956), Chapter IV, "Haec Sublimis Veritas," pp. 84–95, 97–110. Excellent pages on the way of Negation and Analogy.

B. The problem of naming God

1. CAN GOD BE NAMED?

Having seen how the human intellect in this life can attain to some knowledge of God, let us now consider how this knowledge can be predicated of God. This is the problem of naming God. For each thing is named according as it is known. What we say about a thing depends upon what we know about it. Predication is our use of knowledge. Through the triple way of causality, negation, and excellence we can possess a knowledge of God. Now we want to know whether this knowledge can be put into meaningful words that can be predicated of the divine essence? Are such words predicated in a metaphorical or proper sense, a univocal or analogous sense?

2. SOLUTION TO THE PROBLEM

The name that most aptly designates God is *Who Is.* Moreover, other names signifying perfections of being as being are said properly of God, and of creatures and God according to an analogy of proper proportion and of proper proportionality.

[2] From *De Pot.,* qu. 7, a. 5, ad 2m.

A. STATE OF THE QUESTION

Having considered the way God can be known by us, in this section we consider the way God can be named by us. For a thing is named according to the way it is understood. Now God is known by us through creatures, according to the way of causality, excellence, and removal. Thus God can also be named by us. This section, therefore, treats of the divine names, and answers these questions: How can we apply our knowledge to the divine essence? And more precisely, how do we predicate names signifying the divine perfections?

B. EXPLANATION OF TERMS

1) "... *name* ..."—any spoken word (or words), which immediately signifies the concept we have of a thing, and through this concept the thing thus conceived. As St. Thomas writes: "Words are the signs of concepts and concepts are the likenesses of things. And thus it is clear that words signify things through the concepts of the intellect. Therefore, according to the way a thing can be known by us, so it can be named by us." (*S.T.*, I, 13, 1)

2) "... *most aptly* ..." A name signifies some meaning or intelligibility, to which there corresponds in the thing some likeness, which likeness is the cause of this meaning or intelligibility. The name that signifies the perfect intellibility of a thing is its definition. And because the name "Who Is" signifies the quasi-essence of God, and therefore his quasi-definition, it is said to designate God most aptly.

3) "... *Who Is* ..."—subsistent Being itself. Unreceived, and therefore subsistent, Existence.

4) "... *perfection of being as being* ..."—because the act of being is "to be" (the act of existing), a perfection of being as being is one that follows the act of existing as such, rather than its reception in some potency (essence). And because the act of existing is simply act, and is in no way ordered to any other act, a perfection of being as being includes in its signification no imperfection.

5) "... *properly* ..."—this is opposed to metaphorically.

What is said properly of a thing is intrinsic to a thing, and does not merely have some extrinsic relationship (cause, sign, and so forth) to it. Thus, for example, heat is said properly of fire.

6) "... *analogy* ..."—a proportion or likeness of one thing to another. "Analogy" is the proportion or likeness itself between two (or more) things. The "analogates" are the things that possess the likeness. The "principal analogate" is the thing that primarily and most perfectly possesses the analogous perfection. There are different kinds of analogy:

(*a*) *analogy of attribution:* this is had when the analogous perfection is intrinsic to only one of the analogates, but is attributed to the others because of some order which these have to the intrinsic perfection in the one analogate. For example, the perfection of health, which is intrinsic and proper to man, is attributed to medicine inasmuch as it *produces* health in man, to the diet insofar as it *conserves* this health, etc.

(*b*) *proper analogy:* this is had when the analogous perfection is intrinsic to each of the analogates. Proper analogy can be of two kinds:

i. *proper proportion:* the direct order or likeness of two things to each other. Thus an effect is directly proportioned to its cause.

ii. *proper proportionality:* the likeness of two proportions to each other. Thus the analogy between the analogates is not direct, since it is between the proportions. Each analogate has within itself some order or proportion, and because of this there is between the two analogates some proportionality, or proportion of proportions. For example, between four and a hundred there is a proportionality, since just as four is twice two, so a hundred is twice fifty. (See *De Verit.*, qu. 2, a. 11c; ad 4m; qu. 2, a. 3, ad 4m.) The likeness is not directly between the numbers, but between the proportions.

(*c*) *The analogy of being:* the order or likeness that obtains between beings as being, or between two things insofar as they exercise their act of existing and those perfections that follow this act of existing. The analogy of being is an analogy of proper proportionality, based on the proportion within each being of its essence to its act of existing.

C. THE PROOF

1) *The name that most aptly designates God is "Who Is."* (*a*) Because "Who Is" signifies no form, but only act: the act of existing. And it signifies this act as a proper name. Therefore, since names are imposed on things to designate their very essence or nature, and since the divine essence is its act of existing, it is clear that the name "Who Is" most aptly designates God.

(*b*) Because "Who Is" designates God as in no way limited or determined. All other names, such as wisdom, love, the good (God), the truth, imply some composition or determination. And while such names as the One, the True, the Good, are convertible with Being, they nonetheless add to Being a relation of reason. And so the name "Who Is" as signifying something altogether simple and indetermined, most aptly designates God.

(*c*) Because "Who Is" implies existence in the present. And in the case of God this is most befitting, since "his Being knows neither past nor future," as St. Augustine writes in his *De Trinitate* (Book V). (See *S.T.*, I, 13, 11)

2) *Names signifying perfections of being as being are said properly of God.* Any name is said properly of a thing if *what is signified* by the name is found really and intrinsically in the thing signified. But perfections of being as being (or *what is signified* by such names) are found really and intrinsically in God. Therefore, names signifying perfections of being as being are said properly of God.

Proof of the major: To have something properly is to have it as one's property or proper possession (that is, really and intrinsically), and not merely metaphorically or by way of extrinsic denomination.

Proof of the minor: God, as Subsistent Being and Pure Act, possesses all perfections in whose signification there is contained no imperfection. Otherwise God would not be the Perfect Being. Moreover, God, as the cause of these perfections in creatures, must act according to his nature. Hence, creatures are really like God because of these perfections. Therefore, *what is signified* through the names of such perfections is properly said of God. It is clear, however, that *the way* such names signify these perfections is in no way said of God. Finally, whatever there is of imperfection in the creature, such as limitation and potency, is not in the creature because it has been produced by God, but because it has been produced by God *from nothing*.

St. Thomas puts this last point clearly:

There are certain things in creatures according to which they are like God, namely, things in whose signification there is no imperfection, such as life, being, understanding, etc. And these are said properly of God; in fact, they are said more properly and eminently of God than of creatures. But there are other things in creatures according to which they differ from God, and are consequent upon creatures' production from nothingness, such as potentiality, privation, motion, etc., and these are not in God. All those names in whose signification fall such conditions (like potency, etc.), are said of God only metaphorically, such as lion, stone, etc., since they contain matter in their definition. These words are said metaphorically of God because of some likeness of effect.[3]

By "likeness of effect," St. Thomas means that God sometimes acts in his effects like a lion, a fire, a fortress, and so forth. For example, God can metaphorically be called "an angry fire" because of the severity of his punishments.

3) *Names signifying perfections of being as being are said of creatures and God by an analogy of proper proportion and proper proportionality.* (*a*) *of proper proportion:* Every effect is directly ordered to and properly like its cause. But creatures are the effects of God, who is their first efficient, exemplary, and final cause. Therefore, *etc.*

(*b*) *of proper proportionality:* Proportionality is the proportion of two proportions to each other, or a likeness of proportions. But the likeness which obtains between created and divine perfections is a likeness of proportions. Therefore, *etc.* The *major* is the definition of proportionality, which has been explained above.

Proof of the minor: Among all beings there is present some real likeness: every being, as being, is like every other being. (I could not say: this creature is a being, God is a Being, unless the creature and God were like each other as beings.) Hence, the reason for this likeness must be found in the being itself of God and the creature. As we know from metaphysics, each thing holds its grade and perfection of being from its order or relation to its act

[3] From *De Pot.*, qu. 7, a. 5, ad 8m.

of existing. According to the different ways beings exercise their act of existing is due the differences among things, and according to a like exercise of the act of existing is due the analogy or proportion among things.

Now God is the Being he is because he *is* his own act of existing, and creatures are the beings they are because they *have* (more or less perfectly) their acts of existing. It is clear, therefore, that between creatures and God there is some proportionality, because just as the creature is the being it is because of its relation to its act of existing, so God is the Being he is because of his identity with his act of existing.

READINGS

St. Thomas, *Summa Theologiae*, in *Basic Writings of St. Thomas*, by A. Pegis (New York, Random House, 1945), pp. 112–134.

G. B. Phelan, *Saint Thomas and Analogy* (Milwaukee, Marquette University Press, 1941).

J. F. Anderson, *The Bond of Being* (St. Louis, B. Herder Book Company, 1949), Chapter XXII, "The Essence of Metaphysical Analogy," pp. 295–313.

XIII

The Perfections of God

PRENOTE

Thus far in our study of the nature of God we have discussed the following points: (1) how we can know God from creatures and grow in this knowledge by a growth in our understanding of the relationships that creatures have to God; (2) how names signifying perfections found in creatures are used when said of these perfections as existing in God. Now we are ready to go a step further and ask ourselves this question: How do these perfections found in creatures and predicated of God actually exist in God? Are all perfections found in creatures also found in God? and if so, how are they so found?

In this chapter we shall divide our study of the divine perfections into five parts. In the first part we shall discuss the problem of how the divine essence, although absolutely simple or uncomposed, nevertheless possesses all perfection. Secondly, we shall investigate how perfections found in creatures pre-exist in God. Thirdly, since God possesses all perfections, we shall discuss the nature of his divine infinity, and this study of God as infinitely perfect will lead us to consider him as the supreme and absolute good. Fourthly, we will discuss how the divine perfections are distinct from the divine essence and from each other. Finally, we shall treat briefly of the omnipresence, immutability, and eternity of God.

A. Divisions of the divine perfections

Our study of the divine perfections becomes clearer and easier once we have grasped the meaning of the terms involved. A large part of our study, then, will be devoted to the understanding of these terms.

A. GOD

From now on, since we are engaged in a scientific investigation of God, the name God is simply a serviceable substitute for that name which most aptly signifies the divine being, namely, "Who Is," or "Subsistent Being itself." "God" therefore equals "Subsistent Being," the divine essence as known by us and from which flow as from their ontological source the other perfections of God.

B. A DIVINE ATTRIBUTE

A divine attribute is any perfection that I can say of God, any predicate I can make of my subject, subsistent Being. Traditionally, the divine attributes have been divided in various ways.

1) (a) *entitative:* that attribute which flows from the divine being considered in itself rather than in its operation, for example, simplicity, infinity, eternity, and so forth.

(b) *operative:* an attribute that implies some divine action, for example, love, wisdom, justice, mercy, and so forth. Also considered here are those attributes that are the direct sources of these activities, namely, intellect and will.

2) (a) *positive:* any divine attribute that is conceived by a positive concept or expressed by a positive term. By positive is meant the placing of something, rather than its removal, for example, love, mercy, wisdom, and so forth.

(b) *negative:* any attribute conceived after the manner of a negation and expressed by a negative word. By a negative term is meant a term that removes something from God rather than posits it. But here we should note that while the manner of conceiving the perfection and the word used to express it may be negative, what the word signifies is in itself something positive. For example, the word *infinity* denies limitation, but limitation is itself a denial of perfection. Thus infinity is really a negation of a negation, and two negatives make a positive. And this is true of all the so-called negative perfections of God, like infinity, immutability, immateriality, and so forth.

3) (a) *absolute:* a perfection that belongs to God necessarily and independently of any hypothesis or contingency, for example, independently of the contingent fact that creatures exist. Thus, the perfections of infinity, simplicity, knowledge, eternity, and so on.

(b) *relative:* some perfection that is said of God because of the actual existence of creatures, for example, creator, lord, provider, ruler.

4) (a) *incommunicable:* a perfection in God that cannot be shared by the creature since it signifies a removal of an imperfection that is necessarily connected with created perfection. Thus all the negative perfections of God are incommunicable perfections, for example, immutability, infinity, and so forth.

(b) *communicable:* an attribute that can be shared by the creature in a finite way. Thus God's positive perfections like wisdom, goodness, or love.

Two things should be noted about these divisions. First, they are not mutually exclusive. For example, infinity is an absolute, negative, incommunicable, and entitative perfection. In fact, any perfection of God would fall under one of the two sets of the different divisions. Secondly, these divisions have come down to us chiefly from such men as Moses Maimonides and Suarez[1] and not from St. Thomas. But as traditional divisions they should be known by the student.

1. The divine perfection of simplicity

A being is simple insofar as it lacks composition. Hence there will be varying degrees of simplicity within a being according to the different orders within that being in which it is not composed. A composed being is one that possesses parts or principles, but parts so ordered to each other as to effect a unity, a composed unit. The actual union of these parts into a unified whole we call composition. Thus matter and form are parts of a material essence, but they are so ordered to each other as to effect a unity, namely, the composed essence. Thus that thing is simple which is not made up of parts and excludes composition.

There are two kinds of parts and thus two kinds of composi-

---

[1] See Emmanuel Gisquières, *Deus Dominus* (Paris, Beauchesne, 1950), pp. 329–330.

tion. First, there are physical parts, like matter and form, essence and the act of existing, substance and accidents. And these parts enter into physical or real composition, a composition within the actual existing being. Secondly, there are logical parts, like genus and specific difference. These enter into logical composition to form a definition. Thus *animal* and *rational* form the definition of man. That being is absolutely simple which is made up of no parts, either physical or logical. Composition in every order of being is excluded.

2. God is absolutely simple

St. Thomas urges two objections against God's absolute simplicity, which we shall give here by way of setting the problem. Every agent acts according to its nature. But every effect of God's action is a being that is composed. Hence the agent, God, must himself be composed. Secondly, composed things are more noble and perfect than simple things. For example, the composite man is more perfect than his separated soul; a compound is more perfect than an element. And since God is the most noble and perfect of all beings, he must be composed.

3. Solution

Perhaps the best way to prove that God is absolutely simple is to show that he is not composed in any of the orders of being. This is the way St. Thomas proceeds in his question in the *Summa Theologiae* on divine simplicity.[2] Simplicity is in itself a positive attribute, for it denies composition, which is an imperfection. Whatever is composed possesses some potency in its being, since any two parts in order to form a unity must be related to each other as potency to act. Moreover, a composed being needs an extrinsic agent to effect its composition. In denying that the divine Being is composed, we attribute a positive perfection to that Being. Here is our proof that God cannot be composed in any order of being.

1) God is not a body, and so possesses no quantitative parts. Every body is potentially divisible and moves only insofar as it is moved by another, as, for example, our human body is moved by

[2] *Summa Theologiae*, I, 3, aa. 1 to 8.

our soul. But as we have seen in the five ways, God is pure act and the first unmoved mover. And so he cannot be a body.

2) There is no matter in God, and so he possesses no essential parts. For matter is pure potency, and God is pure act.

3) In God, essence and the act of existing are the same, and so God is not composed in the order of being. If in God these were different, two contradictions would follow. Since essence would have to be ordered to the act of existing as potency to act (for from two acts in the order of being, two beings would result), it would follow that there is potency in God, which is impossible. Secondly, these two principles of being, if different, would need an extrinsic agent to bring them together in composition. But God is completely uncaused. Therefore in God essence and the act of existing are absolutely the same.

4) In God there are no accidents, and so he is not composed of substance and accidents, that is, he is not composed in the order of activity. Substance is in potency to its accidents, for it receives them and is perfected by them. But in God there is no potency; thus there can be no accidents.

5) Finally, the perfection of God's essence cannot be classified according to genus and specific difference, as can, for example, the essence of man, which is rational animality. For the essence of God is one with his act of existing—his essence is identified with his Being. And being, as we know, transcends all species and genera. Thus the divine essence has no logical parts.

4. GENERAL PROOF

We place here by way of summary two general proofs of God's complete simplicity:

1) Every composite being must have a cause. For what of themselves are different, do not come together to form a unity unless they be brought together by some cause uniting them. But God as first cause is absolutely uncaused. Therefore, he is also absolutely uncomposed or simple.

2) In every composite there is act and potency. In order to form a unit, one part must be related to the other as potency to act, because two acts cannot make one act. But in God there is

absolutely no potency, for he is pure act. Hence in God there is absolutely no composition.

5. Answering the Objections

The first objection against God's simplicity was as follows. Every agent acts according to its nature. But every effect of God is composed. Therefore, God as agent must be composed. We answer that it is of the nature of a caused being that it be composed, at least of essence and existence. It is of the very nature of uncaused being that it be uncomposed, even of essence and existence. Every agent acts according to its nature insofar as this is possible. God can communicate his perfections to others, but only as participated, and hence as composed. The objection simply applies a principle in a fallacious sense.

As regards the second objection, we say that among us composite beings are more perfect than some that are less composed, because a finite being reaches its perfection through many acts and not simply by existing. Thus man has more parts and is more perfect than an electron. But this is not true in God whose activity is one with his existence.

To conclude this discussion of God's simplicity, we should add that God cannot enter into composition with any other being. He is also simple in the sense that he cannot enter into composition with another as a part. St. Thomas mentions three errors in this regard.[3] Some have said that God is the World-Soul (Animistic Pantheism). Others have said that the divine substance was the formal principle of all things. Finally, David of Dinant held the rather odd doctrine that God is the same as prime matter, since there is no way to differentiate between the two.[4] David of Dinant was a logician, not a metaphysician, and he was the victim of a bad syllogism: God is pure potency; prime matter is pure potency. Therefore God and prime matter are the same.

It is obviously impossible for God to be either the formal or material cause of the world or of anything else. For these causes, as the very intrinsic constituents of the being, are numerically one

[3] See *Summa Theologiae*, I, 3, 8.
[4] See Etienne Gilson, *History of Christian Philosophy in the Middle Ages* (New York, Random House, 1955), pp. 241–43.

with the being. But God is the efficient cause of all being, and an efficient cause can never be numerically one with its effect, for it is extrinsic to the effect. Thus God could not be the material or formal cause of any thing.

6. GOD IS COMPLETELY PERFECT

When we say that God is perfect, we mean that God possesses that act or actuality proper to him as God. Hence, within this context, to say that God is *completely* perfect, means that God is completely in act. We mention this point at the outset so that we will not confuse the problem of the perfection of God with the infinity of God. The two problems are very closely related, but they are not exactly the same, as we shall see.

Etymologically, a thing is perfect that has been *per factum*, totally made or accomplished. And since what is made is reduced from potency to act, the word *perfect* has been transposed to mean *anything in act, insofar as it is in act*. Thus, man is perfect at the level of essence, but he is imperfect, or perfectible, at the level of accident. Each being is perfect in its substantial "to be," but imperfect, or perfectible, in its other modes of being. We say that God is completely perfect, since he is completely in act in the order of being; nothing is wanting or lacking to the Being of God.[5]

7. PROOF

Each thing is perfect insofar as it is in act. Now every agent, as agent, is in act. But we have seen that not only is God an agent, but the first agent. Thus as first agent, as uncaused efficient cause, God is completely in act and hence completely perfect in Being.

B. How the perfections of creatures pre-exist in God

1. PRENOTE

In this second part of our study we wish to do two things. First, to establish the fact that any perfection found in a creature must also in some way pre-exist in God. Secondly, and more impor-

---

[5] See *Contra Gentiles*, Bk. I, Ch. 28. For some objections against the divine perfection, read *Summa Theologiae*, I, qu. 4.

tantly, to show *how* these perfections can be said to pre-exist in the divine Being.

It would seem that not all perfections that exist in creatures pre-exist in God. For some of these perfections are contraries, like hot and cold, black and white, which can hardly be in the same subject at the same time. Moreover, the essence or nature of God is subsistent Being. But *to live* is more perfect than merely *to be;* and *to be wise* is more perfect than merely *to live.* Thus if God's essence is a subsistent "To be," how can he be said to possess the further perfections of life and wisdom?

2. SOLUTION

In God are the perfections of all things. The reason is that God is the first efficient cause of all things. An effect must pre-exist in some way in the power or virtue of its efficient cause. If not, there would be no reason why the cause could produce it. Moreover, the effect must pre-exist in the power of the cause according to the being of the cause. And since God's Being is completely in act and completely perfect, these effects must exist in God according to a completely perfect manner of being. Moreover, each perfection in the creature is a perfection only to the degree that it has being. "The perfections of all things," writes St. Thomas, "pertain to the perfection of being; for things are perfect because in some way they have being."[6] And since God is *subsistent Being,* no perfection of any thing is lacking to him.

It remains to be seen *how* the perfections found in creatures can be said to be in God. Once more we must have an exact understanding of the terminology involved. We have already seen that perfections can be of two kinds. First, those perfections in whose very notion there is contained imperfection, like reasoning, animality, etc. These are called *mixed* perfections, for of their very nature they involve imperfection. Secondly, there are those perfections in which there is no imperfection, like to be, to live, to know, and so forth. These are called *simple* perfections, or perfections of being as being.

We can make the following statements about these two kinds of perfections: (1) both are found in God virtually and eminently;

[6] *Summa Theologiae,* I, 4, 2.

(2) simple perfections are also found in God properly. Let us see precisely what the terms virtually, eminently, and properly mean.

1) *virtually:* one thing is contained, or pre-exists, in another virtually, if the latter has the power or virtue to be the efficient cause of the former. For example, the perfection of a painting exists virtually in the art of the painter. Another term closely associated with virtually is equivalently. One thing possesses another equivalently, if it can produce effects of the same nature as something in which these effects exist formally. For example, the human soul can be said to be equivalently an animal and vegetative soul. For although formally only rational, the human soul is the source of man's sensitive and vegetative functions. The word virtually refers more to efficient causality, equivalently more to formal causality.

2) *eminently:* one thing is contained in another eminently if it is contained in that other according to a higher mode of being than it has in itself. For example, wisdom is in man according to an accidental mode of being, but wisdom is in God as identified with the divine substance. Thus we say wisdom is more eminently in God than in man.

3) *properly:* a perfection is proprely in another when the actuality that is the perfection belongs to it intrinsically and by reason of the very perfection itself. Thus, humanity belongs properly to Paul, and goodness belongs properly to God.

3. Second solution

1) *Every perfection* found in creatures pre-exists in God both virtually and eminently.

(*a*) *virtually:* every thing in the creature is a perfection insofar as it has being or is ordered to being. But everything insofar as it has being or is ordered to being comes from God as from its first cause. Thus every perfection pre-exists virtually in God.

(*b*) *eminently:* whatever is in God, is God, for God's Being is absolutely simple. Hence, as in God, these perfections are identified with the divine Being, and so exist in God in a higher and more perfect way than they do in creatures.

2) *Simple perfections* are also in God properly. To show what we mean, let us take an example of two different perfections, ana-

lyze them, and see in what sense each may be said to be in God.

(*a*) *"to sense"* (*the perfection of sensation*): this is an act by which a sense faculty grasps cognitively a sense object—by seeing it, hearing it, tasting it, etc. The thing to be noted about such an act is this: it includes within itself sensible matter. Sensation is the act of a sense organ, and so cannot exist except as affected by the conditions of matter. Hence this perfection, according to what it signifies, necessarily includes imperfection due to matter.

In what sense can such a perfection be said of God? If I say, "God hears me," this predication must be by way of metaphor, for God has no sense faculties and so cannot *properly* be said to hear.

But I can say that sensation is *virtually* in God, for God has the power to produce beings who can properly sense. This is all that virtual presence means in an efficient cause. It simply states a fact that must be true; namely, since God does possess the power or virtue to produce them, these mixed perfections can be said to exist in this power as in their cause.

Secondly, I can also make this statement about mixed perfections: Since they do exist in the power of God as in their first efficient cause, and since the power of God is one with the Being of God, mixed perfections are in God *eminently*. Just as virtual presence refers to the power that can produce the perfection, so eminent presence refers to the mode of being of this power. Sensation is in an animal properly, since it is there by reason of the perfection itself. But sensation is in God only virtually, since God has the power to produce this perfection in animals. But since this perfection is present in God's power, and since this power is one with God's Being, we must also conclude that the perfection of sensation is eminently in God, for it is present there according to a higher mode of being than in the creature. And this is all we mean when we say a mixed perfection, like sensation, can be said to be in God virtually and eminently. What this two fold presence in God is opposed to is the presence the perfection has in the creature. For sensation exists in the effect (the animal) formally, properly, and according to the mode of being of the thing in which it is.

(*b*) *"to understand"* (*the perfection of understanding*): this also is an act. It is that act by which an intellect grasps cognitively an intelligible object, that is, by understanding it. If we analyze what this perfection is in itself, we do not discover any imperfection. This perfection does not depend upon matter, nor upon any of those conditions that follow dependence on matter, like motion, time, place, etc. Like sensation, understanding is an act; but unlike sensation, understanding is not dependent upon matter in order to be, and hence it is simply act.

With this in mind, in what sense can I say "God understands?" Obviously, I can say God has understanding in the sense that he can produce beings who can understand. In this sense understanding is virtually in God. The understanding that I find in creatures exists in God as in its first efficient cause. Further, since the power by which God causes is his own divine substance, the perfection of understanding also exists in God eminently.

Finally, the perfection of understanding, unlike that of sensing, exists in God *properly*. That is, this perfection belongs to the Being of God by reason of the very perfection itself. It is there intrinsically and in its own right, and not, for example, merely because God can cause it. Just as a perfection like rationality is proper and intrinsic to the being of man, so all simple or unmixed perfections are proper and intrinsic to the Being of God. The perfection itself that is signified is in God, and is God. In relation to the existence that these simple perfections have in creatures, they are said to be in God eminently or according to a more perfect way of being; but the perfection itself is also the proper possession of God. And the reason for this is that such perfections involve no imperfection, and so as in God they can exist according to the fullness and completeness of pure act.

We have made the statement that since the perfection of understanding involves no matter, it was simply act. Why then would it not follow that the perfection of an angelic essence, which possesses no matter, is simply act and thus properly in God? This should be noted about such a perfection of essence. While act in the order of essence, it is potency in the order of being (where act is "to be"), for it is ordered to the act of existing as potency to act. Therefore God, who is pure act in the order of being, cannot possess such a perfection properly. It is possessed properly only by the angel whose essence it is, and by God virtually and eminently.

In a word, the perfection of an angelic essence is not a perfection of being as being, it does not flow from the act of existing; it is the essence itself.

Most authors use the word "formally" where we have used the word "properly." They say that simple perfections are formally in God. There is an advantage and a disadvantage in using this word. The disadvantage is this: the word tends to formalize or essentialize the actuality of simple perfections. These perfections are not forms. They cannot be abstracted by the intellect as forms are abstracted from matter. The abstract terms *wisdom* or *life* are not conceptual abstractions like *man* or *animal*, and do not have the same intentional relation to the existent as do these latter terms. *Formally*, then, has the disadvantage of formalizing these perfections in God. But the word does bring out this fact: simple perfections constitute the very essence of God. God has these perfections essentially; whereas no simple perfection ever constitutes the essence of a creature. Creatures possess these perfections only by participation. In this sense they are not *formally* in creatures, whereas they are in creatures *properly*.

By way of summing up this teaching of how the different perfections that exist in creatures exist also in God, let us analyze a simple example and apply it, by way of an analogy, to our problem. We know that every agent acts according to its own nature. We know also that effects that proceed from a non-univocal cause, such as God, are less perfect than their cause, both as to the nature of the perfection and its manner of being. For example, what is simple and one in the cause is composite and many in the effect. Thus, one agent through a single causal power can produce a diversity of effects. For example, fire can heat, burn, blacken, or liquefy. So, too, God by the single power of his Being can produce a multitude of different creatures.[7]

Let us analyze this example of fire a little further, for it will throw some light on the problem of the pre-existence of perfections in the divine Being. In every effect, whether it proceeds from a univocal or an analogous cause, there is something that is like the cause and something that is unlike the cause. The likeness comes from the form that is educed and the unlikeness from

[7] See *De Pot.*, qu. 7, a. 1, ad 1m.

the matter from which the form is educed. Consider the case of a brick being hardened by fire. Insofar as it is heated by the fire, the brick is like the fire. Both are hot. But insofar as what is heated becomes hard and solid, it is unlike the fire. These last two effects are due to the matter that is being heated. If that in which the brick is like the fire be predicated of the fire, it will be predicated properly of the fire. For heat is properly both in the fire and in the brick. Indeed heat will be predicated primarily and more perfectly of the fire, since heat exists more perfectly in fire than in a hot brick. Fire is naturally hot, while a brick is hot only if heated.

On the other hand, if that in which the brick differs from the fire is said of the fire, the predication would be false. It is simply false to say that fire is hard and solid. But fire is *virtually* hard and solid because it can produce these qualities in the brick.

Now let us apply this example to divine causality. There are certain things in the creature that are like God, and these are those perfections that connote no imperfection in what they signify—perfections like being, life, and understanding. These perfections are properly said of God. Indeed they are said primarily of God and more eminently of God than of creatures. Just as heat was said properly of the brick and the fire, but primarily and more eminently of the fire, so being, life, and so forth, are said properly of God and of creatures, but primarily and more eminently of God than of creatures. God is Being and life essentially, while a creature is, or is living, only by participation.

On the other hand, there are things in creatures by which they are unlike God, just as in the case of the brick and the fire. And these things belong to the creature insofar as it is produced from nothing, just as these other things were in the brick because of its matter. Because the creature is "from nothing," it possesses potency, motion, privations, and so forth. And these things are false when said of God. Therefore, those names in whose meaning the conditions of created being are included, cannot be said properly of God. Of course, as we have already seen in the section on the divine names, such perfections, and even privations, can be said metaphorically of God. I can say, "God is deaf to my cries," or that he is a strong fortress, a purging fire. For in some of his effects God may act like a purging fire, and so on.

4. ANSWERING THE OBJECTIONS

Our first objection was this: not all perfections can be in God, for some, like black and white, hot and cold, are contraries, and can hardly be in the same subject at the same time. The answer is clear. Perfections that have contraries are mixed perfections, and are not properly in God, but only virtually and eminently. It would be the proper possession of these contraries that would constitute a contradiction.

The second objection stated that life says more than being and wisdom says more than life. But if God is subsistent Being, then he does not have the further perfections of life and wisdom, for these are not included in the notion of being. If they were, all beings would be living and wise. Here we must distinguish between being and the Being of God. It is quite true that something can participate in being, that is to say, in simple existence, and not participate in life or wisdom, which are higher ways of being. But the Being of God is subsistent Being, and subsistent Being includes all the perfections and modes of being.[8]

In a word, this objection is based on a faulty notion of the act of existing. For the act of existing is much more than simply that by which a being is outside nothing. Rather, it is the actuation of everything within a being. The act of existing is not perfected by life or understanding in living and intelligent beings; rather, it is the very actuation of living and intelligent beings. In different beings, the act of existing is more or less perfect because it is more or less limited by the essence. And so in God, where essence is the act of existing, the Being of God is subsistent and all-perfect.

C. God is infinite and supremely good

1. PRENOTE

Since the Being of God is completely in act, he is completely perfect; absolutely nothing is lacking to his Being. Therefore,

[8] *Summa Theologiae*, I, 4, 2, ad 3m.

we say that God is also infinite; there is no limit or term to his Being. To be perfect and to be infinite are not the same thing. The former posits in God the complete actuality of being and all the perfections of being; the latter removes or denies any term or limit to this being. But infinity flows from perfection: since God's Being is completely in act, there can be nothing potential or limiting within it.

2. IS THE BEING OF GOD REALLY INFINITE OR WITHOUT LIMIT?

It would seem not. What has some limit or term is finite. For example, a being which is in this place is limited or terminated by this place, so that it cannot also exist in some other place at the same time. Such a being, we say, is finite according to place. In like manner, a being that is this being, so that it cannot be another, is limited or finite in its being. But God is God and nothing else. He is not the world nor any part of the world. Therefore, God is not infinite in his Being.

3. SOLUTION

A thing is called infinite that in some way is not terminated. Literally, it is not finished. In a material being, matter is finished or terminated by form, and form by matter. Matter is terminated by form in the sense that before it received a certain form it was in potency to it and to many others; but having received the form, this particular potency of matter is terminated or finished by the form. Form, in its turn, is terminated or finished through matter, because considered in itself and apart from matter, form is common to many; but as in matter, it is the form of this thing only.

However, there is a great difference between the infinity or indeterminateness of matter without form and of form without matter. Matter is made perfect by the form that determines it. Thus material infinity, or uninformed matter, implies imperfection. Of course, matter does not exist without form, except as potency. All infinity based upon the potency of matter implies imperfection, for it considers the material being as not terminated by form. An example of such infinity would be the infinite divisibility of quantity and its potency to be infinitely added to.

Formal infinity, on the other hand, involves no imperfection. Form is not made perfect by matter, but rather contracted and limited by it. Thus form not determined by matter has the characteristic of that which is perfect.[9] Now that which is most "formal" in a thing is its act of existing. Not in the sense that "to be" is a form, but in the sense that everything in a being is related to the act of existing as potency to act, and that existence itself cannot receive anything. Existence says simply act and in no sense potency. Now the "To Be" of God is not received in anything. God is subsistent Being. And unreceived Being is simply infinite. God is infinite in his Being, without limit or term of any kind.

Furthermore, only God is simply infinite, for only his Being is unreceived. An angel is infinite in the order of essence, for its essence is not received in matter. But its act of existing is received and limited by the essence. And since "to be" is the act of being, the being of an angel is limited or finite. Infinity in Being is the exclusive and incommunicable attribute of God.

4. ANSWERING THE OBJECTIONS

It was objected above that since the Being of God does not include the being of the creature, God is not infinite but finite. Indeed the fact that God is subsistent Being whose act of existing is not received in anything, distinguishes God from all other beings and removes all these beings from God. God is by his very essence, creatures are by participation. But to answer the objection, we say that whatever of being is possessed by the creature God also possesses in an infinitely more perfect way. Thus the fact that there are beings other than God does not mean that God is not infinite in his Being. Moreover, if the Being of God included the participated being of the creatures, God would be finite, material, and so on, which is absurd.

Finally, while the fact that infinite Being co-exists with finite beings gives us more beings than the infinite Being alone, it does not give us more being (*plura entia sed non plus entis*). For example, after a teacher communicates his knowledge to many students we have many more who know (*plures scientes*), but we do not have any more knowledge (*plus scientiae*). So, too,

[9] See *Summa Theologiae*, I, qu. 7; *Contra Gentiles*, Bk. I, ch. 43.

after the creative act of God, by which he communicates being to creatures, there are more beings, but not more being.

5. IS GOD SUPREMELY GOOD?

Let us see where we have thus far arrived in our consideration of the divine Being. We established, after the proofs for his existence, that the essence of God as known by us is most properly grasped under the aspect of subsistent Being. All the properties or attributes of the divine Being are what they are because of this fact. As subsistent Being, God must be pure act. Because God is completely in act, God is absolutely perfect. Because God is absolutely perfect, he has no limit or term, and so is infinite. And now we want to show that an infinitely perfect Being is also supremely good.

What precisely is *good*? Aristotle says the good is that which all desire. A thing is good insofar as it is desirable. The good is being as desirable. But what makes being desirable? It is that which is most perfect and best in being. For example, we say this is a good play, or this is a good basketball game, because each has a certain excellence or perfection about it. A thing is good according as it is perfect. Being as good is being as in some sense perfect. Good and being are the same in the thing; but good adds to being the notion of desirability, which being as such does not expressly include. And so we say that good and being are different according to what they connote.

Let us consider more in detail this difference between good and being, so that on the one hand we will be better able to understand how in God the attribute of goodness differs from the divine Being, and on the other hand, how divine goodness is seen to flow from and depend upon the divine Being.

Since being and good differ in their notion, a thing is not said to be simply being and simply good in the same sense. A thing is said to be insofar as it is in act.[10] Now act has an order to potency. Therefore something is simply being according as it is first distinguished from that which is only in potency. That by which a being is first distinguishable from what is only in potency is its substantial "to be." Thus each thing is simply being because of

[10] See *Summa Theologiae*, I, 5, 1, ad 1m.

its substantial "to be." Because of subsequent and superadded acts, a thing is called being not simply, but "in a certain sense." For example, *being white* is not simply to be, but to be in a certain way. To be white does not remove simple potency, since it accrues to a being already existing in act.

Things are just the reverse as regards the notion of good. Good adds to being the notion of desirability, and hence is said of a thing according to that which is perfect and ultimate in it. Thus it is according to its ultimate perfection that a thing is said to be simply good. Consequently, that thing which does not have the ultimate perfection that it should have, although it does possess some perfection insofar as it is in act, is not simply perfect, and therefore not simply good. It is good only "in a certain sense."

Hence, according to its substantial being a thing is simply being but not simply good. And according to its ultimate perfection of being, a thing is simply good but not simply being. So when we speak of God as good, we are considering the divine Being precisely as ultimately and completely perfect, which is not explicit in the consideration of God simply as Being. The goodness of God, however, flows from and depends upon the Being of God. Since God is perfect Being, he is completely in act and good. Nor does the attribute of good add anything to the Being of God. It is simply the divine Being as more expressly considered; namely, considered precisely as the *fullness* of being.

God is not only good, but the highest good. And he is not only the highest good, but he is good by his very essence. That he is good goes without saying, for he is the cause of those perfections in things which we desire. These perfections are nothing more than participated likenesses of the divine goodness, so that in seeking them we are really seeking the goodness of God. St. Thomas puts this in a striking manner.

All things in seeking their own perfection are seeking God himself, inasmuch as the perfections of all things are certain likenesses of the divine Being. And so of those that seek God, some know him according to himself. And this is proper to the rational creature. Others know certain participations of his goodness, and such knowledge extends even to sensible cognition. Others, finally, have a natural seeking of God without any knowledge, and this is insofar as these things have been inclined towards their ends by some higher knower.[11]

That God is the highest good is also easy to see. Things are good because they participate in the goodness of God. Good therefore pre-exists in God as in the first cause of all things. As we have seen, God is not a univocal cause but an analogous one. Hence, good exists in God according to a manner of being infinitely more excellent than that which it has in creatures. And in this sense God is called the highest good.[12]

Finally, we say that God is good by his essence, which is not true of any other being. Let us see why this must be so. A thing is said to be good insofar as it is perfect; for good is being as desirable, and hence according to its fullness or perfection of being. Now the perfection of a thing is threefold. First, insofar as it has substantial being; secondly, insofar as it has added to it certain accidents necessary to act in a perfect manner; and, lastly, insofar as it reaches its end, which is the final perfection of a being. For example, the perfection of man consists, first of all, in the being that he has through his substantial form; secondly, in possessing such accidents as intellect and will by which he can act perfectly as a man; and, thirdly, in attaining the end of being a man.

Now no one but God holds this triple perfection by reason of his very essence. The essence of God is one with his Being, and that which is said by way of accidents of others, is said essentially of God, for God has no accidents. Finally, God is ordered to no end, but all other things are ordered to him as their final end. It is clear, therefore, that only God possesses all manner of perfection by his very essence. Thus he alone is good through his essence.

D. How the divine perfections are distinct from the divine essence and from each other

The divine Being is absolutely simple, and so absolutely one and uncomposed. Independently of our knowledge of God, his essence is not different from his perfections. Nor are these perfections

[11] *Summa Theologiae*, I, 6, 1, ad 2m.
[12] *Ibid.*, a. 2.

different from one another. God and the perfections of God are one and the same in God. The difference is in our knowledge of these perfections. There is no plurality in God, only in our knowledge of God. This much is clear. But there is another and more difficult question we want to answer here. Is this plurality only and wholly in our intellect? Is the difference between the essence of God and his attributes, and the difference among the attributes themselves, due entirely to the operation of our intellect in knowing God?

To this question we answer no. At the outset, a simple distinction will be of help. The plurality and distinction between God's essence and his attributes and among the attributes themselves, is in our intellect as in its subject. But this plurality and distinction is also "in" God as in its source and foundation. In more technical terminology, we say that there is no real distinction between God's essence and his attributes nor among the different attributes themselves. There is only a distinction of reason. But this distinction of reason is not due merely to the one reasoning. It is also due to the very thing reasoned about, namely, God and the perfections of God. Thus, the difference between God's goodness and his truth is not the same, for example, as that between man and rational animal, where the whole reason for the distinction is due to the act of the one knowing. Rather, the distinction between God's Being and his perfections and among the perfections themselves is like the distinction between being and its transcendentals and among the transcendentals themselves.

And the reason for the distinction in both cases is fundamentally the same. Just as our intellect cannot exhaust in a single concept the fullness of being, but must exploit this fullness by more and more express and explicit concepts—like one, true, good, and so forth, so neither can our intellect exhaust in one concept the fullness of God's Being as knowable through creatures, but must express that fullness in many and distinct concepts. These distinct concepts, therefore, are due not merely to the intellect that knows God, but also to the fullness and transcendence of the divine Being. And just as our concepts like one, true, and good signify being itself, but under different aspects, so all our concepts of the divine perfections signify God himself, but under different aspects. These perfections are not distinct in the thing (God), but only in my knowledge of the thing. Hence no real distinction is involved here, but only a distinction of reason. But it is not a distinction of mere reason, since the *foundation* for the distinction is not merely in the intellect but also in God.

So far these are so many statements of facts. Now let us examine their proof. And since the proof throws much light on the whole question of our knowledge of God, it will be worth our while to go here into some detail. We will put the problem in the form of a question, urge two objections against our answer, and then try to disengage and understand the elements of a solution.

1. QUESTION: DOES THE PLURALITY OF MEANINGS THAT THE DIVINE ATTRIBUTES HAVE EXIST ONLY IN OUR INTELLECT OR ALSO IN GOD?

It would seem that in no way can this plurality of meanings exist in God. Whatever is in God, is God. Thus, if the meanings according to which these attributes differ are in God, they are God himself. But God is one and simple. Therefore, as existing in God, these meanings cannot be many.

Furthermore, that which in itself is absolutely one cannot be the *foundation* for any plurality or distinction. But we have seen that the divine essence is absolutely simple, excluding all physical and logical composition. Therefore this divine essence cannot be the foundation for any plurality or distinction. Hence the plurality of meanings that the divine perfections have seem in no way rooted in the divine essence, but only and solely in our intellect knowing that essence.

2. SOLUTION

In our solution to this problem we maintain that all the divine perfections, like wisdom and goodness, are entirely one and the same thing in God, but they are different in their meanings. We also say that this difference in meaning is not due merely to the intellect knowing God, but also to the very nature of God himself.

To grasp this important teaching, four questions must be answered. First, what is this meaning according to which the

divine attributes differ? Secondly, how is meaning said to be or
not be in a thing? Thirdly, are the different meanings of the
attributes in God or not? Fourthly, is the plurality of these meanings due only to our intellect or are they also in some way due
to God?

We answer the first question as follows. Meaning is that which
is signified by a word; or meaning is that which the intellect
understands when it grasps the representational value of a word.
In the case of those things which are capable of a strict definition,
the perfect meaning would be this definition. But things can have
a meaning even though they cannot be defined, for example, such
things as quantity or quality. The meaning of quantity is that
which is signified by the word "quantity." And this is simply that
by which quantity is quantity. It makes no difference, therefore,
whether that which is said to have a meaning is or is not capable
of being defined. Thus, for example, divine wisdom is not capable
of being defined by the human intellect, since it does not know
this perfection according to the infinite mode of being it has in
God. Yet our intellect does have a notion or idea of divine wisdom, namely, that which the intellect knows when it understands
the meaning of the phrase "divine wisdom."

We are now in a position to answer our second question. How
can meaning be said to be in the thing known? Obviously, meaning itself is not in the thing. Nor is the way a meaning is grasped
by the mind in the thing. For both meaning and its mode of being
are in the mind as in their subject. Rather, meaning is said to be
in the thing known insofar as in the thing known there does correspond something to what the mind has conceived. For example,
when I say *John is lazy*, the meaning of laziness is not in John;
but what laziness signifies has its correspondent in John, for
example, those different acts or lack of acts that fulfill this meaning.

Meaning contained in a concept can correspond to the thing
existing outside the mind in three different ways. Sometimes what
the intellect conceives is the *likeness* of the thing existing outside
the mind. This happens, for example, when the intellect conceives the intelligible content of a word like *man*. Such a conception of the intellect has its proximate foundation in the thing,

insofar as the thing itself, because of its conformity to the intellect, produces the very truth of the intellect, and is the cause why the name signifying this concept is said of the thing.

Sometimes, however, that which a name signifies is not a *likeness* of the thing existing outside the mind, but is something that results from the way the thing outside the mind is understood. These are meanings or notions that our intellect in some way constructs. For example, that which is signified by the word *genus* is not the likeness of any thing existing outside the mind. Rather, from the fact that the intellect understands that the perfection *animal* can be in different kinds of animals, the intellect attributes to animal the notion or meaning of genus. Obviously, what corresponds to the meaning of genus is not something existing outside the mind. With meanings of this kind, the proximate foundation is not in the thing but in the intellect. For it is the intellect which sees that animal can be predicated of many species and thus attributes to it the notion of genus. However, the *remote* foundation is the thing itself. Because the perfection of animal in the thing is of such a nature that it can be found in many kinds of animals, the intellect can attribute to it the notion of genus. And so the intellect is not false or in error when it constructs these meanings.

Sometimes, finally, that which is signified by a name has *no foundation* in the thing, either proximate or remote. For example, the notion of a Chimera—a fire-breathing monster that is part lion, part goat, and part dragon—is a concept that is neither the likeness of anything that exists outside the mind, nor does it result from the way the mind understands some thing outside the mind. And so such a concept is false if said of anything existing outside the mind. Thus the answer to our second point is clear. A notion or meaning is said to be in the thing insofar as what is signified by the meaning is in the thing.

We are now ready to answer our third question. Are the meanings that the mind conceives of the divine attributes in God? According to St. Thomas, there were two main opinions in his day concerning this question. One was that of Avicenna and Maimonides, and the other that of the Pseudo-Denis and Saint

Anselm of Canterbury.[13] Both these opinions deserve careful study, since almost any position we take regarding our knowledge of God's perfections is reducible to one of them.

3. THE OPINION OF AVICENNA AND MAIMONIDES

According to St. Thomas, Avicenna and Maimonides taught that God, as existing outside our mind, is a subsistent Being (*esse*), and nothing else. There is nothing else in God except Being (*esse*).[14] Thus they taught that God was Being without essence. Whatever other perfections we attribute to God are true only by way of negation and causality. For instance, it is true that God is wise in the sense that such attribution removes from him that defect found in things that lack wisdom. Or a given negation may *result* in something that is true of God. When, for example, I say God is undivided, this negation tells me that he is one. Or when I say God is immaterial, I know that he is intelligent. Thus, according to Avicenna and Maimonides, all such names are used by us to remove something from God rather than to put anything in God.

Knowledge by way of causality is also true of God in a twofold sense: either because God produces the perfection found in the creature, or because God conducts himself, so to speak, after the manner of a creature. Thus, for example, I can say God is wise in the sense that he is the cause of wisdom in creatures, or that in producing certain of his effects he acts as a wise man acts.

Let us look for a moment at this doctrine. The first thing that strikes us is that while the doctrine is true in what it says, it does not go far enough. It errs in saying this is all names tell us about God. Moreover, the interpretation Maimonides gives to his doctrine is really agnostic. For he expressly says two things: First, that all the names used of God are used equivocally; and, secondly, that no likeness of the creature to its creator results from the fact that the creature is good or wise or possesses any other perfection whatsoever it may be. According to Maimonides, that which our intellect conceives when it understands an attribute like wisdom or goodness does not refer to God as a likeness of something that

---

[13] *In I Sent.*, d. 2, q. 1, a. 3, *solutio.*

[14] Thomas's references to the works of Avicenna and Maimonides, upon which he bases his interpretation, are found in the text cited above.

is in God. There is nothing in God that corresponds to our notion of the divine attributes. Whence it follows that the meaning of these names are not in God as in their proximate foundation, but only as in their remote foundation. They are just like those relative names that are predicated of God because of time—words like creator and lord. For these relations are not in God, but follow merely from our way of understanding God, just as we have seen above as regards the notions of genus and species.

Thus, according to the opinion of Avicenna and Maimonides, the notions of the divine attributes are only in our intellect and not in the thing—not in God. Rather, the intellect constructs these notions from a consideration of creatures by way of negation and causality. In a moment we will see what is true and what is false about this doctrine. But before we do so, let us turn our attention to the second doctrine, that of Denis and Anselm.[15]

4. THE OPINION OF THE PSEUDO-DENIS AND ST. ANSELM

These two men taught that the perfections existing in creatures exist in God, but in a pre-eminent way. And this pre-eminence is threefold. First, it is a pre-eminence of *universality:* for in God all perfections are found joined together, while in creatures they are dispersed and scattered. Secondly, it is a pre-eminence of *plenitude:* for God's perfections are without defect, whereas this is not true of perfections in creatures. Thirdly, it is a pre-eminence of *unity:* in creatures these perfections are many and diverse; in God they are all one and the same. Not only are these perfections joined together in God, they are all identified with God. In this one Being all things pre-exist, and so by it all things are caused, all things are known, and to it all things are similar, according to a likeness of analogy.

In this opinion, therefore, the notions or meanings that the intellect understands when it knows these attributes, are truly likenesses of that Being which is God, although they are only partial and deficient likenesses. Such notions do not exist merely in our intellect but have their *proximate* foundation in God. That is to say, what proximately corresponds to our notion of (for example)

---

[15] The teaching of Denis is found in Chapter Twelve of his *Divine Names*, and that of Anselm in Chapter Three of his *Monologion*.

divine wisdom is God himself (and not any creature), but not God *in himself*, but as manifested through creatures. Thus this opinion concludes that what belongs to wisdom as such, rightly and properly belongs to God.

5. RECONCILIATION OF THESE OPINIONS

St. Thomas attempts a reconciliation of these two teachings. He begins by pointing out that their apparent difference and opposition flow from the two different sources from which they have arisen. Avicenna and Maimonides have considered principally the created things themselves because of which the different names of the attributes were first given or imposed. For example, the name *wisdom* is given to a certain quality in man, and the name *essence* is said of things that are not subsistent being. And since such things as qualities and non-subsistence have nothing to do with God, this opinion teaches that wisdom is not in God, and that God is Being without essence.

On the other hand, Denis and Anselm have considered not the creatures themselves that possess these perfections, but the very perfections as such. And since God according to one act of Being is perfect by all the modes of perfection which these names imply, these men have said that such names belong positively to God. One opinion does not deny what the other affirms. The first does not deny that any mode of perfection is lacking to God, nor does the second affirm that God possesses qualities or is non-subsistent.

With this rather detailed explanation, the answer to our third question becomes clear. Are the meanings that the mind conceives of the divine attributes in God? The notions or meanings of the divine attributes are truly in God, for the meaning of a name is derived more from the reason the name is given than from the thing to which it is given. For example, the name "wisdom" is given because of the operation of ordering things to an end; but it is imposed upon something that is a quality. Thus its meaning is concerned more with the perfection of ordering than with the quality. This perfection of ordering belongs to God and is in God, but no quality is in God.

We come now to our fourth and last question which concerns the plurality of these notions. We have seen that these *notions* are truly in God. Can we also say that the *plurality* of these notions is also in God or only in our intellect?

First of all, this very plurality of notions comes from the fact that the thing known, namely God, exceeds our intellect. Our intellect cannot receive in one concept all the different modes of divine perfection. And this for two reasons. First, because the intellect receives this knowledge from creatures, in whom there exist different modes of perfection according to different forms or natures; and, secondly, because that which in God is one and simple is multiplied in our intellect. This multiplication flows from the very nature of caused knowledge, just as multitude and difference flow from the very nature of caused things.

To sum up: Since God according to one and the same thing, his divine essence, is perfect with all the modes of perfection, our intellect in one concept cannot integrally grasp his perfection nor, consequently, give this perfection one name. To know God we must have many and different concepts conveying many and different meanings. And so we must have many and different names for these meanings. These names are not synonyms, because they signify different notions or meanings. To the plurality of these notions there does correspond something in the thing, but there does not correspond a plurality of the thing. To the plurality of notions there corresponds the fullness of perfection of the thing, so that all these different names and notions are aptly applied to it. If our intellect were able to see God in himself, it could give to this understanding of God one single name. And this name would not signify merely goodness or wisdom, and so forth, but would include the signification of all these things.[16]

[16] But it should be mentioned that although in heaven we shall all see the divine essence and therefore shall know God as he is in himself, we shall not comprehend God. The vision we have of his essence will not be a comprehensive vision, it will not exhaust the intelligibility of God. As the theologians put it, "the whole God shall be seen by us, but he shall not be wholly seen." God is infinitely knowable and our intellects remain finite in heaven. God will exceed our intellects even in the beatific vision, and from this point of view St. Thomas says that there will be *even in this vision* of God a plurality of names. Here is his explanation: "But nevertheless, if the intellect seeing God through his essence should give a name to the thing which he sees, and should name this thing through the understanding which he has of this thing, the intellect would still have to use many names. Because it is impossible that the conception

When Avicenna and Maimonides said that this plurality is only on the side of our intellect and the effects in creatures, they were in a certain sense right and in a certain sense wrong. If they refer to the cause of the multiplication, then what they say is true, for this cause is our intellect and the effects in creatures, since our intellect cannot conceive the divine perfection in one concept but needs many. If, however, these men are referring to the manner in which these notions are attributed to God, then their position is false. For God is not good because he makes good things or because he acts after the manner of something that is good. Rather, because God is good, he makes good things; and these good things, because they participate in his goodness, can act after a manner that is like the goodness of God. If God had never created, he still would be such that he could be considered according to all those notions that our intellect now possesses when it considers him. The plurality of these names is not merely on the side of the intellect forming them, but also on the side of God himself, insofar as something in God corresponds to all these concepts, namely, the fullness and completeness of God's perfection. Each name signifying these notions is said of God truly and properly. But no diversity or multiplicity is placed in God by reason of these diverse and multiple attributes.

6. Answering the difficulties

We can now answer the two objections that stated the plurality of meanings exists only in our intellect and in no way in God. The first objection was this: Whatever is in God, is God. But God is absolutely one and completely simple. Therefore the plurality of

of a created intellect should represent the whole perfection of the divine essence. Therefore, for the one thing seen, it would form different conceptions and would use different names, for God is not seen by the intellect with a comprehending vision. But that conception which perfectly represents God is the Uncreated Word, and thus this Word is one only. Therefore it is clear that the plurality of names comes from this fact, that God himself exceeds our intellect. And that God should exceed our intellect is due to God himself (because of the plenitude of his perfection), and to our intellect (which is unable to comprehend God). And therefore also the plurality of notions is not merely because of our intellect but also because of God himself, insofar as his perfection exceeds any conception whatsoever that our intellect can form of it." *In I Sent.*, d. 2, qu. 1, a. 3, *solutio*. Words in parentheses added.

notions can exist only in our intellect. We answer this difficulty by saying that just as the meaning of the word "man" is not something in the existing man, but is in the intellect as in its subject and in the existing man as in the source of its truth, so in like manner the meaning of the words "divine goodness" is in the human intellect as in its subject, but in God as in that which corresponds by some likeness to this meaning, giving this meaning its truth.

Our second objection was this: That which is absolutely one cannot be the root or foundation for any plurality. But this is the case with the divine essence; therefore the plurality of meanings is in no way rooted in the divine essence, but only and solely in our intellect knowing that essence. We answer this objection as follows: Something can be said to be rooted or fixed in another if it has from this other a certain stability or firmness. Now intellectual meanings possess a twofold "firmness"—that of their existence, and that of their truth. The first kind of stability a meaning has from the intellect in which it inheres, just as any other accident derives its existence from its subject. But a meaning has the stability of its truth from the thing to which it is conformed. The way a thing is or is not determines our understanding of it. The meanings, therefore, of the divine attributes are fixed or rooted in the human intellect as regards the stability of their existence, since our intellect is their subject; but they are rooted in the divine essence as regards the stability of their truth. And this "rooting" in God, since it is not as in a subject, in no way compromises the divine simplicity.

7. SUMMARY

"God is absolutely uncomposed (simple), and yet a completely perfect Being. For in him pre-exist virtually and eminently all perfections found in creatures. Perfections of being as being also exist properly in God. He is, therefore, absolutely infinite and supremely good."

A. STATE OF THE QUESTION

Having seen in Chapter 12 how names signifying perfections first found in creatures can be said of God by way of analogy, in this chapter we discuss how these perfections themselves, signified by these names, are contained in the divine essence.

1) "... *simple* ..."—lacking parts or composition. Simplicity is really a positive perfection, since it denies composition, which implies potency and hence limitation.

2) "... *absolutely* ..." God is not composed in any order of being (essence, existence, activity, logical order, and so forth). This is true only of God, since every creature is at least composed in the order of existence.

3) "... *completely perfect Being* ..." A thing is perfect (*per factum*) insofar as it is in act. God, as completely in act, is completely perfect.

4) "... *perfection* ..." A perfection is anything that has existence, or is ordered to existence. As we have seen, a thing is called perfect insofar as it is in act; hence, perfection is denominated from the act, or order to the act, of existing.

5) "... *virtually* ..." To be present in a thing virtually is to be in the causal power of that thing.

6) "... *eminently* ..." To be present in a thing eminently, is to be there in a more perfect manner (than in something else).

7) "... *properly* ..." To be present in a thing properly is to be there as the intrinsic property and possession of that thing. Moreover, to possess a perfection properly is to possess it by reason of the perfection itself.

8) "... *perfections of being as being* ..."—perfections in whose notion there is contained no imperfection.

9) "... *infinite* ..."—without limit or boundary. A thing is absolutely infinite if it has no limit or term whatsoever to its being. Only God is absolutely infinite, since all creatures are limited in their being by their essence.

10) "... *good* ..."—being as desirable; hence, being considered according to its ultimate perfection, since a thing is desirable insofar as it is perfect. The supreme good would be the most perfect Being. This is God.

C. THE PROOF

1) *God is absolutely simple.* (*a*) What is composed must have an efficient cause of its composition, since diverse parts cannot

form a unity unless they are brought together by some cause uniting them. But God has no cause. Therefore, *etc.*

(*b*) In every composite there is act and potency; for from two acts we cannot have one act, or unity. But in God there is no potency. Therefore, *etc.*

2) *All perfections found in creatures are virtually present in God.* Nothing gives (causes) what it does not have. But God is the first cause of all perfections found in creatures. Hence, all perfections found in creatures pre-exist in the causal power of God. But this is to be virtually present in God. Therefore, *etc.*

3) *All perfections found in creatures are also eminently in God.* The causal power of God is one with the essence of God, since, as we have already proved, God is absolutely simple. Hence, perfections that pre-exist in this power, pre-exist as identified with the divine essence. But this is to exist according to a higher mode of being than these perfections have in creatures. Hence, all perfections found in creatures are eminently present in God.

4) *But only perfections of being as being exist properly in God.* (*a*) Mixed perfections, as including within their very signification some imperfection, cannot exist in God by reason of themselves, but only in the sense that God can cause them (virtual presence), and cause them with a power that is one with his divine essence (eminent presence). God, as Pure Act, can contain no imperfection.

(b) But simple perfections, as including within their signification no imperfection, can exist in God by reason of themselves, since, as simply act, they can exist in God according to their complete fullness and perfection of act.

5) *God is absolutely infinite.* A being is absolutely infinite if there is no term or limit to its act of existing. But God's act of existing is not limited by, or received into, any potency or essence. Therefore, the Being of God is absolutely infinite.

6) *God is supremely good.* Good is being considered according to its ultimate perfection. Hence, that being which is completely perfect, and in no sense perfectible, is the supreme good. But God, as completely in act and absolutely infinite in being, is completely perfect. Therefore, God is supremely good.

READINGS

St. Thomas, *Summa Theologiae*, in *Basic Writings of St. Thomas*, by A. Pegis (New York, Random House, 1945), Vol. 1, pp. 25–62. *On the Power of God* (*De Potentia*), translated by English Dominican Fathers (Westminster, Newman Press, 1952), three books in one volume, Book III, pp. 1–46.

E. The omnipresence, immutability, and eternity of God

Only the Being of God is everywhere, entirely unchangeable, and eternal.

A. STATE OF THE QUESTION

Having considered the simplicity, perfection, goodness, and infinity of the divine Being, we are logically led to a consideration of his omnipresence. For what is infinite has no limit, and so God as infinite in his Being would seem to be everywhere. In this section, then, we consider the omnipresence and immutability of God, and the eternity what flows from such immutability.

B. EXPLANATION OF TERMS

1) "*. . . is everywhere . . .*" can mean two things: to be in all *things* (omnipresent) or to be in all *places* (ubiquitous). To be in all places and in all things is true only of the Being of God. A body is in a place *circumscriptively*, that is, by the contact of its quantity with the quantity of the surrounding bodies. A spirit is in a place *virtually*, that is, by the contact of its power (*virtus*) with the body it is affecting. A spirit is where it acts. Thus the human soul is in every part of the body, since it actively informs the whole body and all its parts. Moreover, the whole *essence* of a spirit is present in each part of the place where it acts. Having no quantity, and hence no extension, a spirit can be wholly present (that is, according to its whole essence) in each part where it acts. Thus the soul is present according to its whole essence in each part of the body, and God is present according to his whole essence in all things and in all places.

2) "*. . . entirely unchangeable . . .*" To change is to become other, that is, to lose or gain some perfection. That being is entirely unchangeable which can in no way become other than it is.

3) "*. . . eternal . . .*"—to be without beginning or end or any succession whatsoever in one's duration of being. Put positively, this means the totally simultaneous and perfect possession of one's being.

C. THE PROOF

1) *Only God is everywhere*—in all things and in all places. (*a*) An agent is present where it acts. But God acts in all things, causing and conserving their being. Therefore, *etc.*

(*b*) A place is a certain reality, namely, a body insofar as it is commensurate with or contains other bodies. Hence, God is in all places insofar as he gives being to all places.

2) *Only God is entirely unchangeable.* That which is pure act, absolutely simple, and infinitely perfect is entirely unchangeable. But this is true only of God. Therefore, only God is entirely unchangeable.

(*a*) Whatever is changed possesses some potency or capacity for the change. But God, *as pure act,* is entirely without potency. Hence, he is entirely unchangeable. Every creature, as possessing some potency, is changeable.

(*b*) Whatever is changed becomes other than it is, and thus possesses something that remains the same and something that changes. Hence, a changeable being is a composed being. But God is *absolutely uncomposed* (which is not true of any creature). Therefore, God alone is entirely unchangeable.

(*c*) Whatever is changed loses or gains some perfection. But God, *as infinitely perfect,* can neither lose nor gain any perfection (which is not true of any creature, for a creature can always gain some new accidental perfections). Therefore, only God is entirely unchangeable.

3) *Only God is eternal.* A thing is eternal insofar as it is unchangeable. But only God, as we have seen, is entirely unchangeable. Hence, only God is eternal in the strict sense. For to change is to undergo some succession in one's being. And to be eternal is to possess one's being without any succession or variation whatsoever.

READINGS

St. Thomas, *Summa Theologiae*, in *Basic Writings of St. Thomas*, by A. Pegis (New York, Random House, 1945), Vol. 1, pp. 63–84. *On the Truth of the Catholic Faith (Summa Contra Gentiles)*, translated by A. Pegis (New York, Hanover House, 1955), Book One, pp. 158–170.

XIV

God's Knowledge and Will

A. God's knowledge of himself and other things

Having seen something about the perfections of the divine Being as these can be known by us, we are ready now to take up a new problem in natural theology. In this chapter we wish to discuss the operations of the divine Being as these can be known by us through the operations of creatures. The transition from the study of the divine Being to that of its operations is a logical one, since a being operates according to the way it is. Operations are of two kinds: those that remain in a being and perfect it, like operations of knowledge and will; and those that proceed from a being and perfect some external effect. Thus our order will be the following. First, we shall study God's knowledge of himself and of things distinct from himself. Then we shall study God's love of himself and of things distinct from himself. Next we shall study the divine operation as a principle of an external effect in the creative act. This will lead us to a study of God's providence over these external effects.[1]

STATEMENT CONCERNING GOD'S KNOWLEDGE

God understands and comprehends himself through his divine essence. Hence his knowledge and his Being are one, and his divine essence is subsistent truth. Moreover, through his same divine

[1] In order to understand the difficult doctrine of God's knowledge of himself and of things distinct from himself, the student is urged to read the entire fourteenth question in the First Part of the *Summa*. It is one of the best questions in the whole of the *Summa*. Along with this the student should also read the Second Question of the *De Veritate*.

essence God knows things other than himself, and he knows these things in themselves with a proper, perfect, and immutable knowledge.

A. STATE OF THE QUESTION

Operations are of two kinds, those that remain within and perfect the subject acting, and those that proceed from the subject and perfect some external matter. We begin our study of the first kind of divine operations. And since knowledge is such an immanent operation, upon which depends all subsequent immanent and transient operations of the divine Being, in this section we treat of God's knowledge of himself and of other things.

B. EXPLANATION OF TERMS

1) *". . . understands . . ."*—an act of intentional identity between subject and object, in which the subject becomes aware of the object in a strictly immaterial fashion.

2) *". . . comprehends . . ."*—to understand perfectly, that is, to know an object to the degree that it is knowable.

3) *". . . his divine essence . . ."*—that intrinsic and infinite act by which God is God: the divine Being itself in itself.

4) *". . . Truth . . ."*—the conformity of the intellect and the thing. Finite intellects share or participate in truth insofar as they receive the forms of other things. God's intellect is subsistent truth insofar as it is identified with his Being that contains the forms of all things.

5) *". . . things other than himself . . ."*—anything that can imitate God or be caused by God. Hence God knows all possible and actual beings.

6) *". . . in themselves . . ."*—that is, God knows each thing that is distinct from him according to its own individual and proper nature.

7) *". . . proper . . . knowledge . . ."* Here proper knowledge of a thing means knowledge of each and every perfection within the individual.

8) *". . . perfect . . . knowledge . . ."*—a comprehensive or exhaustive knowledge of the thing.

9) *". . . immutable knowledge . . ."*—an act of knowledge

that is incapable of any change whatsoever. By one and the same unchanging act God knows changeable things and the changes of things, since this act is the very cause of things and the changes of things.

C. THE PROOF

1) *God understands himself.* A thing is knowable insofar as it is removed from matter and potency, and a thing can know insofar as it is removed from matter and potency. Hence, the Being of God, as supremely immaterial and completely in act, is perfectly knowable and perfectly knowing. And so the divine Being, as absolutely transparent to itself, knows itself.

2) *God comprehends himself.* As completely without potency, God's Being is infinitely knowable: there is nothing within it that is impervious to knowledge. And as completely in act, God's power of knowing is infinite: nothing escapes his act of knowledge. Hence, God not only knows himself, but comprehends himself; that is, he knows himself to the degree that he is knowable.

3) *God knows and comprehends himself through himself.* God's Being is absolutely simple and uncomposed, as we have proved in a previous chapter. Hence, in God there is no real distinction between what God knows and the form by which he knows. But what God knows and comprehends is himself. Thus he knows and comprehends himself through himself, and not through some super-added form or intelligible species.

4) *God's knowledge and Being are one.* Just as the "to be" of a thing follows upon the presence of a physical form, so "to know" follows upon the presence of an intentional form. But we have seen that the divine essence (by which God is) is one with the intelligible form by which God knows. Hence, since God is and knows by one and the same act (his divine essence), it follows that God's Being and God's knowledge are one and the same.

5) *The divine essence is subsistent truth.* Truth is the conformity of the intellect with the thing. But God's intellect is conformed with the thing (the divine essence). In fact, it is identified with it. As conformed through identity with the essence, this divine intellect is true, and since this essence is subsistent Being, the divine intellect, as identified with this essence, is subsistent truth.

Moreover, just as logical truth is the conformity of the intellect with the thing, so ontological truth is the conformity of the thing with an intellect. And since the divine essence is identified with the divine intellect, in God logical and ontological truth are the same subsistent truth.

6) *God knows things other than himself.* (*a*) In knowing himself perfectly, God knows his divine power perfectly; and in knowing his divine power perfectly, God knows the things to which that power extends. But that power extends to all things. Hence, God knows things other than himself.

(*b*) God's act of knowledge and Being are one. Now every effect must pre-exist in its cause, for no cause gives what it does not have. Thus all things must pre-exist in the divine Being (and hence in the divine knowledge). Thus God must know things other than himself.

7) *God knows things other than himself through himself.* Here we prove that the divine essence is the intelligible species by which God knows things other than himself. Because God knows his essence perfectly, he must know that essence as imitable. But in knowing that essence as imitable, God must, by that very fact, know whatever imitates or can imitate that essence. Just as one who knows an image knows by that very fact the thing whose image it is, so God, in knowing himself as imitable, knows all other things. Moreover, God by one and the same act knows himself and all other things through himself. For it is the same simple and uncomposed essence by which he knows himself and things distinct from himself. Multiplicity and composition are on the side of the different things that imitate God, and these things are outside God. By an infinitely perfect image (his essence as the cause of things), God can know perfectly a multiplicity of finite objects.

8) *God knows other things in themselves.* God knows whatever is proper to each individual existent. For as a subsistent act of existing, God possesses whatever finite perfections are shared in by each individual existent.

9) *God's knowledge of other things is perfect.* In comprehending his own Being, God must likewise comprehend (know perfectly) all other things which share in his Being.

10) *God's knowledge is immutable.* The act by which God

knows himself and all other things is one and the same act. And this act is one with the divine Being, which is absolutely unchangeable. Hence God knows all things by an absolutely unchangeable act of knowledge. By this unchanging act, God knows changing things and the changes of things. For God's knowledge is the cause of all things, and hence of changing things and their changes.

READINGS

St. Thomas, *Summa Theologiae*, in *Basic Writings of St. Thomas*, by A. Pegis (New York, Random House, 1945), Vol. 1, pp. 135–161. These pages cover the all-important Fourteenth Question of the First Part of the *Summa*. The student should read at least articles 5, 6, 9, 13, and 15. *Truth (De Veritate)*, translated from the definitive Leonine text by R. W. Mulligan, S.J. (Chicago, Henry Regnery Company, 1952), Vol. 1, pp. 59–76. These pages cover the two very important articles of God's knowledge of himself and other things.

Etienne Gilson, *The Christian Philosophy of St. Thomas Aquinas*, (New York, Random House, 1956), pp. 110–114.

B. The perfection of will in God

Having considered God's knowledge both of himself and of other things, we now want to consider that perfection which follows upon knowledge, namely, the perfection of willing. This is the act by which God is said to be inclined to his own divine goodness and the goodness of other things. We want to consider, therefore, how God wills and loves himself and creatures. This problem we will divide into three sections: first, how God wills and loves himself and creatures; secondly, in what sense there is free choice in the divine will; and thirdly, how this free choice is reconciled with the immutability of God. We will then say a word about a very difficult and mysterious problem: the reconciliation of God's unchanging will with man's free choice.

1. STATEMENT CONCERNING GOD'S WILL

God wills and loves himself necessarily and things distinct from himself freely. There is present, therefore, in the divine will the perfection of free choice. This free choice in no way contradicts the immutability of God's Being, nor does this immutability contradict free choice in man.

A. STATE OF THE QUESTION

Having seen that God knows himself and other things, we now want to see in what sense he wills himself and other things. Beings endowed with intelligence are also necessarily endowed with a will or rational appetite. For the good is that which all desire. And since beings endowed with intelligence can understand something as good, they can want or will such good. Thus they are endowed with a rational appetite or will—an inclination toward intellected good.

B. EXPLANATION OF TERMS

1) ". . . *will* . . ."—the power or faculty by which a being is inclined toward a thing seen by the intellect as good, that is, as perfect in itself and perfective of the one knowing it. Any act (actual inclination) of this power is called an act of willing. In God, this act and power are identified with the divine Being. Moreover, the good that God knows and wills necessarily is this same divine Being. Hence, in willing himself God is not *inclined* toward something that perfects him, but rather delights in and enjoys the infinite perfection that he is.

2) ". . . *love* . . ."—an act of the will in which good is wanted for oneself or another. There are different kinds of love; for example:

(*a*) *Love of concupiscence:* an act in which we love something for the good we can derive from it.

(*b*) *Love of benevolence:* an act in which we love another for the good that he has or that we wish him to have. If this love is between equals it is called the *love of friendship.*

(*c*) *Love of complacence:* an act in which one delights in and enjoys the good of another or of himself. God loves himself with a love of complacence, and things other than himself with a love of benevolence.

3) ". . . *to will or love necessarily* . . ."—to be inclined by the necessity of one's nature toward the known good. Thus God cannot not will and love his infinite goodness. Such a necessary act is *voluntary* in the sense that it is not forced upon God from without, but flows from the inner nature of his will (*voluntas*).

4) ". . . *to will or love* . . . *freely* . . ."—to exercise an act of

choice. A known good is chosen freely in the sense that it need not be chosen. An act of choice is of means, not of the end. And an act of choice is free when there are more than one means to the end, or if the means are not necessary for the end.

5) "... *the perfection of free choice* ..."—the power or faculty of willing, insofar as it can direct itself indifferently toward different known goods. Hence, the essence of free choice does not consist in being able to choose between good and evil, but between good and good. Such an act of choice is a perfection of being as being, since it contains no imperfection. In God, this act is one with his essence.

6) "... *the immutability of God's Being* ..." Since God's act of free choice is one with his Being, and since his Being is absolutely unchangeable, God's act of free choice is absolutely unchangeable. This does not contradict the notion of free choice, which consists not in the ability to change our choices (this is due to the imperfection of the one choosing), but in the ability to will indifferently different goods. God immutably, but freely, chooses whatever creatures he wills, and he does so by an act that is one with his essence.

C. THE PROOF

1) *God wills and loves himself necessarily.* That act of the will is necessary when the known good, toward which it is inclined, cannot not be wanted. But God cannot not want his own infinite goodness, since it is one with his Being and will. Hence, God wills and loves himself by a necessity of his nature. And since God is not necessitated to this act by any thing outside himself, he enjoys supreme *liberty of being,* for he is absolutely free from all coercion. Insofar as the divine goodness is one with his act of will, we say that God *wills* himself necessarily, and insofar as this divine goodness is God's supreme and infinite perfection, we say that God *loves* himself necessarily.

2) *God wills and loves creatures freely.* That act of the will is free when the known good can indifferently be willed or not willed. Insofar as God knows things distinct from himself, he *can* will them. But insofar as these things are not necessary for the divine perfection, he *need not* will them. If God wills them, he wills

them freely. That no creature whatsoever is necessary for the divine perfection is clear from the fact that God is completely perfect in himself, and whatever perfection there is in a creature has been derived from God. Hence, God freely, and not by any necessity of his nature, wills whatever creatures he wills.

3) *Therefore, God has the perfection of free choice.* Since God has chosen creatures freely, it follows that he possesses the power of free choice. And since this power to choose among different goods implies no imperfection, there is no reason on the side of the power why it cannot be in God. But several things should be noted here. First, God's power of free choice is one with his act of free choice, and this act is identified with his essence. Secondly, the fact that God actually wills himself necessarily and creatures freely, puts no composition within the pure act that is God. For just as God by one and the same act knows himself and creatures (in knowing himself as imitable), so by one and the same act God wills himself necessarily and creatures freely.

Nor does this *way* of willing creatures (freely) put any composition into God's will-act. For this way is due to the things willed (creatures) and not to the one willing. What *moves* God to will creatures is his divine essence as communicable, and this is one with God. Thirdly, and finally, the fact that God wills creatures from all eternity, and by an act identified with his Being, does not mean that he is not free to will or not will them. From all eternity God freely wills that creatures should begin to be at different times (according to his will). When creatures begin to be, God in no way changes. The change is on the part of the creature. And even had God willed no creatures at all, he would still exercise from all eternity (and that by an act identified with his Being) his power of free choice; namely, in choosing not to will what he could will. In all this there is no change in his Being, since the only thing affected is the object of God's will; namely, the creature.

4) *Free choice in God does not contradict his immutability.* The act of free choice in God would contradict his immutability if God were to change a free choice once made. For this would be to change his *act* of free choice and hence his Being which is identified with that act. But this God cannot do. Hence, free choice

in God does not contradict his immutable nature. Men change their mind about an object either because of new knowledge or because the attitude of their will toward the object changes. But there is no room in God for either any new knowledge or any new good; for both his knowledge and goodness are infinite. Thus while God is free to choose or not choose, or to choose this good rather than that, he cannot change his free choices. For this would be a sign of imperfection, either in his knowledge or goodness. Hence, on the supposition that God chooses some good, he immutably chooses it. He freely, but immutably, wills changing things and the changes of things.

5) *The immutability of God's choices does not destroy free choice in man.* God, as we have seen, is the first cause of every effect. Every effect, insofar as it shares in existential act, has God as the first and proper cause of this act. Thus man's acts of free choice, as existential, have God as their first cause. Now such acts would not be free if under the influence of God's causality they could not be other than they are. But this is not the case. First of all, the will of man, as a certain power of free choice, is a participation in God's perfection of free choice. Secondly, when the will places its free act (as secondary cause) under the influence of God (as first cause), the motion of God is in the will according to the nature of the will. That is, God freely moves the will. This "free motion," is *in* the will but *from* God, as from the first free Being. And since whatever is received is received according to the nature of the one receiving, this motion moves the will freely, that is, in such a way that it is not necessitated to choose the good. Just as God immutably, but freely, chooses creatures, so God infallibly, but freely, moves creatures to their free choices. And just as God's immutable Being is in no way incompatible with his perfection of free choice, so neither is his infallible causality incompatible with the free choice of the creature. For the efficaciousness of the divine will is so transcendent that, as St. Thomas teaches,[2] not only do the things that God wills take place, but they take place in the way he *wills* them to take place, that is, freely or necessarily.

----

[2] See *Summa Theologiae*, I, 19, 8, and ad 2m.

READINGS

St. Thomas, *Summa Theologiae*, in *Basic Writings of St. Thomas*, by A. Pegis (New York, Random House, 1945), Vol. 1, pp. 195–211. These pages cover the important Nineteenth Question concerning God's will. The student should read at least articles 1, 2, 3, 7, 8, and 10. *On the Truth of the Catholic Faith*, translated by A. C. Pegis (New York, Hanover House, 1955), Vol. 1, pp. 239–271.

Etienne Gilson, *The Christian Philosophy of St. Thomas Aquinas* (New York, Random House, 1956), pp. 114-120.

XV

God's Creation and Providence

A. Creation

The manner in which the world comes from God

In our last chapter we saw that God freely wills creatures and that therefore things are not caused by him through any necessity of his nature. God's causality is free, and hence proceeds by way of an act of his will. We know that whatever a cause produces is in some way like this cause, and so in some way must pre-exist within the cause. We have seen, moreover, that what is in another is there after the manner of the thing in which it is. And since God's Being is also an act of knowing, creatures pre-exist in God as in an act of knowledge. Now whatever is in an intellect, does not proceed from it or is not produced outside it except through the mediation of the will. The will is the executor of the intellect, and it is the intelligible form that moves the will. Thus whatever comes forth from God does so by way of his will.[1]

But this procession of creatures from God constitutes a problem for the metaphysician. On the one hand, creatures must be produced by an action of God. But any action of God must be absolutely identical with the substance of God. And as the action and perfection of God, it must be an immanent act. On the other hand, precisely because of this act, the creature is produced. The act posits an external effect. Hence at least the efficacy or power of this act must, so to speak, pass over to the creature. To this mysterious act we give the name "creation."

[1] See *De Pot.*, qu. 3, a. 15.

In this section on creation we will answer the following four questions: (1) In what manner has the world or visible universe been caused? (2) What is the nature of this act by which it has been caused? (3) Is creation anything real in the creature? (4) What is creation in the creature?

1. STATEMENT CONCERNING CREATION

The way in which the world has come forth from God is through creation. Creation considered actively is a formally immanent but virtually transient act. Considered passively, creation is nothing else than a relation to the creator as to a principle.

A. STATE OF THE QUESTION

Having considered how God knows and wills things other than himself, we want to see how things have come forth from God, their first principle. Since God freely wills things other than himself, we know that these have proceeded from him freely and not by any necessity of his nature. Moreover, the entire effect, nothing presupposed, has come from God. And so we say that things have come forth from God by a creative act.

B. EXPLANATION OF TERMS

1) "... *world* ..."—all things other than God at the ontological moment that they came forth from God.

2) "... *creation* ..."—the production of a thing according to its whole substance, nothing whatsoever presupposed. By a creative act, the matter, form, substance, accidents, and act of existing of a thing are all simultaneously produced.

3) "*Creation considered actively* ..."—that is, considered as the act of the agent. In this sense, creation is a divine action that is identified with the substance of God.

4) "... *immanent* ... *act* ..."—an act that remains in, and is the perfection of, the agent acting.

"... *formally immanent* ..."—an act that in its own intrinsic and proper nature remains in, and is the perfection of, the agent acting.

5) "... *transient act* ..."—an act that proceeds from the agent but is in the patient and perfects the patient.

"... *virtually transient* ..."—an act that, while formally imma-nent, has the virtue or power to do what is done by a formally transient act; namely, to effect something outside the agent.

6) "... *creation considered passively* ..."—the act of creation considered as in the creature. This will be that because of which a creature is a creature.

7) "... *relation* ..."—some kind of order of one thing to an-other.

8) "... *principle* ..."—that from which something proceeds in some way or other. Here "principle" is a synonym for efficient cause.

C. THE PROOF

1) *The world has come forth from God through creation.* (*a*) By elimination: There are three possible ways the world could have come forth from God: (1) by strict emanation, (2) by strict formation, or (3) by creation. But the first two ways are impos-sible. In strict emanation (or by a necessary overflow of a nature), the thing produced is of the same nature as the one producing it. But God is infinite and pure act; whereas the world is finite and potential in its being. An act of strict formation (or an eduction of forms from matter) supposes pre-existing matter. But if matter were uncaused and eternal in its nature, it would be pure act, which is a contradiction, since matter is pure potency. Thus the world could not have come forth from God by either emanation or information.

(*b*) Positively: the world had to come forth from God accord-ing to its whole substance, nothing pre-supposed. But this is to be created. Therefore, the world was created. Moreover, God can create, since as infinite Being he has infinite power, and so can produce the total actuality of a being.

2) *Creation considered actively is a formally immanent but virtually transient act.* (*a*) Considered actively, creation is that act by which God produces the whole substance of the creature. But as the act of God, creation must be identified with the sub-stance of God, since God is pure act and absolutely uncomposed. As identified with the divine substance, creation is the intrinsic and proper perfection of God. Therefore, it is formally an imma-

nent act. What creation adds to the essence of God is a relation of reason to the creature.

(b) But this same act, while formally immanent, is virtually transient, since because of its power (virtus) some effect is placed outside God. Since the power of the act effects the creature, this act does what a formally transient act does. Hence, it is virtually (has the power of) a transient act.

3) Considered passively, creation is a real relation in the creature. Creation considered passively is creation as in the creature. It is that because of which a creature is a creature. But a thing is a creature because of its total dependence upon God as upon its cause. Real dependence upon another is a real order or relation to that other. Hence, creation as in the creature is a real relation to the creator. Finally, this real relation is a predicamental accident. By it, the whole creature is wholly related to God. If this relation were identified with the substance of the creature, the creature would be a substantial relation. But the creature is not a relation but rather something that is related. Thus it is related by a relation that is distinct from its substance. Creation, then, as in the creature is an accident.

READINGS

St. Thomas, *Summa Theologiae*, in *Basic Writings of St. Thomas*, by A. Pegis (New York, Random House, 1945), Vol. 1, pp. 433–442. *On the Power of God* (*De Potentia*), translated by the English Dominican Fathers (Westminster, Newman Press, 1952), Book I, pp. 78–123, especially pp. 91–96.

Etienne Gilson, *The Christian Philosophy of St. Thomas Aquinas* (New York, Random House, 1956), pp. 120–129.

J. F. Anderson, *The Cause of Being* (St. Louis, B. Herder Book Company, 1952), Chapter II, "Creation, Active and Passive," pp. 31–50.

B. Divine providence

The transition from a consideration of creation to that of providence is a logical one. In our study of the divine operations we considered God's knowledge of himself and of things other than himself. Next we studied that operation which follows upon knowledge; namely, God's love of himself and of things other than himself. These acts are formally immanent in God and are concerned with his intellect and will. Next we discussed that divine action which concerns both God's intellect and will; namely, that act by which God makes things outside himself. This act we called creation. As the action or operation of God, it is the divine essence with a relation of reason to the creature. Thus actively considered, creation is a formally immanent act identical with the divine substance. But this same act is virtually transient since it causes external effects. As in the creature, we saw that creation is a relation; namely, an order of having existence from another.

Now in point of fact, creatures are not merely ordered to God as to their first beginning. They are also ordered to him as their ultimate end. And each creature is also ordered to its own immediate end. Creatures, furthermore, are ordered to each other, as becomes obvious from an analysis of their different operations. It is to the order of these creatures to their ends, proximate as well as ultimate, that we now turn our attention. That this order exists, we take for granted. The precise point we want to establish is whether God knows this order. And since the knowledge of this order constitutes providence, our questions become: (1) Does God have a providence over his creatures? (2) Does he have a providence over each and every one of his creatures? (3) Does he have an immediate providence over everything? Then we shall try to show how the presence of physical and moral evil in creatures in no way contradicts the providence of God. Finally, we shall pass from providence in God, namely, the existence in the divine mind of the order of all things to their end, to the external execution of this providence. Here we shall see that God achieves this execution through the mediation of creatures. This execution of divine providence is called government.

1. STATEMENT CONCERNING GOD'S PROVIDENCE

God has an immediate providence over all things, nor do the evils in the world contradict this providence. God governs creatures (executes his providence) through other creatures.

A. STATE OF THE QUESTION

Creatures come forth from God as their first principle and, as we shall see, are ordered to God as their last end. But creatures are also ordered to other more immediate and proximate ends. Does God know these ends, and does he order his creatures to them? Since this is nothing else than to have providence over his creatures, in this section we want to know: (1) Has God an immediate and universal providence over his creatures? (2) How is such providence compatible with evil in the world? (3) How does God execute this providence?

B. EXPLANATION OF TERMS

1) ". . . *providence* . . ."—the knowledge of things as ordered to their ends.

2) ". . . *immediate* . . ."—to possess this knowledge of oneself and not through another.

3) ". . . *evil* . . ."—a privation (or absence of a perfection that should be present).

(a) *Physical evil*—a privation of some physical good. Thus blindness is a physical evil for a man.

(b) *Moral evil*—sin; that is, an act of man's free will that lacks the proper order to its end. Thus, for example, lying is such a disordered act, since the end of communicable speech is the manifestation of the truth.

4) ". . . *governs* . . ."—the execution of providence, or the actual direction of things to their proper ends.

C. THE PROOF

1) *God has immediate providence over all things. There is providence in God*, since God knows all creatures and the ends of all creatures. All natures act for an end, and so God in establishing these natures has pre-established their ends. And providence is nothing else than the knowledge of these natures as ordered to these ends.

This providence is immediate, since the knowledge of God is one with the essence of God. And so God has this knowledge of himself, and not through another.

This providence is universal, since divine knowledge is co-extensive with divine causality (God's knowledge is the cause of things), and all things have God as their first cause.

2) *Evil in the world does not contradict divine providence. Not*

physical evil, since in a hierarchical universe, where there are many and diverse particular goods, God, as universal provider, allows the privation of a lesser good (evil) to achieve the presence of a greater good. For example, God allows the death of plants to achieve the growth and perfection of animals.

Not moral evil or sin, since God prefers the presence of some greater good to the absence of some lesser evil. And so, for example, God will allow the cruelty of the persecutor, which results in the heroism of the martyrs. Notice, God in no way causes this evil, but only tolerates it. The whole cause is within man's free will, with which God will not interfere—for then man would not be free—would not be man. Moreover, God would not tolerate evil, unless he were able to "draw from it" greater good. Finally, this greater good is not the reason (final cause) God tolerates evil (for evil has no final cause), but merely the occasion of his tolerating it.

3) *God governs creatures through other creatures.* Government, or the execution of God's providence, is the actual direction of things to their ends. But creatures achieve their ends through their activity. Hence creatures are active. But as active, creatures can cause other creatures and the operations of other creatures. Hence, creatures reach their ends through the causality (physical and moral) of other creatures. Thus while God knows immediately the ends of all creatures (providence), he mediately (through creatures) executes this providence.

READINGS

St. Thomas, *Summa Theologiae,* in *Basic Writings of St. Thomas,* by A. Pegis, (New York, Random House, 1945), Vol. 1, pp. 229-237 (On the Providence of God); pp. 950–961 (On the Government of God); pp. 259–269 (On the Power of God). *Truth (De Veritate),* translated from the definitive Leonine text by R. W. Mulligan, S.J. (Chicago, Henry Regnery Company, 1952), Vol. 1, pp. 220–251, especially 202–204; 209–210; 222–223; 232–234. *On the Power of God (De Potentia),* translated by the English Dominican Fathers (Westminster, Newman Press, 1952), Book One, pp. 1–41.

XVI

God as the End of Man

We turn now to our final question in natural theology. In what sense is God the final term or goal of all created being? God is not only the first efficient cause of the universe, he is also its final end. But what do we mean by this?

1. DEFINING SOME TERMS

To understand our solution, let us begin by defining three different kinds of ends. First, there is the *finis operantis*. This is the end or goal of the *one performing* the action. Secondly, there is the *finis operis*. This is the end or goal of the action or *work performed*. Thirdly, there is the *finis quo*. This is not so much an end as a means. The *finis quo* is that by which the *finis operis* is attained, that by which the thing produced achieves its end.

Let us take a simple example to illustrate these three different ends. A man makes a watch. The *finis operantis* is the end or goal he had in making the watch. It is that which "moved" him in the order of finality to make the watch. Let us say it is to earn a living. But what is the *finis operis*, what is the end of the watch that he has made? This flows from the very nature of the watch. The end of a watch (*finis operis*) is to tell the time. Finally, what is the *finis quo?* How does the watch achieve its end, how does it tell the time? By moving its hands around its face.

2. APPLYING THESE TERMS TO GOD

Let us apply these terms to God and the creature. God has made the creature. Why? That is to say, what moved God in the order of finality to produce creatures? What is the *finis operantis*, the end of God creating? God is his own end, he cannot be moved by anything other than himself. The only end that could attract his will to the making of anything is himself. What moved God to produce creatures was his own infinite goodness, not, however, considered in itself, but considered as communicable to others. The *finis operantis*, the end of God creating, is the infinite goodness as communicable to creatures. Since this is so, once this goodness is actually communicated to creatures by way of participation, these multiplied and finite participations will automatically and necessarily mirror forth the uncreated goodness of God.

This is a simple but important truth. God is like an artist who paints a self-portrait. And God paints his own picture because he wants to communicate his likeness to the canvas. God wants to manifest himself by his painting. The painting, by the mere fact that it exists, mirrors forth the painter. And so creatures, by their very natures, manifest God. The *finis operis* of the self-portrait is the painter. And the *finis operis* of the creature is God. Notice what we are saying: that which the creature manifests is God. Hence God as *manifested* is what terminates (ends) the creature. The final end of the creature is not the *manifestation* of God; this is the *means* by which the end is attained. The manifestation is the *finis quo* by which the *finis operis* is achieved. The end of the creature is achieved by manifesting God; but God, who terminates the manifestation, is the end of the creature. God himself is the *finis operis* of every creature.

Let us make this idea more clear by a simple example drawn from the order of knowledge. What is the end, or *finis operis*, of a concept? It is to give us a knowledge of things. And how does the concept achieve this? What is its *finis quo*? A concept gives us a knowledge of a thing by representing it. We know the thing because of its representation by the concept. What I know is the thing, but I know it because of a representation. The end of the concept (*finis operis*) is the thing known.

Let us apply this example to God as our final end. There is, of course, only one perfect word, or exhaustive representation of God, and that is the Word, the Second Person of the Blessed Trinity. This is the internal and divine Word of God, consubstantial with his nature. But there are countless imperfect and deficient words of God, externally spoken by God and outside his nature. And all these words speak of, represent, his essence. Such words are the creatures of God.

What is their purpose? To manifest God. Creatures are so many finite words, created tongues, speaking the same thing, but speaking it in different words and with different sounds. All creatures, each in its own way, are talking about God. He is the term of their speech, that is to say, the end of their being. And how do they attain God? Simply by being what they are and doing what they should do. How does the self-portrait manifest the painter? By simply being what it is, a likeness of the painter. God has communicated his likeness to the creature, as the painter has communicated his likeness to the canvas. So all creatures necessarily manifest God. He himself is the end of his creation.

With this consideration we have come full circle in the order of finality. We know from metaphysics that the final cause is the first in the order of intention and the last in the order of execution. The *finis operantis*, or the end of God creating, is the first in the order of intention, for it is that which "moves" God to create. And what is this end? It is the infinite goodness of God as communicable to the creature. The *finis operis*, or the end of the thing created, is the last in the order of execution. And what is this end? It is this same infinite goodness of God, for it is this goodness that terminates the manifestation (*finis quo*) of the creature. Just as it was the divine goodness that was the end of God creating, so it is the divine goodness that is the end of the thing created. The *finis operantis* and the *finis operis* are one and the same: God as manifestable through creatures and (after creation) God as manifested through creatures.

But man is a special creature. Because of his intellect and free will, he does not merely manifest God by being what he is and doing what he should do, but he also can formally possess God. All creatures "materially" possess God, insofar as they necessarily and automatically manifest his goodness. But man through knowledge and love can formally possess God. He does so in this present life insofar as he knows and loves God in and through his creatures. On the natural level this is done through natural creatures; on the supernatural level, this knowledge and love is achieved through supernatural creatures; for example, divine faith and charity.

In heaven, God will be the end of our being in a very special manner. Here we will not merely manifest God, we will possess him; and we will not merely possess him through creatures, but through himself. For in heaven we will see God, not as mirrored by creatures (imperfectly) or by faith (darkly), but through the splendor of his own countenance. Here, once more, God himself is our end (*finis operis*), the Beatific Vision being the means (*finis quo*) of possessing him. God himself will terminate that vision, possessed now in a very special way. In this vision, which is called beatific, we will know God with the knowledge he has of himself, and we will love God with the love he has of himself. And this knowledge and this love will bring us perfect joy and happiness.

But, as should be obvious from what has been said, even those who go to hell still have God as the end of their being. For although they have lost the Beatific Vision, and hence the supernatural end for which they were created, they still manifest God, but especially now his justice.

3. Conclusion

With this discussion of God as the end of creatures, our study of natural theology comes to an end. Starting with creatures, we have mounted up to God, seeing him as the first principle and last end of all things. In seeing how all things are ordered to God as their final end, the work of wisdom is achieved. Achieved, that is, at a certain level of speculative knowledge, and according to a static contemplation of the truth. But the practical achievement of our end and the dynamic movement toward God must be the work of love. And this knowledge of itself can never give. But knowledge can make the work of love more enlightened and profound. And when the love of God enters the student's heart, he will not only be wise, but holy.

Readings

St. Thomas, *Summa Theologiae*, in *Basic Writings of St. Thomas*, by A. Pegis (New York, Random House, 1945), Vol. 1, pp. 431–432.

On the Truth of the Catholic Faith (*Summa Contra Gentiles*), Book Three: *Providence;* translated, with an Introduction and Notes, by Vernon J. Bourke (New York, Hanover House, 1956), pp. 97–125.

Etienne Gilson, *The Christian Philosophy of St. Thomas Aquinas* (New York, Random House, 1956), pp. 130–143.

Index

Boldface numbers indicate definitions; italicized numbers, footnotes

absolute nature, 66, 68, 76, 105
abstraction, 9-10, 10-11, **24,** 26-27, 48, 58, 60-61, 62-63, 65-66, 112, 123, 306
  degrees of, *47, 52*
  formal, 10, **24,** 62
  second-level, 10
  total, 9-10, **24,** 61-62
accident, 97-98, 103, **116,** 117, 120-121, 124, 128, 212
  as being, 132
  logical, *97*
act, 125-126, 142, 147-148, 301
  and potency, 139, 230, 239
    correlation, 139-140, 321, 322
    distinction, 127-128, 161
    knowledge of, 136-137
    limitation, 132-134, 273
    priority, 143
  as intelligibility, 126, 262
  first and second, 138
  God as pure act, 233
  of existing, *see* existing, act of
  state of 86-87, **90,** 125, 289, 324
acting, **165**
action, **165,** 171-172
  immanent **116,** 150, 178, **363**
  transient *116,* **165,** 178, **363**
activity, 114-116, 128-129, 147, 290, 301
actualism, *see* phenomenalism
agent, 114-115, 164, **165,** 205, 283-284, 286, 297-298, 301
  kinds of, 168
  see also cause, efficient
agnosticism, 308

aimless, 178
Albertson, 99
analogate, (analogue) **76, 314**
analogous, **76**
  primarily and secondarily, *71*
analogy, 69-71, 75, 78, 189, **314**
  causal, 162-164
  of attribution, **314**
  of being, 131-132, **314**
  of composition, 98-100, **116-117,** 131, 169-170
  of eminence, 164, **167,** 170
  of individual communicaton 71-73, **76,** 77
  of proportion, 99-100, **117,** 121, 132, *139,* 163-164, **314,** 316
  of proportionality, 76, 77, **314,** 316
  structure of, 69-73
  see also proportionality
analytic, *56*
Anderson, 25, 317, 365
angel, 110-111, 158, 253, 257, 328
  knowledge of, 62-63
Animistic Pantheism, 323
Anselm, St., 342, 343
anthropomorphism, 291
a posteriori, *see* demonstration
appetite, *141*
apprehension, 61
  complex, 50, 53-54, **57**
  simple, 11, 48, **57,** 111
a priori, *see* demonstration
argument from design, 292
Aristotle, 90, *114,* *117,* 167, 238, 256, 261, 288

attributes (divine), **319-320**
Augustine, St., 211, 315
Averroës, *32, 39*
Averroism 38-40
Avicenna, *32,* 341, 342, 343

beatific vision, 372
beauty, 208-209
becoming, **89,** 160
  see also change
behaviorism, 34
being, 29, 46-47, 55, 60, 65, 68, 112-113,
  120, 123, 212
  as being, **57**
  being and being-known, 212
  common to many, 67-68, 77
  in common, 27-28, 188-189
  of metaphysics, 52, *68,* 187-188
  of reason, 10, 192-193, **210,** 212
  philosophy of, *see* philosophy of being,
    metaphysics
  primitive notion of, 47-49
being-for-another, 196-197
being-in-itself, 196-197
Bergson, 238, 292, 293, 297
Berkeley, 43
Bourke, 373
Boyle, *75*
Breton, 189
Buchner, 296

Cajetan *49, 68*
Caldin, 25
causality, 145, 148-149, 156-162, **165,**
  301
  analogy of, 162-164
  of material agent, 150
  principle of, *156*
  theorem of, 156-162
cause, **165**
  analogous, **166,** 307
  cause and change 150-151, 230
  cause and effect correlation, 152, 157,
    242
  efficient, *127,* 135, 145, 147-149, 149-
    150, **165,** 241-242
  equivocal, 152-153, **167**

cause—*continued*
  exemplar, 155-156, 272
  final, *172,* 241-242
  formal, 146, **165,** 185-186, 242
  instrumental, 154-155, **166,** 169,
    245-246
  kinds of, 185
  material, 146, **165,** 185-186, 242
  per accidens ordered, **241,** 248, 249
  per se ordered, **240,** 241-246
  primary, 152, **166**
  principal, 154-155, **166,** 169
  proper, 299, 300, 301, **302**
  reciprocal, 233, 236
  secondary, 152-153, **166,** *182*
  telic, *127,* 146, *172,* 173, **183,** 185
    see also end, goal, purpose
  univocal, 152-153, **166**
certitude, 26
Chambat, 264
chance, 180-183, **184,** 204, 289, 290-291
  absolute, 182, **184**
  relative, 182, **184**
  total, **184**
change, 80-81, **89,** 90, 91, *113-114,*
  119-120, 142, 175, 229, 230-233,
  237, 238-239
  accidental, 93-95, 96-98, 103, **117**
  and composition, 91
  and succession, 91-92
  essential, *see* substantial
  subject of, 85
  substantial, 100-102, 118
Charlsworth, 58
Clarke, 22, 58, 228
Collins, *32*
coming-to-be, 88
common sense, 4
compenetration, *107*
composition, 90, 122, 320, 321-322
Comte, *32,* 308
concept, 9, 11, 313, 370
  see also simple apprehension
condition, 144
  active, **164**
  passive, **165**
constancy, 175
construct, 192-193
contingence, 159, 161, **166**

contingent being, 254-255, 257-258, **263**
corruptible beings, 252-253, **263**
 need for a cause, 255-256, 257, 265
cosmology, 45
creation, **363-364,** 365

Darwin, 288, 296
David of Dinant, 323
deduction, transcendental, *201*
defect, 174
definition, *84,* 313, 321, 339
degrees of abstraction, *see* abstraction,
 degrees of
Democritus, 288, 296
demonstration, a posteriori, 225-226
 of God's existence, 227-228
demonstrative knowledge, *see* knowledge,
 demonstrative
Denis (Pseudo-) 312, 340, 342, 343
denomination, extrinsic, *207*
dependence, causal, 162
Descartes, 248, 249, 251
Descoqs, 264, *288, 293*
Determinists, 288-291
difference, 83-84, 106-107
 essential, *84*
dimensions, *108*
Dionysius, *see* Denis
disposition, *144-145,* **168**
distinction, 82-83, **90**
 in God, 336-338
division, 108
doubt, 290

effect
 analogous, 309
 univocal, 309
 pre-contained in cause, 283-284
Eleatics, 238
emanation, 364
Empedocles, 296
empiricism, 11
end, *172,* 283-286, **296, 369**
Epicurus 288, 296
epistemology, 15, 105
equivocal, 64-65, **76,** 78, 120, 169
Eslick, 119
esse, 143
 see also existing, act of

essence, *48,* 94, *112, 114,* **116,** 121-122,
 124, 253, 254-255, 257-258, 267
 and esse, 121-122, 269-270, 299-301
 knowledge of, 84, 95
 of God, 354-355
essentialism, 37-41, 43-44, **57,** 81, *149*
eternal, **350**
ethics, 15
evil, 202-203, 214-216, **367**
 abstractly and concretely, **210, 211**
 moral, 294-295
 and divine providence,, 367-368
evolution
 creative, 292-294
 materialistic, 288-291
exemplar, 156, **166,** 173
 see also cause, exemplar
existence, 194
existentialism, 41-42, 44
existing, act of, 48-49, 67-68, 79, 111-
 114, 115-116, **117,** 118, 124,
 129, 136, *146,* 161-162
 distinct from essence, 299-301
 how conserved, 242-243
 how lost, 257-258
 how produced, 242, 254
experience, 4, **24**
extrinsic reference, 69

Faith and reason, 18
 see also philosophy and religion
false, 200-201
Feibleman, *12*
fiction, *31,* 46, *105*
finality, *172,* 283, **296**
 demands an intellect, 285-287, 290,
 291-292, 298-299
finalization, *172*
form, 108, 109, 120, 124, 253, 255, 257-
 258, 262, 301-302
 as being, 132
 substantial, 101, **117,** 118
formality, 38
free choice, **358**
 in God, 358-359
 and man's free choices, 360
 as immutable, 359-360

generalization, 49
Geny, 264

Gilson, 25, *32,* 58, 78, 119, 167, 184,
    187, 208, 211, 224, 228, *288, 292,*
    303, 312, *323,* 356, 365, 373
goal, 172, 173, 181-182, **183,** 185, 204
    see also end, final cause, purpose
goal-directedness, 206
goal orientation, **184**
Goblot, 297
God, 27, 40, *207*
    as cause of being, 299-302
    as end of man, 369-372
    as knowing Himself, 352-354
    as knowing other things, 355-356
    as willing Himself, 356-358
    as willing other things, 358-360
    demonstration of His existence, 225-228
        proof from causation of existence,
            299-302
        proof from change, 229-239
        proof from corruptible beings, 252-
            265
        proof from efficient causes, 239-252
        proof from existence of order, 280-
            299
        proof from grades of perfection,
            265-280
good, 71, **210,** 215
    divine, 334-335, 335-336, **347,** 348
    proper, 202-205, **210**
    transcendental, 205-208, **210**
government of God, **367,** 368

haecceity, 38
Haeckel, 296
Hamilton, 308
Harmon, 167
Hawkins, 25
health, 70-71
Hegel, *68,* 297
Heidegger, 41
hell, 372
Henle, 3, 58
Heraclitus, 80-81, 88, 238, 296
Hobbes, *32*
Hume, *32,* 308
Huxley, Julian, 288

idealism, 43
Ideas, Platonic, 37, 104

identity, 82, **90,** 93-94
Illuminati, 307-308
immanent action, *see* action, immanent
immaterial, *53-54*
immutability of God, 349-350
    of God's free choices, 358, 359-360
    and man's free will, 360
inclination, natural, 286, 335-336
    see also appetite, tendency
incorruptible being, 253-255, 257-258,
    263
individual, 67, 72, 76, 95, 103-104, 107,
    118
individual communication, *see* analogy of
individuality, **117**
individuation, principle of, 104, *105,* 108,
    117
inferior, 64, 70
infinity
    formal, 333
    material, 332
    of God, 333, 348
information, 364
instrument, *see* cause, instrumental
integral part, *16,* 89
intellect and sense, 26
intelligibility, 10, **24,** *126,* 194, **210,** 213-
    214, 275-276, 279
    formal, 7, **22**
intelligible, 272-273, **306**
intentional existence, 284, 293
intuition, *306,* 308-309
Ionians, 238
is, 46, 49, 52, *54, 68,* 187

Johann, 167
judgment, 48-49, 55-56, **57,** 61, 111
    negative, *see* separation
    perceptual, 49

Kant, *32, 56,* 250-251, 259-260, 264,
    291, 296-297, 308
Klubertanz, *9, 17, 19, 47, 50, 73,* 78, *88,*
    94, 115, 183, 184, *194*
knowledge, *209*
    abstractive, 306
        see also abstraction

knowledge—*continued*
  analogous, **307**
  common, 64-65
  demonstrative, 7, **23**
    see also demonstration
  humanistic, 4-5
  liberal, 4
  matter of, *see* matter of knowledge
  mediate, **306**, 309
  mode of, 3-6
  non-quidditative, **307**
  purpose of, 3
  scientific, 5-6, 7-11, 11, *196*
  spontaneous, 3-4
  universal, 8, 104-105
Kossel, 130, 211

Laplace, 183
Lauer, 119
Leibniz, *32*
Le Roy, 292, 297
life, *209,* 233-234
limitation, 161-162,
  by efficient cause, 135
  of act by potency, 132-135, 272-273
Littre, 296
living thing, *160*
logic, 15
Loisy, 308
Lonergan, 119, 142
love, **357-358**
Lucretius, 296

Maimonides (Rabbi Moses) 261-262, 308,
  320, 341, 342, 343, 345
Mansel, 308
many, 195
many-to-many, *see* analogy, structure of
many-to-one, *see* analogy, structure of
Maritain, 25, 59, 91, 119, 142, *193, 208,*
  211, 224, *236,* 303
Marxism, 34, 296
materialism, 33-36, 42, 43, **57**, 151, 197
materialists, 288-291
material thing, **24**
matter, 43, 120, 124, 332
  as being, 132
  in general, 35-36

matter—*continued*
  intelligible, *110*
  of knowledge, **22**
    abstract, 7
    concrete, 6
    proper, 7, **23**
  primary, 102, 108-109, **117,** 118, 126-
    127, 252-253, 262
Maurer, 119, 224, 312
meaning, 338-340, 343, 346
means, 204, 285-286
metaphor, *75,* 193, 316, 327
metaphysics, 11
  certitude of, 28
  nature of, 26-27
  object of, 28
  same science as natural theology, 16,
    220-221, 222-223
  subject of, 9, 59-60
  see also philosophy of being
Michelangelo, 242
Mill, 308
Morris, 59
motion, **89,** 142, 229-230, **237,** 239
movers, 231-232
Mulligan, 356, 368
multiplicity and unity, 122
multiplicity in a species, 122

names, **313**
  as applied to God, 315
  of God, 313, 315, 319
natural theology, 15-16, **219,** 220, 221,
  224
  as a science, 222
  as the same science as metaphysics, 16,
    222-223
nature, 94, **116,** 272
  absolute, *see* absolute nature
necessary being, 253-255, 257, **263,** 265
necessity, 156-158, **166, 263-264**
  essential and existential, **166**
negation, 192
Newtonian law of motion, 235
nominalism, 104, *149*
normal, 174
notion, *see* meaning

occasion, 145, **165**
omnipresence, 349-350
one, **210**, 214-215
  accidental, **210**
  per accidens, 98, **210, 215**
  per se, **210**
  see also unity
one-to-one, *see* analogy, structure of
Ontologists, 308
order, 285, 286, 287, 289, 291-292, 294, **295**
orientation in being, 179-180
orientation to goal, *see* goal
Owens, 78, *156*, 224, 228, 303

Paley, 292
Parmenides, 80, 81, 89, 238
part, 89
participation, 270, 271, 277-278, 333
  see also analogy of
passing-away, 88
passion, 149-150, **165**
passivity, *127, 149, 179*
patient, 149-150, 164, **165**
  kinds of, 168
  see also effect
Pegis, 211, 224, *239*, 312, 317, 349, 351, 356, 365, 368, 372
per accidens unit, *see* one per accidens
perfection, 141-143, **278, 347**
  mixed, 325-327
  simple, 325-328
person, 41, 44-45, 73-75, 112
Phelan, 211, 317
phenomenalism, 32-33
phenomenology, 39-40
philosophy, **23**
  and religion, 17-20, *23-24*
  first, 28
  of being, 11-12, 12-14, 16, **24**, 31, 47, 51, 96, *105, 114*
    see also metaphysics
  of human nature, 15
  of nature, 15, *101, 104, 107, 113*
  reason for, 12-15, 21-22
  Thomistic, *see* Thomism
place, 349-350
plant, 174-175
Plato, 104

Platonism, 37
Plotinus, 308
plurality in God, 343-345
positivism, 11
possibility, 191
possible, 55, *159*, 190-191, **210**
potency, 126-127, 262, 321-322
  intelligibility of, 273
  operative, 126, 129-131
  passive, 126-127, 231, 232, 233, 239, 253
  state of, 86-87, **90**, 125, 160
  see also act and potency
potency and act, distinction of, 161
power, *115, 130, 179,* 141
  see also potency, operative
predetermination, *183*
predicate, 187
predication, proper and improper, 69, 315-316, 329-330
  analogous, 316-317
  univocal, 330
premotion, *179*
presence
  eminent, **326, 327, 347,** 348
  proper, **326,** 328-329, **347,** 348
  virtual, **326,** 327, 330, **347,** 348
principle, **25,** 27, 89, **364**
  first, 54-55
  of being, **25,** 131-132
  of causality, *156,* 247
  of contradiction, 55, 56-57, 230-231
  of knowledge, **25,** 54-55
principles, knowledge of, 62
priority, *112,* 158
privation, 192, 202, 215, 290-291
property, 162
proportion, **314,** 316
proportional predication, 69
proportionality, *71,* **314,** 316-317
  proper, 72-73
  see also analogy
providence (of God) 365-368, **367**
purpose, 172, 173, 177, **184**
  in animals, 173

quantity, 107-108
quiddity, *48,* 114

real, 30-31, 42-44, 44-45, **57,** 58, 189
  extended sense, 30
  strict sense, 31
realism, *104-105*
reasoning, 24
reduction, transcendental, *201*
Reese, 119
regress in causes, impossibility of infinite,
  231-232, 246, 251, 265, 298-299
relation, 70, 192-193, **364**
  of creation, 365
  transcendental, *74*
religion and philosophy, 17-20
  see also faith and reason
Renan, 297
Richet, 297
Russell, *162*

sacred theology, 224-**225**
Salmon, 59
sameness, 82
Sartre, *68*
Schmitz, 59, 78
Schrödringer, 59
science, 5, **23,** 35
Scotism, 38
self-evidence, *156*
semantics, general, 34
sensible, 51
sensible matter, 267
sensible thing, **24**
separation, *10, 47,* 53, 54, **57,** 58, 61-62
Sertillanges, 142, 184
Sheldon, 59
signification, 339-340
simple, **210**
simplicity, (of God), 320-324, **347**
sin, 203, **367**
singularity, 38, *110*
Smith, 59
something, *46,* 190, **210**
soul, 234-235, 253, 258, 349
  separated, *110*
species, intelligible, 306
Spencer, 288, 296, 308
Spinoza, 264
Suarez, 320
subjectivity, 41, 74, *197*

subject matter, *see* matter of knowledge
subsistent being 313, 319, 331
substance, 97, 98, 103, **116,** 117, 120-
  121, 124, 128, 212, 301
  as being, 132
succession, 85

teleology, 116, *172,* **184**
  principle of, *179,* **184**
  see also finality
tendency, 141
  see also appetite, inclination, purpose
term, 9, 64-65
  common, 76, 78
  see also analogous, equivocal, univocal
that-which-is, **117,** 118
theology, 28
  see also sacred, natural theology
thing 24, 73-75, 190, **210**
Thomas Aquinas, St., 19, 22, 25, 47, 58,
  77-78, *102,* 118-119, *129, 132,*
  138, 141-142, *148, 153,* 167, 184,
  188, 200, 211; in part II, *passim*
Thomism, 21-22, 22, 42-43, *44, 68, 73,*
  113
Tournier, 59, 78
transcendental, **210**
transient activity, *see* action, transient
truth, 61, 197-200, 346, **353**
  logical and transcendental, **210**
  subsistent, 354-355
Tyrrel, 308

ubiquitous, 349-350
unchangeable, *see* immutable
unity, 70, 94, 194-196
  kinds of, 195
  per accidens, 98
  see also one
universal, 11, 65, 104, *105,* 194
  existence of, 66
univocal, 8, 9, 11, **24,** 65, 70, 73, **76,**
  120, 168
  see also knowledge, universal

Van Riet, 4
Van Roo, 119, 142
verb, *46*

virtual, *48,* 137
  see also presence
Vogel, 168

Walton, 119
Ward, 185
way
  of causality, 307, 309-310, 311
  of negation, 307, 309-310, 311
  of transcendence, 307, 309-310, 311
Weltanschaung, 21
whole, 210

Wild, 26, 59, 91, 142, 168
will, 233-234, **357**
  in God, 356-360
    as free choice, **358,** 359
    as immutable, 358, 359
wisdom, 26, 294, 311-312, 372
word, 370-371
  of God, *344-345*
world, 44-45, **363**

Zeno, 238